Kate O'Brien and
Fiction of Ident

GW01452691

Kate O'Brien and the Fiction of Identity

Sex, Art and Politics in
Mary Lavelle *and Other Writings*

AINTZANE LEGARRETA MENTXAKA

McFarland & Company, Inc., Publishers
Jefferson, North Carolina, and London

LIBRARY OF CONGRESS CATALOGUING-IN-PUBLICATION DATA

Mentxaka, Aintzane Legarreta, 1967–
    Kate O'Brien and the fiction of identity : sex, art and politics in
Mary Lavelle and other writings / Aintzane Legarreta Mentxaka.
      p.   cm.
    Includes bibliographical references and index.

    ISBN 978-0-7864-4873-9
    softcover : 50# alkaline paper ∞

    1. O'Brien, Kate, 1897–1974. Mary Lavelle.   2. Politics in
literature.   3. Sex role in literature.   I. Title.
PR6029.B65M355   2011
823'.912 — dc22   2010052798

BRITISH LIBRARY CATALOGUING DATA ARE AVAILABLE

Cover image: Kate O'Brien in 1926, during rehearsals for *Distinguished
Villa*, by Sasha (photograph reproduced courtesy of the Glucksman
Library, University of Limerick)

Manufactured in the United States of America

McFarland & Company, Inc., Publishers
  Box 611, Jefferson, North Carolina 28640
    www.mcfarlandpub.com

Table of Contents

Preface:
The Canon

Introduction

In the year 2000, I became aware of Kate O'Brien's work and was instantly drawn to it. I was particularly interested in the Basque connection to *Mary Lavelle*, but I could not find any relevant information as to how the novel had come into being. I conducted a search on the Internet, and only one reference, one Web page, came up. It publicized "The Kate O'Brien," a lesbian bar in San Francisco. Critical analysis of O'Brien in 2010 is still overshadowed by the fact that her work has been kept in the margins for so long. One can detect a "sense of a mission" in all those MA theses on O'Brien from the 1970s and 1980s and feel the passion and commitment of the fan in the handful of articles that got published in the 1980s and 1990s. Today, this is about to change. Her work is on the verge of becoming an academic field, and "Kate O'Brien" is also about to shift from a site of wonder, to a spectacle, to an icon for an Ireland that wants to think of itself as mature, tolerant, and modern. A queer Irish woman is the perfect sphinx to match our pyramids.

⌒

Why does this book concentrate on *Mary Lavelle*? *Mary Lavelle* is a remarkable experiment. It represents a new direction for Kate O'Brien. It will affect all her future work in different ways, but many elements related to this novel will not be repeated again. Chronologically, *Mary Lavelle* is only the third major work in a career that spanned over 50 years and included ten novels, as well as nine plays, two film scripts, two biographies, two travelogues, short stories, copious criticism, and journalism. Kate O'Brien is considered a novelist, and most research to date has concentrated on her fiction, which is regularly perceived as conservative in style and outmoded in tone, but the critical understanding of her work is hopelessly inadequate. *Mary Lavelle* is a particularly good example of O'Brien's interest in redrafting and mixing a variety of genres, forms, and even mediums. Within her work, *Mary Lavelle* has elicited some

1

interest from critics, but it is not considered either particularly accomplished or particularly representative. Despite being a scholarly blind spot, it continues to be one of O'Brien's most popular books.

We will start by considering a number of possible contextualizations of *Mary Lavelle*, from Kate O'Brien's own work and some nineteenth century sub-genres and movements, to activist fiction and modernism. Then we will consider the relevance of history, biography, and autobiography to *Mary Lavelle*, bringing in all major and minor works by O'Brien, to conclude with some reflections on her representations of subjectivity. But before all that, let us take a brief look at Kate O'Brien's shifting position in the literary canon.

Middle-Class Catholicism and the Canon

Mary Lavelle is practically untraceable in critical accounts of literature in English or European literature, to give just two examples of areas in which the book made an important contribution. Occasional academic papers and articles have signaled a continuing low-key interest in Kate O'Brien's work up to 2010. No relevant piece of criticism has concentrated on *Mary Lavelle*, and rarely on any other specific books, probably because the urgent task was to encourage an interest in O'Brien's work as a whole. Two monographs on her work, from 1987 and 1990, included sections on *Mary Lavelle*, while the 2000 UK edition of the novel included a critical introduction. After a discreet revival of O'Brien's work in the 1980s, which saw the reissuing of some of her novels, including *Mary Lavelle*, two collections of lectures and criticism in 1993 and 1994 evidenced the continuing interest in O'Brien. A series of conferences and events from the mid–1980s onwards promoted interest in her books, but it was the publication of the first full biography of O'Brien in 2006 and the reissuing of her last novel, *As Music and Splendour*, in 2005, that inspired an unprecedented interest among the public and the critics.

The Anteroom, the 1934 novel published by O'Brien before *Mary Lavelle*, has regularly been highlighted by Irish critics as her most accomplished book. The implicit assumption is that after a creative peak at the beginning of her career, Kate O'Brien's work quickly fell into decline. Yet there are indications that the favoring of *The Anteroom* has been dictated by politics. *The Anteroom* was included in the canon-forming *Irish Classics* by Declan Kiberd in 2000. Another canon-forming effort, *The Penguin Book of Irish Fiction*, edited by Colm Tóibín in 1999, included both *The Anteroom* and *The Land of Spices*, while a collection of 20 "Irish Classics" published by *The Irish Times* in 2005 again chose *The Anteroom* from O'Brien's works. *The Anteroom* is, in a sense, a "safe bet," as the novel accommodates to the posthumously constructed, acceptable view of Kate O'Brien, as alert chronicler of the moral and imaginative constraints of middle-class Irish Catholic family life, but it is highly debatable how representative of O'Brien's work and O'Brien's abilities this novel really is.

All of Kate O'Brien's production up to 1936 seems to have concerned itself with the specific moral dilemmas of the middle class, mainly the Catholic Irish, a trend that was to continue in her work. This fact is regularly underlined by commentators as Kate O'Brien's main contribution to Anglo-Irish literature, and is often perceived as "filling a gap" in the map of Irish letters. For example, Joan Ryan sees Kate O'Brien as "introducing a new Ireland into literature" (125), and Adele Dalsimer opens her study of O'Brien as follows: "Kate O'Brien is a pioneer. She is the first writer of Irish fiction to represent fully and meticulously the Catholic upper-middle class" (xi). The same claim is repeated with variations again and again. "[S]he persuades us that if we overlook this Ireland [of the Catholic middle class], and these people, then we are overlooking ourselves," says Eavan Boland ("Legacy" 7). This appreciation of middle-class visibility is revealing of the priorities of Irish criticism. Colm Tóibín's comments are characteristic:

> Kate O'Brien was starting from scratch.... There was no Irish fiction to help her, and there was something heroic about her insistence on dealing with this world, sticking to it, rather than describing a rising Catholic class which she could satirize and laugh at. She took these people seriously; she gave them enough money so that they could have choices [xxv].

The use of the term "heroic" for an artist drawing from her background is frankly striking. Perceived class allegiances are too often a smokescreen, as sins of omission at home show; the belated assessment of the Irishness in Elizabeth Bowen and Iris Murdoch, for example, shows that a modicum of attention may be granted to a woman writer in Ireland, provided that she is part of the clan. Arguably, in the critical response to Kate O'Brien, her concern with middle-class life is not valued, but rather it is her interest in middle-class *catholic* life that is rewarded.

Mary Lavelle would appear to corroborate Kate O'Brien's interest in upper-middle-class Catholic family life, this time as manifested in the Basque Country. In the novel, the bourgeois Pablo Areavaga is married to a woman from a family of industrialists, Consuelo; their son Juanito is married to an aristocrat, Luisa. The Areavagas exemplify the contemporary consensus on the marks of newly acquired wealth: costly dresses, art deco furniture, a musical appreciation, a perfect Castilian Spanish, and a working knowledge of one or two European languages are desirable. Formal education plays a part for the men. Leftist politics should not. Both Pablo and Juanito signal their class unorthodoxy by their sober and careless appearance. By contrast, Irish governesses working for the likes of the Areavagas are trapped in spinsterhood and poverty, and they band together in a parody of a middle-class family, obsessed by a respectability born of their "good old Irish small-town notion that [they're] 'ladies'" (O'Brien *Mary*

204). They don't quite get it right, and their make-up is over done, their hats fall off, their carefully rehearsed salutations are ignored by eligible males.

To an extent, however, with *Mary Lavelle* Kate O'Brien's work moves away from family matters, understanding "family" as a physically stable (genetically and geographically speaking) entity. Tellingly, the protagonist Mary reminisces about her brothers, Jimmy and Donal, but neglects to even mention the name of her "little sisters" (228). Most references to her widowed father and her aunt, who is part of the household, are negative; her father is at least fair, being "crankily unjust to his children whom he seems to resent and, without discrimination, to dislike" (24). A self-contained community that functions as surrogate family makes its first appearance in Kate O'Brien's books in the Café Alemán, the meeting point for immigrant governesses in *Mary Lavelle*. It will return in far more positive terms, in the guise of a convent (*The Land of Spices*), a group of friends (*Pray for the Wanderer*) or schoolmates (*The Flower of May, Constancy*), or an artists' colony (*As Music and Splendour*). Giulia Lorenzoni has shown that Kate O'Brien was one of the first Irish writers who "envisioned alternative and more fluid views of family" outside heteropatriarchy ("Visions"), and a major break in this direction is signaled by *Mary Lavelle*. After this novel, every O'Brien protagonist fulfills Mary's childhood dream of becoming "a free lance" (27).

Much has been made of the fact that Frank McCourt's *Angela's Ashes* deals with Limerick city in the same period covered by O'Brien (see for example Boylan viii) but focusing on the appalling poverty of a large sector of the population rather than on the middle-class. City slums do appear in a number of books by Kate O'Brien, and it is always a momentary flash from a visitor who is just "passing through." *Mary Lavelle* is not her first novel to pause on the slums; *Without My Cloak* had already described in detail the slums of Mellick/Limerick (see 126–7). Kate O'Brien's books are ignorant of the experience of poverty, but they are aware of its existence at least — which serves as a gloss to the comfort in which the main characters live. Interestingly, O'Brien is keen to redefine the term "aristocracy." Individualism, a knowledge of languages, oversensitivity, an egalitarian spirit, can all be "aristocratic" (see *Music* 331, *Anteroom* 176, *Flower* 369), and the same applies to an "intellectual ascendancy" (*Cloak* 291; different from Noel Annan's use of the term — see Lee *Virginia* 51). In *Mary Lavelle*, the Basque are described as "a hopelessly aristocratic people, in a world which has outstripped the aristocratic principle," which seems to mean that they are polite and have "moral integrity" (123; see ibid., 75, 76). O'Brien was to extend this observation to the Spanish, and it is interesting that George Orwell would make a similar comment in his book about the Spanish Civil War, *Homage to Catalonia*, where he claims that the Spanish "have, there is no doubt, a generosity, a species of nobility, that do not really belong to the twentieth century," to add: "[i]t is this that makes one hope that in Spain even Fascism may take a comparatively loose and bearable form. Few Spaniards possess the damnable efficiency and consistency that a modern totalitarian state needs" (178). O'Brien shared this view with Orwell and, like him, aligned "nobility" to an "anarchic" temperament. It is worth recalling that in Oscar Wilde's first play a character declares that "in good democracy, every man should be an aristocrat" (*Vera* 665).

Miraculous escapes from poverty and crippling dependence, in the form of a scholarship (*The Land of Spices*), an inheritance (*The Flower of May*), and artistic success (*As Music and Splendour*), give freedom to penniless protagonists in O'Brien's fiction. The critics' emphasis on her middle-class sensibility needs to be qualified. These women and their stories are *framed* by middle-class contexts, but they are themselves, for the most part, merely "daughters of educated men"—in Virginia Woolf's crucial distinction ("Guineas" 160). Only one female protagonist in the entire oeuvre of O'Brien, Ana de Mendoza (*That Lady*), starts out in the security of inherited wealth at her command, and it is not by chance that, austere to a fault, she attempts to join a nuns' order and ends up with ethics as her only asset, and her only companion, like a new Antigone. Most O'Brien characters, emphatically because they are women, face financial uncertainty. Mary Lavelle returns to Ireland half-hopeful on her ability to earn a living, and confident at least that the 100 pounds left to her in her aunt's will guarantees a head start. These 100 pounds buy freedom for all subsequent Kate O'Brien heroines.

Feminism and the Canon

Mary Lavelle's feminist and internationalist politics have not been of much interest to critics. The canonization of Kate O'Brien's *The Anteroom*, a novel that happens "indoors," accommodates to the "domestic" framework associated to women's writing (Gerardine Meaney, in conversation December 2005). In this context, it is troubling that a 2005 canon-forming collection of ten key novels of the twentieth century from the feminist publishers Virago in England has included *The Anteroom*, endorsing the focus of Irish criticism on the early, less political, part of O'Brien's career, even if her presence in the selection is a welcomed sign of the growing attention paid to her work. Neither the most feminist, nor the most stylistically stimulating of her books, the association of Kate O'Brien with *The Anteroom* is a disservice to her range. It would appear to be inconceivable (since it remains to be done) to place O'Brien in the context of European literature or of socialist activist writing, for example. Yet a close look at *Mary Lavelle* makes this erasure a near impossibility. This is not to say that politics, in the most general sense of the term, do not play a part in every one of O'Brien's books, and this is not to say that feminism is not crucial to her work. But the "Kate O'Brien" that continues to be filtered down through criticism is a domesticated version of the original.

The feminist canon has been more welcoming of *Mary Lavelle*. It was one of the O'Brien novels reprinted by both Dublin's Arlen House and London's

Virago in the 1980s. In an early book of feminist literary criticism, Margaret Lawrence's remarkable *We Write as Women* (*The School of Femininity*), first published in 1936, the author declares *The Anteroom* to be an example of "a matriarchal answer to the little games of men; the little tower they build out of blocks; the little states they build in the sand; the little ideas they have about this country or that country and what it may mean in the general plan" (199–200). Despite this early example, feminist writers and commentators after the 1970s have been inordinately cautious on the subject of O'Brien's feminism. Eavan Boland wondered, "Was she then a feminist writer? I think it is a difficult question to answer" ("Legacy" 8), while Lorna Reynolds described O'Brien as "writer *and* feminist" [emphasis added] and went on to claim that "her feminism was a subtle, covert feminism" (51). The artist and writer Anne Le Marquand Hartigan emphasized, in a 2004 paper, how important Kate O'Brien had been for Irish feminist *readers* in a world with no referents. Gerardine Meaney, in a 2003 paper, described the then long-out-of-print *As Music and Splendour* as a novel "waiting for the twenty-first century," and "a utopian novel," in that it presents the figure of the woman artist as a "taken for granted thing."

Novelist Anne Enright was commissioned to write the introduction to the long anticipated reissue of *As Music and Splendour* in 2005, but it was clear from her tone that the twenty-first century had yet to dawn in Ireland. "Clare may be a lesbian ... but this is not the point of the character, quite"; "Lesbianism is not Clare's problem"; "[p]erhaps Clare's lesbianism has a function," "Clare's problem is, first and foremost, a spiritual one"; "the question is not what kind of flesh Clare should indulge in..."; "the only explicit conversation in the book about Clare's intractable heart turns out not to be about lesbianism" (v–ix). It would be idiotic to claim that Clare Halvey, co-protagonist of *As Music and Splendour*, is nothing more than her sexuality, but to try to explain it away, and with such frantic insistence, seemed at this point in time nothing short of a betrayal. Nevertheless, it is useful to see this lesbophobia in the context of other taboo topics in O'Brien criticism, such as socialism — that is, as a reminder that lesbianism can be perceived as a political threat. The expounding of anarchist and communist theory in *Mary Lavelle*, which is such a crucial feature of the book, rarely gets a mention, and when it does, it is in passing. O'Brien's contextualization as a Catholic, middleclass author also turns her into an apolitical, genderless, sexless author.

This has been regularly contested by feminist commentators, and it is their efforts that have resulted in what Michael O'Toole, in a 1995 article, calls "the rehabilitation" of Kate O'Brien in the 1990s ("Peasants"). The phase is now coming to a close, but a range of critical commentaries that are more than illustrations of particular themes is yet to come. As Tina O'Toole realized when she researched O'Brien, her work belongs to a rich tradition of Irish literature by and about women seeking alternative models, and we must recover that tradition too ("Kate"). Feminists understandably have had to focus on the groundbreaking, positive aspects of O'Brien's work, but they have been more willing to *critically* engage with it than anyone else. It is another kind of legacy left by O'Brien —fearlessness, self-reliance, compulsive scrutiny. It has provided some of the most exciting criticism available on *Mary Lavelle*. For example, Lorna Reynolds' much-derided but excellent early study of O'Brien (see Donoghue "Noises," Walshe "Note") includes the occasional Olympian pronouncement against this or that structural problem, and *Mary Lavelle* does not escape her wrath (see for example *Kate* 59). In a lively pamphlet, Katie Donovan rallies against *Mary Lavelle*; her "polemic" antics are misdirected, because of Donovan's reading of the protagonist as "ultimately acquiescent" (*Writers* 21). Anne Fogarty's focus on the "undecidability" of the limits of Romance conventions in O'Brien —"the question remains open" on *Mary Lavelle*, Fogarty claims (113) — lays down a series of interesting problems, but her quietly defeatist conclusion seems unsatisfactory somehow. Patricia Coughlan's robust engagement with O'Brien's potentially objectifying descriptions of female beauty — including how they affect the "minefield" of Lavelle's sexuality (70) — is exasperating at times in its oversimplification of a complex issue, but her approach is at least thought-provoking. We need more worship-free feminist criticism of O'Brien's work which does not lose sight of the greater issues at play. One of many urgent tasks is to review the construction of canonical modernism that ensured the exclusion of writers such as O'Brien, an undertaking already begun by critics such as Gerardine Meaney (see "Modernism"). Feminists have created an alternative set of referents as a palliative to the silencing of official accounts of history and literature. The result is that, in Ireland at least, we have two different versions of the significance of Kate O'Brien's work. For example, in two critics who were writing around 2005, Hugh McFadden concedes that *The Land of Spices* is "a subtly feminist book" ("Introduction" 406), while Elizabeth Butler Cullingford describes it as a blatant lesbian feminist activist novel ("Nuns" 63). Christine Battersby points out that "[f]eminist criticism is a *collective* enterprise" (emphasis in original, 157). I see my own work as part of that enterprise, and I feel it is imperative that we go beyond building an alternative canon or an alternative O'Brien canon, to honor that collective approach by dismantling a hierarchical ordering of Irish literature, which can only perpetuate exclusion and distortion.

Banning

Mary Lavelle was banned in Ireland upon publication, at a time when the Irish government had reached a peak in its concern with "protecting national identity" (Fischerova "Writer"). The banning has been described by John Jordan as "the debacle of *Mary Lavelle*" ("Kate" [1976] 234). The cause, Reynolds quoted *Pray for the Wanderer*, was "the vagaries of the new Calvinism in Irish society" (*Kate* 75). Eibhear Walshe explains that *Mary Lavelle* was banned "on the grounds of obscenity on 29 December 1936. It was her first novel to be banned in Ireland and, unlike *The Land of Spices*, it was never the subject of a revocation order and so remained on the list of forbidden works" (*Kate* 67). As Michael Adams has documented, after the Censorship of Publications Act of 1929, one of the most commonly used grounds for banning a book was its being "in its general tendency indecent or obscene," with *indecent* defined as including text that was "suggestive of, or inciting to, sexual immorality or unnatural vice, or likely in any other similar way to corrupt or deprave"; Jana Fischerova notes that this definition was clearly being stretched to accommodate other unspoken concerns, as was made clear in 1942, when the banning of Kate O'Brien's *The Land of Spices* was controversial enough that it caused an argument in the Seanad: How could this novel be considered of an immoral tendency, when only one (rather chaste) sentence referred to homosexuality? The book stayed banned despite the debate, but Fischerova is right to highlight this particular "controversy" and to suggest that the novel's attack on the nationalist priorities of de Valera's government was a more likely cause for the banning than its "immorality" ("Writer"). In 1941, novelist Sean Ó'Faoláin protested in the Dublin journal *The Bell* against the censor's claim of indecency in *The Land of Spices*: "Clearly this is a lie" (quoted in Walshe *Kate* 89). As Eibhear Walshe explains, Kate O'Brien was persuaded by senator John Keane and other supporters to appeal against the ban in 1946, which determined her "public profile in Ireland as a controversial writer" (ibid., 90).

The earlier banning of *Mary Lavelle* has not been scrutinized as much as that of *The Land of Spices*, perhaps because an Irish girl *demanding* sex of a married man must have undoubtedly raised eyebrows in 1930s Ireland (see Reynolds *Kate* 101). The book granted "self-government" to its protagonist (O'Brien, *Mary* 27), a political provocation to the establishment. At a 1937 lecture in London, Irish feminist activist Hannah Sheehy Skeffington complained about the banning of *Mary Lavelle* (see Walshe, *Kate* 69). Emma Donoghue contends that Agatha's unrepentant lesbianism in the novel may have also been grounds for banning ("Order" 41), and she may be right, even though Agatha's ultimate chastity may have gone some way to calm down the inquisitors. However, the novel itself highlights the main "perverse" episode (see O'Brien *Mary* 296), an illicit heterosexual sexual encounter, and the main narrative moves inexorably towards the sex scene in the Basque mountains, which, to quote Patricia Coughlan, "brings the plot (and the male lead) to a climax" (68). Reynolds suggests that the fact that this sinful behavior "could not be ascribed to the customs of a 'pagan' country" must have mobilized the Catholic censors into action (*Kate* 102). It is important to keep in mind, however, that O'Brien was not a lone victim. As John Jordan reminds us: "The banning of *Mary Lavelle* in 193[6] was not, of course, an isolated affront to Irish writers. The same year Francis Hacketts's *The Green Lion*, Seán O'Faoláin's *Bird Alone* and Austin Clarke's *The Singing Men at Cashel* were chopped. Nineteen-thirty-six was a vintage year for the Censorship of Publications Board" ("Kate" [1987] 237).

Farewell Spain was never banned in Ireland, yet several commentators see its publication as the reason why O'Brien was forbidden entry into Spain for 20 years (see for example O'Neill xii–xiii; Reynolds, *Kate* 97) — a controversial topic that remains contested (see for example Walshe *Kate*; Ramblado "Kate"). In 1972, O'Brien declared at a public lecture that "all my works were long ago totally banned in Spain — and so remain" (emphasis in original, "Spain" 4), and this was also contested by critics. As we will see, Marisol Morales Ladrón and Ute Mittermaier have put the debate to rest after some impressive research in Spanish archives, proving that *Mary Lavelle was* banned in Spain.

The publication history of Kate O'Brien, with many of her books remaining out of print for decades, might be considered evidence of another form of censorship. The often puzzled-about delay in reprinting *As Music and Splendour* was in fact owed to the fact that the copyright holders were attempting to secure publication for both this novel and the lesser-known *The Flower of May* as a "package" (Donough O'Brien, in conversation, November 2003). In an academic context, established literary critics may have ignored her work in general because it was at one time too popular (see Jordan "Kate" [1973] 230) or, as Emma Donohue points out, they may have been responsible for another form of silencing, by under-researching O'Brien's two novels with explicit lesbian content, *As Music and Splendour* and *Mary Lavelle* ("Order" 37). On the other hand, scholars faced unusual difficulties; as Mary Coll put it, in the late 1970s and early 1980s "[i]nformation about O'Brien was as hard to discover as the third secret of Fatima" ("Introduction" xii). Patricia A. Cawley explained in 1981 that "25 years of obscurity" were just coming to an end, with the publication of a special edition of the *Stony Thursday Book* devoted to O'Brien's work, a television adaptation of her novel *The Anteroom*, and, also in the same year, a Civic Week in her native Limerick, which was reported in *The Irish Times* under the heading "A City at Last Forgives Kate O'Brien" (Cawley 38). It was not enough to have been banned, she had to be forgiven for it, and then only after rage could no longer shake her (to paraphrase Swift's epitaph). In 1984, the mainstreaming of her work took a steady course with the annual "Kate O'Brien Weekend," set up by the poet and O'Brien scholar Louise C. Callaghan on behalf of Arlen House, the publishers that had begun to reprint O'Brien's novels four years earlier. By 2003–2006, when the conference "An Evening with Kate O'Brien" was organized in University College Dublin (by myself and, in 2006, Shannon Byrne), a considerable pool of O'Brien scholars was emerging. Despite the difficulties in earlier years, another important consequence of the ban of *Mary Lavelle* and *The Land of Spices* was that Kate O'Brien became a sort of unofficial hero for those readers — particularly for the artists among them — who felt oppressed by the Irish government's intervention on arts and culture from the 1930s to the 1950s, and for those who disagreed with Irish policies and the role of the church in the following decades.

Kate O'Brien avoided discussing the banning of *Mary Lavelle* in Ireland (see Jordan "Kate" [1973] 229), but it is evident that it conditioned all her subsequent output. *Pray for the Wanderer* was a direct response to the banning, a "literary revenge" in the words of James Cahalan (208), and a critique of censorship which is not entirely coherent, according to Brad Kent ("Argument"). Reynolds suggests that setting *That Lady* in sixteenth century Spain may have been "a deliberate strategy" to avoid the censor (*Kate* 104). The discreet approach to eroticism in *The Land of Spices* was a retreat in terms of explicitness. For protagonists after *Mary Lavelle*, it was to be all allegory and suggestion. It is impossible to know how much self-censorship affected O'Brien's working practice. There is evidence that filters were in place as early as her first novel, but a desire to avoid difficulties must have been exacerbated after the banning. Donoghue suggests that it was only "[a]t the end of her career, when Irish censorship was easing up, [that] Kate O'Brien allowed herself to return to a lesbian theme" ("Noises" 183). Reynolds believes that the bans "deflected her from doing what she might otherwise have done, show a mature Irish woman defy the narrow conventions of her day *in Ireland*" (emphasis added, *Kate* 104). The national and international politics too, after the rage of *Pray for the Wanderer*, were to be discreetly articulated — no more direct references to socialism, nor to authoritarianism of de Valera's kind. Religion was also a problematic topic, and Reynolds further suggests that the agnostic O'Brien did not chronicle loss of faith in fiction partly because "she knew such a novel would be banned in Ireland" (118). At a formal level, subsequent works were to play safe too. It is of enormous significance that even as late as 1962, in her penultimate book, *My Ireland*, O'Brien is still referring to censorship as a very real concern: "were it not so tricky nowadays about printing what one has in mind..." she laments (28). It is impossible to know where the experimentation of *Mary Lavelle* may have taken Kate O'Brien, had she been allowed to continue exploring formal and thematic possibilities to the extent she does in this novel. There is no question that she had to hold the reins and pull back after 1936.

ONE

Some Contexts

Introduction: Flaws

No other book by Kate O'Brien crosses so many borders nor crosses them with such ease. *Mary Lavelle* is an activist novel, as well as an autobiographical novel, an experimental modernist novel, a fictional biography, a "governess abroad" bildungsroman, a documentary, an existentialist novel, and a romance, perhaps in that order. If we consider allegory to be a genre (see Quilligan 1979), *Mary Lavelle* also belongs to it. As we will see, Adele Dalsimer is baffled at how late the romance plot takes off in *Mary Lavelle*, with the love interest, Juanito, making his appearance halfway through the book (see 40). This is an "anomaly" only according to certain reader expectations. Clearly, Mary's encounter with a foreign country, with a new profession, a new social circle, and a new freedom, are the main concern of the novel, *at least* until Juanito appears, if not for the duration of the book. *Mary Lavelle* has been, to this day, marketed as a romantic novel, and critics and readers seem to have internalized this assumption too. *Talk of Angels*, the 1998 film version of the novel, provides a striking example. When the film was at the pre-production stage, the romantic content in O'Brien's story was foregrounded to such an extent that the producers considered shifting the setting to Portugal, as they deemed the location and politics of the book a mere cosmetic enhancement to the drama of passion. The contextualization of *Mary Lavelle* is crucial to fully appreciate its idiosyncrasies. *Mary Lavelle* can be placed in many literary contexts, and I will look at two of them in detail in this section: the governess abroad bildungsroman and the generation of 98. There are a number of possible frameworks, so for example *Mary Lavelle* can be approached as a realist, romantic, or historical novel. There has been no attempt to consider *Mary Lavelle* as a multiple-genre book, alert to contemporary experimentation while carrying on a dialogue with tradition. Contextualization of O'Brien, half-heartedly attempted by many scholars, has created a number of problems when her books have been forcibly fitted into a number of available models. As a result, her work has been severely distorted, and many multi-generic, inter/sub-textual features have been misread as flaws. One of the most striking features in O'Brien criticism is the fact that the overwhelming majority of scholars see flaws wherever they look. It is an unfailing source of amusement to wait for the inevitable admission in an essay. Anne Haverty actually opens her 2006 review of Eibhear Walshe's biography of O'Brien with the following:

> Really, Kate O'Brien should not have been a particularly good novelist. Her preoccupations could be said to be narrow and were continually recycled. Bent on idealising her middle-class Limerick background and the milieu she came from, she had propagandist tendencies. She was almost devoid of the illuminating qualities of humour and irony. She could be careless or even unimaginative.... And her ear for cadence and rhythm was not the best — her sentence construction is often clumsy and clotted.
> Yet she is a deeply impressive and satisfying writer. One reads her, not exactly with pleasure perhaps, but at the least with an invigorating sense of connection with a subtle and liberated mind — which is arguably what literature is ultimately for [12].

One of the tasks I set out for this book is to refute every one of the arguments in that first paragraph, which happen to be representative of much O'Brien criticism. As for the second paragraph, also representative, the self-justification of commentators is reminiscent of the nervous legitimating operations of scholars of noncanonical literature that we rarely encounter nowadays. In the case of O'Brien, this tendency reaches astonishing proportions. For example, Anne Fogarty in 1993: "The literary output of Kate O'Brien ... is of interest because of its flawed and hybrid character. Her novels are compelling because they are misshapen, open-ended and lacunary" ("Desire" 101). Fogarty goes on to claim, "It is their imperfect meshing of the conventions of women's romance with social critique which leaves the reader both with an impression of the probing acuity of O'Brien's fictions and also with an abiding sense of their imbalance" (ibid.). If there is some acknowledgment here of the multi-generic nature of O'Brien's work, this feature is irrevocably linked to failure. In the same collection, Patricia Coughlan makes practically the same statement, claiming that O'Brien produced "a series of novels which are, it should be admitted at the outset, of uneven quality, largely lacking in stylistic elegance and apparently innocent of the great modernists' developments in narrative technique, if not altogether in vision. Yet under the dismayingly wordy surface..." (60). If at least Fogarty allows for the possibility that O'Brien's particular approach to "meshing of conventions" is what is "imperfect," rather than the practice itself, Coughlan highlights what she sees as "inelegance" and the failure of O'Brien to display a high modernist style as "the problem." Coughlan follows this with an interesting move, suggesting that flaws are crucial to the survival of works of art and referring to Pierre Macherey, "who proposes that it is precisely the fissures and fractures in the smooth surface of writings which offer leverage to a truly productive criticism, and that the conditions of possibility of a text, which by definition it cannot itself make manifest, are the ultimate objects of critical inquiry" (83–4). In addition to perpetuating the view of O'Brien's work as flawed, these comments assume that criticism is the natural environment of fiction, with the critic as embalmer devoted to the survival of a trade cut off from any immediate social/cultural relevance.

Haverty, Coughlan, and Fogarty at least attempt to articulate their sense of "flawed texts" within some useful parameters. Most other O'Brien critics simply register their discomfort. A freak example of "the flaw school" is Eavan Boland's paper "The Legacy of Kate O'Brien," where she uses O'Brien to attack feminist publishers for giving a platform to unworthy texts (that is: severely flawed as opposed to relatively flawed). Another worrying example is Declan Kiberd's highlighting of "grat[ing]" flaws in O'Brien, "flaws she appears to share with [George] Eliot," such as the "wise woman syndrome," comments followed by his attempt at disclaiming responsibility, by stating that "these objections are often less strenuously prosecuted against a male than a female author who tells readers what they may think" (*Classics* 559–60). Some critics, such as John Jordan, highlight a specific "flaw" or "weakness" in character construction ("Kate" [1976] 234–5). Others point to certain plot features that they see as defective. Lorna Reynolds's *Kate O'Brien — A Literary Portrait* (1987) is peppered throughout with such comments. Adele Dalsimer's *Kate O'Brien: A Critical Study* occasionally draws attention to such "flaws," as when she claims that "Vincent's suicide in *The Anteroom* is a weak ending to this powerful book" (32). At another point, however, considering *Mary Lavelle*, Dalsimer perceptively notes that Juanito's "awkwardly placed appearance late in the novel, after Mary has begun her self-discovery, suggests that their love story is not as crucial to the novel as Mary's quest for individuation and self-definition" (40), the implication being that a potential flaw in a romantic novel is no such thing in a bildungsroman. A reader's conviction that Juanito's appearance is "awkwardly placed" is therefore entirely dictated by her expectations. This is to me the key to the bafflement and awkwardness that touches most O'Brien scholarship. I do not wish to claim that O'Brien's work is perfect, which would be a meaningless statement, but rather, that positioning her texts is crucial to each reader's and critic's perception of them. *That Lady*, for instance, seems to me irreparably flawed as a historical novel (despite critical persistence to allocate it to that role), yet a powerful example of political novel at its very best (see Byron "Drawing-Room"). *Mary Lavelle* certainly belongs to a number of traditions— some of which may superficially appear to cancel each other. Approaching this multifarious text from a number of angles seems to me the only appropriate way to critically engage with it. Allow me to borrow some props from the novel itself to illustrate this point. *Mary Lavelle*, considered as a single tool — say, a gramophone — will only "perform" when required to play pre-recorded tunes; if it is then expected to fulfill a function as another tool — say, a wireless — it will fail to give us a news broadcast. Why not see this novel as a trunk containing a number of novels, all of which engage with each other but have distinct qualities and uses? When doing so, many perceived "flaws" simply dissolve without a trace. The hands of Oisín Kelly's 1977 statue *Jim Larkin* in Dublin's O'Connell Street — like the hands of Michelangelo's sculpture of *David* in Florence — are out of proportion with the rest of his body, being far too big. No one would dare to suggest that this is a flaw. In good faith, critics/observers assume that there is a purpose to this "problem"—it heightens drama, it suggests the empty hands of the dispossessed, it represents the transformative power of Larkin's eloquence, it is the only "weapon" of the working class—in other words, this "flaw" is no such thing. A certain good faith from commentators is crucial to reading *Mary Lavelle*, arguably more so than when dealing with other O'Brien texts because much of the experimentation in this particular novel relies on a multi-generic, multi-textual approach.

The multi-genre character of *Mary Lavelle*, as we will see later, is just one of the important aspects to the novel that has been overlooked. Another is the intertextuality or intratextuality between *Mary Lavelle* and a number of other books by O'Brien. The first context for *Mary Lavelle* is its close interaction with *Farewell Spain*, which provides historical and biographical clues to the novel; another is *The Anteroom*, which provides a sketch of *Mary Lavelle* with alternative plot developments; another is *Without My Cloak*, which offers one of O'Brien's first attempts at telling Lavelle's story; and a final crucial reference is *As Music and Splendour*, which rewrites the protagonist of *Mary Lavelle* forcing us to reassess the earlier novel. It may be useful to begin with *Farewell Spain* because its intertextual relationship with the 1936 novel needs to be considered somewhat independently, given the specificities of a dialogue between a factual and a fictional account. Then, we can consider the fictional interplay between *Mary Lavelle* and other versions of the novel, beginning with an analysis of the way in which symbolism and subtext operates in O'Brien's work. In the case of the intertextuality of *Mary Lavelle* with other O'Brien novels, there is a traceable central narrative/experience so crucial to her work that she constantly revised it, from a first sketch in 1926 to a final rewrite in 1958, and which came into its fullest (yet still clearly unfinished) form in 1936. This may suggest something like a subatomic model in which a series of minor works gravitate around *Mary Lavelle*, but the fact is that the connections between all five books (and, to an extent, all of O'Brien's work) are more akin to a series of energy waves transforming all in their path according to what book one is holding, in relation to which other. Once we have considered *Mary Lavelle*'s relationships within the universe created by O'Brien, we can move on and consider other contexts. There is consensus on seeing *Mary Lavelle* as a bildungsroman, but looking at the characteristics of the subgenre that I am calling the "governess abroad" bildungsroman makes evident the revisionist attitude of O'Brien to a type of narrative that is itself quite invested in redrafting conventions. A neglected yet equally interesting context in which to place *Mary Lavelle* is that of the literary movement known as the "Generación del Noventayocho" ("the generation of 98") in Spain, a context in which much of O'Brien's work after 1936 can be placed comfortably. There are other contexts, as we will see in subsequent chapters—focusing on activist literature, modernism, and fictionalized history — and no doubt many more will resurface as new readers come to *Mary Lavelle* bringing their own interpretations, carrying their own trunks.

Companion Book

Mary Lavelle is unique in Kate O'Brien's output in that a companion piece to the novel was published the following year, *Farewell Spain*. There are two important issues relating to their intertextuality: highlighting the relevance of the politics of *Farewell Spain* has a similar effect on the novel, and collating the references in *Farewell Spain* with those in *Mary Lavelle* makes evident that an autobiographical reading of the novel is very deliberately encouraged. The last chapter of *Farewell Spain* in particular, devoted to Bilbo/Altorno, is a political and aesthetic testimony of intent. It is not, however, a simplified attempt at authenticating *Mary Lavelle*'s factual basis, because the painstakingly worded recreation of memory in this piece of nonfiction is clearly a creative endeavor. Looking at *Farewell Spain* in the light of *Mary Lavelle* alters our perception of the travelogue, opening history and identity to fictionalization, distortion. In other words, *Farewell Spain* is "glossed" by *Mary Lavelle* too.

The political content in O'Brien's work has been invariably sidelined by critics. This singular blindspot in Irish criticism may also be reponsible for the neglet of another remarkable book set in the Basque Country, *The Spirit and the Clay*, published by the Irish author Shevawn Lynam in 1954; it offers a fictionalized account of a personal testimony (in a series of interconnected stories) retelling the "adventures" of Basque political prisoners escaping from the fascist army in the aftermath of the Spanish Civil War. The common practice of describing *Farewell Spain* as a travelogue of Spain without further details is an example of the versatility of the notion of genre, easily turned from velvet rope into lynching prop. The landscapes of *Farewell Spain* are clear political landscapes, just as the main plots in *Mary Lavelle* are political plots. *Farewell Spain* stands, in relation to *Mary Lavelle*, in a similar position as Virginia Woolf's 1938 *Three Guineas* to her 1937 novel *The Years*. Both *Mary Lavelle* and *Farewell Spain* originate from a single political impetus; their differences are related to the rapidly changing political climate during their composition in those crucial years. That is, if O'Brien's 1936 novel could be used as a vehicle for the revolutionary ideas that inspired the leftist Republic in Spain, like a Trojan horse (I am thinking of Jeanette Winterson's description of *Orlando* as "a Trojan horse"; see *Art*), the 1937 book had to demand that Franco's troops be stopped and firmly state, "No pasarán" ("They shall not pass") (102), half aware of its own future status as an elegy.

This political dimension is not an anomaly in O'Brien. For example, Michael O'Toole has described *Pray for the Wanderer* as "Kate O'Brien's novel of protest" ("Peasants"), and the book's rage against de Valeraism warrants it. Feminist politics and sexual liberational politics are everywhere in O'Brien's work and are also crucial to *Mary Lavelle*. But *Mary Lavelle* and *Farewell Spain*, together with the 1946 *That Lady*, as responses to the immediate threat of fascism, are unequivocally also political *acts*. In *Farewell Spain*, O'Brien sets herself the task of informing her Anglophone readers of the present political landscape in Spain. In doing so, she has an agenda; her book (and this applies also to *Mary Lavelle*) is the literary equivalent of the revolutionary murals by Mexican artists in the 1920s and 1930s. O'Brien *explains* that General Franco's forces are "the returning Moor" (147)—that is, to her, an imperialist army, foreign to the Spanish temperament — and his attack of the leftist Republic is "criminal" (220) because this war is "openly aimed at the murder of every democratic principle, and for the setting up of [Franco's] little self as yet another Mussolini — such a war strikes not merely for the death of Spain, but at every decent dream or effort for humanity everywhere" (221).

Descriptions of places and retellings of events as the narrator remembers them are constantly interrupted by references to the current state of the war. In the introductory chapter, for example: "As I write Irún is burning. There's a photograph in this morning's *Times*..." (6). The same interruptions take place in Woolf's *Three Guineas*, written in the winter of 1936–1937, like O'Brien's book, and also as a response to the threat of fascism. In February 1937, as O'Brien writes the final lines of *Farewell Spain*, control of the Madrid-Valencia road (the supply route to a Madrid under siege) was crucial to the survival of the democrat camp, and the fascist forces were trying to close the road. Kate O'Brien exclaims: "May it be held open for ever and for all our sakes!" (229). O'Brien's 1937 *Farewell Spain*, Woolf's 1938 *Three Guineas*, and George Orwell's 1938 *Homage to Catalonia* are three responses to the Spanish Civil War which can be seen to be complementary in that they are personal responses from fiction writers who supported the cause of the leftist Republic in Spain, all of whom were sympathetic towards anarchism. There are a number of interesting punctual coincidences among these three texts, such as O'Brien's derision of the British taste for pageantry as it translates in an emphasis on uniforms and rituals; both the tone and the list included (see O'Brien *Spain* 167–8) are uncannily similar to Woolf's more extensive and politicized dealing with the topic in *Three Guineas*.

Whether one sees it as politically or geographically minded, *Farewell Spain* is not a travelogue of *Spain*, if we take into account that the traveler-narrator only visits the northwestern half of the Iberian Peninsula. O'Brien was self-admittedly not familiar with the east and south — nor interested in them. There is something almost perverse in this focus, as the most popular/publicized regions to foreign tourists are, of course, the sunny east and south. The route of the book starts in Santander, moves to Santillana, Covadonga, Altamira, Santiago, Salamanca, Avila, Madrid, Segovia, Burgos, and ends in Bilbo (the Basque spelling of Bilbao), where O'Brien had spent several months working as a governess in 1922–1923, and where she had set *Mary Lavelle*. In the chapter titled "Mainly Personal," dealing with Bilbo/Altorno, O'Brien consciously follows Lavelle (without once mentioning the novel), from Portugalete/Cabantes, to San Vicente/San Geronimo, to Begoña/Allera. The real names of the locations take over the fictional ones, and our traveler retraces the steps of Mary, to enjoy the view from a bench by "Our Lady's shrine," just as her characters had done, while

regularly "dropping" autobiographical information related to the novel. "[L]ook-
ing down from Begoña towards the bridge and the Arenal where I search for my
own ghost" (*Spain* 211), for example, just as Mary, in the same spot, had referred
to her "double" (*Mary* 200) dancing in the square that O'Brien now overlooks.
"I sometimes sat up here," O'Brien explains, "on this same bench, 12 years ago"
(*Spain* 208–9). As we will see, many details from O'Brien's nonfiction account
work in tandem with *Mary Lavelle*, and add to the sophistication of the conceptual experiment that the novel represents. The Bilbo chapter ends *Farewell Spain*,
with the author crossing the border by train in Irun, uncertain if what she leaves
behind will remain intact. Lavelle's border crossing was also the end of the novel,
and there was no doubt that she was traveling towards the ruins of one of her
possible futures— as model wife. Lavelle was also leaving Spain just before the
world she had known and loved collapsed, with the coup d'état of General Primo
de Rivera in 1923. Other O'Brien books were to soar out of *Farewell Spain*
(prefigured by sections on Teresa of Avila and Philip II), but this is the terminus
for the Basque Country. Yet Kate O'Brien was well aware that when one crosses
the border between Spain and France in Irun, one is still on Basque soil. The last
two pages of *Mary Lavelle* (the brief section called "A Matador's Cape"), then,
are set in a utopian space where ends are meaningless, limits breachable. However, this is also a space where closure is impossible and the past inescapable.
When Mary arrived, she was on "the errand of keeping alive" (*Mary* xvi), and
now her host country will have to do the same. Written with hindsight of a time
preceding dictatorship, and in the awareness that the present fragile democracy
may not last, *Mary Lavelle* and *Farewell Spain* were of one mind in their attempt
to derail "the far too easy and platitudinous derision of ... history" (*Mary* xvi).

Symbolism and Subtext

Before discussing *Mary Lavelle*'s intertextuality within O'Brien's fiction,
it is useful to consider the ways in which the textuality of the book is manifest.
Wanda Balzano has remarked on the different layers of writing in *Mary Lavelle*,
which at one level is about Mary and John, at another about Mary and Agatha,
at another about O'Brien herself ... and there is always something underneath,
waiting to be unearthed in turn ("Question"). There are three related techniques
used by O'Brien to bind the novel internally and with other books: symbolism,
allegory, and subtext. In symbolism, a word or image referring to something
specific is suggestive of something else. In allegory, the narrative (or a strand)
is suggestive of another narrative. Both symbolism and allegory may be added
onto a given story without disrupting its main focus. In subtext, however, a
hidden parallel narrative works *against* the text of the surface narrative. For
example, Agatha wears a Tara brooch, symbolizing her discrete yet relevant
allegiance to Ireland and emphasizing an Irish-Spanish link (the hill of Tara,

Tea Mur, was the burial place of the much loved Spanish Tea, wife to an Irish king — see MacManus 54). For example, Mary can be seen to represent the Irish Free State, and her adventure can be read as an allegory of a journey towards independence (she yearns for "self-government," and her journey begins in 1922). The presence of a brooch as part of Agatha's attire, or the suggestion that Mary is Ireland, does not undermine the cohesion of these characters or of the main story in any way; yet other "elements" in the novel decidedly look out of place. For example, Patricia Coughlan rightly points out to the "preposterou[s]" spectacle of an "untravelled and provincial" Mary Lavelle comparing Luisa Areavaga to an angel in an Italian primitive nativity (83). And yet, what is preposterous in the context of realism, or plausibility, is no such thing if we bring symbolism, allegory, or subtext into the equation. Mary's comment can be seen as a "disruptive signal," an indication that something else, outside the realist narrative, is relevant to the story. Discussing O'Brien's first novel, Lorna Reynolds notes that early on in the book "[s]he introduces the oblique methods of poetry to intimate folds of meaning not yet available" (*Kate* 47). The same occurs in *Mary Lavelle*, where a number of characters are likened to angels, something which plays an important part in an allegorical plot which we shall discuss later. Given that *Mary Lavelle* is considered unanimously to be a realist novel, this must mean that "preposterous" occurrences are rare in the book. In fact, the novel peels off its skin on every page to reveal a symbol. For example, Agatha's description of home as "flat[land] ... with millwheels" (208) points to a Quixote from Co. Wexford. For example, Mary and Juanito's dancing to the tune "I met my love in Avalon" (189) speaks of once and future utopia. For example, Luisa and Mary's first meeting, proving that "Greek ... usually knows Greek" (151), is nothing other than a lesbian reckoning. In *Mary Lavelle* there are countless other examples of strained turns of phrase and oddly sitting bits of information, all of which disrupt realist convention, if only momentarily. After *Mary Lavelle*, such handling of symbolism will be trimmed up and consolidated in Kate O'Brien's subsequent work. This "disguised symbolism," to borrow Erwin Panofski's term from the visual arts (141) — useful despite some poststructuralists' tantrums — is rather blatant, relying as it does on a hammering of repeated suggestions and on the intrusion of awkward turns of phrase, clamoring for the attention of the reader. Yet surprisingly this feature of O'Brien's writing has yet to be considered by critics, although it may be one of the reasons why John McGahern described her in 1999 as "a poet writing in prose" (quoted by Kiberd, *Classics* 574).

Symbolism, a staple of poetry, is not used with such eclecticism and frequency in any other novel by Kate O'Brien. *The Flower of May* is consistently divided in a pattern of light and dark, while *As Music and Splendour* equates musical proficiency to sexual maturity, and these ideas work in tandem with the narratives. *Mary Lavelle* uses a number of symbols — notably the bullfight to signal an awakening to aesthetics and eroticism in Mary. In this novel, however, symbolism is also used to destabilize the main text by signposting a series of subtextual narratives. What I refer to as the "main text" is, in the case of *Mary Lavelle*, as follows: a bildungsroman of Mary, a young heterosexual Irish woman who attains financial independence, freedom of movement, and ethical self-reliance in a foreign city, Altorno/Bilbo. What I refer to as "subtext" is any submerged narrative in the novel which contradicts that main text. A reader can access a subtext by tapping onto certain signs, such as a specific use of symbolism. So for example, in *Mary Lavelle* the constant repetition of words such as "natural" and "orthodox" creates a disturbance, a ripple in the surface suggesting that some form of alter-life stirs below.

A number of symbolic images are used only once, such as the linking of Mary (in the sex scene) to a martyred San Sebastian, but there are also many "symbolic layers" running throughout the text. An allegory will retain the basic developments in the narrative, respect its plot, and suggest the "substitution" of one set of events for another: "Mary falls in love with Juanito" can be substituted by "Irish Free State falls in love with Spanish Revolution." But a subtextual narrative will undo one set of events through another: "Mary falls in love with Juanito" can be substituted by "Mary is lesbian." In allegory, the same container is used to carry different contents; in subtext, the container is disabled. This is what happens in Meret Oppenheim's sculpture *Fur-covered Cup, Saucer, and Spoon* of 1936, where the "main text's" function is annulled while, ironically, its shape is highlighted. In writing by women, as Elizabeth Abel, Marianne Hirsch, and Elizabeth Langland have pointed out, "[t]he tensions that shape female development may lead to a disjunction between a surface plot, which affirms social conventions, and a submerged plot, which encodes rebellion" (12). No other novel by Kate O'Brien invests and releases as much energy in subtextual narratives. Several of them coexist in *Mary Lavelle*, and it is not merely a feat that they retain their coherence, but the management of their interrelation to the main text is an extraordinary accomplishment. Speaking of Kate O'Brien's previous novel, Declan Kiberd detects a variance of selves in the protagonist and regrets that the author is not up to the technical challenge to represent this modern quandary, which calls, as he sees it, "for a multiplanar narrative that will capture all the fragments of that experience" (*Classics* 562). *Mary Lavelle* (as *The Anteroom* had in fact done to a lesser degree) will create such a "multiplanar narrative" through an astonishingly ambitious subtextual program, taking fragmentation to an extreme by dividing the protagonists into a multiplicity of characters.

One subtext branches out (in different directions) of the novel's biographical concern with the figure of Enrique Areilza, the model for Don Pablo in *Mary Lavelle*. Kate O'Brien met him in 1922, and he made a considerable impression on her, so much so that this novel is part biography, part homage, as we will see later. Enrique Areilza, a famous and much loved surgeon, reformer, and intellectual from Bilbo, appears in the novel in a thin disguise (as Don Pablo), is projected onto a fictional son (Juanito) and a daughter (Milagros), and is presented side by side with an antithetical version of himself (Dr.

Lavelle). In *Mary Lavelle*, Don Pablo/Enrique Areilza is not a surgeon, although Juanito, "the recreation of [Don Pablo's] youth" (144), is given "to analogies from physiology to clarify his belief" (160). There are numerous indications that Juanito is intended as a "double" of Don Pablo. One example is Mary's reaction when Juanito is about to leave for France: "'I shall see him every time I look at Don Pablo,' she thought contentedly" (190). *Mary Lavelle*'s subtextual conflation of Don Pablo and Juanito simply makes no sense in relation to the main text, but it grants Don Pablo/Enrique Areilza a co-starring role in the novel, in what Reynolds sees as an (unsuccessful) attempt "at making Don Pablo's bad health encompass an enveloping action" (*Kate* 61). But his role is far more complex than that. Not only is Juanito "spiritually [his father] enhanced, corrected," but his sister Mila is also presented as Don Pablo's "echo" (*Mary* 335), and this link redrafts the nature of Mary's relationship with the siblings.

At another level, Don Pablo, Juanito, and Mary's triangular relationship reads well as a lively update of the Arthuriad. Thomas Malory's version of the Arthurian legend, written around 1495, is referred to in the novel, highlighted by Nieves, who declares the book to be her favorite read at present (see 136). In addition to the well known Arthur/Lancelot/Guenevere narrative, given Agatha's self-acknowledged "hag/witch persona" (Donoghue "Order" 47; see O'Brien *Mary* 297), she can also be read as an update of Arthur's half-sister, Morgan la Fay (see Malory 23), a figure that has been read as lesbian (see for example Marion Zimmer Bradley's 1982 *The Mists of Avalon* and Marilyn Farwell's analysis of the novel). The implications of these links reverberate throughout the book.

Other subtexts present parallel storylines for Mary. One links Nieves, Mary, and Agatha to offer a lesbian bildungsroman. The "blatant signal" that disrupts the normative story is here the unusual quality of their blue eyes, suggesting the same way of looking at the world. From the girl who dreams of being "an English boy at Eton" (*Mary* 16), to the young woman at first "glad to be orthodox in feeling" (31) in a heterosexual attachment and later exploring her sexuality in a foreign country, to the mature woman who accepts her lesbian feelings, this storyline cannot be accommodated into the main heterosexual narrative of the novel and obviously functions on a different timescale, by offering snapshots of a single woman at around 15, 20, and 30 years of age.

An allegoric and subtextual "frenzy" that goes beyond alternative plots makes *Mary Lavelle* a unique effort in Kate O'Brien's work. The chapter titles, for example, which Kate O'Brien treats with detached restraint in all her books, are in *Mary Lavelle* occasionally "at a slant" (to borrow from Emily Dickinson — see 1024), unstable signifiers in bold conceptual experiments. The chapter titled "In the Calle Mayor" ("In Main Street") for example, switches the narrative *without warning* into a new setting — after taking the reader through the streets and sights of Altorno/Bilbo for 200 pages— to the capital city of Spain and the geographical center of the state, Madrid. The title "In Main Street" rewrites Altorno as a suburb irrevocably attached to a center and reconfigures Spain as a massive urban space.

Another example is the chapter titled "Romance." It deals not with the protagonist's love affair (as the reader might expect), which has yet to take off, but is concerned instead with unorthodox love in a double subplot involving two Irish governesses, one of whom marries a (bald, fat, middle-aged, poor) Basque shopkeeper, while the other confesses her passion for Mary. The chapter title can be seen as a diversion, or as a head-on charge against the conventions (and the reader's consequent expectations) of heteronormative romantic fiction. This creative use of titles is *not* realistic in a conventional descriptive sense; it is oppositional, disconcerting, as unpredictable in its familiarity as the turns of a dream.

Borrowings

INTRODUCTION

Some characters from *Mary Lavelle* appear in three other novels by Kate O'Brien. We find sketches of Pablo/Juanito and Mary in *Without My Cloak* and *The Anteroom*, while Mary and Luisa reappear in *As Music and Splendour*. The repetition of characters in an author's work is not in itself exceptional — we have the famous twentieth century precedents of Clarissa Dalloway and Stephen Dedalus, for example, both borrowed by Woolf and Joyce from their own first novels. Also in Kate O'Brien, three secondary characters in *Without My Cloak*, Vincent, Marie-Rose, and Agnes, become the protagonists of *The Anteroom*. These are straightforward borrowings, which do not affect the plot of either book. O'Brien has a tendency to explore a limited set of "types," and there are numerous echoes to be found, in chains of characters, sometimes purposefully highlighted by the repetition of similar/same details or even names. For example, there are similarities between Marie-Rose (*The Anteroom*), Rosie O'Toole (*Mary Lavelle*), and La Rosa d'Irlanda (*As Music and Splendour*). The critic Akiko Kaijima also sees links in the personalities of Lilian, Caroline, Marie Rose, Ana Murphy, and Fanny (47–48). In *Mary Lavelle*, however, there are three striking, elaborate, and crucial borrowings *from* two previous novels and *by* a future novel, which force us to reread *Mary Lavelle* under a different light.

THE ANTEROOM

Don Pablo is a "reincarnation" of William Curran in *The Anteroom*. Doctors recur in Kate O'Brien novels, but in Dr. Curran we have another clear portrait of Enrique Areilza, or "Dr. Areilza," as he is still remembered today in Bilbo/Altorno. In *The Anteroom*, Dr. Curran is a "man of detachment and intelligence" (52), "inwardly ... burn[ing] in the usual hell of human longing which it had been his studied intention to escape" (ibid.), but plagued with "a cold sense of the futility of life" (53). A practicing Catholic, "[a]s a doctor he observed [prayer] to be the most salutary of medicines" (58), even though "[m]ysticism and its chance to ennoble, or at least to alleviate, granted, Doctor Curran would be rationalistic" (ibid.). He believed that "the Catholic Church provided as good a system as might be found for keeping the human animal in order ... because, through thick and thin, it exacted a soul of every man and instilled in the very lowest of its creatures an innocent familiarity with things not apprehended of the flesh" (ibid.). Don Pablo put it more succinctly, considering Catholicism "the only system of faith at once impassioned and controlled" (*Mary* 61). Dr. Curran and Don Pablo think alike and are described in exactly the same terms, but in *Mary Lavelle* we are also given an account of Areavaga/Areilza's political beliefs (a crucial point to the novel), as well as a detailed biography that includes a brief history of his family. In *Mary Lavelle*, "Don Pablo, the philosopher" (169), has a richer inner life than Dr. Curran (or perhaps he is so much more important in the later novel that the reader just gets to know him better), but we have only the vaguest information about his professional activities. Finally, like Dr. Curran, Don Pablo finds himself unexpectedly attracted to a beautiful, intelligent, introverted woman younger than himself.

Anthony Roche has stated that "through the figure of [William] Curran, Kate O'Brien examines the pathology of male romanticism in the late nineteenth century" ("Anteroom" 91). Yet it is not William, but *Vincent*, who proposes to Agnes that they elope. It is Vincent who dreams that they could "stay away together, so that no mud flung by the righteous should disfigure them," and live "among the simple, ancient peoples who ... take their courtesy from the sweet morning of their world" and who would not disapprove of their adventure, given that "her beauty would be their fatal explanation everywhere on those shores where men have eyes" (O'Brien *Anteroom* 224). It is Vincent who, after imagining this, actually looks at Agnes, smiling, and decides that "she must give him children," and those children will "play their first games on the Ægean hills and Adriatic rocks," after which "she would grow old with a divine, non-combatant reluctance, a rueful grace like that which was his mother's," after which "then there would be death and for their sin whatever theologians meant by hell" (224–5). We find a delightful example of the best dry humor in O'Brien when, following this pile of gibberish, the next paragraph opens with the chiseled: "Agnes wondered why this alternative had never once occurred to her" (ibid.). In a later novel, however, O'Brien's attitude seems to have softened, with an autobiographical character claiming that "romantic love is not an invention so much as a discovery, like America or radium. It's an expression of life's latitude and possibilities" (*Pray* 188–9).

Vincent and William have more in common than their passion for Agnes. We can see Vincent as a double of Dr. Curran (which explains the somewhat confusing similarities between them), in a similar relationship as Juanito and Don Pablo. A number of passages from the 1934 novel seem to have been redrafted into *Mary Lavelle* without altering the relevant ideas—and often using the exact same language. For example, Vincent's recalling of his former passion for his wife and its disappointment (see 8–9) is very much the same as Don Pablo's (*Mary* 54–7). The reason why the "borrowing" of Dr. Curran and his reappearance as Don Pablo is important, as well as striking, is that it allows us to read Curran's frustrated love for Agnes as a rehearsal for Pablo's inarticulated love for Mary, while Vincent is also a rehearsal for Juanito. I do not wish to imply, by using the word "rehearsal," that the earlier novel is more imperfect in any way, but merely that O'Brien was to find a more accurate way of *portraying* Enrique Areilza.

However, the significance of *Mary Lavelle's* "borrowing" from an earlier novel does not stop at the male characters. On the surface the two protagonists, Agnes and Mary, are very different women, but the way they speak and react is often uncannily similar. Given that both women face the same moral dilemma — how to repond to the advances of a married man — we may conclude that these two novels provide alternative endings to the same romance plot. Their circumstances are certainly different socially, financially, etc., and the implicit assumption seems to be that, to an extent, those circumstances dictate the outcome. As for the other woman in *The Anteroom*, Marie Rose, she seems a more extensive "version" of the later Luisa de Maraval (Juanito's wife) in *Mary Lavelle*. It is important to keep in mind that, just as O'Brien was to do with other borrowings, in the case of Dr. Curran/Don Pablo, she ensured that the links between the characters were traceable. The intertextuality or intra-textuality *within* O'Brien's books has this extraordinary dimension: she leaves a trail, so that different versions of stories and characters are simultaneously visible to the reader of her work. As an aesthetic practice, as an ethics, and as a philosophical approach to identity, the method is quite unique.

WITHOUT MY CLOAK

If *The Anteroom* provides a close model for the relationships that dominate *Mary Lavelle*, there are some remarkable commonalties between O'Brien's first novel and *Mary Lavelle*. *Without My Cloak* may be seen to fill in gaps or provide alternatives to the two later narratives, in much the same way as we have discussed of *The Anteroom*. Perhaps the "main" story in the choral novel that is *Without My Cloak* involves Denis, of the well-established Considine family, and Christina, a woman without means, falling in love in Mellick and secretly beginning an affair in the countryside. In *The Anteroom* and *Mary Lavelle*, the male suitor is already married, but in *Without My Cloak*, the main obstacle to the affair is the woman's lower status, which is seen as a threat by his family. There are many points in common between the Christina/Denis subplot and the romance between Mary and Juanito, including some strikingly similar exchanges between the lovers and, remarkably, a very similar setting for their meetings, with Christina's leaning of "her whole body ... against the tree" (291), reminiscent of Mary Lavelle in the sex scene in "The Good Basque Country" chapter. Much of the subplot in *Without My Cloak* lends itself to be read as an appendix to Mary's breakup with Juanito. For example, Mary twice claims to be aware of the risk of pregnancy before having sex with Juanito and leaving the country. The possibility that Christina may get pregnant is discussed and dropped twice. When the lovers reunite after a separation, Christina makes a sudden decision (we find similar reactions in Mary and Agnes), leaves Denis by pretending she is engaged to another man, and we hear no more of her fate. The cloak of the title ostensibly refers to a cape owned by Denis, and it is mentioned in a conversation that would not look out of place in *Mary Lavelle* (see O'Brien *Cloak* 324–5).

Christina considers his proposal of marriage, but their different backgrounds make it difficult to envision a future together. Denis poses the risk of pregnancy as the main reason to marry, in another exchange that could be easily ascribed to Juanito and Mary (see ibid., 326). Except, of course, that Juanito is not free to marry, although he explains that introducing divorce into Spanish legislation is a priority for him — one of the occasions in the novel where he sounds more like a legislator than a revolutionary (a disturbing link to "Mr. Lawgiver," Mary's occasional nickname for her forceful fiancé, John).

> "And listen, love." He gathered her up again into the consoling darkness of embrace. "Listen — supposing you have a child — " She stirred as if she wanted to speak, but he held her head to his breast and hurried on: "If you have a child! How do you suppose I would consent to have you unmarried then? Don't you know the world even that much, Christina? And after all, you'll admit that I too would have some right in the child, don't you?"
>   She raised her head.
>   "Denis — that's true. If I were to have a child I'd be afraid. I know the way they treated my mother — and the way they sometimes treat me. If I were having a child, Denis, I'd be terrified, and I'd want your help. But if you stood by me — "
>   "Stood by you! Christina, will you stop talking like a lunatic? I love you, I tell you, I love you! I'm your husband whether you like it or no — I'm yours, do you hear? You can't escape me!" [326].

Denis loses his cape a few days later, when Christina fails to meet him because she has been sent away (see 338). When Denis finds her in New York and they resume the affair ten weeks later, the narrative reads, in retrospect, like a supplement to the unfolding of the love story in *Mary Lavelle*, giving us a richer version of the reason for the lovers' final parting. Their first kiss after their reunion "carried Christina over a wide range of debate" (409), because "she had discerned that which Denis had half hidden from himself and of which in this glad and tender hour he was determinedly incredulous, that he loved now but no longer imperiously desired her" (410). Denis is not acting out of love as much as obligation now, and Christina, like Mary, makes the unilateral decision to end the affair, and she does it in much the same way: "There must be now no sweet, half-careless arguments such as used to be in the wood. The only endurable thing was to be quick as lightning in killing the last chance of such a thing, and then get away [from him] for ever" (412).

Denis is as childish in his language and behavior as Juanito, by comparison with Mary, had been. His ludicrous outbursts ("Dear Christina! Loved and deflowered..." [ibid.]) show him to be ultimately unworthy of his partner, much like the male interests in the two O'Brien novels that were to follow. Psychologically, emotionally, and in terms of circumstances, the lovers in *Without My Cloak* are very much like the lovers in *Mary Lavelle*. Mary's future after her return to Ireland is somewhat uncertain, but it seems likely that, rather than marrying John, she will take whatever little money she can and she will leave Mellick. O'Brien's first novel suggests a different resolution for that romance plot, in a marriage of convenience which will confine the woman to a metaphorical "small, dark room that looked on the blank wall" (412).

As Music and Splendour

The borrowing of Lavelle and her reappearance in *As Music and Splendour* changes our reading of *Mary Lavelle*. Mary's story is a branch in a serpentine family tree that includes Christina in *Without My Cloak*, Agnes in *The Anteroom*, Louise — "there's at least two of everyone" — Lafleur and "Belle" Nell in *Pray for the Wanderer* (212), and touches upon all the female characters that carry the "beauty gene" (and there are many) in the work of O'Brien. We can see Mary Lavelle in the Anna Murphy of *The Land of Spices* for example, and read the girl's fascination for her classmate Pilar in the context of Lavelle's relationship with Spain. It is not by chance that Miss Anita Murphy is the Areavaga governess immediately preceding Mary in the household. Also, as we have seen, Marie Rose Mulqueen can be seen as a prototype of Luisa de Maraval. Discussing *Mary Lavelle*, Patricia Coughlan describes the meeting of Mary and Luisa in terms of an "unspoken competition which produces some of the novel's sillier passages" ("Kate" 151, see also 168–9). But Mary and Luisa admire each other's beauty and strength of character, and Mary, we are *specifically* told, "had no sense of competitiveness against other women" (*Mary* 151).

> [Luisa's] grooming, dress and manner were of simplicity so perfect that they should have deceived as naïve a person as Mary, and had she not been by accident herself of formidable beauty, perhaps she would at first have missed the true ring of steel. But Greek, however unsuspecting and untried, usually knows Greek [ibid.].

Despite her own cheap cotton dress, Mary is able to appreciate Luisa with "a lively mixture of astonishment, curiosity and delight" and "to marvel innocently at the audacity of Juan Areavaga y Parajo in marrying such a miracle" (ibid.). The passages in question only seem silly if one is blinded by the normative main text; that is, they appear as "silly" as a third eye on a cubist portrait. It is imperative that we read this scene with another understanding of *reality* in mind. First and foremost, we must believe, as one commentator put it, that with Kate O'Brien "we are in safe hands" (Boland "Introduction" xv). That is, we must trust the ability and purposefulness of the author, or we will run the danger of getting utterly lost in *Mary Lavelle*, face to face with a Minotaur. When the two women meet again in Madrid, Mary reflects: "Curiously, as her nerves acknowledged the atmosphere of unforced beauty and therewith the passionate intelligence of Luisa, ... a thought repeated itself from the Cabantes meeting: How brave of [Juanito] to marry such a miracle!" (*Mary* 233). The Madrid drawing-room "moment" is inconsequential to the main plot but crucial to one of its subtextual plots. Certain turns of phrase are meant as flashing alarm signs, an order to exit the main story and *turn* to a subtextual one. For example, Pepe says of Conlan that "she understands [the bullfight] like a matador!" (277), and when his wife retorts that he should have married Conlan instead of her, he shakes his head and murmurs, "Brave indeed would be the man —" (ibid., 278). This comment links Luisa to Agatha (see the quote above)—a surprising move, if it were not for a series of other equally strange comments scattered throughout the text. As we see in the long quote earlier, Mary and Luisa are referred to as "Greeks" (151)—when "Greek love" has been used for centuries as a byword for homosexuality. It is not the only time the expression is used like an Archimedean point to shift the text: Mary's resemblance to a "Greek boy" (67), for example, stirs up a dormant fire in Don Pablo, while references to the painter known as El Greco are carefully aligned to sexuality in the novel, as we will see later. In the relationship between Mary and Luisa, the stated fact (via Greece) of their lesbian inclinations simply cannot co-exist with the main story (it certainly appears "silly" *as part of* the main text). The explicit signaling of Castile as Mary's (and Agatha's) favored region is, among other things, a symbolic underlining of the fact that the Castilian Luisa, should the choice be available, would be a more suitable destination for Mary than the Basque Juanito. We are also presented here with a subversive conceptual remapping of "the Spains" (152), as a set of contiguous yet distinct erotic landscapes.

The blue-eyed Irish Mary Lavelle and the grey-eyed Castilian Luisa Areavaga reappear in Kate O'Brien's last novel, as the blue-eyed Irish "Clarabelle" Halvey and the grey-eyed Castilian Luisa Carriaga. In *As Music and Splendour*, they become lovers. That is, they are allowed their own love story, which would have been impossible in an Irish novel of 1936, and it is of course ironic that they should be granted the freedom to love each other in the 1890s instead. Clare is not only referred to a number of times as "Clarabelle" (see for example *Music* 73), but she is also "Halvey," divided. Despite the position of *As Music and Splendour* at the end of O'Brien's career, the Clare-Luisa romance is not the definitive rewrite of *Mary Lavelle* but simply the offer of yet another coherent development from the same initial premise/character. The romance between Clare and Luisa is not a plain heroic lesbian narrative either, irrespective of the ending of the love affair, because, as we will see later, the "halved" Clare is provided with a double, Thomas, which stands for a homophobic subjectivity. The intertextuality of characters and plots *readjusts* the heterosexual romance narrative in the earlier novel. Is it possible, on the strength of this connection, to read *Mary Lavelle* as a frustrated lesbian romance? It is a complex operation. In one of the subtexts, Mary is attracted to Luisa, while in the main text, Agatha declares her love for Mary, while in another subtextual strand, as we will discuss later, Agatha is likened to Juanito through the wording used to describe their appearance and facial features. These are the equivocations of a dream, but a dream treated with the respect generally afforded to the real, as in a surrealist painting.

The Mary/Clare connection certainly provides at least an alternative reading of some scenes, such as that first encounter with Luisa, which inspires "fear" and "excitement" in Mary. It is unquestionably a perceptive description of a young heterosexual woman, Mary, as she begins to realize that she is attracted to her companion's husband, Juanito. There is no more to say about it if we consider the scene by itself. However, knowing as we now know that Luisa and Mary are to become lovers in *As Music and Splendour*, Mary's nervousness, inexplicable to her in the passage, can be read legitimately as Mary's first intimation that she is attracted to Luisa (157). This is merely a flash, a sort of subliminal message that will be subsumed in the main narrative of heterosexual romance. In the alternative subtextual lesbian bildungsroman that aligns Nieves, Mary, and Agatha, we can in fact read Juanito and Mary's love affair under a radically different light. As Karin Eva Zettl has pointed out, "Mary Lavelle decides to becom[e] Juanito's lover in order to set herself free," and to that end "her engagement — the last remaining link to her past — must be broken" ("Search" 99–100). Zettl, who reads this in terms of Mary's need for *heterosexual* sexual fulfillment, illustrates her point with a quote from the novel, where the protagonist thinks "with casuistic pity" that having sex with Juan will make things easier for John, because "[a] moony story about being in love with a Spaniard would render him prolongedly unhappy and half-hopeful — but this other news, revolting him, would turn his heart away from her, and cure it" (*Mary* 308). In a lesbian reading of *Mary Lavelle*, the protagonist (who as Zettl points out is the one who directs every step of the affair) *uses* a heterosexual attachment to break all possibility of such future attachments, starting with the most pending, her engagement to John. This seems to be suggested even at the point of Mary's and Juanito's first kiss, which provides an unexpected thrill to the protagonist: "It occurred to her now that whatever she might do or not do in future she could never be more purely faithless to John than she had been in the second of that kiss," and "*she had already, in her gaiety of to-day, a notion that she had cast her lot. Not with Juanito,* whose fate was shaped already, in Spain and Spain's future, and with his wife and child" (emphasis added, *Mary* 252). Even as early as this, we are told, "she was beginning to suspect that she might have to sell the orthodox order of her own life" (ibid., 252–3). The alternative reading whereby Mary's illicit heterosexual affair opens up a path to lesbianism may "explain" the otherwise absurd stylistic decision of giving the same name, John, to the two male suitors (Juanito means "little John" in Spanish). It also "explains" why Mary, who should have at least *considered* the possibility of deceiving her husband-to-be and keep quiet about the affair, is determined to return to Ireland "with a brutal story" (344). That is, we can read Mary's decision, and Mary's reflections on it, as a relishing of the brutality (and the freedom) to come: "There were truths that were indefensible, truths that changed and broke things, that exacted injustice and pain and savagery, truths that were sins and cruelties," and Mary was going home with "a wicked story that would be agony to John, and had no explanation, no defense. And afterwards—she would take her godmother's hundred pounds and go away" (344). As the main and the subtextual narratives come to a close, through her new commitment to "truth," Mary has fulfilled her desire to be "a free lance" (27). Her deliberate loss of virginity seems intended to secure a passport out of marriageability.

To read *Mary Lavelle* with Mary as lesbian can only be a partial exercise. What this subtext does very effectively is to question the authority of the heterosexual romance. It is striking that a novel that builds its "official" plot on a story of unorthodox love would seek to displace that plot by way of an even more radical story. If Juanito and Mary's affair would have been conventional, this may have been more understandable, but the lawlessness of the couple should have aligned them with all other proscribed loves without need for further destabilization. The inclusion of a lesbian subtext suggests that, at some level, heterosexual love/sex cannot help but be normative, which does not seem to be the case even within the novel's own logic. On the other hand, an obvious effect of making this subtext visible is the greater prominence of Luisa Areavaga, who emerges, after taking into account her doubling as Luisa Carriaga, as potentially lesbian or bisexual. The ambiguities that result from bringing an awareness of *As Music and Splendour* into *Mary Lavelle*, point to a triangular relationship in which the primary erotic interest is that between Mary and Luisa, despite the fact that Juanito is placed at the center of the novel (literally, in structural terms). The emerging set of relationships is like that in John Luke's 1945 painting *The Three Dancers*, with a Daphne-like figure aligned to a man, reaching for a woman who reciprocates her interest. The painting and the novel present a segment of time, but irrespective of the current ordering of the dancers, the emphasis is, inevitably, on movement itself.

The Governess Abroad Bildungsroman

O'Brien built a very complex relationship between her books, and this is particularly evident in the versions of the plot and characters of *Mary Lavelle* that we have discussed. Her work was also in dialogue with a number of literary and artistic traditions, seeking to further them, and often revealing their inner contradictions in the process. In *Mary Lavelle*, the most obvious of those traditions is the bildungsroman genre.

TRAVELING GOVERNESS

As Lorna Reynolds points out, *Mary Lavelle* is the only one of O'Brien's titles that is "straightforwardly descriptive" (*Kate* 124), inviting the reader to see the book as the portrait of a young woman. Reynolds suggests that this novel "may be taken as Kate O'Brien's *bildungsroman*" (ibid., 106), while Katie Donovan sees Joyce's *Portrait of the Artist As a Young Man*, published in 1914–1915, and O'Brien's *Mary Lavelle*, as "the first 'Bildungsroma[ne]' of twentieth century Irish literature" (*Writers* 19). *Mary Lavelle* is, among other things, a female novel of development, belonging to a branch of that tradition, the "governess abroad" bildungsroman. As Lucía Etxebarria has noted, "[i]t would seem that in literature men travel to conquer, and women to escape" (132, my translation). From Anne Brontë's 1847 novel *Agnes Grey* to Sandra Goldbacher's 1997 film *The Governess*, there have been countless stories of governesses traveling in search of freedom to a *foreign* place. Many French, Prussian, Swiss, and German women traveled west in the nineteenth century to work as governesses. Midcentury, there appeared to be a "surplus" of educated women seeking employment. Governessing was the only job available to them, and the competition was high. After the 1860s, many women who were British subjects emigrated to the colonies. In England, they had help from the Society for Promoting the Employment of Women, and the Female Middle Class Emigration Society. The governesses were, of course, middle class, or more accurately, "daughters of educated men" (Woolf, "Guineas" 160), and many commentators have explored their contradictory position as impoverished outsider-insiders in the household, resulting in a "status incongruence" (see Peterson). The governess was likely to elicit more sympathy than her working-class sisters, who endured far harsher conditions, for this very reason (ibid., 4). In Molly Keane's *Good Behaviour*, the posh narrator mentions in passing that her servants in Ireland "ate Robin starch from the laundry, partly as a thinning diet and partly because they were hungry" (45). Concern was proportional to status, and around the 1840s, a number of charitable institutions were created to help governesses in distress. In London, in 1843, the Governesses' Benevolent Institution opened its doors. In Dublin, as early as 1838, the Harcourt Home for Aged Governesses was set up in Harcourt Terrace to ensure they ended their lives with some dignity, and a communal grave was provided for them at Mount Jerome to ensure they had some dignity in death.

Irish governesses tended to go to Spain, a country with a solid Catholic tradition where their moral integrity was expected to remain intact. Instead, they often found and embraced sexual, financial, and intellectual freedom. Movement is inextricably associated with the governess. In fact, a type of carriage was designed to assist her in her duties: "the governess cart," a small vehicle drawn by a pony or a donkey, where the governess would sit sideways while driving, in one of the parallel seats that allowed her to keep an eye on her charges (Broughton and Symes 44). Sommerville and Ross famously used a

governess cart in the tour of Connemara which resulted in a remarkable trav-
eloque, published in 1892 — an early contribution to the Irish Revival.

Maura Laverty, another Irish writer, may have written her "governess
abroad" bildungsroman of 1944 *No More Than Human* in response to *Mary
Lavelle*. As the poet and O'Brien scholar Catherine Byron highlights, in a striking
coincidence Laverty and O'Brien were in fact governesses in the same year, 1922,
and Laverty's novel presents a governess in Madrid briefly traveling to Bilbo with
her charges, whereas Lavelle goes on the reverse journey (Catherine Byron in correspondence February 6, 2003). Ireland did "export" governesses, and also
employed many, including Mary Wollstonecraft, who in 1787 traveled to Ireland
to work for the Kingsboroughs, in Mitchelstown Castle (which she called "the
Bastille") and in their house in Dublin's Henrietta Street. A few months later, she
was sacked, charged with corrupting the children and unladylike behavior. Home-
less, jobless, and referenceless, Mary Wollstonecraft took to writing to survive.
She portrayed her employers in the 1788 novel *Mary, a Fiction*, a book that, according to her biographer Claire Tomalin, represented "the first battle on record in
which a governess emerged with at least equal honors from the field and revenged
herself in print, instead of being simply crushed and swept aside" (64).

"Abroad" did not always assume the crossing of a border. To nineteenth century provincials like Agnes Grey, who had never been more than 20 miles away
from home, reaching her new job, a day's travel by carriage to a house 70 miles
away from her village, was effectively a trip to the moon. Miss Grey sums up the
hopes of impoverished young ladies for the next 100 years as the book opens:

> How delightful it would be to be a governess! To go out into the world; to enter
> upon a new life; to act for myself; to exercise my unused faculties; to try my unknown
> powers; to earn my own maintenance.... And then, how charming to be entrusted
> with the care and education of children! [12].

The rest of the novel will chronicle the shattering of each and every one of
her dreams. Governess novels are full of unhappiness and toil. "[G]overnesses
formed one of the largest single occupational groups to be found in insane asy-
lums," according to Harriet Martineau (quoted in Peterson 3). Sigmund Freud
would develop his influential interpretation of hysteria partly through his 1901
study of "Lucy R."— a governess with a nervous condition. Madness hovers on
the edge of governess stories. Lucy Snowe, the protagonist of Charlotte Brontë's
Villette, published in 1853, actually has a nervous breakdown. But Agnes and Lucy
could not have predicted this work hazard, not at the time. Their stories were
partly written as a warning to others. Only escapist Hollywood musicals dared
defying this tradition, but the 1956 *The King and I* or the 1965 *The Sound of Music*
(despite being based on autobiographical accounts) parade their own fictionality.
Even the current metamorphosis of the governess novel, the "au pair novel," follows
the same dark trail, in the tradition-aware work of Jamaica Kincaid or Willem
Herman. In the governess novel, Kate O'Brien's *Mary Lavelle* and Dorothy Richard-

son's *Pilgrimage*, published between 1915 and 1935, seem to stand alone. Richardson's autobiographical protagonist, Miriam Henderson, finds her governessing experience "enrich[ing]," without qualification (351). Like *Agnes Grey*, O'Brien's novel also opens with an enunciation of Mary's expectations (see 37), and her modest hopes also prove wrong, but because her experience will be far more positive than anticipated. Nevertheless, Richardson indicates that governessing is primarily an escape from "poverty and discomfort" (351), while O'Brien ruthlessly deglamorizes the "profession." Agatha explains to Mary, "We came out in our green youth because our parents had no money to spend on us, and saw no likelihood of getting us husbands," and asks what other job would consider as qualifications the facts that "you are a Catholic and can speak English fluently, if badly? We're not even required to know how to teach. It's jam for the stupid" (O'Brien *Mary* 204). When Mary replies, "You're very hard on your profession," Conlan retorts, "Profession? ... We're a lot of incompetents and we know it" (204–5).

SELF-GOVERNMENT

As Lorna Reynolds points out, "Kate O'Brien turned the accepted idea of the governess upside down" ("Artist" 54). She did so deliberately, even ostentatiously, by giving her heroine an extraordinary beauty, an attribute that marks her as the reverse photographic image of the most famous governess in fiction, Jane Eyre. Beauty, in a "job specification" that often includes chaperone/companion of marriageable ladies, is a handicap for a governess, as we are constantly reminded in *Mary Lavelle* and as exemplified in the dog-like features of the title character in Richard Sheridan's 1775 play *La Duenna*. But the assumption of knowledge in a governess is also mocked, with Agatha Conlan claiming, "If we had any brains or education ... we wouldn't be here" (O'Brien *Mary* 204). In another snub to tradition, *Mary Lavelle* incorporates a *plausible* love story. Governesses, real and fictional, were assumed to be in pursuit of idealized romance. An 1862 article in the satirical British magazine *Punch*, entitled "The Governess Abroad," dealt with supposed public concerns about the fact that "the intending emigrants carry two faces under one hood. While ostensibly going out to cultivate the waste lands of mind their real destination is the Eden of matrimony.... We don't believe a word of it" (quoted in Broughton and Symes 164). Nineteenth century "governess abroad" novels end up in marriage. Editorial pressure to pair off the governess with a suitable man was resisted by many female writers, who registered their protest in different ways. Charlotte Brontë, for example, simply withheld the ending of her 1853 *Villette* from the reader. A popular strategy, used by Louisa May Alcott in her sequel to *Little Women*, titled *Good Wives*, was to cast doubts on the plausibility of a match of passion through the crude but effective method of presenting the suitor as a much older man. Alcott complained about her publishers, who demanded that "my little women must grow up and be married off in a very stupid style" (quoted in Langland 118), but reluctantly complied. Even taking into account Victorian ideals, the recurrent emphasis on old age is startling and may best be understood as a stereotypical marker of asexuality, like in the Christian iconography of Mary and Joseph. But there is something else. Governesses are attached to knowledge, a knowledge that is embodied in the mature men they marry. This is perhaps a ritual union, then, a metaphor. The centrality of Don Pablo to *Mary Lavelle* would appear to be partly indebted to that trope — a scar of forgotten wars.

The affair between Juanito and Mary also has another dimension. Charlotte Brontë's Jane Eyre/*Eire* and Lucy Snowe *Bretton*, boldly inscribe "the governess" in an unacknowledged political tradition entwining feminism and nationalism. Charlotte may not have been too supportive of Irish independence in her public statements, but just how much her Irish ancestors influenced her imagination and her politics can be seen in William Wright's extraordinary account *The Brontës of Ireland: or, Facts Stranger Than Fiction*, from 1893. Eyre's marriage to an English lord can only happen as a union of equals. Sometimes, the heroine of governess abroad novels, a headstrong but impoverished young woman exiled from her own deferred possibilities, represents the will without the means, the nation without a state. Mary Lavelle's communion with her Basque surroundings puts forward the same idea. Crucially, she is also a young Irish woman exploring her newly discovered freedom in 1922 — the year of the establishment of the Free State. Her affair with Juanito, who embodies the revolutionary hopes of a new generation, can be seen as an invitation to Ireland to follow suit. We know what the official response to O'Brien's novel was at home. There is an allegorico-political tradition of "melodramatic romance" (see Roche "Anteroom" 88) within which *Mary Lavelle* could have been inscribed, but Mary wants to "belong to no one place, or family, or person"; she hopes for alliances that will not disturb her childhood dream of "perpetual self-government," an ideal which she equates to being "free and lonely" (O'Brien *Mary* 27).

In Louisa May Alcott's novel of 1868 *Little Women*, the March sisters liven up the boring task of mending sheets by dividing them in four, each representing one of the four continents. It is not a coincidence that when the sisters are described, the narrator explains that one is a "snow maiden," another fair, another rosy, and another brown, a rather peculiar variation. Josephine, or Jo, March, governess to be, has a brown complexion, and she also has "a decided mouth" and "a comical nose" (4). In other words, she is of a different race. This subtext of racial or national aspirations is simply made explicit in Sandra Goldbacher's 1997 film *The Governess*, by presenting a young woman who is actually Jewish and who must "pass" as a white Christian in order to get a governessing job. Jane Eyre is "faery born" (Brontë *Jane* 438), which may just amount to the same thing: governesses are, and remain, foreign in their heart and soul.

Mary Lavelle and *Pilgrimage* subvert tradition in the protagonists' passionate interest for their surroundings. O'Brien's governess abroad bildungsroman — much as Iris Murdoch's 1963 *The Unicorn*, set in the Burren, in the West of Ireland—also exploits the metonymic potential of an unusual landscape. Governesses tend to be self-centred to the point of obsession, and even when they land in vibrant urban centers, we learn nothing about the places they visit. Charlotte Brontë's Lucy Snowe describes her first meal in Brussels as "meat, nature unknown" (*Villette* 68). This could as easily be applied to the Belgians. In Alcott's *Little Women*, Miss March's crucial trip to New York to become a governess is also primarily an inward journey, a "voyage in" (see Abel et al.). In *Mary Lavelle*, the imperviousness of the misses in the Café Alemán to the culture of their adoptive home is so ridiculous that it must be handled in comic vignettes. However, *Mary Lavelle* is conventional in the fact that learning Euskera, the Basque language, is not even conceivable to the novel. Within the parameters the story sets itself, which is the xenophobia of foreign governesses towards all things "Spanish," Conlan and Mary (who learn the Spanish language) together with O'Toole (who adopts Altorno's *language* in dress and makeup) shine in the dark like votive candles. They represent a new kind of governess abroad who takes interaction with her environment to heart, to the extent that she can become a representative of her host culture. In this way, O'Brien's novel gives the secondary characters Agatha and Rosie their very own narrative, by clearly presenting them, through their looks and sparkling banter, as female versions of the most famous characters in Spanish fiction, Don Quixote and his faithful squire, Sancho.

The Unruly Governess

There are two opposing staples in the genre: the unruly governess, suffering from what we may term "an excess of knowledge," and the figure of the "innocent governess abroad"—and *Mary Lavelle* offers examples of both. We find the archetypal "innocent" in Katherine Mansfield's short story of 1915 "The Little Governess," in a historical context, as Foucault would have it, where knowledge and sex are in "interplay" (*History* 72). When a "governess abroad" appears as a secondary character, like the Irish Mrs. Sweeney in *Villette* or the governesses in Joseph Sheridan le Fanu's 1864 *Uncle Silas: A Tale of Bertram-Haugh* and Molly Keane's 1981 *Good Behaviour*, for example, she tends to be incompetent and unruly, in proportion to her relevance in the novel—the smaller the part, the wilder the character. Criminal intent, drunkenness, or malevolence are common traits, and so is deviant sexuality. It is sometimes introduced by unorthodox gender allegiances, at least since Lucy Snowe (see Rabinowitz), and the unorthodox Nieves Areavaga has more in common with the protagonist of *Villette* than her name (*Nieves* means "snow" in Spanish). Josephine March claims that "I'm the man in the family" (Alcott *Women* 11) and, like Nieves Areavaga, she is expected to become a "great m[a]n" (O'Brien *Mary* 64). If the evil governess in Henry James's 1898 *The Turn of the Screw* is "[t]he first literary appearance of lesbian corruption of a child by an adult" (Foster 111), by the 1890s the governess figure had already become commonplace in the Victorian pornographic repertoire (see Broughton and Symes 180). Avoiding thrills, sensationalism, or moralizing, the three deviant governesses in *Mary Lavelle* are presented as courageous in their shunning of convention. O'Toole marries a local shopkeeper, Conlan declares her love for a woman, and Lavelle has a brief affair with a married man. The three have broken the code of the governess, and this has been prompted by their interaction with a foreign cultural setting that they have grown to love. When Mary arrives in Altorno, she tells herself that she is merely "a four days' journey away from [John], and from all she was and again would be" (O'Brien *Mary* 36). But this frozen, continuous landscape of her lifetime before her has already begun to thaw. And yet, as we will see later, another way in which *Mary Lavelle* seems to subvert the bildungsroman tradition as delineated by Susanne Howes in 1930, Jerome Buckely in 1974, etc., is in its ambiguous approach to development. Does Mary change at all, or is it merely her circumstances that change? Perhaps her innate "awayness" (O'Brien *Mary* 29), which John considers a problem, turns itself inside-out. That is: by going "away," her original homelessness dissolves, and she officially becomes the stranger that she secretly always was. In this and other ways, O'Brien is in dialogue with the governess abroad bildungsroman tradition, a critical engagement seeking to renew the genre.

Generación del 98

The contextualization of *Mary Lavelle* has been dictated by general assumptions on the work of Kate O'Brien. Her writing has been aligned for the most part to realism and the nineteenth century, as well as romance, all considered outmoded or unchallenging, stylistically timid and ideologically moribund. Even when her competence is praised, she is always placed in frameworks without currency. For example, Elizabeth Bowen suggested that O'Brien could be "the Balzac of Ireland" (quoted in Hogan "Introduction" [1986] xi), and Hannah Sheehy Skeffington called her "[t]he Irish Galsworthy" (quoted in Walshe *Kate* 69). Anne Fogarty has described O'Brien's fiction as "a fusion of the conventions of romance and realism" ("Desire" 104), while Patricia Coughlan sees it as mixing realism with sensationalism (see "Kate" 60). The nineteenth century is regularly presented as the natural referent to O'Brien's work. For example, Adele Dalsimer refers to "[h]er traditional literary style, far more akin to that of the Victorian novel than that of contemporary *avant-garde* fiction..." (xvii), while Eavan Boland believes that O'Brien "fell into the general category of romantic novelist, a category which critics of realistic fiction, in a later generation, were quick to diminish and reject" ("Legacy" 7; see also 8). I largely disagree with those claims, but I want to make the case that O'Brien *did* look back to an outmoded school of writing, that of the "Generación del Noventayocho" in Spain, and that in adapting their model to *Mary Lavelle* she produced "a novel of 98" of dazzling originality, a daring novel which was of relevance to her times.

98 in *Mary Lavelle*

The Generación del 98 is an artistic, mainly literary, movement in Spain that spearheaded self-reflexivity and reform after the fall of the Spanish empire (Spain was the first European power to lose its main colonies), sealed in 1898 with the independence of Cuba (see Mir "Introducción"). The loss of the Cuban war was referred to in Spain as "el desastre" (the disaster), and the work of the writers of the 98 generation was promptly described as "the literature of the disaster" by Miquel Oliver ("Literatura" 69). Writers such as Miguel de Unamuno, Pío Baroja, Antonio Machado, and "Azorín" were concerned with the search for an authentic Spanish identity, a task pursued through a retreat into core values, austerity, individualism, moral integrity, and communion with the landscape. The movement has many points in common with the Irish Renaissance, such as the aim of regeneration, the quest for authenticity, and the recovery of "national" motives. Decades on, much like the Irish Renaissance, the impact of the Generación del 98 on the curriculum remains unscathed, and its relevance as referent for subsequent writers is still strong.

Mary Lavelle includes direct references to the Generación del 98. For example, Don Pablo reflects on "Unamuno's 'Man of Flesh and Bone'" (164), which is the title of the first chapter in Miguel de Unamuno's *Del Sentimiento Trágico de la Vida* ["On Tragic Sentiment in Life"], first published in English in 1921. The group was said to have a "devotion to melancholy" (Oliver "Culto" 61), exemplified by the pessimist Pablo. Ninety-eight is often described as the Spanish "version" of existentialism, a movement with which O'Brien can certainly be aligned (see Reynolds *Kate* 118–9). *Mary Lavelle* in fact includes a summary of the origins and beliefs of the 98 group.

> [Consuelo] saw serious harm in [Pablo's] despair against the Spanish scene at the opening of the twentieth century. He belonged to the generation now remembered in Spain as that of '98 — a generation so diversely gifted as to include Unamuno, Azorin (sic) and Benavente. Startled into attention to Spain's plight by the revelations of the disastrous Cuban war, and encouraged in rebelliousness by the period-vogue for Nietsche (sic), this outcropping of talent had little in fact to unify it and was perhaps no more than a display of many greatly gifted and highly individualised writers very busily at cross purposes, but the gifts and promises were great, and the beginnings seemed indeed like a profound renascence. Pablo smelt the air of his time and wanted to be where it blew freely. He wanted to enter political life and in its struggle work out, in writing and oratory, his difficult creed of anarchy and faith [60–1].

This subtle, knowledgable, and interesting description of the 98 movement for the benefit of the Anglophone reader is a rare intervention by the overseer-narrator in the novel. It anticipates current debates on the *construction* of the group by critics, who pitted the 98 generation (as represented by Unamuno) against High Modernism (as represented by Rubén Darío), creating a false dichotomy that has been debunked by scholars such as Richard Cardwell. O'Brien was, apart from an original thinker, very proficient (and somewhat anxious) at managing her sources, and it seems to me that she was inspired by Salvador de Madariaga's 1930 book *Spain* (he is mentioned in *Farewell Spain* 73), which includes a full chapter, comprehensive and insightful, on the Generación del Noventayocho (see Madariaga 127–147).

The description of the movement in *Mary Lavelle* suggests a context for Don Pablo. As we will see later, Enrique Areilza, the model for Don Pablo, was in fact identified by his biographer as "a man of 98," and Areilza, as O'Brien was undoubtedly aware, was close to many of the writers and thinkers in the group, such as his lifelong friend Miguel de Unamuno. O'Brien's description also provides a context for the novel itself, which can be considered a belated example of the literary production of the group. "Noventayocho," named after the year in which the Cuban war made a mark on a group of young writers, is usually dated by the year of birth of these writers, falling between 1864 and 1875, and O'Brien was born in 1897. How can *Mary Lavelle* be said to be representative of "98" then? This novel puts forward a specific idea of Spain (one that requires the obliteration of Basque uniqueness), it hails austerity as the moral response to industrialization, it delineates some typical "98 characters," and it is concerned with the search for an authentic (national) self in a Spanish context.

Considering O'Brien as a 98 writer opens up her work to an interesting reading, while making a valuable contribution to the movement itself. For example, it helps redraft the role of women writers in the group. Félix Maraña has pointed out that "the time of the 98 is far more intense than the period signaled in history books," and writers born after 1875, such as the Basque women Ernestina de Champourcin and Carmen Baroja, are also part of the Noventayocho (xiii). Women's lives play a small part in the group's best-known fictional production, and a specific interest in feminist issues is, with minor exceptions such as some powerful essays by Azorín, absent from their work. The centrality of women's freedom in *Mary Lavelle*, considering the novel as an example of "el Noventayocho," represents a radical contribution to the movement. It also helps delineate a group of existentialist novels concerned with choice and freedom for women, from Simone de Beauvoir, through O'Brien, to Iris Murdoch.

CASTILE

"The Spain of Kate O'Brien is markedly Castilian," says Michael Cronin (144), discussing *Farewell Spain*. O'Brien's obsession with this region has puzzled many scholars, but within the context of 98, the focus is unsurprising. Nearly all writers from the group devoted an important part of their work to Castile, the poor, bare, dry land that this generation saw as the symbol of a new Spain that would regenerate itself through austerity and introspection. This discourse often acquired the tone of a religious quest, exemplified by Unamuno's "Poem," of 1907, opening with "You lift me up, land of Castile." This agenda is spelled out in *Mary Lavelle* (214–5), courtesy of a train trip by the protagonist to Madrid, through Castile, which seems designed, in a somewhat contrived way, to eulogize the region. *Mary Lavelle* is the first of a number of O'Brien's books to articulate an interest in Castile as site of Spanish authenticity. The main 98 writers were from regions which had little in common with this part of the peninsula. In fact, the numeric dominance of Basque writers in the movement is often highlighted, and an elucidation of possible explanations is a continuing topic of debate. Because the beginnings of the Generación del Noventayocho roughly coincide with the emergence of Basque nationalism, in my view it is plausible to see the movement in part as a reaction to it—Unamuno's hostility was so public and virulent that he remains a controversial figure in the Basque Country. The founder of Basque nationalism, Sabino Arana Goiri, sent a telegram to president Roosevelt in 1898, congratulating him on the success of the American campaign in support of Cuba and against Spain; the telegram was intercepted and Arana was imprisoned (see Anasagasti 34). Joaquín Costa, one of the intellectuals of 98, once claimed that Basque people represented the essence of the Castilian spirit (see Oliver "Literatura" 120), but such a claim would be considered ludicrous today.

The reification of Castile is akin to the Irish Renaissance's investment in the West of Ireland as a source of authentic Irishness; in fact, O'Brien herself would claim in her travelogue *My Ireland* that there is a "sisterhood" between Castile, Palestine, and the Irish Burren, on account of their shared virginity/austerity (32). In *Mary Lavelle*, "Christian" Castile is described as "the Spanish heart" (215) and "the greatest of the Spains" (216). It is as if, in 1898, the expansion of the empire had been reversed, turning into a shrinking which performed the same cultural elisions, only this time they happened within Spanish borders. Cinta Ramblado, in a paper of 2007, described O'Brien's idea of Spain as a "monocultural" view, coinciding somewhat with the image of the country promoted by Francoism in the 1940s: Catholic, rural, Castilian, self-sufficient ("Farewell"). O'Brien's ambivalent treatment of her Basque setting makes some sense if we see her as a 98 writer. In a talk at the University of Valladolid in 1971, Kate O'Brien named the writers in the Spanish language which had influenced her, and the list shows the impact of the 98 movement.

I am not concerned about the fact that O'Brien was not a Spanish citizen and never wrote in Spanish. No one would claim that an existentialist novel must be written in French, and the same applies to the Spanish language. The "Noventayocho" was well acquainted with transnational/transregional reconfigurations. Eugenio d'Ors, for example, normally wrote and published in Spanish, Catalan, *and* French. To my mind it is beyond doubt that O'Brien implicated herself in this artistic and philosophical movement, and did so to the extent that *Mary Lavelle* may be considered one of the last novels of the Generación del Noventayocho.

TWO

Activist Fiction I:
Politics

Introduction

Mary Lavelle belongs to a tradition of political fiction. "[A]s entertaining as it is instructive" was the promise on the 1516 title page of *Utopia* (quoted in Turner 7); whether the instruction in Thomas More's novel involved Catholic *or* proto-communist propaganda, as critics were to debate, we were not told. Political analysis in literature is not always driven by commitment to a particular cause; this is the case, for example, with Oscar Wilde's 1880 play *Vera, or The Nihilists* and Henry James's 1886 novel *The Princess Casamassima*. In an important survey of 1957, Irving Howe described the political novel as one where its characters' actions or thoughts show "some coherent political loyalty or ideological identification" (21). *Mary Lavelle* belongs to the genre of *activist* fiction; that is, fiction conceived or perceived as a political act or intending a call to action. Unsurprisingly, activist fiction has dealt with a wide variety of issues. For example: denouncing the abuses of the prison system (William Godwin's *Things as They Are, or The Adventures of Caleb Williams*, 1794), exposing the horrors of war (Dalton Trumbo's *Johnny Got His Gun*, 1939), decrying Stalinism (George Orwell's *Animal Farm*, 1945), or promoting lesbian-feminist separatism (Monique Wittig's *The Guerrilleres*, 1969). Fiction could reach where political tracts would not, and novels have sometimes changed popular perception of a controversial issue to the extent that it brought about historical change. For example, Harriet Beecher Stowe's *Uncle Tom's Cabin*, published in 1851–1852, is often credited with prompting the American Civil War and bringing about the end of slavery in the United States. Another example is *The Sportman's Sketches*, published in 1852 by Ivan Turgenev, which inspired Tzar Alexander to abolish serfdom in Russia. Turgenev's public acknowledgment of the influence of Maria Edgeworth's *Castle Rackrent* was proudly highlighted by Kate O'Brien in a 1971 lecture on Irish fiction, where she referred to the political effect of his book.

Kate O'Brien's *The Land of Spices* has been steadily increasing its credence as a politically subversive text (see 1987 with Reynolds *Kate* 63 & 66; 1990 with Weekes 122–3; 2007 with Cullingford 63), but many O'Brien books are yet to follow suit. *Farewell Spain* is the one most often described as political, but the assertion is invariably neutralized by saying that the travelogue is not "really" or not "exclusively" political (O'Neill "Introduction" xii and Foley "Novels" 23, respectively). In addition, its politics are rarely specified, so that they end up in a no-man's-land. This is perhaps the most outrageous example of a general determination to de-politicize O'Brien's work. Some passing references to politics, however, can be gleaned from critical accounts. *The Anteroom*, for example, is said to be framed within "the political crises of the summer of 1934" (Fogarty "Desire" 114) and to engage "the political world at the highest level" (Reynolds *Kate* 102), *That Lady* is generally seen to contest "tyranny" in a generic sense, and *Mary Lavelle* has been described as "a mixture of romantic fantasy and political fact" (Dalsimer 43). More is the pity when these able scholars rarely attempt to explain what kind of political analysis, from what perspective, in what context, and with what possible aim can we discern in O'Brien's books. This silence is itself politically motivated, of course. Branded, or crowned, as a "middle-class Irish Catholic author (of feminist leanings)," this monochrome sketch is better left undisturbed. Despite what the critics say, and don't say, there is a clear and consistent politics in O'Brien. Broadly, her books are soaked in a socialism and a feminism very much informed by her historical context. Individualist feminism is crucial to her work — and so is a libertarian attitude. Libertarian, anti-authoritarian politics are crucial to every one of O'Brien's novels, normally articulated through the right of individual women to full freedom and full equality. Other very specific strands of political theory, such as Christian anarchism, are also important to her thinking and her aesthetics. *Mary Lavelle* and *Farewell Spain* provide clear evidence of support for anarchism, as well as solidarity with other left movements, including those advocating state-communism. The publication of *Mary Lavelle* is most concerned with the political climate in Spain at the time of writing, 1935, when a rare consensus on the left was about to be reached in order to oust the conservative government. Although the novel was set in 1922, O'Brien's knowledge of Primo de Rivera's dictatorship and the revolutionary upheavals in the intervening years were crucial to its composition. She was writing at a time when anarchist ideas undercutting the work of many artists and intellectuals were reaching momentum in Spain, feminist authors unable to step into a clearly delineated tradition were coming up with their own idiosyncratic approaches, and a new understanding of sexuality was overdue in Ireland. Emerging out of these contexts, as we will see, *Mary Lavelle* allied itself to popular culture to put forward an agenda of radical politics in a unique way. Like Ahdaf Soueif in *The Map of Love*, a novel published in of 1999, O'Brien uses romance to smuggle politics.

O'Brien was also writing at a time when socialist realism was forcing authors to consider the political implications of their stylistic choices and presenting itself as the supreme form of activist fiction. Throughout the twentieth century, many leftist writers considered it *their duty* to produce fiction that would rouse social change. In 1934, at the Soviet Writers' Congress, socialist authors were called upon to realistically depict the conditions of the working class and join, in the words of A. Zhdanov, "the army of [proletariat] writers" (20). In order to develop Joseph Stalin's definition of communist writers as "engineers of human souls," Zhdanov prepared a list of literary "musts," which began with the "dut[y]" of "knowing life so as to be able to depict it truthfully in works of art, not to depict it in a dead, scholastic way, not simply as 'objective reality,' but to depict reality in its revolutionary development," a "truthfulness and historical concreteness" which "should be combined with the ideological remolding and education of the toiling people in the spirit of socialism. This method in *belles lettres* and literary criticism is what we call the method of socialist realism" (21). Rooting fiction in experience and approaching it as social molder do not appear to be altogether unreasonable aims for the politically committed writer. The trouble started when this model was used to denounce the majority of existing literature as "bourgeois," both on account of its content and its style. For example, at the congress, *Ulysses* (which happened to be written by a socialist) was to be singled out by Karl Radek, who famously described it as "[a] heap of dung, crawling with worms, photographed by a cinema apparatus through a microscope" (152). Detailed descriptions of minute details, such as those included in Joyce's book, were (and in this Radek showed some astuteness) just a furthering of naturalism (181); a great vista of society should be prioritized instead (157); psychological probing was to be eliminated (158) and only "types" portrayed, by showing "the typical in the individual" (181). That these approaches were seen as intrinsically unpolitical is disconcerting from a distance. Modernism was clearly under fire, but this narrow prescriptiveness had the potential to destroy all forms of creativity. In an address Kate O'Brien gave in 1963 to an international group of writers meeting in the Soviet Union, she declared: "The novelist's responsibility is immense — since his intention is to be read — by millions! But it is his sole responsibility, his inward duty, what he writes." The writer is a mediator between reality and art, O'Brien continued, which may sound like "a dangerous fact," but "[h]e has to do it alone," and "[t]he world which may or may not read him has to take its chance with his inspiration, and his possible moral authority" (1).

In his address to the Soviet Writers' Congress 27 years earlier, A.I. Stetsky gave the novels of Maxim Gorky as the supreme example of socialist realism, because "[h]is works are all so fashioned that the mass reader can understand them excellently" (270). In a way, this was the crux of the matter: politically committed fiction in general, and socialist realist fiction in particular, had to be *popular* (to recall More's editor, "entertaining" as well as "instructive"). *Mary Lavelle* "wanted to be read by millions," partly because of the peculiar circumstances of its conception, as Kate O'Brien knew herself to be in a unique position to publicize the developments in revolutionary Spain to an English-reading public, and she took up the challenge. O'Brien's novels do not fit in the socialist realism agenda, but there is a consonance in their stylistic imperative, as she was driven by financial necessity *and* political commitment to ensure a wide readership. We will start this chapter by considering two related, key pre-occupations of O'Brien: the Spanish situation and an anti-capitalist agenda. This will be followed by a closer look at two political strands which are particularly relevant in *Mary Lavelle*: Christian anarchism and individualist feminism. Kate O'Brien's interest in sexual liberation will be looked at in subsequent chapters. These recontextualizations, then, aim at showing the relevance of politics to the work of O'Brien. We will see how *Mary Lavelle*, in particular, is beyond doubt an activist novel, publicizing socialist, feminist, and queer politics, while also publicizing revolutionary politics *in Spain*, as shaped by O'Brien's chosen spokespersons, upper-class Basque socialists.

Spain

THE REPUBLIC

No matter how easy it is to dismiss the propaganda machine of Stalinism, the use of fiction as a medium to spread *information* was as legitimate and necessary in the 1930s as it is today, when the media in democratic countries is subjected to the tyranny of the spectacular headline and the maximum-impact image. The 1995 political film *Beyond Rangoon*, for example, made a point of justifying itself when the protagonist's voice off explained: "What the Chinese did in Tiananmen Square was televised. But Burma wasn't. So, for most of the world, it just didn't happen." *Mary Lavelle* and *Farewell Spain* are witness accounts of "what was happening" in Spain, seeking to *inform* an Anglophone audience. Ironically, mass-marketability has become the main obstacle to activist fiction. Ironically, because one thing that *did* matter to politically aware writers in the 1930s was intelligibility—they all engaged in this aspect of the controversy (see for example Woolf "Bennett"; Orwell *Road* 71). The debate came to a halt in 1937 when the pressing matter of the fascist uprising in Spain forced writers to move fast.

However, the tension had been mounting from the early 1930s, as anti-communist hysteria and the growth of fascism fed each other all over Europe and in the United States. Diego Rivera's 1934 socialist realist mural *Man at the Crossroads* was, like O'Brien's novel, a political act, and it was met by an even more savage form of censorship: commissioned for the Rockefeller Center in New York, John D. Rockefeller ordered the mural to be destroyed when Rivera refused to erase a portrait of Lenin included in the painting. Many artists resorted to subtext in order to survive creatively—the work of composer Dmitri

Shostakovich after 1934 is a case in point (see Shostakovich). In Ireland, the church was instrumental in giving breathing room to fascism from the pulpit; in some cases driving the population to violence, as in March 1933, when a congregation vandalized the offices of the Revolutionary Workers Union in Dublin's Connolly House after an incendiary sermon (see Bob Doyle's account of the attack 41–2). The most visible sign of fascism in the country was the Blueshirts, an organization claiming a membership of 100,000 in 1933 and regularly assisted by a violent group known as the "animal gang" because of their inhuman methods. The fascist cause had ideologues such as Michael Tierney (president of University College Dublin between 1947 and 1964) and the support of leading intellectuals such as W.B. Yeats as well as the church at large (O'Riordan 25). As crucially, the Irish press was fueling mass hysteria on the supposed menace of anti–Christian communists, manipulating information and relying on apocalyptic headlines, which only worsened during the Spanish Civil War (see Oran 187–8).

Kate O'Brien traveled to Spain in the summers of 1933, 1934, and 1935 (see Reynolds *Kate* 37) and had an opportunity to take the temperature of the political climate and compare it to what was happening at home, and in England, where she had been based since 1923. *Mary Lavelle* emerged from O'Brien's commitment to the revolutionary aspirations in Spain, shaped by her firsthand assessment of the state of the country between 1933 and 1935. If *Mary Lavelle* closes just before the coup of General Miguel Primo de Rivera, O'Brien is writing the novel in 1935, in full awareness of the changes in the intervening years. A brief sketch of historical events is useful to us here. Primo de Rivera led a dictatorship in Spain between 1923 and 1930 with the tacit support of King Alfonso XIII, but both dictatorship and monarchy collapsed under the pressure of economic crisis, workers' demands, and the growth of Basque and Catalan nationalism. A new democratic period then began with the instauration of the Second Republic, and three subsequent governments were elected, in 1931 (left), in 1933 (right), and in 1936 (left). The first leftist government in the new Republic was a momentous occasion. Such was its impact in the popular consciousness, that the overseer-narrator in *Mary Lavelle* refers to it as "a revolution" in the "Prologue" to the novel: "In 1922, for instance — the year of our story — [Mary] did not know any more than anyone else that nine years later a revolution would practically wipe out her obsolete and ill-defined profession" (xvii). The mention proves how important it was for O'Brien to contextualize the narrative, incorporating the knowledge of what happened *after* Lavelle's departure from the Basque Country. In 1931, a coalition government of socialists and leftist republicans undertook a number of reforms. Devolution was granted to regions such as Catalonia, Euskadi (the Basque Country), and Galizia; secular marriage was introduced and divorce legalized ("In the Spain of which I'll be Premier," Juanito had said to Mary, "there'll be divorce"; 259); and a general move towards diminishing the role of the church in public services was undertaken (the banning of crucifixes from school walls was a particularly sore point for the conservatives). The bulk of the reforms went into agriculture and education. Within the next two years, about 10,000 new schools and countless libraries would be built, but the new laws allowing the state to expropriate landowners and hand over the property to poor peasants was very timidly enforced. In September 1931 the debate on women's suffrage began in the Spanish parliament, dominated by two women deputies, Clara Campoamor and the lawyer Victoria Kent. The fierce argument between these two feminists was driven by the fear that, granted the vote, women (by and large under the influence of the Catholic church) would vote for the conservatives. Women got suffrage and, in the next election in 1933, both Campoamor and Kent lost their seats following the victory of the conservatives. The result of the election had to do in part with the apathy on the left, given that governmental reforms had not been taken far enough. Also, the secularizing agenda of the leftist government had mobilized a considerable segment of the population in support of the church. Anarchists also played a crucial part in election results. Anarchists abandoned some of their tenets a number of times in Spain during this period, as we will see, in a series of remarkable and controversial actions that were decisive to the unfolding of events.

FEDERALISM

As a young man, Pablo had sought "the classification of himself in shooting off his impossible theories against immediate issues, and perhaps arrive eventually at a practicable code and a movement" (O'Brien *Mary* 61). The practicable code and movement that Pablo dreamt off in his youth was well established in the Iberian peninsula by the 1920s. The first anarchist journal ever published, *El Porvenir*, had in fact appeared in Catalonia in 1845 (see Woodcock 335). In October 1868, the Italian anarchist activist Giuseppe Fanelli had arrived in Spain bringing news of anarchism, without speaking any Spanish, despite which he made such an extraordinary impression on a gathering of federalists that the historian George Woodcock described the meeting as "Pentecostal" (339). The Catalan Francisco Pí y Margall — whose first substantial book, *La Reacción y la Revolución*, was published in 1854, and who was notable for his translations of the work of the anarchist Joseph Proudhon into Spanish and for his incessant work for the federalist cause — had already inspired many with a first inkling of what an anarchist structuring of society may mean. Pí y Margall explained that "Federalism starts out, not from humanity, but from the individual. From the individual it sees emerge, in spontaneous and natural development, the family, the town, the province, the nation, the groups of nations," to add that Federalist thought "denies the State even the right of intervention in the internal organization of provinces and towns" (82 — my translation). Federalism did not eliminate the function of the state altogether, like the anarchists hoped, but it was just one step away from doing so; as Woodcock puts it, federalists and anarchists are "cousins" (341). Most importantly, in the context of *Mary Lavelle*,

Pí y Margall's ideas were tuned to the demands of Basque nationalists (see Pí y Margall 87 and 91). In the turbulent 11 months of the First Spanish Republic in Spain, in 1873, Francisco Pí y Margall became president (the second of four in the period) and with the backing of congress proclaimed Spain a Federal Republic; many regions in the south declared themselves free cantons before legal ratification came through, which together with a new Carlist upsurge in the Basque Country, brought about a new government which enforced centralization.

Juanito Areavaga and Mary Lavelle's affair can be seen as a *federation* of two autonomous entities. Anarchists tend to shun the institution of marriage, favoring "free unions"; in the Basque Country, anarchists only began to marry as a matter of course during the Spanish Civil War, when the high numbers of casualties spurred them to secure state financial aid for orphans or partners—many of these marriages (officiated in anarchist syndicalist centers) were a "gesture of solidarity" between people who were not acquainted with each other (Chiapuso 313). In the Basque Country, towns used to have a specially designated tree which would perform the role of "offical witness" to a commerical transaction or an oath, and given that Mary and Juan seal their union under a tree, this may be read as a ratification of vows under a pre–Christian, natural law. This approach to relationships has had an enduring appeal for anarchists, as can be seen in Ursula Le Guin's science fiction novel of 1974 *The Dispossessed*, set in an anarchist planet where society, culture, education, politics, and sexual and affective attachments, are all organized under libertarian principles, which in the book are partly formulated by a thinker named Odo. "An Odonian undertook monogamy just as he might undertake a joint enterprise in production, a ballet or a soap-works," we are told, because "[p]artnership was a voluntarily constituted federation like any other. So long as it worked, it worked, and if it didn't work it stopped being. It was not an institution but a function. It had no sanction but that of private conscience," and although it may seem, in Odo's development of social theory, "that her insistence on freedom to change would invalidate the idea of promise or vow, in fact the freedom made the promise meaningful" (203). In this context, Luisa de Maraval and Juanito Areavaga represent the Unitarian and Federal vision respectively, as Luisa explains to Mary in an important scene: "The Kings of Castile have been kings of all the Spains for a very long time. Myself I cling to the long tradition, but Juanito says ... that some form of federated autonomies will have to be conceded" (O'Brien *Mary* 152). "Conceded," that is, after a communist revolution and the instauration of a communist state, as we learn later: "He simply saw that Spain's aching need was for the ruthless establishment in every cranny of the peninsula of justice, order, health and knowledge," and "the only relatively quick way to such a goal was by an antiseptic scouring out of all precedented establishments, and the enforcing of the main principles and practices of Communism" (ibid., 160).

"[R]uthless," "order," "scourging," "enforcing" ... do not sound too promising as a democrat's manifesto. And it is even more disturbing when the description of Juanito's "political faith" (159) is mixed in the novel with the story of how himself and Pablo fell in love, at the very same age, with comparable aristocratic women (and presumably, this suggests, with similar results). The novel blurs the distinction between idealism in politics, and in romance. A disappointed Pablo was soon forced "to consider the value and inevitability of the spirit's solitary confinement" (57). A marriage of equals may have had little chance with Consuelo given her coldness, but it also seems doomed with Luisa, given her conservatism and Juanito's remarkably unromantic notions. Realizing that "I am my own political party" and lacking a single "soldier," he had decided that "I must take a wife to remedy that" (162). After making this decision, in a quirk of fate, he had fallen in love with the stylish aristocrat Luisa, "the perfect flower of all he proposed to sweep away" (ibid.).

ANARCHISM

Juanito is not, however, the average tyrant. In accordance with Marxist theory, he expects the centralized state to dissolve itself after it has served its function (the equation of this thesis to the anticipated evolution of his marriage is, needless to say, disheartening). "Juanito saw Spain as the field in which the eventual inevitable battle would be fought against centrali[z]ation and the slave-state"; a "long-sighted" view, in that "he believed it his political duty to help to found something which he must rely on his grandsons to overthrow," because he hoped that Communism would come "within 50 years, and within a hundred, if Spanish individualism could at all be trusted, it would be gone, leaving knowledge, the only true good, behind it" (159–161). Don Pablo would listen, "shudder tolerantly," and tell his son: "No end can justify the risky imposition of citizen-servility" (161). The objection is clear, but not unambiguous. This is the traditional anarchist stance, except for the word "risky," which leaves some room to conceive of a slave state as potentially good at least *in theory* if too risky in practice.

The traditional aims of anarchism have been: dismantling power structures, promoting and facilitating education, and redistributing capital and goods (see also Kornegger 2–3). Power is the primary target of anarchists. O'Brien did devote two of her novels to study abuse of power, *The Last of Summer* (see Reynolds *Kate* 80) and *That Lady*, and used one novel to describe a just ruler, *The Land of Spices*. In this last novel, Mother Superior Helen Archer is a just ruler in the Daoist sense of "ruling without ruling" (see Marshall 53–60 for the Daoist link with anarchism). Rather than organizational systems, O'Brien was interested in how individuals were affected by power — by having it, and by being victims of it. Domestic power structures, the tyranny of a Catholic conscience, and the negotiation of freedom in relationships, are central to all her work.

There are a number of branches in anarchism, the main ones being: individualist anarchism, collectivism, anarchist communism, anarcho-syndicalism, pacifist/Christian anarchism, anarchist/social ecology, and anarcho-feminism.

The differences between the various anarchist schools, as George Woodcock points out, "actually lie in two fairly limited regions: revolutionary methods (especially the use of violence) and economic organization" (19). Some examples from "classic anarchism," the anarchism of the nineteenth century, prove the diversity within the movement: Pierre Joseph Proudhon was a federalist anarchist who believed in the right to private property, Mihail Bakunin was a collectivist believing in property in the hands of voluntary institutions, and Pieter Kropotkin was an anarchist communist believing in common property (that is, no property). Anarcho-syndicalism saw the trade union movement as playing a key role in bringing about the fall of the state through the general strike, while anarchist individualism envisaged the gradual dismantling of the state's structures. Anarchists are keenly aware of the ethics of power-distribution between individuals at an everyday level, but one of the main goals of anarchism is the abolition of the estate — any state, including parliamentary democracies.

COMPROMISE

This is how *Mary Lavelle* sums up Don Pablo's ideas: "He was in fact an anarchist — with a difference. As perhaps every Spaniard is whatever he is — with a difference" (61). To an anarchist, voting in a parliamentary system is the equivalent of relinquishing one's right and ability to be a social agent, and the epitome of endorsing the authoritarian structure that supports any given government. To an anarchist, voting makes a mockery of collective decision-making, the equivalent of reading out from an obsolete script. Yet, as George Woodcock explains, in the Spanish municipal elections of 1930 which signaled the end of the monarchy in the country, "many anarchists had gone to the polls — against all their publicly proclaimed principles — for the tactical reason that a republic seemed more favorable to their aims than a monarchy," while in 1933 the anarchist union CNT "carried on a vigorous abstentionist campaign [and] the lack of the million votes which it controlled meant defeat for the Left and two years of reactionary right-wing government" (363).

In 1933, this new right-wing government rescinded all previous reforms and moved towards dictatorship. In response, the main anarchist and socialist unions (CNT and UGT) planned a rising, but because of lack of coordination, the revolt only broke out in two regions in October 1934. In Catalonia, it was led by the semi-autonomous nationalist government and did not amount to much because of the lack of unified support from workers' organizations. In Asturias, however, it took the form of a popular revolt, with socialists, anarchists, and communists instituting a revolutionary regional committee that lasted all but nine days, before being violently crushed by the Spanish army. Kate O'Brien had followed these developments closely. It is in Asturias that the most important incident of civil unrest in *Farewell Spain* takes place, while elsewhere in the book O'Brien refers directly to the commune and its repression (by government troops sent from the Spanish colonies in north Africa), making a striking historical link to the Christian-Arab war: "That invader — the Moor — never returned within sight of the cross of Covadonga until Spanish officers marched him up there in October, 1934, to shoot at Asturian miners" (67). The upsurge, often referred to as "the failed revolution of 1934" or the "Asturian commune," was of enormous significance. It polarized political positions, bringing together the left in the Frente Popular (Popular Front) and moving the right towards an extreme conservatism of fascist leanings. The establishment of the commune was also the immediate precedent for the Spanish Civil War.

New elections in 1936 gave the victory to the Frente Popular, partly thanks to the votes of thousands of anarchists who once more went against their own beliefs and co-operated with the parliamentary system in order to put an end to conservative rule. It is not by chance that *Mary Lavelle* incorporates a debate on the potential moral justification of government, in the eyes of a Christian anarchist, the young Pablo, who sees state centralization as anathema but seems at least willing to consider compromise: "A system of faith was essential, he thought — indeed perhaps the only essential system. But as to secular government, to be acceptable at all, how it would have to be reconceived, in what terms of looseness and simplification!" (61). Both claims make Pablo rather unusual among anarchists.

As it happens, when revolution came, its priority was not the creation of a centralized state. In Spain after the 1936 elections, as soon as news of the victory of the Frente Popular arrived, thousands of people were convinced that this represented the end of the system as they knew it. A revolutionary movement swept across Spain, with workers and peasants seizing property, tools, weapons, taking control of factories, collectivizing lands, and creating self-regulated communities; it was a social revolution. Later, when news of the fascist uprising arrived, the revolutionary movement took on a renewed impetus and, for a few months, "in those parts of Spain not overrun by Franco's troops, about 3 million men, women, and children were living in collectivized communities" (Ward 23). The Spanish revolution has been described as "the farthest-reaching movement that the Left ever produced" (Bookchin 1).

It is rarely stressed outside Spain that the Basque Nationalist Party (together with nationalists from other regions), despite being rather conservative in outlook, sided itself with the leftist republic and with democracy. Although many people in Navarre supported the rising, most other Basques did not, and like everyone else on the side of the Republic, they had to pay the price in the war and during the dictatorship — not only in terms of personal suffering, but also in terms of a brutal repression to their culture. The prevalent custom in anglophone countries of referring to the Spanish fascist contingent as "the nationalists" is completely misleading and it should be reviewed at once; in Spain, the Francoist army is generally referred to as "the nationals" ("los nacionales"), and there is no reason for this term not to be adopted instead.

September 1936 saw an even more serious breach of anarchist ideas than casting a vote in the elections, when in the emergency government set up to respond to the fascist uprising, some anarchists became ministers with the backing of the most important anarchist organizations in the country, the CNT (Confederación Nacional del Trabajo, "National Workers Confederation") and the FAI (Federación Anarquista Ibérica, "Iberian Anarchist Federation"). In the "emergency" governments set up to respond to war, the famous anarchist writer, intellectual, and activist Federica Montseny became Minister for Health ("Sanidad"), the first female minister in Spanish history, and the anarchists Juan García Oliver, Joan Peyró Belis, and Juan López Sanchez became Ministers for Justice ("Interior"), Industry ("Trabajo"), and Commerce ("Comercio"), respectively. It was a fiercely contested move that has remained controversial with anarchists despite being taken "in extremis"; the fact that the gesture was well-meaning was never disputed — nor the four individuals' credentials — but it clearly signified "a virtual abdication of anarchist revolutionary hopes," because "it meant that the anarchist leaders were strengthening the governmental institutions which were their natural enemies" (Woodcock 369). It has been suggested that the presence of anarchists in government encouraged the internal coup of May 1937, which resulted in weeks of street battles (as recalled by Orwell in *Homage to Catalonia*), when Marxists attempted to take control of the leftist Republican side and stop revolutionary efforts from the POUM (communist) and the CNT (anarchist) organizations. They succeeded, and a USSR-led war effort marked the rest of the conflict. As Woodcock points out, the willingness of some anarchist leaders to compromise was not to blame for the failure of the Spanish revolution, because "[b]y compromising they did not make their failure less certain; they merely made it more humiliating" (370).

PUBLIC POSITIONS

Kate O'Brien was writing in 1935, before any of this happened, but a crucial point in *Mary Lavelle* is that the political ideals of both Pablo and Juan are practicable and not merely an intellectual pastime (for Pablo see 54). The same "practical" tendency is inherited by his son, who "was too Spanish to be any kind of Utopian," and who spends his time studying constitutional history and law (162). This emphasis is found elsewhere in O'Brien. For example, Dr. Curran in *The Anteroom*: "But he was not a poet. He was a Victorian bourgeois, rationalist in the idiom of his mind. Catholic in tradition and practice, a man eager to harness feeling into usefulness" (*Anteroom* 57). Or, for example, in O'Brien's filmscript *Mary Magdalen*, Jesus is not only a spiritual leader but also a political activist and, one of his followers claims, "no foolish idealist," because his mission is "just plain materialism" (n.d.a. 45). Juanito explains to Mary that "I'm after a Communism very different from Lenin's. I want it understood as what it is, pure Utilitarianism, plain, materialistic justice. With no spiritual attack or message" (260). Let us look at these claims more closely.

Juanito, a lawyer, would have been very familiar with utilitarianism, developed by the jurist Jeremy Bentham. In 1789 Bentham put forward the idea that whatever brings happiness to the greatest number of people is good, and that legislation should aim at the happiness of the greatest number, being applicable "not only to every action of a private individual, but to every measure of government" (*Morals* 12). Nineteenth century utilitarianism was often placed at the service of egalitarian causes. Bentham himself, for example, was the first person to publicly demand the decriminalization of sodomy in England, in 1785 (see "Offences"). Among those inspired by his theories, we find William Godwin, whose 1793 *Political Justice* is often considered the first anarchist treatise (as well as an example of utilitarianism), and John Stuart Mill, who in addition to a popular introduction to utilitarianism of 1861, also published, in 1869, *The Subjection of Women*, one of the first feminist treatises and one of the most influential, a plea for equality based on utilitarian principles. Juanito's utilitarianism is in line with the insistence of *Mary Lavelle* on the viability of the political projects on offer. However, the novel does not pursue this line of argument, and Juanito seems only too aware of the fatal limitations of utilitarian politics, when he explains to Mary that "the real issues will always be unmanageable. There is no such thing as legislation for happiness" (260).

Juanito's distancing himself from Lenin's communism may be an antidogmatic stance or, given that O'Brien was writing in 1935, she may want to distance him more generally from the Soviet Union (Gerardine Meany in conversation June 28, 2007). Since the Kronstadt massacre of 1921 (see Newell 10–12), anarchists and other dissidents had made public outside Russia the repressive methods of the regime, which may explain Juanito's emphatic claim that a communist state would have a very distinct character in Spain. Although Juanito refers to "communism" throughout, he clearly means a centralized communist state with a single leader (himself). Communism merely means social ownership and sharing according to need. Most anarchists may be said to be anarcho-communists, in that they believe in non-hierarchical organizational structures and common ownership of goods, availed of according to need; the black and red flags so associated with anti-fascist resistance in the Spanish Civil War were anarcho-communist flags. "The Communistic theory, [Juanito] would say, could be no more than a means to the truly vital creature — never, never, in any bearable world, an end" (O'Brien *Mary* 160). Here may lay the crucial point of disagreement with his father, given that "anarchists believe that the means create the ends" (Kornegger 2).

Mary Lavelle seems to defend the viability of a state-communism "with a difference" (the difference being, apparently, that "Spanish" individualism will make it bearable), but it is perhaps in its defense of the *sanity* of anarchist beliefs that the book distinguishes itself. Pablo is a graduate in Modern History, whose library includes Aquinas, Spinoza, Pascal, Marx; he is a devout Catholic, a respected factory owner, a philanthropist, a pillar of society, and an anarchist.

This (unlikely) combination is calculated to pre-empt objections to his politics. The prevalent accounts of anarchism in the media in Anglophone countries have been and continue to be relentlessly hostile, inaccurate, and manipulative. The demonization of anarchists and the reviling or ridiculing of their beliefs is widespread. The most consistent tactic has been to associate anarchism with violence, to the extent that sympathetic histories of anarchism invariably open by attempting to dispel this assumption (see Woodcock 1970 [1962], Marshall 1993 [1992], Ward 2004). It is symptomatic that one of the best known Basque anarchists is Casilda "the bomb girl," Casilda Meńdez Hernáez, from Donostia/San Sebastian, a prominent fighter in 1934 and in the Spanish Civil War (and later in the French Resistance), who in fact opposed the use of violence other than in self-defence, and who was considerably involved in syndicalist and feminist activism (see L.M. Jiménez). Although rarely acknowledged by commentators, anarchism was a mass movement in Spain, as indicated by the membership of its main organizations up to the beginning of Franco's dictatorship, with the anarchist union CNT reaching about 2 million, and the FAI reaching 150,000 in 1938 (see Woodcock 369). Leaving aside the numbers, in anarchist historiography Spain is seen as "the country where anarchism put down its deepest roots" (Ward 20). Critics have failed to engage with the political radicalism of *Mary Lavelle*, arguably because of the persistent silencing of anarchism, which remains something of a "blind spot" if, like in this novel, it is approached sympathetically by the author.

Given that the black flag is the anarchist symbol (while the red and black flag, as we have mentioned, stands for anarcho-communism), it may not be a coincidence that *Mary Lavelle* refers to black as "a national uniform" (105) in Spain. More significantly, Don Pablo is, like his father Don Juan, "profoundly a Spaniard — that is, convinced to the last drop of his blood of the absolute dominion of personality over system" (50), which is a libertarian statement. Spanish commentators like Heleno Saña also see anarchism as an ideology particularly tuned to the Spanish character; in an essay of 2006, he claimed that there is an anti-authoritarian tradition predating nineteenth century anarchism, traceable in popular revolts and religious writings, something which can be linked to a "natural" democratic spirit in Spain (41). Saña's essentialist claims, punctuated by his attacks on Marxism, are in my view inaccurate and unhelpful in an egalitarian context. Nevertheless, they are noteworthy in the context of *Mary Lavelle*. Perhaps Don Pablo is "[a]n armchair anarchist" ["Un Anarquista de Salón"], the turn of phrase used by the anarchist from Bilbo Emiliano Serna to describe himself in his (rather eventful) autobiography of that title. Don Pablo may be alarmed by his son, and Juanito may consider his father "a dreamer" (O'Brien *Mary* 261), but the fact is that the novel presents a Marxist and an anarchist in good terms with each other. This is partly explained by the historical context in Spain. Things were to change dramatically on the year of publication of the novel, and relationships between Marxists and anarchists were to deteriorate steadily with the evolution of the war.

In the period between the military insurgence of 1936 against the leftist Spanish Republic and the instauration of a fascist regime in Spain, that is, during the civil war, an unprecedented number of international artists and intellectuals, often implicitly seeing themselves as *European* or Euro-American, focused their energies in gathering support for the cause of democracy in Spain. Some, like Ernest Hemingway, immediately began to give public speeches and to write articles in support of the Republic. Some wrote poems in a call to join "the struggle," like W.H. Auden in "Spain." Some helped raise funds, like Virginia Woolf, who donated for auction the manuscript of *Three Guineas* to the committee supporting Basque refugee children. Some produced paintings, like Pablo Picasso, whose *Guernica* represented Spain at the International Exhibition (shortly before the Nazis began to publicly burn "degenerate art"). Some traveled to Spain to join the Red Cross on the Republican side, like Silvia Townsend Warner and Valentine Ackland. Some, like Charles Connolly or George Orwell, joined the International Brigades to fight in the trenches. Others made films, in rushed, desperate attempts to influence public opinion and pressure their governments to take action. The 1938 film *Blockade*, for example, a tale of political betrayal set in the Spanish Civil War directed by William Dieterle and starring Henry Fonda, ended with a zoom to close-up of the hero and a desperate appeal to the cinema audience: "[This is] not war; war is between soldiers. It's murder! Murder of innocent people. There's no sense to it. The world can't stop it? Where's the conscience of the world?!" *Farewell Spain* belongs in this context, as it is clearly an attempt to offer a favorable witness account of the causes and development of the civil war in the face of hostile propaganda, and it is shaped by a sense of urgency. The case of *Mary Lavelle*, however, is different, because the novel was written before the fascist uprising. O'Brien is unique in that her response to the situation in Spain *preceded* the general alarm and frantic public positioning of intellectuals and artists throughout Europe. It was the climate of proto-revolutionary fervor in the Spain of the early 1930s that went into *Mary Lavelle*. The novel was published in 1936, coinciding with the developments that triggered the Spanish Civil War, but the conception and execution of *Mary Lavelle* were informed by the political tensions preceding the event. There was no need to be loud then. A cold exposition of the reasonableness of anarchist and communist goals was all that was needed. Class issues did not need to be simplified at that stage, nor political ideologies invisibilized in a "catch-all" call for "democracy." Because *Mary Lavelle* was written before the civil war, the novel could pursue an aesthetic of composed interweaving and an ideology of plural complexity that would have become impossible just one year later.

According to Lorna Reynolds, Kate O'Brien was "a hater of war" (*Kate* 16). In *Farewell Spain*, O'Brien described herself as "that funny old-fashioned thing, a pacifist" (220), although still managed to register her theoretical support for a communist army (in self-defense of democracy) as opposed to a fascist army (seeking to overthrow it). It is relevant that Kate O'Brien chose to live in England, rather than on neutral Ireland, during World War II. By 1943, in *English Diaries and Journals*, she was making jokes on the horrors of war in rather poor taste. This attitude may be characteristic of those who lived through the blitz in England (as Gerardine Meaney suggests, in conversation, March 11, 2007), but perhaps the time-gap accounts for O'Brien's irony as a distancing measure, in the context of a general disillusionment on the left after Stalin's pact of nonaggression with Nazi Germany and the outcome of the Spanish Civil War. Irish neutrality was a point of contention for the anti-fascist writers of the period, and we find a striking link between O'Brien and Elizabeth Bowen, in the remarkably similar short stories that both devoted to the perception of World War II in the minds of ordinary Irish people. Both declared having worked for the British Ministry for Information (Walshe doubts O'Brien's claim in *Kate* 98; but see 96). O'Brien's vocal anti-militarism cannot be squarely equated with pacifism, as shown for example in her problematic admiration for the "cleansing" campaign of the "Reyes Católicos" ("Catholic Monarchs") in the Spain of the fifteenth century or, of more relevance to *Mary Lavelle*, in her call to arms in the final chapter of *Farewell Spain*.

Anti-Capitalism

CAPITALISM AND APOCALYPSE

Mary Lavelle's anti-capitalist strand is idiosyncratic, focusing as it does on a (penniless) middle-class woman and two upper-class men, all of whom are presented in a positive light in the novel. This focus is partly the result of the important autobiographical input in the drafting of the novel, which is based on O'Brien's acquaintance with the upper-middle-class Areilzas in the Bilbo of 1922, as we will see later. Other writers' political focus was prompted by a direct contact with working class experience. For example, in 1937, the year of publication of *Farewell Spain* and one year after *Mary Lavelle*, George Orwell's *The Road to Wigan Pier* documented the life of coal miners in Yorkshire and Lancashire, describing in detail the appalling conditions of the workers and their families. These are very different books, yet *Mary Lavelle* and *The Road to Wigan Pier* are both stylistic hybrids seeking to document critically some of the consequences of capitalism. The city of Bilbo had once been described as "the California of Iron" (see Montero's book of the same title), but by the 1920s the mines' role had diminished greatly. By contrast with the poorer Asturias, a neighboring region with an economy relying on the mining industry, the Basque Country, as O'Brien encountered it in Bilbo, was prosperous, with an economy based on commerce, shipping, and foundries. On the one hand it was an uncompromising financial center, aptly referred to by O'Brien as "Bank-encrusted Bilbao" (*Ireland* 19). On the other hand, there was a reformist impulse in an important sector of the Basque bourgeoisie. This class-map is crucial to *Mary Lavelle*, a book that is less concerned with the plight of the workers on the ground than with the revolutionary ideas that were sweeping across all segments of society at the time. This is not to say that an anti-capitalist novel that emphasized the abuses of the workers as suffered in the mines and factories of Bilbo was not also possible to a literary visitor in the city. Vicente Blasco Ibáñez, a writer sometimes aligned to the generation of 98, proved it in 1904 with *El Intruso* ("The Intruder"). As we will discuss later, incredible as it may seem, this novel shares some characters with *Mary Lavelle*, notably the protagonist of *El Intruso*, who is a fictionalized version of Enrique Areilza, the man who inspired Don Pablo, here portrayed as a politically radical doctor.

Kate O'Brien, in her *Irish Times* column of August 2, 1967, referred to "tycoons and materialists," saying that "we belong to them now. They own the twentieth century" (*Long Distance* 34). The anti-capitalist strand in *Mary Lavelle*, firmly planted on a metropolitan context, develops a similar approach in O'Brien's first novel, *Without My Cloak*, where another Mellick/Limerick-born outsider, Denis Considine, has an apocalyptic vision prompted by his encounter with another capitalist hub, the city of New York in the 1850s (O'Brien had been inspired by her own visit to the city in the early 1920s). We have seen how Denis's wealthy family has dispatched his lower-class lover, Christina, to New York. Christina says of her new home that "[i]t whirled with passion towards some greedy ruthless dream that no one seemed to have time to explain or to examine" (*Cloak* 405). Denis travels to the United States in an attempt to find her and learns that the merciless city he encounters is not conducive to his romantic idealism. In New York, he observes that money is "first principle and holy grail" (ibid., 386), thanks to the "new alchemy" of petroleum (385). He declares: "This country had what was left of time before it, and all the sins and warnings of a hundred fallen empires and jaded cultures to point its way" (386). In the same vein, Mary Lavelle will retake the biblical imagery and go on to describe gold as "Altorno's God," with the book including references to Sodom and Gomorrah and taking a conceptual leap to liken the androgynous Mary to an angel and Don Pablo to Lot, the biblical survivor to the destruction of Sodom. As we will see later in more detail, *Mary Lavelle*, the novel itself, therefore becomes a warning/announcement of impending apocalyptic collapse; the capitalist haven of Bilbo is about to fall, O'Brien implies, but there is hope "for the socialists among ye."

There are numerous precedents for anti-capitalist outsiders resorting to biblical metaphors when faced for the first time with a dehumanized urban center. One example is the allegorical 1948 novel *The Plague*, by the existentialist and libertarian Algerian writer Albert Camus. Examples inspired by New York include the 1882 poem "Big City Love" ("Amor de Ciudad Grande") by the Cuban José Martí, and the poem sequence "Poet in New York" ("Poeta en Nueva York"), written between 1929 and 1930 by the Spanish Federico García Lorca; both give voice to outraged visionaries, visitors in a city where capitalism has barred "humane love" ("amor humano"— Lorca 166), who register their despair at the impossibility of either retreat or surrender. However, apocalyptic dénouement is often underpinned by a circular view of history. In our own time, in

Ireland, we may be tempted to retrospectively read the neo–Egyptian architecture of "celtic tiger" Dublin, and the postmodern apotheosis of Seán Hillen's Irish Gizeh, as sure signs of impending ruins. Conversely, the "devaluation of the contemporary moment" in apocalyptic discourse is often part and parcel of "regenerat[ive]" politics (Eliade 132).

Shabby, Beautiful

Apocalyptic references in *Mary Lavelle*, for all their relevance, are discreetly articulated, and the novel's position amounts to a *subtle* comment on the harms of industrial capitalism. Mary signals an allegiance to the working class through small gestures by, for example, wearing rope soled shoes, the Basque "abarketas," certainly not part of the accepted "uniform" for a governess. However, she doesn't quite side herself with the poor but with the unpretentious, the unshowy, the shabby. In her first excursions to Altorno/Bilbo, Mary notes the "very showy" city center, the "pretentious" shops, the fancy cars, the "self-indulgence" and "glossy splendour" everywhere. The showy appears side by side with the shabby; there are "shabby trees," a "shabby bandstand," and, more importantly, there are very "shabby" slums (73). In the logic of the novel, the sin of the city is not so much the accumulation of capital, as its display. The adjective "shabby" had already been invested with moral connotations in *Without My Cloak*. To give just one example, the only New Yorker in that novel who doesn't lust after money is a "shabby" gay sculptor from Greenwich Village who makes an unsuccessful pass at Denis (387). In *Mary Lavelle*, Pablo and Juanito Areavaga may be upper class, but they are both contemptuous of wealth and status and, crucially, both of them look "shabby." This time, unlike Denis, the protagonist will fall for the shabby and will have an affair with Juanito, thereby shunning her own duties to her class. Reciting pastoral poetry to the Areavaga girls, stalking their mansion in her rope-soled shoes, this proper young lady from Limerick must have looked like the sphinx (perhaps "crouching towards Bethlehem to be born"—see Yeats "Coming" 235). In this, she may appear to be as *anomalous* as her boss and her lover. However, two crucial aspects of the presentation of class in the novel must be taken into account: O'Brien's use of "wealth" as a malleable trope and the contemporary association of socialism to the middle class. We will look at them in turn.

Kate O'Brien once referred to "significant beauty," modifying a famous coinage by art critic Clive Bell, who in his book *Art*, of 1914, claimed that modernism in the visual arts is a quest for "significant form"; according to O'Brien, Cézanne's paintings were the first to show that beauty "can lie in a rumpled table-napkin, and a half-empty glass" ("Rage" 12). Lorna Reynolds titled her analysis of *Mary Lavelle* "A Girl and Her Beauty" (*Kate* 59), and her beauty is clearly the most relevant thing about Mary—together with her contempt for it. Beauty is never decorative in an O'Brien novel, but rather it functions as a reliable prop. Physical beauty is imposed on the female protagonists ("thrown" at them, in a sense), and it is in their response to it that the reader can delineate their spiritual and intellectual worth. "La Belle" is not even aware of her beauty; her beauty is therefore irrelevant to her. In this context, one of the most striking moves in O'Brien's work is how often beauty equates wealth. In her novel *The Flower of May*, for example, Lucille is looking at Lilian: "'How *absolutely* beautiful she is,' she thought coldly, 'how much she is mistress of her beauty. She wears it like a weapon, like a coat of arms. Already she has mastered it completely; she knows it to be her state; she will invest it for sound dividends all her life," (206). Mary's disregard for her beauty functions on the same level as the socialism of the upper-class Areavagas in *Mary Lavelle* and the austerity of the princess of Eboli in the novel *That Lady*. It functions on the same level as the Prima Donna's singing voice (Rose) in *As Music and Splendour*, a voice which she will not force, refusing to show off, or Reverend Mother's power, in *The Land of Spices*, a power which she will not abuse. Beauty, like inherited wealth, artistic ability, fame, or authority, is an "accident." Incidentally, so are nationality (in *My Ireland*), sanctity (in *Teresa of Avila*), and homosexuality (in *Farewell Spain*), all of which are described by O'Brien as "accidental." All these things do not make us who we are but, rather, it is the way we deal with them that is the measure of our character. As Lorna Reynolds pointed out, "Catholic Ireland [in the thirties and forties] seemed not to know ... that without freedom to choose there can be no virtue" (*Kate* 105). O'Brien's heroes are given "riches" so that their integrity has a background to shine on.

COMFORTABLE REVOLUTIONARIES

George Orwell claimed in 1937 that socialism as a theory was "confined entirely to the middleclass," to add that "[t]he typical Socialist is not, as tremulous old ladies imagine, a ferocious-looking working man with greasy overalls and a raucous voice" (*Road* 161). Orwell humorously described himself as belonging to "the lower-upper-middle class" (ibid. 128) and decried "the grand old Socialist sport of denouncing the bourgeoisie" (167). The anarchist Don Pablo and the communist Juanito don't talk about poverty, not once — they seem to understand socialism in terms of soul-saving (the collective soul of Spain). This is perhaps less striking given that they are in an awkward position as upper-class gentlemen. However, an emphasis on redistribution of capital, although the common goal of all forms of socialism, is stressed differently in Marxism's near-exclusive focus on economic oppression and anarchism's placing of a greater emphasis on authority as the basis of hierarchical systems. In Orwell's words, it is easy to imagine a collectivist world, "that is, with the profit principle eliminated — but with all political, military and educational power in the hands of a small caste of rulers and their bravos. That or something like it is the objective of fascism" (ibid. 200). Anarchism focuses on dismantling concentrations of power, from which the end to the concentration of wealth in a few hands will inevitably follow. In this context, it is important to remember that part of the mythology of anarchism in the late nineteenth century, as exploited by the media, was the supposed proliferation of educated members of the upper classes who had rebelled against their background after embracing anarchist beliefs. Popular historical figures, such as "Prince" Piotr Kropotkin, the once aristocrat Mihail Bakunin and, most famously, the landowner who redistributed his property among his serfs, Leo Tolstoy, gave some credence to the perception. Oscar Wilde's Prince Paul, and Henry James's Princess Casamassima, provided similar fictional figures to the popular imagination in an oversimplified form. Wilde's anarchist sympathies, persistently ignored by biographers and critics, were more apparent in the consistent mockery of authority and exuberant libertarian "amorality" of his subsequent plays than in any overt references to politics, although his beliefs were clearly stated in his essay-manifesto of 1890 "The Soul of Man (Under Socialism)," as we will see later. Other representations of anarchists, such as the motley crew in Joseph Conrad's 1907 *The Secret Agent* and the Carbonari Professor Pesca (see Sucksmith 622, and Rath) in Wilkie Collins's *The Woman in White,* published in 1859–1860, portrayed respectable members of the middle classes ranging from psychotics to terrorists.

There are also some sympathetic examples, however. Tolstoy's 1899 *Ressurection* deals with a Russian aristocrat who comes to realize the absurdity of the judicial system and the sinfulness of capital and has a political epiphany which "resurrects" him. In a passage of the novel, interesting in the context of Mary Lavelle's characterization, a former prostitute of peasant extraction named Katusha, wrongly condemned to hard labor, spends some time with political prisoners during the trip to Siberia: "[Katusha Maslova] understood that they were for the people and against the upper classes, and, though themselves belonging to the upper classes, had sacrificed their privileges, their liberty, and their lives for the people. This especially made her value and admire them" (410). Katusha is particularly impressed by Mary Pavlovna, "whom she was not only delighted with, but loved with a peculiar, respectful, and devoted love" because "this beautiful girl, who could speak three languages, the daughter of a rich general, gave away all that her rich brother sent her, loved like the simplest working girl, and dressed not only simply but poorly, paying no heed to her appearance. Mary's " complete absence of coquetr[y] was particularly surprising and therefore attractive to Maslova" (411).

The autobiographical 1903 novel *A Girl Among the Anarchists*, narrating how a young upper-middle-class Victorian lady joined the anarchist underground in London and went on to become the editor of an anarchist newspaper, aimed at a realistic, demystifying portrait of the feared anarchist "criminal" network. Written by Helen and Olivia Rossetti (nieces of Christina and Dante Gabriel Rossetti) under the pseudonym Isabel Meredith, the novel was based on the two sisters' experience of publishing *The Torch: A Revolutionary Journal of International Socialism,* as teenagers, from the basement of their family home, between 1891 and 1897, after reading Kropotkin's essay "Appeal to the Young" and setting up their own press (see Jennifer Shaddock's introduction to the novel). It is remarkable that they were tolerated by their parents, who saw their anarchist ardor as a passing phase, although they were not themselves unfamiliar with radical politics; Professor Pesca in *The Woman in White* was said to have been inspired by Gabriele Rossetti (see Sucksmith in Collins 605), the grandfather of the authors. Many of the characters in *A Girl Among the Anarchists* are originally upper class or from the liberal professions and share, apart from their devotion to the cause, various degrees of "shabbiness" in their appearance. As in *Mary Lavelle*, this novel also has a female protagonist who is forward in love matters and a number of distinctly nonsensationalist portraits of anarchists.

Despite the long list of hostile commentators, there was a parallel public discourse sympathetic to anarchism available to O'Brien, that of Romanticism and Aestheticism, which, according to Ruth Vanita, helped "develop an anarchist feminist worldview" (10). It is also noteworthy that writers of the Noventayocho like Azorín and Ramiro de Maeztu showed interest in anarchism, while "[Blasco Ibáñez] would immortalize Fermín Salvochea in his book *La Bodega*, Pío Baroja wrote his novel *Aurora Roja* inspired by the libertarian militants José Prat and Ricardo Mella," and Unamuno once admitted that "my readings on economy (more so than on sociology), turned me into a socialist, but I soon realised that my foundation was and is, above all, anarchist" (Saña 42–43 — my translation). O'Brien was certainly aware of the stereotypical representations of political radicals available and specifically sought to undermine anti-anarchist propaganda, for example by insisting on the fact that the Areavaga father and son have "irregular" features (*Mary* 175 and 51), a characteristic highlighted by criminologist Cesare Lombroso in 1876 as the telling sign of an anarchist. O'Brien perversely gave *this face* to her gentle heroes, who are the opposite of what Lombroso had in mind.

In *Mary Lavelle*, there is an interesting ideological progression between Don Juan, his son Don Pablo, and his son Juanito (patent in the latter's adoption of a "friendlier" name), perhaps intended as an allegory of the raise of "political consciousness" among the intellectual bourgeoisie from the nineteenth to the twentieth century. Don Juan is a proto-socialist, but his allegiances are "complicated" by his status as businessman, because he realizes that his "circumstances" are the result of "false premises," and he sees "the evil plight of the industrial magnate, but *neither his tradition nor his temperament would allow him to believe that the solution of it, if there was one, lay in the abolition of his class*," so that, in the final assessment, he may be nothing more than "a rich man with a conscience" (emphasis added, *Mary* 50).

Mary Lavelle is an anti-capitalist novel, yet terms such as "the capitalist system" don't make much sense when discussing O'Brien. She is concerned with consumerism, with excess, with display, with unethical (mercantilist) behavior, with decadence. These are more obvious in a metropolis. Cities play an important part in many O'Brien novels, but New York and Bilbo are unique in her work in that they are a force that must be resisted. Dublin may be added to the list, with the narrator's description of the shopping haven of Grafton Street as "a state of being" in *Without My Cloak*, "a persistent and contradictory piece of Ireland's self-expression" (150). In *Mary Lavelle*, capitalism and inherited wealth are not sources of collective oppression, but a challenge to individual strength of character. The novel does not demand the redistribution of capital, but focuses on emphasizing inalienable personal freedom, the ability and need to resist the tyranny of status, social imperatives, religious dogma, and consumerism, at an individual level. O'Brien's revolutions are always located in the personal, exemplified by characters who freely choose austerity, as well as solidarity. This is one of the reasons why the famous factories and blast-furnaces in Bilbo are not highlighted in *Mary Lavelle*, as they are in Vicente Blasco Ibáñez's *El Intruso*. However, as if to make up for her shift of focus, in her novel O'Brien renamed the city, and called it Altorno, in reference to "Altos Hornos de Vizcaya," the most emblematic blast furnace in Bilbo. Through this allegorical move, the city itself becomes a factory, a furnace, a soul-less and violent shaper of those who enter it. In *Mary Lavelle* capitalism is not attacked (or socialism promoted) by highlighting the plight of the working class. Morally uncontaminated middle-class individuals, by virtue of their radical Christian beliefs, are the ones with the ability to resist and overthrow "the system."

Christian Anarchism

CHRISTIAN POLITICS

Given that Kate O'Brien was agnostic, one of the most interesting features in her work is her willingness to avail of the Christian tradition, specifically Catholic, to draft her plots of moral conflict, to construct a European identity, and also as a store of reference — as a kind of shorthand. In *Mary Lavelle*, the social codes of Bilbo are articulated in religious terms. For example,

> Altorno's wealth, always growing at that time, always deepening, inexhaustibly available, it seemed, to the astute and watchful, was naturally, after god, Altorno's god. Neophytes who conducted themselves with proper respect in the sanctuary were welcome, though it was permissible for the faithful-born to smile at small ritualistic errors [49].

O'Brien, like many other artists, took the dictum of building on existing knowledge to the letter. As Declan Kiberd puts it:

> Most Irish writers before O'Brien and most after her too have treated religion in terms of its social effects. She is unusual in her alertness to the spiritual dilemmas posed for conscientious young intellectuals by its exacting claims. O'Brien wrote as an agnostic but as one who had a deep respect for the drama of the Catholic conscience [*Classics* 559].

A "Catholic agnostic" according to Reynolds (*Kate* 118), O'Brien's work went beyond merely acknowledging the influence of the Catholic tradition. Christianity was useful, as a civilizing force, as a source of ethical grounding, and as a builder of community. This may be striking in a writer committed to leftist politics, given that there is a strong anticlerical tradition on the left, but there are also precedents of a militant Christian socialism of the kind publicized by Leo Tolstoy, for example. In 1897, specifically addressing the situation in Ireland to propose anarchism as the way to end colonial oppression, Tolstoy described the class system as "immoral" and called for those "force-maintained anti–Christian combinations called states" to be destroyed ("Reply" 178). The massive popularity of Tolstoy publicized Christian anarchism across the world, but the socialist movement in England also had a peculiarly Christian character, sometimes attributed to the influence of John Ruskin.

Christian anarchism or, as Maxim Gorky dismissively referred to it, "mystical anarchism" or "[t]he gospel of 'Eros in politics'" (49), has had an enduring influence to the present day, most notably on the development of Liberation Theology (communist inflected), which spread globally from Latin America thanks to publications such as Leonardo Boff's 1972 *Jesus Christ Liberator*, and caused unprecedented panic and internal purges during the papacy of John Paul II. In the first decades of the twentieth century, Christian anarchism had inspired many radical movements of growing public presence, such as the Catholic Workers' Organization in the United States. Rethinking Christian values as a response to the excesses of capitalism was also articulated in more modest ways. For example, the protagonist of the film *Mr. Deeds Goes to Town*, directed by Frank Capra and released the same year as *Mary Lavelle*, is a sudden multimillionaire who thinks of his riches as a burden and proceeds to give them away. Political, radical Christianity pervades *Mary Lavelle*. Christian referents are invoked throughout the novel in subversive mode, from the apocalyptic subtext concerned with industrial capitalism as a system bound to implode, to the naming of the characters. The evangelists Pablo and Juan, the martyr Saint Agatha, and the virgin Mary, however unique as individuals they may be in O'Brien's novel, are also the product of a very specific cultural tradition. In the case of Agatha, who can be read as a figure of resistance to colonialism, a *Basque* Christian tradition. A Christian martyr, Saint Agatha resisted the sexual advances of a Roman governor, claiming to be consecrated to Christ. Her breasts were cut off to signal her unwomanliness; the wounds healed miraculously, but she was then burnt alive, in February of the year 251. Agatha is the patron saint of the Basque Country, and festivals in her honor are an important part of the Basque calendar today; at one time, the festivals included the transferral of all political power to local women for a number of days (see Mentxaka "Witch").

THE ANARCHIST RELIGION

In a 2006 article surveying the anarchist press at the turn of the twentieth century, entitled "The Good News," Lily Litvak points out:

> Religious fervour permeates the entire acratic ideary and it is patently in evidence in the adoption of certain modes of expression through the Christian formulations and images. Postrevolutionary society is called paradise, the Chicago martyrs are worshiped, solidarity is hailed as a religious virtue, often expressions close to the Gospels are used and a certain messianic prophetic tone is taken from the Bible [7].

She is not the first commentator to point to a "moral-religious element which distinguishes [anarchism] from ordinary political movements" (see Woodcock 359). There is a strong anti-clerical tradition in anarchism, yet Gerald Brenan once claimed that "in the eyes of Spanish libertarians the Catholic church occupies the position of anti–Christ in the Christian world. It is far more to them than a mere obstacle to revolution"; Brenan went on to say that "the anger of the Spanish anarchists against the church is the anger of an intensely religious people who feel they have been deserted and deceived" (quoted in Woodcock 360). In *Farewell Spain*, Kate O'Brien recalls overhearing that some people plan to turn churches into markets and garages to at least preserve their structures from anarchists intent on destroying all religious symbols. O'Brien exclaims: "Give me an anarchist every time rather than these bright, utilitarian dullards" (99). In the same book, she went on to describe General Francisco Franco as "the enemy of all that is individualistic, free and libertarian" (150). She was writing about politics in Spain in 1937, significantly after a workers' state had become a new referent with the Russian revolution (unlike at the time of Tolstoy's remarks quoted earlier). It was in this context that O'Brien made a remarkable connection between anarchism and the Christian framework: She claimed that one either likes communism or doesn't, but it is there (in the USSR), yet one must *believe* in anarchism, as in Christianity, because it is utopian, always in the making. To those who equate anarchy and chaos, O'Brien replies: "Anarchy? Don't you know that that impossible condition would be Heaven — Heaven on earth?" (*Spain* 33). (M. Cronin unaccountably reads this as suggesting a link between *communism* and Catholicism, 145.)

A common criticism of anarchists, who are still regularly referred to as "utopian socialists," was their refusal to offer a clear program. Emma Goldman addressed this issue in 1917:

> "Why do you not say how things will be operated under Anarchism?" is a question I have had to meet thousands of times. Because I believe that Anarchism can not consistently impose an iron-clad program or method on the future. The things every new generation has to fight, and which it can least overcome, are the burdens of the past, which holds us all as in a net. Anarchism, at least as I understand it, leaves posterity with its needs. Our most vivid imagination can not foresee the potentialities of a race set free from external restraints. How, then, can any one assume to map out a line of conduct for those to come? [43].

Like Goldman, O'Brien makes a distinction between anarchy (an anarchist world) and anarchism. Like Tolstoy, O'Brien implicitly dismisses the futurity of the "kingdom to come" by emphasizing the importance of politico-moral beliefs as *lived* experience, a notion summarized in the title of Tolstoy's famous book of 1894,

The Kingdom of God Is Within You. Presenting fictional models of this lived experience in 1936, and subsequently addressing it in her nonfiction of 1937, O'Brien made a thought-provoking link between living *as a* Christian, and living as an anarchist, understanding both as commitment, not to an abstract cause, but to a way of life. Such a link eliminates in one stroke the perception of anarchism as perverse/alien, criminal, and unrealistic, instead presenting it as pan-topian rather than utopian. O'Brien is, on the one hand, aware of a leftist Christian tradition, and on the other, she wants to eliminate the Christian objections to the revolutionary movement in Spain, objections which were brandished in Ireland as the main excuse for nonintervention in favor of the leftist Republic, or indeed as the main motivation for blue-shirt aid to Franco (whose coup, let us not forget, had the bene placito of the Vatican). *Mary Lavelle* and *Farewell Spain* can be seen as Christian propaganda, not from a Christian, but aimed at Christians. For example, the figure of the priest Don Jorge in *Mary Lavelle*, a sexual predator and the symbol of a corrupt organization, was perhaps introduced in the narrative in order to "explain" the anticlericalism of the leftist Republic. The novel more than balances this out, however, by insisting on Don Pablo and Juanito's Catholicism. A crucial distinction is made (in this novel and throughout O'Brien's work) between Catholicism as organization and as set of beliefs. Don Pablo and Agatha have an unshakeable personal faith independent from the church as institution. This is a distinctly "protestant" attitude and an approach to belief that serves well as a metaphor for a certain politics, based on an scrupulous respect for individual choice.

Individualist Feminism

THEORIES

Oscar Wilde represented the most important precursor, for Kate O'Brien's generation, of a different way of being Irish, of a commitment to individualism, and of an anti-authoritarian aesthetics. He was also a popular author convinced of the quasi-religious role of the artist in bringing about social change. An anarchist feminist, Wilde succinctly expressed his views in "The Soul of Man Under Socialism," of 1890:

> Individualism, then, is what through Socialism we are to attain. As a natural result the State must give up all idea of government. It must give it up because, as a wise man [Lao Zi] once said many centuries before Christ, there is such a thing as leaving mankind alone; there is no such thing as governing mankind. All modes of government are failures [1087 — see Zi].

The insistence on contesting power as an individual is an aspect of O'Brien's work which seems attuned to anarchism. Alexander Berkman, writing in 1929, described individualist anarchists following Max Stirner and Benjamin R. Tucker as being at variance with other anarchists in two crucial aspects: on the one hand, "[they] do not believe in revolution. They think that present society will gradually develop out of government into a non-governmental posi-tion," and, on the other hand, "[they] believe in individual ownership as against the communist anarchists who see in the institution of private property one of the main sources of injustice and inequality" (*ABC* 49). In the last 30 years or so, a number of thinkers have developed an ideology using the work of Stirner, Tucker and others, culminating in the neoliberal appropriation of the term *libertarian* for the creation of the Libertarian Party in the United States. It is now regularly stated, even by anarchist historians, that there is a form of "right wing anarchism," and there is also a worrying trend to equate individualist anarchism with the American neoliberal extremists (see Ward 62–9). Certainly at the time when O'Brien was writing, this was not the case, and any references to individualist anarchism in the present study reflect the traditional left-wing understanding of the term.

As Martha Ackelsberg points out, in Western Europe socialism and feminism arose more or less simultaneously, around "the promises of freedom and universal citizenship offered by the French Revolution and the promises of abundance and economic growth offered by the Industrial Revolution" (206). Anarcho-feminism, theory and practice, has had an illustrious figure in Emma Goldman, whose essays on women have not lost their strength since they appeared in book form in 1917. In Spain, the association Mujeres Libres (free women), founded in 1936 and rooted in anarcho-syndicalism, "mobilized over 20,000 women and developed an extensive network of activities" (ibid. 21). Second-wave feminism, particularly after the upheavals of 1968, had some important affinities with the anti-author-itarian movement in methods and theory. For example, Cathy Levine explains that the women's groups in the USA of the late 1960s "began functioning without the structure, leaders, and other factotums of the male left, creating independently and simultaneously, organizations similar to those of anarchists of many decades and locales. No accident, either" (quoted in Kornegger 8). Some feminists believed that: "When we say we are fighting the patriarchy, it isn't always clear to all of us that that means fighting *all* hierarchy, *all* leadership, *all* government, and the very idea of authority itself" (emphasis in original; Kornegger 9). Individualist fem-inism, however, exceeds the anti-authoritarian context, having been put forward by a number of theorists since the eighteenth century, most notably John Stuart Mill and Mary Wollstonecraft.

The politics foregrounded in *Mary Lavelle* are centered on personal liberties, which must be negotiated and exercised before they reach outwards. The free-thinking Pablo has an effect on Milagros and Juanito, who in turn affect Mary. The self-expression of anti-authoritarian individuals, rather than community-based militancy, is presented as having a knock on effect, whereby lies its ability to produce social change. This does not strictly correspond to the anarchist valuing of individual sovereignty as merely the natural foundation to the development of networks, as a sort of compulsive federalism. In anarchist theory (with the excep-tion of Max Stirner), libertarianism is always compelled towards solidarity. Mila-gros, Juanito, Pablo, and (by the end of the novel) Mary, implicitly endorse this solidarity rather than exercising it in an obvious way — their "individualist social-ism" is intellectual. Despite Pablo's support of the "Working Man's College" and Juanito's political involvement, the novel focuses on radical *individualism* as agent of progress, and the characters concentrate on a "politics of everyday life" of ques-tionable value as agent of collective change. Mary's childhood dream is to be "a free lance" (O'Brien *Mary* 27). As Eavan Boland put it, Kate O'Brien's main con-cern is women who are "imprisoned in a code of response, a minuet of pro-grammed answers and expectations," and her novels show how these women may be "freed by moments of insight" (quoted in Cawley 1; Boland "Kate" 46–7).

In Kate O'Brien's novel *The Land of Spices*, the suffragette Mrs. Robertson referred to her own actual imprisonment as "an accident of time and place" (210). As Michael G. Cronin pointed out in a paper of 2006, "the objectives of feminism can not be achieved by accident," but only through a concerted, col-lective effort. However, O'Brien's heroic characters are always modest, and that must also be taken into account when considering statements such as Robert-son's. In any case, when so much of *Mary Lavelle* is given over to expounding socialist beliefs, a similar articulation of feminism seems to be missing. Feminism was a given in socialist theory, from Charles Fourier to Alexandra Kollontai, through Marx, Engels, and Charlotte Perkins Gilman (see Charvet 48–96). Fem-inism was also a given in anarchism, which acknowledged no bounds to indi-vidual freedom other than the infringement of others' liberty, transcending "accidents" such as biological sex. This "given" often resulted in a problematic invisibility of patriarchal oppression. As we have seen, a famous 1931 parlia-mentary debate in Spain saw female ministers from different political parties discuss the wisdom of granting the vote to Spanish women given that the major-ity were conservative. A similarly ironic situation was seen in France in 1936, when another socialist alliance (under the same name as the Spanish one, the Popular Front), brought three women to the government in a country that did not grant suffrage to women. Mary Lavelle's implicit support of Juanito's cause is caught up in this conundrum, surrendering her rights as a woman for the sake of a general improvement in the conditions of citizens at large. Mary's fem-inist politics can only be articulated through action, by her exercising of personal freedom (whether legally acknowledged or not): in choosing a job, in choosing a lover. She does both despite opposition, after overcoming her own doubts.

FICTIONS

There is now some agreement among critics on the pervading feminist politics in Kate O'Brien's work, even if as we have seen this feminism was once regularly qualified by commentators. O'Brien was committed to feminism to the extent that she gave it as a motivation behind her biography of Teresa of Avila, "a genius of the large and immeasurable kind of which there have been very few and only one a woman," which prompts the author to declare: "Let the feminists who, anxiously counting up their Sapphos, Jane Austens and Mesdames Curie, always ignore Santa Teresa — let the feminists pull themselves together and get this square correctly named once and for all" (102–3). Teresa was, O'Brien insists, "a feminist" (111), and the book itself is a good example of feminist historiography. Without doubt, some of O'Brien's novels can also be considered feminist activist literature; in the case of *The Flower of May*, according to Lorna Reynolds, the feminist agenda of the author got so out of control as to undermine the plausibility of the narrative (*Kate* 59). Despite this, Reynolds has also claimed that "The subject of feminism is never raised openly in her work" (ibid., 128). This is not really true. Direct references to feminism are made not just in *Teresa of Avila* but also in *As Music and Splendour*, while *The Land of Spices* includes an important sympathetic secondary character, as we just mentioned, who is a suffragette. However, Reynolds, who was in fact one of the first critics to clearly identify O'Brien's books as feminist (Margaret Lawrence was, strictly speaking, the first), added: "But the theme of her novels is the necessity of woman to be as free as man" (ibid., see also 126). Tina O'Toole has identified a number of precursors of Kate O'Brien in Ireland: "Sarah Grand, George Egerton, 'Iota,' and L.T. Meade had also written about women's need for educational and pro-fessional equality, women's sexuality, and at least in the case of Egerton, women's struggle for autonomy from family and legal structures" ("Autonomy").

Mary Lavelle belongs to a tradition of feminist fiction that is individualist and anti-authoritarian. Mary makes this link explicit in her desire for "self-government" (O'Brien *Mary* 27). In considering *Mary Lavelle* within contexts such as the female bildungsroman, it is already clear that O'Brien's novel shows a preoccupation with the experiences of women — and with the particular oppression that an individual woman suffers *as a woman*. It seems equally clear that the book does not sit comfortably within a number of strands of feminist fiction, such as the novels which seek to "denounce," novels which push for "reform," or novels which publicize a "manifesto." It may be useful to consider those strands in turn. An example of works marked by the explicit demand for women's equality voiced by a female protagonist is Mary Wollstonecraft's 1798 *Maria: or The Wrongs of Woman*, which (post French Revolution) spells out patriarchal oppression as "tyranny" and "despotism," and equates "born a woman — and born to suffer" (133). No such outburst is found in *Mary Lavelle*. O'Brien's novel does not belong to the reformist or "assimilationist" feminist tradition either, a politics that inspired a number of works specifically concerned with the restrictions placed on women's lives. George Moore's 1886 *A Drama in Muslin* is an example of this type of novel because it seeks to document (and redirect) women's progression towards "freedom" as "the gloom of the female mind clears" and they realize they have rights and the means to attain them (152–3). Mary Lavelle's life-changing decisions to deviate from gendered expec-tations rely on her sudden impulses to avail of opportunities rather than reflec-tion/analysis or an unusually strong temperament. She has no intellectual ambitions but hazy "dreams," and by the end of the book her political self-awareness is as vague as her future. As a consequence, *Mary Lavelle* does not belong either in the group of novels with a plot explicitly or allegorically driven by the desire to publicize a feminist agenda. An example of these is Charlotte Perkins Gilman's 1915 socialist-feminist *Herland*—a precursor of the feminist speculative fiction of the 1960s and 1970s—with its emphasis on the social constructedness of a two-sex/gender system which is "in no way essential" (59). The narrative in *Mary Lavelle* has multiple political interests, but the only clearly delineated critique involves Juanito's state-communist model for regeneration of Spain, a model that fails to show any awareness of women's experience and how/if this is likely to change in the future he envisions.

The activist feminism of *Mary Lavelle* is not concerned with articulating a theory, with enabling female solidarity (the Café Aleman is an all-female dystopia of sorts), or with making any demands for women *as a group*. Instead, the novel offers an example of an individual woman's awakening to her previously unimagined possibilities. Mary, as a conservative (by default) and inexperienced young woman, seems an unlikely candidate as heroine, let alone role model, but it is precisely because of her own limited ambitions that the enormity of her transgressions is all the more threatening, or alluring, to the reader. *Mary Lavelle* makes it its business to publicize the potential of the *individual*, in all its frightening "vastness," within reach of even the lesser equipped for the adventure. In this, O'Brien's novel has much in common with Zora Neale Hurston's *Their Eyes Were Watching God*, published the year after *Mary Lavelle*, a feminist novel that focuses on an individual woman exercising her freedom to love outside normative dictates. Interestingly, Hurston's book is also—even primarily—concerned with documenting a specific historical and geographical reality, the black town of Eatonville, Florida, in the 1930s, just as O'Brien "preserved" in fiction the Bilbo of 1922. Hurston's protagonist's complaint to her husband that "Mah own mind had tuh be squeezed and crowded out tuh make room for yours in me" (133) is the closest the novel gets to an articulation of inequality, and her subsequent taking a lover despite her community's objections is, like Lavelle's relationship with Juanito, the ultimate transgression and a point of no return. The feminism in *Their Eyes Were Watching God*, like that of O'Brien's novel, is framed within personal experience. The feminism of *Mary Lavelle*, however, is set on a spelled-out backdrop of socialist theory and practice linked to an anti-authoritarian politics.

THREE

Activist Fiction II: Sexuality

Introduction: Ireland

Mary Lavelle also belongs in a tradition of activist literature seeking to challenge normative views on sexuality and to present deviant/demonized sexual behaviors and orientations in a positive light. A libertarian approach to sexuality is central to O'Brien's fiction, which repeatedly suggests that, to quote Alan Goldman, "[t]here is no morality intrinsic to sex, although general moral rules apply to the treatment of others in sex acts as they apply to all human relations" (95). Within this framework (taken up by queer theory in the 1990s), "perversity" is "a deviation from a norm, but the norm in question is merely statistical" (ibid., 97). The sensitive portrayal of lesbianism and homo/bi/sexuality in *Mary Lavelle* sits comfortably in this context, but the illicit heterosexual romance pursued by the female protagonist, central to the book, would appear to belong to a different category altogether. Mary does not think so and refers to churchgoers, including Agatha and herself, as "[s]eeking strength against the perversions of their hearts and escape from fantastic longings. Seeking mercy, explanation and forgiveness because they are so vicious as to love each other" (*Mary* 285–6). The novel goes to considerable lengths to liken all forms of sexual deviance, in fact suggesting, as in this passage, that love is itself a threat to the status quo.

Elizabeth Bowen once claimed that Irish fiction "is sexless" (quoted in Tóibín xxvi), presumably meaning it lacks explicit sexual content — and Bowen herself published two important "asexual" lesbian novels, *The Hotel* in 1927 and *The Last September* in 1929. Notwithstanding the explicit sexuality in the medieval saga from the Ulster Cycle *Táin Bó Cuailnge* ("The Cattle Raid"), and in *Cúit an Mheán Oíche* ("The Midnight Court"), written by Brian Merriman around 1790, her conclusion seems correct. The *Táin*'s central story shows how queen Medbh would stop at nothing to secure the famous brown bull of Ulster, in order to match a sacred white bull owned by her husband. The saga is noted for its feisty and multitalented female characters, as well as for a remarkable explicitness in bodily matters—including sexuality—which only became widely known after Thomas Kinsella's translation in 1969. Kate O'Brien may have read Mary Anne Hutton's translation, published in Dublin as early as 1907 (reprinted in 1924), or she may have been familiar with a version in modern Irish language. Deirdriu's seduction of the "game young bull" Noisiu may have been a referent (Anonymous [Kinsella tr.] 12) for *Mary Lavelle*. "The Midnight Court," by the "eighteenth century Utopian" Brian Merriman (O'Connor 11), may have been another. It included a derision of celibacy in the Catholic priesthood, a Rousseau-inspired use of illegitimate offspring as "symbol of natural innocence" (ibid.), a call for the abolition of marriage, and a series of angry diatribes by sexually frustrated women.

Mary Louisa Gordon, in her fictionalized biography of the ladies of Llangollen, *Chase of the Wild Goose*, published in the same year as *Mary Lavelle*, has Sarah Ponsonby telling Eleanor Butler before their elopement: "you are my Ireland" (139). Gordon's protagonists leave their country in 1778 because they are otherwise condemned to live stunted lives, as women who love each other, *and* as women (see ibid., 140). "Nation" and "belonging" acquire different meanings for those who inhabit social gaps. As Tina O'Toole puts it, highlighting the significance of *Mary Lavelle* as site of contestation, "the colonization of women within the Irish Free State was one way in which new political and social discourses were forged" ("Autonomy"). O'Brien herself pitted a British suffragette against an Irish nationalist man in *The Land of Spices*. In Ireland, there are a handful of commentaries on the *fruitful* intersections between feminism and nationalism, in literary criticism, historiography, and popular culture (see for example Meaney "Territory," Byrne "Conflict," and *Young* 2:1 and 2:2 respectively), but the conflict had been underlined in 1937, the year which, in the words of Emma Donoghue, "saw the publication of an influential heterosexual fiction: the Constitution of Ireland" ("Noises" 179).

Kate O'Brien wrote *Mary Lavelle* after the "scandal" of Joyce's *Ulysses* in 1922, which provided a "case study" for contemporary authors interested in stretching the limits of what was permissible in literature. *Ulysses* includes a rather comprehensive survey of queer sexualities and desires (mostly queer heterosexual), but perversity in the book remains either inferred or clouded in stylistic pirouetting. Lillian Faderman has claimed, following Edmund Wilson, that modernist authors such as Gertrude Stein developed experimental forms of writing precisely in order to give expression to non-normative sexuality (*Love* 399–405). The portrait of Agatha in *Mary Lavelle* has been justly hailed as a groundbreaking depiction of lesbianism in Irish literature by Emma Donoghue and others. Molly Keane is the other author (Bowen goes unmentioned with astonishing regularity in accounts of queer Irish fiction) whose lesbian characters are sometimes highlighted, particularly the hysteric lesbian couple she describes in *Devoted Ladies*, published two years before *Mary Lavelle*. O'Brien's last novel, *As Music and Splendour*, Kay Inckle has persuasively argued, presents a "utopian lesbianism" that offers a unique appraisal of non-monogamy at the time of its publication in 1958.

Monogamous heterosexual eroticism was itself difficult to articulate in Ireland, as we see in Maeve Binchy's novel *Echoes*, set in 1950s Dublin, which seems to resonate with O'Brien's *The Land of Spices* in its central mentor-pupil relationship. In *Echoes*, the intellectually ambitious, independent-thinking protagonist Clare O'Brien can't help but face the same moral qualms that had tormented Mary Lavelle three decades earlier, deciding not to go to church because her affair with a man "was a sin, and that was that. There was no point in acting the part of a person who was praying. If Clare were the Lord she'd prefer those kind of people not to come to church at all" (347; compare to O'Brien, *Music* 208). As Emma Donoghue notes, "O'Brien's books celebrate passion-at-a-price; they are never anti sex" ("Order" 183). This also applies to Binchy's novel.

When we consider *Mary Lovelle*, it is not immediately clear which may be more threatening to "official Ireland": an individual Irish woman initiating a sexual encounter with a Basque/Spanish man, or an invitation to her country to join the socialist revolution. We have seen that Mary Lavelle is the symbol of a nation searching for self-expression, and it is interesting that a number of recent narratives have linked queer female sexualities to the formation of national identity. The 2004 film *Butterfly*, for example, set in China at the time of the Tiananmen massacre, makes an analogy between the suppression of the democratic movement in the country and the futile attempts at self-repression of lesbianism in the protagonist. The 2005 film *El Calentito*, set in Spain in the years after the end of Franco's dictatorship, a period known as "the transition," makes an analogy between the movement towards democracy in the country and one of the characters' journey as a "transitioning" pre-operative male to female transexual. As early as 1929, Elizabeth Bowen's novel *The Last September* offered a dazzling example of a subtextual queer narrative in the link between the danger of lesbianism, hovering over the protagonist, and the danger posed by the underground rebellion against the colonial powers in Ireland. In O'Brien's novel, as in all of these examples, the assertion of female eroticism is the expression of a democratic impulse.

In recent narratives, we have seen similar attempts creatively linking unorthodox sexuality to the consolidation of Europe as a political entity. For example, Krzysztof Kieślowski's 1993 film *Three Colours: Blue*, a political allegory of the background to the birth of the "bastard child" that is Europe, or Maureen Duffy's 1992 novel *Illuminations*, in which the "heterosexual myth" of the maiden Europa being seduced by Zeus-as-bull is rewritten, as Donoghue points out, to symbolize "the individual's courageous journey into new political and erotic territories ("Boundaries" 94). *Illuminations* has the parallel plots of a lesbian coming-out romance narrative and an academic investigation into the story of a medieval nun — plots that come together at a conference on European identity, so that the book presents the emergence of lesbian eroticism as the equivalent of the dramatic changes brought about by the formation of the EU.

As we will see, *Mary Lavelle* subtextually metamorphoses Mary and Juanito into bull and bullfighter, offering a version of the origin of Europe, a feminist version in which Europa overpowers Zeus. In "The good Basque Country" chapter, Zeus/Juanito metamorphoses into a bull/his car — his aimless velocity and their "zig-zagg[ing]" upwards (see 302), a modernist update of the original tale. Mary does more than acquiesce, she instructs her lover to bring together her eros and tanatos drives. In an Irish context, Mary's financial, moral, sexual independence is part of a decolonizing process. Her fiancé John follows the logic of tyranny, because "he was never more of a lawgiver than when he was frightened" (*Mary* 139).

Lesbians and Queer Men

LESBIAN

Portraits of lesbians at the time of publication of *Mary Lavelle* were often vampiric or evil, as Lillian Faderman has discussed in her 1981 *Surpassing the Love of Men*. The 1936 film *Dracula's Daughter* is a case in point, with a vampire protagonist who appears to favor women (in a number of erotically charged scenes) and, consumed by guilt, contacts a psychiatrist. Agatha Conlan is "tall and thin" (O'Brien *Mary* 84), like the lesbian vampires Carmilla, in Joseph Sheridan Le Fanu's story of the same title from 1872, and Christabel, in Samuel Taylor Coleridge's poem, written between 1787 and 1800. As Akiko Kaijima has pointed out, "all intelligent heroines in Kate O'Brien are tall" (52). Agatha is also as metaphorically "starved" (O'Brien *Mary* 210) as those lesbian vampires. According to her fellow governess Keogh, in old age Conlan will become "the sort of muttering hag children throw stones at" (297—for O'Brien and Irish hags, see Reynolds "Women" 17–18). When Mary asks her why she loathes life, Agatha responds matter-of-factly, "My evil nature. I'm at cross purposes with it" (206). She is clearly not "evil" in Mary's eyes, yet critics regularly place Agatha beyond the pale of normalcy in other ways. Both Patricia Coughlan and Emma Donoghue see in her character and facial features the influence of "the invert" popularized by Radclyffe Hall's novel *The Well of Loneliness* (Coughlan "Kate" 74; Donoghue "Order" 42), with Donoghue also suggesting a link to the "fanatical, religious Cecilia" in George Moore's *A Drama in Muslin* ("Noises" 180). Agatha is no more an "apparitional lesbian," to borrow Terry Castle's term (from her 1993 study of that title), than Juan and Pablo, with their "pallor and tragically sculpted strong-set facial bones" (*Mary* 146, 331), and, as we will see later, her distinctive look follows a different code.

Radclyffe Hall, who preferred to use the name John, believed that homosexuality was an inborn condition. As the author's biographer Michael Baker explains, Hall was much influenced by contemporary sexologists who had offered the idea of the "invert," a term used to describe a woman who "rejected her femininity, was attracted to women not men, and engaged in masculine pursuits" (217). The psychiatrist Carl von Westphal had coined the term "congenital invert" in a case study published in 1869. It was the first step towards the consolidation of lesbianism as a sexological pathology. As Lillian Faderman explains, Westphal's most influential disciples, "Richard Krafft-Ebbing (*Psychopathia* Sexualis, 1882) and Havelock Ellis (*Studies in the Psychology of Sex: Sexual Inversion*, 1897) ... cast love between women in a morbid light" (*Love* 241), and congenital *pathology* was to remain associated with the theory of inversion. The library of Stephen Gordon's father includes books by Karl Henrich Ulrich and Richard Krafft-Ebing (see Hall 23, 207). The library of Don Pablo Areavaga includes a book by Havelock Ellis, part of a selection of favorite reads by his bed (see O'Brien *Mary* 329).

Havelock Ellis wrote the preface to the first edition of *The Well of Loneliness*. The novel, a landmark in queer activist fiction, was not only "a heroic gesture" (Foster 281), it was also a carefully thought out strategic move. As Lillian Faderman explains, the protagonist, Stephen Gordon, possesses "heroism and nobility," but these are "overshadowed by her self-pity and self-loathing, which are explainable by Hall's conviction that tolerance would be most effectively wrung out of her heterosexual readers by eliciting their pity" (*Love* 321). Unlike Stephen Gordon (the phonetically kin), Agatha Conlan is not self-loathing. O'Brien is pursuing a different strategy than Hall: rousing "empathy" rather than "pity." After Agatha tells Mary that she has a crush on her, their relationship in fact deepens (Donoghue "Fictions" 47). Mary's love for Juanito means that "her understanding of feeling in others, as, for instance, in O'Toole and Pepe, was immediate and natural" (295–6, see also 285), and similarly, "her voice and manner with Agatha had automatically become easier and more sisterly, not so much because Agatha fantastically and perversely loved *her* but because, like her, she was fantastically and perversely in love" (emphasis in original, 296; see 295).

O'Brien was undoubtedly familiar with the historical obscenity trial that followed the publication of *The Well of Loneliness* in 1928 (see Walshe *Kate* 39). Jeannette H. Foster, in her 1956 study *Sex Variant Women in Literature*, a magnificent survey that remains essential reading, gives details of novels sympathetic (and hostile) to the cause of lesbian, bisexual, and transgendered women between 1925 and 1935, identifying "a first peak in variant literature" in 1928 (154). Among activist fiction in which an entire book specifically seeks to improve public perception of queer women, Foster highlights *The Well of Loneliness*, together with Virginia Woolf's *Orlando*, of 1928: "Mrs. Woolf pled as it were in the abstract, Miss Hall in passionate particular, for the variant, even the lesbian woman of personal integrity" (286–7). There are enough common points to indicate a close relationship between *Mary Lavelle* and *The Well of Loneliness*. For example, Hall's recurrent play with the word *nature* (Hennegan xi), the claim that inverts tend to be religious (see Hall 412), or the persistent links to "othered" communities, such as the Irish (Stephen is half–Irish), the Bretons, or African Americans. But, without wishing to deny the influence on *Mary Lavelle* of what has become "*the* lesbian novel" (emphasis in original, Barker 213), O'Brien's narrative and characters unfence new realms of connotation.

Perhaps it is legitimate to see Agatha's characterization as a study in "female masculinity," a concept introduced into the mainstream by Suzanne Vega in an article of 1991 and by Judith Halberstam in a photographic essay of 1998, both promoting an understanding of multiple-gendered identities disassociated from biological sex (for an interesting list of genders, see Hale). 1936 was, after all, the year when the cross-dressing adventurer *Sylvia Scarlett* (Dir. George Cukor, from the novel by Compton Mackenzie) was kissed by another woman on the screen. In *The Well of Loneliness*, Stephen Gordon explains, "As a man loves a woman, that was how I loved — protectively, like my father [loved my mother]" (Hall 204). Agatha Conlan's remarkably straight-forward declaration of love to Mary, "I like you the way a man would" (*Mary* 285), may, on the surface, suggest an understanding of lesbianism as aping of a heteronormative model, with Agatha as "invert," or a man in a woman's body. However, the turn of phrase (in 1936) is primarily an unmistakable declaration of carnal desire. "I never can see you without," Agatha continues, "— without wanting to touch you" (ibid.). This is not necessarily a masculinization/authentication of lesbian eroticism, nor is it necessarily an allegiance to a butch gender identity. Jane Eyre's famous claim that "women feel just as men feel" (Brontë *Jane* 109) had been boldly translated into a lesbian context by Woolf's Mrs. Dalloway, who articulated her own erotic attraction to women by reflecting that, "She did undoubtedly then feel what men felt" (Woolf *Dalloway* 34). O'Brien's novel is determined to unsettle gender expectations by presenting a host of assertive women, and, in my view, their sexual deviance is a byproduct of their assertiveness (an unfeminine quality), rather than the other way around.

In *Mary Lavelle*, Luisa's elaborate gender presentation is an exquisitely refined "female masquerade" (see Riviere), contrasted with Agatha's "unfeminine" prioritization of intellect over appearance. In line with the politics of the novel, Agatha is not a feminist *in theory* (her disappointment with the human race is indiscriminate), but she is a feminist in practice, making the most of her financial limitations to expand her horizons, and refusing to conform to the cosmetic trappings of marriageability as much as to the polite deference expected of a governess; as we know, her host families merely "tolerate" her because she is a good teacher (see *Mary* 298). As I see it, Agatha is less an "invert"— or, in the more nuanced contemporary term, transgendered — than she is an unconventional, intellectually able and ambitious woman, thwarted by oppressive gendered expectations at a particular historical time.

Several commentators point out that the bullfight chapter of the novel "is structurally parallel to the sex-scene between Juanito and Mary" (Coughlan "Kate" 68). A number of critics, such as Patricia Coughlan, Emma Donoghue, and Wanda Balzano, highlight the fact that it is Agatha who invites Mary to the bullfight. In a paper of 2002, Balzano further suggests that "[i]n a sense, [Mary] looses her virginity at the bullfight" ("Question"), the implication being that she looses it at the hands of Agatha. "Mary understood a little Conlan's comment on *the first performance*. She was well *initiated* in one programme" (emphasis added, 117; compare to 311). Not only is Mary first introduced to the bullfight by Agatha, but the guide to her second experience of the ceremony is Milagros (see 231).

In a novel of 1934, *Delay in the Sun*, Anthony Thorne tells the story of two female English friends holidaying in Spain. Having attended a bullfight, a later visit to an empty bull ring prompts them to jokingly imitate the performance: "[Jean] played at bull fighting for the sake of a pretty girl in a yellow dress who sat in the *barrera*. Playing together, they mocked a dangerous game. And dangerously they entered a secret world in which they had so great a need of each other" (quoted in Foster 307). This episode forces the two women to reassess their friendship: "What had happened to them last night was something beyond their control," and they decide to "let this strange force follow its own law — let it part them forever or join them forever. It was something too big for their reason, and too delicate.... Of no use to fight, reason, or wonder" (ibid.). The novel hurriedly closes, letting the reader decide the progression that the narrative may take. Whether Kate O'Brien was aware of *Delay in the Sun* or not as she was writing *Mary Lavelle*, her own appropriation of the conventions of a sport representing the extreme test and validation of a certain masculinity is remarkable. There are intertextual links between *Mary Lavelle* and Ernest Hemingway's idiosyncratic treatise on bullfighting of 1932, *Death in the Afternoon*, as we will see later. These links include Agatha paraphrasing Mr. Hemingway a number of times, for example in her admission that "Death interests me" (209), which also opens his book. Hemingway's persona was entwined with his writing, and the massive influence of his direct style in the 1930s, as Jeanette Forster pointed out, was noticeable in lesbian writing (see 314).

Kate O'Brien made regular use of subtext to hide lesbian content. Her biography *Teresa of Avila* is particularly interesting. Perhaps the book sought to supplement Vita Sackville-West's celebrated 1944 biography of the saint, *The Eagle and the Dove*. In O'Brien's introductory section, the simple experiment of substituting the word "genius" with "lesbian" opens up the hidden text and prepares the discerning reader for the queer project about to unfold. O'Brien opens the book by saying that "I write of Teresa of Avila by choice which is passionate, arbitrary, personal. No one need agree with anything I have to say — but they must not, either, be hurt thereby," and explaining that she will "examine Teresa" as "a woman of genius," specifying that "[w]omen of genius are few" in the context of literature (*Teresa* 10). After such a politically innocuous statement, something progressively "feels" out of kilter in O'Brien's turns of phrase and her overemphases, and that something is the indication that a subtextual message is being conveyed:

[L]et us enumerate our precious things and people. Let us say our personal says. I say, with great regret, that within the two thousand or so years that my very poorly trained vision can take in, genius has rarely ever flowered in a woman. We can jump back beyond those two thousand years and boast of Sappho. But we have only fragments, rumours of her — and in any case we have to wait for a woman to match her until England and the nineteenth century. It is strange; all the variable, definable furies, styles and freedoms could pass over Europe — we could have Virgil, Lucretius, Dante, Ronsard, Shakespeare, Racine, Madame de La Fayette and Miss Jane Austen — but there was still no tracking down of a *woman* who could be called genius until Emily Brontë's burning shadow flung out. Not as broken, not as indefinable as Sappho's, but strangely sympathetic to her legend, and just as unsatisfactory. And they are the only female geniuses of our recorded knowledge in literature [emphasis in original, 10–11].

O'Brien adds that "for our consolation, there have been women who, had they not been too large and too much perplexed by the old dilemma of being woman, might have been almost as immeasurably great" (11). It is only by resorting to a set of subtextual and intertextual references that a bold outing of Teresa could be printed. For example, there is a tradition of reading Emily Brontë as lesbian (see Foster 129–134), but it would be easy to miss the significance of the mention if one is not acquainted with that tradition. Emily Brontë is, apparently, "strangely sympathetic to Sappho's legend," a legend fraught by "rumors." Bridging the gap between the two, O'Brien claims, we find Teresa. O'Brien used similar strategies elsewhere, for example in *Pray for the Wanderer*, where Nell is compared to "Madam du Defand, for instance, he thought mischievously — or Saint Catherine of Siena. Or some might have said Sappho" (13). Similarly, in *English Diaries and Journals*, O'Brien remarked on the "*rumours* about [the] private lives" of Madame de Genlis and Madame de Stael (italics in original, 32), while doing her utmost to encourage fresh rumors about, for example, Dorothy Wordsworth and Katherine Mansfield. The passage from the hagiography quoted above is clearly not about literature, nor about feminism: *Teresa of Avila* is an unrecognized yet important example of lesbian historiography. O'Brien's mischievous use of the key word *genius* strikes a chord with a key passage in Oscar Wilde's *De Profundis*, an essay-letter written in 1897 to his lover, Alfred Douglas, while Wilde was in prison for engaging in homosexual acts, a text in which he claims that the French understand "the peculiar quality of my genius" because they know "[t]hat along with genius goes often a curious perversity of passion and desire," a subject which "belongs to Lombroso," although "the pathological phenomenon in question is also found amongst those who have not genius..." (42).

As Faderman has noted, "the literature of lesbian encoding" has been almost universally neglected (Faderman *Cloe* 441–445), but there are considerable difficulties even for critics who are alert to it. Writing in 1979, Akiko Kaijima described *The Flower of May* as "an experimental study of [lesbianism]" (51), but Emma Donoghue claims it has no lesbian content ("Order" 48–49), and

Adele Dalsimer believes that the protagonist is a lesbian in denial about her sexuality (102). In my view, *all of them* are right: the novel is concerned with romantic friendship (something also suggested by Donoghue "Embraces" 24 and Tina O'Toole "Autonomy"), a form of female bonding that can certainly be read as lesbian (see Faderman's *Surpassing the Love of Men* 63–144); it offers a lesbian self-portrait; it is a modernist experiment, an attempt at duplicating a single subjectivity in the dark-light *couplet* of Fanny-Lucille.

　　Mary Lavelle's description of the main characters as "angelic" is also aligned to a word for homosexuality, *Uranian*, a term borrowed in the nineteenth century by the pro-homosexual-rights reformer Karl H. Ulrichs from Plato's *Symposium*, where the philosopher had linked uncommon/heavenly love to "Aphrodite Urania" (180 d; see Robb 53). Between 1916 and 1940, Irish lesbian writer and activist Eva Gore Booth (sister of one of the leaders of the 1916 rebellion, Constance Markievicz), together with her partner Esther Roper and three other editors, published the journal *Urania* in Liverpool, promoting radical sexual politics and the abandonment of orthodox gender binaries (see Tiernan "Journal"). In addition to "heavenly" creatures, in *Mary Lavelle* there is also a game of cross-referencing, which draws attention to classic novels dealing with female deviancy. For example, it seems likely that O'Brien was redrafting the golden eyes of the Spanish Paquita Valdez, the bisexual protagonist of Honoré de Balzac's 1835 *The Girl with the Golden Eyes*, onto Luisa Areavaga and Luisa Carriaga, in *Mary Lavelle* and *As Music and Splendour* respectively. Another example is the comment that Nieves would like to "be a boy and go to Eton," which is also made by the father of the protagonist of *Lesbia Brandon*, written by Algernon Charles Swinburne between 1864 and 1867 (see Faderman *Love* 273), when as a young woman, Lesbia had fallen in love with a governess. *Lesbia Brandon* was published after O'Brien wrote *Mary Lavelle*, but the manuscript was available in the British Museum since around 1930, and a biography of Swinburne including a comprehensive analysis of *Lesbia Brandon* had been published by George Lafourcade in 1928 (see Forster 78–9).

　　If we obediently follow the subtextual signs, it turns out that Agatha is not the only character in the novel with lesbian leanings. Nieves and Mary are also lesbian, while Luisa is bisexual. We have the crucial postscript of the lesbian affair of Luisa and "Clarabelle" in *As Music and Splendour*, already discussed, a clear invitation to reread Mary Lavelle and Luisa Carriaga's mutual appreciation as lesbian attraction. Duarte explains to Clare, "'Luisa has never been in love with me — as you know, Clara. And indeed it would have been wrong and grotesque had she been'" (*Music* 296). He further explains that "'What Luisa thought she was doing when she made me her lover was to set up guards for herself against a kind of love she knew about already and which frightened her.... But the trouble was ... that she was already *in* that love before she took me,'" to which Clare replies, "'She told me that always she has been attracted to women — and afraid of the attraction'" (emphasis in original, ibid.). This suggests that one's orientation/preference is not only unrelated to sexual behavior, but may be defined by one's ability to *fall in love* with men, women, or both. Our enlightened times have failed to theorize the force of such an argument, drafted by O'Brien in 1956. In *As Music and Splendour*, this means that Luisa Carriaga is a lesbian who has sex with men. If we apply it retrospectively to *Mary Lavelle* (text and subtext), this means Mary is bisexual: She falls in love with a man, and in her double life as Agatha, she falls in love with a woman.

In the light of all this, one of the literary contexts *Mary Lavelle* belongs to is clearly that of activist lesbian/bisexual fiction. Despite the secondary role of the lesbian character in the main narrative, *the entire novel* can be read as a plea for tolerance on the basis that lesbian love/desire is comparable to other targets of repression, such as interracial and interclass liaisons, women victimized by the stress on virginity/purity/ignorance, and the reification of the marriage bond. In addition, *Mary Lavelle* offers an encoded lesbian bildungsroman (Nieves-Mary-Agatha), as well as the first chapter of a lesbian romance narrative (Mary-Luisa) that will reach its conclusion in *As Music and Splendour* (Clare-Luisa). O'Brien approaches this intricate project with remarkable lightness, even humor; for example, when someone says to Mary that "'Your double would take a bit of finding,'" Agatha quickly adds, "'That's a fact'" (200). It is only by bringing "out" the subtextual queer women in the novel, that a full assessment of *Mary Lavelle* in the context of lesbian/bisexual literature can be made. The secrecy of the encoding may be seen as working against an activist intent, but it could be also argued that subtext represents an ingenious attempt to foil censorship and provide queer readers with narratives that would otherwise be beyond their reach.

QUEER MEN

There are four male characters in *Mary Lavelle*: Don Pablo, Juanito, Pepe, and Don Jorge. All of them are marked as sexually non-normative in one way or another. Pepe breaks from convention when he marries a foreigner, the Irish governess Rose, who is also (in his estimation and that of the governess colony) above his station. Don Jorge, a Catholic priest, sexually harasses Mary and the girls to whom she teaches music. Don Pablo and his son are also beyond the demarcations of sexual normalcy. The senior Areavaga has been celibate and, it is implicit, asexual, since halfway through his marriage, until his first sight of Mary, whose "boyish" and "Greek" look, in a telling combination, stirs up a forgotten/suppressed fire in him. The novel further emphasizes his queerness, as we have seen, by pointing out that Don Pablo owns a book by Havelock Ellis, the popularizer of the theory of inversion, suggesting that Pablo's suppressed sexuality has a distinctly homosexual tonality.

Havelock Ellis and Krafft-Ebbing are also read by the protagonists of Elizabeth Bowen's "The Cat Jumps," a 1934 story dealing with marital murder, described by one critic as "a baroque joke about the battle of the sexes" (Lee

Bowen 144). As Graham Robb points out, "By the end of the [nineteenth] century, it was possible to create a distinctively homosexual interior that included
a selection of significant books" of "symbolic value" (226), as well as significant
paintings and objects. Perhaps more accurately, Don Pablo's "odd range" and
his "aesthetically indiscriminate" collection of treasures, in an arrangement
which "might even please Luisa" (*Mary* 329), could be read as a marker of bisexuality. Given the account of his marriage in the novel, Don Pablo's cooling down
of heterosexual desire has to do with his wife's unresponsiveness rather than his
own, so the "addition" of homoerotic feelings would mark him as bisexual. Theories of inversion, however, invested in a dual model: The invert was either a
heterosexual man in a woman's body *or* a heterosexual woman in a man's body.

The "Greek" model, another recurrent reference in gay literature, presented an older man (*erastés*) and a younger boy (*erómenos*) in clearly demarcated active and passive roles respectively. We know that Mary transforms into
a "Greek boy" under Pablo's eyes (61), so it is possible to think of Mary as
Ganymede, with Pablo/Zeus temporarily transformed into Juanito. Pablo and
Juanito's mirroring bond can be read as a form of narcissism; not only is self-
love queer in itself, but also, via Freud, it is often linked to homosexuality.
Despite all these possible readings of Pablo's sexuality, it seems to me that he
cannot be accurately described as bisexual, invert, or *erastés*, but that he is best
described as sexually unconventional or queer, given that the text does not
clearly settle for a specific orientation.

Pablo is, however, clearly celibate. Celibacy crosses over sexual orientations
and is a recurrent preoccupation in O'Brien (see *Mary* 3, *Anteroom* 208, *Ireland*
26, 32, for example). Examples of celibate characters include Eleanor in *The
Flower of May*, Agatha in *Mary Lavelle*, and Paddy in *As Music and Splendour*.
Given that Pablo's self-restraint and individualism are linked to his politics, we
may also see a parallel between his sexual and ideological history: from limited
choices, to alienation, to compromise. In this light, his celibacy would not be
so much a renouncing of passion, but rather a sign of his withdrawal from the
world; celibacy would not be a way of enhancing integrity (physical, emotional,
political), but a last resort to ensure (psychic, ideological) self-preservation.

As we have seen, Juanito is marked as Don Pablo's double at a number of
points in the novel, and the hints are often made by highlighting the queerness
of both men. Mary looks "Greek" to both, for example. One is reminded of the
line "Lapsed Latinate and Half-Lucid Greek" in a poem of 1955 by Blanaid
Salkeld (see the same idea in O'Brien *Land* 140). A more interesting subtextual
connection is made between Juan and Pablo in the references to the painter
Domenikos Theotocopoulos, known as El Greco (the Greek), an idiosyncratic
artist who is sometimes considered to be proto-modernist on account of his
loose brushwork and "cubist" organization of space (see Smith 98). Born in
Crete in 1541, El Greco spent most of his life in Spain after becoming the favorite
court painter of Philip II and, as we will see, has often been associated with a

"gay sensibility." Don Pablo has a replica of El Greco's the *Burial of Count Orgaz* hanging in his "celibate's bedroom" (328), where he agonizes at the end of the novel, and it is significant that the painting offers a double portrait of Orgaz, as a dead man, and after his resurrection. At the same time, his son, in the "painful" ecstasies of his sexual encounter with Mary, sees her transformed into "a wounded San Sebastian" (309). El Greco's depiction of San Sebastian's death presents the martyr in the traditional way, propped against a tree, just like Mary when she is penetrated by Juanito's arrow. El Greco approached the topic on two occasions, and it is conceivable that Juanito may have seen either or both paintings. He is certainly familiar with El Greco's work, which he discusses with Mary and with his family at different points, and which is unsurprising for a cultured Basque living in Madrid, with El Prado museum and near Toledo (where the painter lived and worked). Mary makes a derisory joke about her uncle's admiration for El Greco, while Juanito claims that the painter is "overrated, hysterical" (236 — interestingly, in *Farewell Spain* O'Brien refers to El Greco's "frantic and rigid formula" 145–6). At some level, Mary and Juanito could be signaling their heterosexuality to each other by publicly distancing themselves from someone associated with "Greek love." An El Greco fan, Mary's uncle Tim from Dublin is described as "eccentric" (226), likely to be an encoded reference to homosexuality in this context (compare to, for example, O'Brien *Diaries* 22, 34, 42). One of the illustrations in *Farewell Spain*, by O'Brien's one-time partner Mary O'Neill, depicts the garden in El Greco's house.

It is of course possible to use El Greco as a referent for something other than queer sexuality; the protagonist of Maura Laverty's governess abroad novel, *No More Than Human*, has an epiphanic dream-vision as she lies consumed by scarlet fever (an episode modeled on Lucy Snowe's hallucinatory wanderings in *Villette*) in a room overlooked by a reproduction of El Greco's *Saint Jerome*. In a flash, she realizes that her solitude must end, not by marrying the man she is engaged to in Spain, but by returning home to Ireland (and marrying an Irish man): "The emaciated suffering of the saint became confused in my mind with my own sickness. The confusion filled me with a queer foolish pity for the man" (220). However, the death of San Sebastian has been a favorite theme in homoerotic painting, particularly after the Renaissance, and the combination of El Greco and Sebastian in O'Brien's novel is a double-strength connotation cocktail.

It is likely that Kate O'Brien confirmed the popularity of the homosexually-queer significance of El Greco, and was inspired to adapt it to her own purposes, when reading Ernest Hemingway's *Death in the Afternoon*. In a crucial passage of his book of 1932 about the bullfight, worth quoting in full, the paladin of hypermasculine heterosexuality described El Greco as someone who, "consciously or unconsciously, paints saints, apostles, Christs and Virgins with the androgynous faces and forms that filled his imagination," and recalled asking one of Greco's biographers, "Do you make him a maricón [faggot]?" When she replied, "No.... Why should I?," Hemingway gave a detailed response:

"Did you ever see more classic examples anywhere than he painted? Do you think that was all accident or do you think all those citizens were queer? The only saint I know who is universally represented as built that way is San Sebastian. Greco made them all that way. Look at the pictures. Don't take my word for it."
...El Greco believed in the city of Toledo, in its location and construction, in some of the people who lived in it, in blues, greys, greens and yellows, in reds, in the holy ghost, in the communion and fellowship of saints, in painting, in life after death and death after life and in fairies. If he was one he should redeem, for the tribe, the prissy exhibitionistic, aunt-like, withered old maid moral arrogance of a Gide; the lazy, conceited debauchery of a Wilde who betrayed a generation; the nasty, senti-mental pawing of humanity of a Whitman and all the mincing gentry. Viva El Greco El Rey de los Maricónes [sic] [Long Live El Greco King of Faggots] [204–5].

Kate O'Brien rarely used the word *homosexual*. In *Pray for the Wanderer*, in a discussion on the "pagan" Matt, we are told that: "Adultery and homosex-uality were entirely respectable so long as their practitioners had the *savoir faire* to keep them so.... But *tolerance and discretion* were the passwords in regard to actual life. Go as you please and make no scenes" (emphasis added, 109). The word is also used in *Farewell Spain*, as a reference to none other than El Greco: "He is said to have been homosexual, but that suggestion can be of little use to us in considering his work." O'Brien adds: "More mighty than he have been touched with that peculiarity, but the residue of all emotional experience tends in spirits large enough to be at last of natural and universal value, whatever the personal accidents of its accretion" (146). Here we find the crucial placing of the term *accident* annexed to *homosexuality*. I have mentioned that O'Brien was to define a number of attributes as "accidental" in her work: beauty, wealth, artistic ability, sanctity, authority, love, nationality.... Her use of the term strongly sug-gests a radically anti-essentialist approach, in this case, to sexuality.

The role of El Greco in *Mary Lavelle* is similar to the role of the name John. *Farewell Spain* singles out, in the old quarter of Bilbo/Altorno, "the little battered church of the two Saints John" (*Spain* 208), a discrete intratextual link to Mary Lavelle's male suitors, John and Juanito. John the Baptist had chosen death over breaking his celibacy in Wilde's play *Salome*. John "the young" (Juan-ito) is more relevant because Christian visual art has a tradition — popular, of widespread visibility — of feminizing representations of the apostle, on account of his role in the Passion, his leaning on the chest of Jesus at the last supper, and his being described in the gospels as "the disciple [whom] Jesus loved" (Jn 13:23–25; 19:26; see *Jerusalem* 1774, 1786), a suggestion often read in homoerotic terms. Kate O'Brien, for example, making the most of sexual ambiguity, has a character in *As Music and Splendour* comparing Clare to "John the Beloved." In *Mary Lavelle*, the use of the name John/Juan also suggests that Mary's choice of independence is a farewell to all "Don *Juans*" (O'Brien *Mary* 318). Interestingly, but also strik-ingly, Silvia Townsend Warner would use the legend of the Spanish Don Juan in 1938 as a symbol of fascism, in *After the Death of Don Juan*, a "political fable" set in eighteenth century Andalucía (quoted in Mulford xvi and v–vi).

The subversive homosexual links to El Greco and Havelock Ellis notwithstanding, Don Pablo and Juanito may be read as heterosexual men who have been forced to acknowledge an attraction towards androgynous women (or *an* androgynous woman, Mary, given that they have previously loved and desired their hyper-feminine spouses Consuelo and Luisa). This does not make them homosexual, but it certainly makes them queer. A desire for a "masculine" woman does not conform to normative standards of gender divisions in heterosexual eroticism. Further, even supposing that these two men have barely acknowledged (to themselves) homoerotic fantasies, this does not make them homosexual either, since fantasy, identity, and behavior do not correlate in such a simplistic way. To my mind, O'Brien does not clearly intend to imply that Pablo and Juan are gay. I would see all the main characters in *Mary Lavelle* as queer, but not necessarily as closeted homosexuals or bisexuals. O'Brien is on a mission to disrupt normativity, and the male leads in the novel are recruits in that mission.

Some queer theorists prefer to restrict their work to the celebration of certain queer sexualities, but the critical scope of a theory of the non-normative is wider than that. Its concerns extend, in my view, to all behaviors and orientations perceived as being non-normative, including rape or pedophilia. Stereotypical masculinity, it has been argued, is the pillar of heteropatriarchal culture (see Rubin "Traffic" and "Thinking"). As the recent work of Miriam Galvin shows, sexual interaction between adults and children must be seen in relation to the construction of normative gender identities (see "Masculinities"). Sexual coercion is an issue that hovers over *Mary Lavelle*, not just in the subplot of Don Jorge but at other unexpected points, such as in the emphasis on Juanito's forcefulness when he meets Mary in Toledo (see 243, 245). O'Brien had considered the issue before, in *The Anteroom*, where Vincent threatens to rape Agnes, and she responds that the only person to get "nothing out of [that] bargain" would be Marie-Rose, his wife and her sister (232). The shocking scene illustrates how rape, and abuse, are *not* actually non-normative behaviors, but *normative*, entirely in keeping with the "proper" sexuality of heterosexual adults (in 1883, or in 1934). That is, aggression, including sexual aggression, is considered an intrinsic part of archetypal masculinity.

"Consent" is at the definitional center of sexual abuse, and O'Brien seems to deliberately confuse its boundaries: Mary must *persuade* Juanito to have sex (see *Mary* 307), while Vincent compares sexual initiation to "tortur[e]" for the woman, just as Juanito does (*Anteroom* 234). As Val Hennessy caustically puts it, "the narrator assures us that although Mary does not have an orgasm on this occasion she experiences the spiritual equivalent. So that's all right then" (xii). The distinction between bodily and intellectual knowledge, the irreconcilable differences between different modes of physical pleasure, and the limits of consent were to be considered again by O'Brien in her unpublished short story of 1964, "Manna." The title is probably taken from a passage in Milton's *Paradise Lost* describing one of the fallen angels, Belial. We are told of this demon that "a fairer person lost not heaven," that "he pleased the ear" and seemed "graceful and humane," and yet: "all was false and hollow; though his tongue / dropt manna, and could make the worse appear / the better reason, to perplex and dash / maturest counsels" (Book I: 108–118; see Milton 25). O'Brien's "Manna" describes an incident of sexual abuse of a child by an adult. The six-year-old Josie wanders into a "Medical Hall" and instantly finds the young male attendant "very beautiful" (5). After a friendly discussion, he asks the curious child if she would like to go to the back of the shop.

> "Would you like to kiss me?" he asked, and she wondered why his voice was husky. She thought he was unhappy; he seemed to be pounding against her somehow and in the sunlight [sic] she thought that his beautiful face was even more beautiful than it seemed upstairs. She laid her hand on it.
> "You're burning hot," she said. "I'd love to kiss you. I think you're lovely."
> ...He ran his burning hands along her legs, forcing them apart. This roughness surprised her, but she liked the hot hands on her.
> "Are you upset?" she asked him.
> He laughed, and then he threw himself very hard against her.
> "Oh, please — ," she wondered.
> "Be still, be quiet, pet — I won't hurt you — I swear I won't hurt you — "
> "I know you won't," said Josie. "But what's the matter? Oh, what's the matter?"
> She was not afraid, exactly. She loved his golden head, and loved those hot hands pressing her down. But in the dim light she could not see him clearly or make out what he wanted [7–8].

In *The Last of Summer*, Angèle Maury's matter of fact reference to a "handsome" man who "surreptitiously petted her" when she was fifteen (89) is reminiscent of the Areavaga girls' tolerance of the "handsome" Don Jorge (*Mary* 198) — the only male character in the novel to be described as such. The villain who sexually preys on children in *The Land of Spices* is known as "The Judge," and when dealing with Don Jorge's sexual molestation, Mary's striking and irresponsible initial reaction is to tell herself that "'I'm not here to judge if anybody is right and wrong...'" (133). Don Jorge himself implies that his abuse is comparable to Mary's affair with Juanito (see 198–9). This may be effective in highlighting the arbitrariness of moral values, but it is an extremely problematic move.

Sexually assertive women have prominent roles in most of Kate O'Brien's books, and so have women who are coerced or charmed into compliance — in fact, they are often the same. It is extraordinary that the two only explicit sexual scenes in the entirety of O'Brien's fiction, in *Mary Lavelle* and "Manna," are both troubling regarding equality and/in pleasure. Mary gives informed consent, but without being ahistorical (if anything, Mary seems more informed than many inexperienced heterosexual women at the time would have been), she is clearly unprepared for the feelings she experiences. She had explained upon arrival in Altorno that "I'm a green sort of creature"; she claims to have "grow[n] up fast in this foreign soil" (198, 105), but there is a sense in which Juanito's lover is still a child when they first have sex. I believe that, despite the ostensible — perhaps over-emphasized — parity of Mary and Juanito, the scene suggests that there is an insurmountable imbalance between them. Their encounter is not a fruitful exchange, but more like war, a devastating change. I believe it can be argued that there is a continuum between the sexual imbalance of experienced-unexperienced adults (such as Juanito-Mary) and other sexual scenarios involving children and adults in O'Brien's work. When O'Brien sets her eyes on a black and white issue, we can be sure that her brush will paint it gray — but the violence in the key love scene in *Mary Lovelle* surely indicates a deep mistrust of the notion of eroticism as a potentially democratizing human impulse.

Queer Heterosexuality

QUEER HETEROSEXUALITIES

The most often repeated protagonist in Kate O'Brien is the queer heterosexual woman who falls in love/lust with a married man (Mary Lavelle, Agnes Mulqueen, Ana de Mendoza), or the woman who, being married, falls in love/lust with a man outside marriage (Caroline Considine, Lilian Morrow, Gladis Woodford), or, in a third variant, the woman who pursues a relationship without marriage in mind (Rose Lennane). Eibhear Walshe describes the affair between Ana and Antonio in *That Lady* as a "covert mating of transgendered lovers" ("Daughters" 161), and, as Anne Fogarty pointed out in a paper of 2003, heterosexual marriage can also be based on "a queer bond," which is the case with Nurse Cunningham and Reggie in *The Anteroom* ("Anteroom"). Another notable feature in the representation of queer sexualities in O'Brien's work is the abundance of sexual triangles, in homosocial attachments with an erotic component. Eve Kosofsky Sedgwick defined "the homosocial" as bonds between men that range in a continuum between the sexual and the social which has a component of desire (see Sedgwick *Men* 1–2). I use "homosocial" in this context to include a lesbian continuum, taking into account that Sedgwick's formulation is, as I see it, adapted from Adrienne Rich's 1980 notion of the lesbian continuum (see Rigby "Perversity"). In the triangles we regularly find in O'Brien, often involving incestuous eroticism, we have a pair, and a third person who functions as a sexual mediator, as conduit for charged physical closeness. For example, Vincent's love for Agnes through her sister/his wife, Marie Rose (*The Anteroom*); André's attractiveness to Fanny on account of his physical similarity to his sister, Lucille (*The Flower of May*); and Clare's considering of the possibility of "accessing" Luisa's body through contact with Luisa's lover, Duarte (*As Music and Splendour*). *Mary Lavelle* contains one such triangle in the bond between Juanito, Don Pablo, and Mary. As we have seen, we can read the novel as a version of the Arthurian legend, in which Juanito/Lancelot literally "replaces" Don Pablo/Arthur, setting up a chain of events that will eventually result in the death of the older man; if we read Agatha as an update of Morgan la Fay, this may suggest yet another triangular formation, between Mary, Luisa, and Juanito. It is worth remembering here the relevance in Thomas Malory of a person's ensuring sexual access to another through enchantment, with a "disguised" King Uther begetting Arthur through Igraine, while King Arthur "unknowingly" begets Mordred through his own half-sister, the wife of one King Lot (see 5, 21). Implied incestuous feelings are also a common occurrence in O'Brien's fiction. It is often the case in O'Brien that a suitor will remark on an incestuous attachment as an obstruction to an affair. So Vincent accuses Agnes by saying, "You love [Marie-Rose] more than me" (231) in *The Anteroom*, or Christina listens to Denis talk about his father "with a faint jealousy" (299) in *Without My Cloak*. There are many other such examples in O'Brien's fiction. Incestuous attachments in O'Brien involve parent and child — as in Anthony and Denis in *Without My Cloak*, Teresa and Reggie, and Vincent and his mother in *The Anteroom*, Hanna and Tom in *The Last of Summer*, or Joseph and Fanny in *The Flower of May*— or siblings— as in Caroline and Eddie in *Without my Cloak* (see Donoghue "Order" 40–1), Agnes and Marie-Rose in *The Anteroom* (see Fogarty "Desire" 111), or Ana and Charlie in *The Land of Spices* (see Dalsimer 24).

Another regular non-normative feature in the work of Kate O'Brien is the woman as sexual initiator. Interestingly, when Don Pablo reviews his disappointed expectations in life, he highlights his realization that his wife could/would not become his equal in a sexual partnership: "A woman's love apparently was, as all the generalisers said, a passive and receptive thing" (57). Mary is to prove him wrong. Her demanding of sex, although not to be repeated in O'Brien's fiction, is related to a number of scenes in other books where women "snatch" a kiss from a man. For example, Christina "taking" a kiss from Denis (409) in *Without My Cloak* or Agnes kissing Vincent in *The Anteroom* after she has decided not to have an affair with him: "She thought that they might part in tenderness; her idea was to reach him in a gentle expression of love, a caress of resignation. That would explain and pacify, and somehow set him free" (235). The decision is uncannily reminiscent of Mary Lavelle's, as is the gesture: "It seemed that his eyes resisted her, and were afraid, but she drew his head down unrelentingly till their mouths met" (ibid.). And we find another strikingly similar example in *The Flower of May*, where Fanny unexpectedly kisses André Marie, in what Lorna Reynolds describes as "a reversal of the usual seduction scene," interpreting this kiss as "an expression of freedom, not of love" given that Fanny is elated after unexpectedly gaining financial independence ("Artist" 60, 108). Reynolds compares the situation to Ana de Mendoza's, a free and rich widow who, "[a]lmost as a whim, we [readers] feel, perhaps to exercise for the first time in her life a sexual choice, ... takes [Antonio] as her lover" (103). Karin Eva Zettl points out that Mary is the one who shocks Juanito by suddenly kissing him in Toledo, and the one who decides "not to take him" then; it is Mary who, in their final meeting, "pulls his head down" for a kiss ("Search" 91). Zettl insists that, by contrast to Mary as "desiring subject" (ibid., 94), throughout the affair Juanito "is depicted as helpless, confused, at a loss as how to interpret the relationship" (92–3). Zettl is here engaging with Patricia Coughlan's assertion that "Juanito and Agatha can be lined up as active agents, desiring *subjects*, each opposite Mary, projected as *object* of desire" (emphasis in original, Coughlan "Kate" 77). I agree with Zettl's reading, and would further contend that desiring female subjects are given prominence in O'Brien's work.

The most explicit reference to sexuality in *Mary Lavelle* is heterosexual and, I argue, also queer, not merely on account of adultery, but also because of its focus on a woman's sexual assertiveness. Heterosexuality is under-theorized as enabling site of radical feminist contestation. Feminist queer theorists have described "queer" as referring to all non-normative "acts, identities, desires, perceptions, and possibilities" (J. Butler "Queer" 228) and as "a sexual specificity of proscribed object-choice, aim, site, or identification" (Sedgwick "Reading" 2). However, queer theory is still today too often reducible to gay and lesbian sexualities, despite attempts to counter the trend. Although practices such as BDSM (bondage, domination [and submission], sadism, masochism) and, lately, movements such as intersex and transgender have elicited some attention, they have the aura of "houseguests" rather than live-in companions, and their transversing/consolidating of "monosexual" orientations (heterosexuality and homosexuality) has failed to elicit critical responses on a par to the challenges they pose. Some commentators, such as Maria Pramaggiore and Clare Hemmings, have addressed the biphobic operations of much analysis on sexuality, but an implicit dismissal of heterosexual practices and identities in queer theory must be further challenged. An important essay of 2000 by Calvin Thomas, "Straight with a Twist: Queer Theory and the Subject of Heterosexuality," in the collection of the same title, focused on the legitimation of heterosexual theorists employing queer theory, rather than the articulation of a specific queer heterosexual approach (for earlier works see Katz and Richards).

Heteronormativity and heterosexuality are implicitly conflated in much queer theory, yet, as Michael Warner puts it, "to be fully normal is, strictly speaking, impossible. Everyone deviates from the norm in some way," and "even if one belongs to the statistical majority in age group, height, weight, frequency of orgasm, gender of sexual partners, and annual income, then simply by virtue of this unlikely combination of normalcies one's profile would already depart from the norm" (*Trouble* 54–55). Or, as Sedgwick puts it, the topic of sexuality is "the locus of so many showy pleasures and identities" that "sexuality in this sense, perhaps, can *only* mean queer sexuality" (emphasis in original, "Queer" 20). It seems to be a case of "degrees" of normalcy with an unlimited potential for the queer constituency, but queer theory is about morally/politically enshrined "norms," not statistics. For a number of reasons, queer commentators have invested in strengthening the divide between norms and deviances. Monique Wittig, for example, famously claimed in 1980 that "[l]esbians are not women" because the term *woman* "has meaning only in heterosexual systems of thought and heterosexual economic systems" ("Mind" 32). Mary

Lavelle, demanding sex of a married man, does not accommodate either to the meaning of *woman* in heteronormative discourse, which requires (in the Ireland of 1922) that she retains her virginity until marriage and that she be passive and content before and after. Gustave Flaubert's 1856 *Madame Bovary* and D.H. Lawrence's 1928 *Lady Chatterley's Lover* prompted scandal because they focused on illicit female (hetero)sexualities. Edna O'Brien's *The Country Girls* was controversial in Ireland in 1960, not because of explicit (hetero)sexuality, but because of its assertive *female* sexuality; while in 1967, Francoist censors took issue with Bilbaian filmmaker Pedro Olea's first feature, *Days of an Old Colour* ("Dias de Viejo Color") and forced him to cut a scene in which a woman initiated a sexual encounter (see Arriola 41). Denis Diderot's 1790 (w. 1760) *The Nun* and Emile Zola's 1880 *Nana*, the targets of another form of censorship, were regularly dismissed as pornographic (as was Henry Miller's 1932 *Tropic of Cancer*, brought to court in 1960 for obscenity); the important lesbian content in both novels no doubt aggravated the charge. In fact, all of these texts were considered at one point or another to be pornographic, and it is true that only in pornography, so often context-free, did one expect to find portraits of female sexual assertiveness.

VIRGINITY

Another thing that one expected to find in pornography is the blatant eroticization of innocence, as opposed to its implied eroticization and/or valuing within social contexts, which obviously plays a part in much canonical fiction, with early examples such as Frances Burney's 1778 *Evelina*. Scenes of heterosexual sexual initiation in Western fiction have often been predicated on two assumptions: that virginity can only be understood as a hymen which should be ruptured by a penis and, consequently, that only women are virgins. Current understandings of virginity are significantly different. Noreen Giffney, in a survey of key concept in Queer Theory, defines *virgin*, following Marilyn Frye (correspondence with N. Giffney, September 7, 2009), as "[s]omeone who has not engaged in a sex act with another person," and adds: "In the Western sex-gender system, virgin is used narrowly to denote all those who have not had sexual contact with a penis." In heteronormative fiction, occasionally the innocence of women has been itself presented as a threat to masculinity in men, as in D.H. Lawrence's *Women in Love*, of 1921. At other times, a woman's innocence is the extension of a vulnerability that may be enhanced rather than neutralized by sexual experience, as in Jean Rhys' *Voyage in the Dark*, of 1934. O'Brien's radical approach to virginity was made clear in a political and existentialist fable, her film script *Mary Magdalen*, where she puts forward the suggestion that the Virgin Mary and the whore of Magdala were in fact one and the same. Mary Lavelle may be assertive in initiating a sexual encounter but, according to Patricia Coughlan, the description of the sex scene insists on her passivity, in a narrative that "gives far more imaginative energy to that *relinquishing* of agency to which Mary is moved by her awakened passion for Juanito than to the representation of Mary's making her own of her life which is the larger concern of the novel" (emphasis in original, 70). The association of passivity and femininity in the West had been shown to be culturally determined rather than natural by anthropological studies published shortly before *Mary Lavelle*, such as those by Margaret Mead and B. Malinovski in the late 1920s and early 1930s. According to the anthropologist Rodney Gallop, who was writing in the late 1920s and documenting the survival of pre–Christian customs in the Basque Country, as a people, the Basques "severely condemn adultery, although they do not object to sexual activities between unmarried people" (57). The pioneering work of Richard Burton had been published at the height of the Victorian era. Burton developed a theory of the "Sotadic Zone," an area of the globe cordoning the equator (between N. Lat 43 and N. Lat 30) and including the Iberian Peninsula and therefore Bilbo/Altorno in the Southern Basque Country. In 1886 he claimed that in this area, due to the climate, "there is a blending of the masculine and feminine temperaments, a crasis which elsewhere occurs only sporadically" and which explains "the male *féminisme* [femininity] whereby the man becomes *patiens* [passive] as well as *agens* [active], and the woman a tribade, a votary of mascula [man-like] Sappho, Queen of Frictrices or Rubbers" (204).

Whether under the influence of her "tropical" surroundings or not (the Basque climate is actually far more similar to that of Ireland than to that of central or southern Spain), Mary manages to transcend her upbringing without great difficulty when the occasion presents itself, persuading the resistant Juanito that she knows all she needs to know, and listing the downsides, such as pain and the risk of pregnancy (see 307). Understandably, some readers found Mary's declaration implausible. Kate O'Brien's brother in law, Stephen O'Mara, actually confronted the author on this point: "If anyone seduced Juanito in the wood, it certainly was not Mary Lavelle; it was quite a different girl — one whose chief characteristic from early youth was solitary brooding and secret self-education in sexual knowledge" (quoted in Walshe *Kate* 68). O'Brien does not seem to have answered to this particular charge. Like the protagonist in Honoré de Balzac's *The Girl with the Golden Eyes*, of 1835, Mary "may be a virgin, but innocent she was not" (iv).

The "wound of the bullfight" (O'Brien *Mary* 128), as we will see, represents a loss of virginity regarding the aesthetic, the politic, the ethic. The facing of the bull is a confirmation of a certain kind of archetypal masculinity, and (as it stands today) is designed as a *male* performance, which includes, by way of the costume and gestures of the bullfighter, a controlled, staged feminization. Many commentators see the ritual as the re-enactment of a misogynystic prototype of the "seduction game," whereby the torero/female seduces and destroys the bull/male. The sport is, nevertheless, associated to a "macho-latino" stereotype (and bullfighters are regularly given an aura of hetero-sexual competence in the Spanish media). The role most obviously allocated to Mary in the sex scene is that of a bull. In Ernest Hemingway's treatise on bullfighting, *Death in the Afternoon*, which as we will see O'Brien seems to have consulted when writing *Mary Lavelle*, he claims that "[a]ll of bullfighting is founded on the bravery of the bull, his simplicity and his lack of experience," and while "there are ways to fight cowardly bulls, experienced bulls and intelligent bulls, ... the principle of the bullfight, the ideal bullfight, supposes bravery in the bull and a brain clear of any remembrance of previous work in the ring" (145). In other words, the ideal *toro bravo* in the ring, wild, courageous, elegant, lethal, must be a "virgin."

Perhaps Mary has been waiting for "Mr. Right" (Roberts xi). Or perhaps she just wants to give the man she loves, in a grand gesture, the only thing that — as a woman — she truly "owns": "She had given him *all she had*" (O'Brien *Mary* 312, see also 307). Another possibility, however, is that Mary wishes for her virginity to be "taken away from her." That is, Mary may be purposefully "devaluing" herself as a female body, within an economy of heteronormative marriage which will ignore her if she lacks currency. As Adele Dalsimer notes, "Mary knows that her passion for Juanito will destroy her life with John" (43). This single sexual act will simultaneously "cur[e]" John and "take [the] pain away" from Juanito (*Mary* 308, 312), when Mary is about to leave them both. *Mary Lavelle* is partly a rewrite of Charlotte Brontë's 1847 *Jane Eyre*, but while Eyre had refused the call from the "visionary messenger" St. John to commit herself to a worthy cause (402), Kate O'Brien amends the story so that her protagonist rejects both St. John and Rochester, suggesting that the two men demand the same unacceptable self-obliteration of their beloved. O'Brien's virgin Mary knows she must preserve her voice, from Juanito as much as John — her virginity is not merely a "gateway" through which she is "entered" (*Mary* 128), but also a drawbridge that facilitates her escape.

PAIN AND MASOCHISM

Patricia Coughlan sees the sexual encounter in *Mary Lavelle* as dwelling "in an undeniably sado-masochistic way on images of Mary's specifically feminine vulnerability and pain *as themselves erotic* and constitutive of Juanito's pleasure" (emphasis in original, 69). In the same collection of essays, Anne Fogarty also claims that Mary "reshap[es] her identity by means of her masochistic passion for Juanito" ("Desire" 113). Leo Bersani's theory proposed in 1987, in a context of certain gay male sexual practices, that, as Lynne Segal puts it, "sexual excitement is itself primarily a 'tautology for masochism'" (253). This has been taken up by queer theorists such as Michael Warner in 1999 and Lee Edelman in 2004, both of whom follow Bersani, rather than Simone de Beauvoir's related discussion of 1949 (see Beauvoir 418). Don Pablo has been "undone" through sex, because his wife has failed to respond to his passion, and Juanito's self-image is shattered by his extramarital affair — "I am undone" he exclaims at one point (*Mary* 307). Segal's feminist appropriation of sexual activity as "ego-shattering" within a heterosexual couple has her claim that "[i]n particular, however, sex places 'manhood' in jeopardy, with its masculine ideal of autonomous selfhood threatened by the self-abnegation, the self-obliteration, that sexual desire engenders" (254). She continues by questioning the assumption that "it is through sexual activity that we consolidate gender and penile/phallic dominance," as suggested by Norman Mailer's claim that "'a man can become more male and a woman more female by coming together in the full rigors of the fuck'"; Segal wonders: "But do they? I think the opposite. As soon as we look into this overworked, heterosexualized normativity, we see what it is working so hard to hide," which is that "[s]exual relations are perhaps the most fraught and troubling of all social relations precisely because, especially when heterosexual, they so often *threaten* rather than confirm gender polarity" (emphasis in original, 254–5). Segal fails to address how this self-shattering of sex affects gender identity *in women*, but her main aim is the reclamation of heterosexual women's sexuality as site of feminist contestation, and she ignores the inconsistencies in her argument.

It is crucial to distinguish between the eroticization of pain or domination/submission as sexual practices, and as metaphors or theoretical levers for the formation and negotiation of gendered identities. The sadomasochistic dynamics detected by Coughlan in what she describes as a "dismaying passage," are at least in part a stylistic parallel to the bullfight ceremony, as Coughlan admits ("Kate" 69). The bullfight does not reify physical pain, but courage (and skill) in the face of the ultimate challenge — in Mary's case, the risk of "social death." Linking pleasure to violence and coercion is part of canonical literature since M.G. Lewis's 1796 *The Monk* (if not since Thomas Nashe's 1594 *The Unfortunate Traveller*), while an eroticization of suffering may arguably have been popularized since medieval times through the "biographies" of Christian martyrs (to the shock of post–Enlightenment non–Catholic observers such as the protagonist of *Villette*). The writings of Sade may be irrevocably associated with perverse sexuality, but the first attempts to present sadomasochism as a sexual practice to a wide public in realistic terms did not occur until the 1970s. BDSM remains one of the least understood and most demonized forms of sexuality, being, as Jay Wiseman noted in 1992, all too often linked to brutality and abuse by uninformed people (see 16–17). Wiseman defines BDSM as "the knowing use of psychological dominance and submission, and/or physical bondage, and/or pain, and/or related practices in a safe, legal, consensual manner in order for the participants to experience erotic arousal and/or personal growth" (10). He goes on to say that: "[BD]SM play differs from abuse in much the same ways that a judo match differs from a mugging" (41). The kind of "consent" implicit in Coughlan's assessment, essential to sadomasochism outside pornography/fantasy, is missing from the sex scene in "The Good Basque Country." Mary certainly does not subscribe to an "enjoyment of pain" in demanding sex that she expects to be painful, and her motivation seems to me equally alien to an eroticization of submission/dominance. As Simone de Beauvoir puts it, "Pain ... is of masochistic significance only when it is accepted and wanted as proof of servitude," but there is no difference in the way pain may affect women's and men's sexuality in general: "As for the pain of defloration, it is not closely correlated with pleasure; and as for the sufferings of childbirth, all women fear them and are glad that modern obstetrical methods are doing away with them" (*Sex* 419). Conversely, I fail to see that Juanito takes a sadistic pleasure in the encounter, although the politics of pain in the scene are certainly worth considering.

It seems problematic to say the least that a caring and sensitive partner such as Juanito is unable/unwilling to make the sexual initiation enjoyable for Mary. A painful loss of virginity has been the experience of many women's "archetypal" heterosexual sexual initiation, as de Beauvoir noted in *The Second Sex* (see 403–412), where she made the — to my mind, unsustainable — claim that vaginal penetration by a penis "always constitutes a kind of violation" (394), to later add that "however deferential and polite the man may be, the first penetration is always a violation" (404). A painful loss of virginity may be common with inexperienced and/or uncaring partners, but the fact is that the rupture of the hymen does not have to be necessarily painful. The scene in *Mary Lavelle* implies that this is not the case. Given that Juanito's masculinity is presented as non-stereotypical, gentle and kind (see O'Brien *Mary* 308), the emphasis on pain may be read as a warning to women. I can think of no other such scene in literature by women: physical pain is mentioned repeatedly during the description of the sexual encounter, and it is also alluded to later in a joking fashion by both lovers: "'You are going to Ireland [tomorrow] — though I very much doubt —' he laughed at her, 'if you'll be fit to travel!' / 'Ah, sweet!'" (311).

For women's references to painful loss of virginity, we must turn to autobiographical accounts. Valentine Ackland's autobiography, *For Silvia*, relates the prolonged suffering brought about by the demented approach to normative sexuality prevalent in Britain when she became a bride in 1925. Isadora Duncan, in *My Life*, refers to her heterosexual sexual initiation in terms strikingly similar to those used by Mary Lavelle:

> I, too, was aroused and dizzy, while an irresistible longing to press him closer and closer surged in me, until one night, losing all control and falling into a fury, he carried me to the sofa. Frightened but ecstatic and crying out in pain, I was initiated into the act of love. I confess that my first impressions were a horrible fright and an atrocious pain, as if someone had torn out several of my teeth at once; but a great pity for what he seemed to be suffering prevented me from running away from what was at first sheer mutilation and torture.... Next day what was at that time no more than a painful experience for me continued amidst my martyred cries and tears. It felt as if I were being mangled [quoted by de Beauvoir *Sex* 405].

Mary Lavelle's frank description of a painful rupture of the hymen is unusual in canonical fiction of the period, and the introduction of "emotional" and "moral" pain into the scene is as interesting. Anne Fogarty describes Juanito as an "aggressive" lover ("Desire" 112, 113), but it is important that he is said to be suffering, even as they are engaged in sex: "His heart hurt him as if it might in fact break" (309). When he says, "I have half-killed you, ... I have hurt you horribly. And yet you seem to like me still, you seem quite happy," she replies, "Yes, you hurt me terribly.... Oh, my love, I'm perfectly happy!" (313). Coughlan claims that the viewpoint in the scene is that of Juanito ("Kate" 69), but both lovers are given segments of stream of consciousness, while the overseer narrator steps in at several points to bridge the gap (see O'Brien *Mary* 305, 309, 314). "[B]oth" lovers give courage and take pain (ibid., 304, 309), and the attempt at presenting them as equals, however ultimately unconvincing, is there. The scene does not follow romantic clichés, but dismantles them, because it re-enacts the meeting of bull and matador. If the life of the bullfighter were not at risk, the bullfight would have no meaning.

The gradual acquisition of sexual knowledge is pointed out at several points in the sex scene in *Mary Lavelle*. The musical training of Clara and Rose in *As Music and Splendour* can be read as a metaphor for sexual experience, as when Clare explains she prefers to be a singer rather than a model: "'Because at least, however idiotic, I'll be doing the thing myself! Not just having it done!' / Thomas threw her an amused look" (O'Brien 68). Another example is the narrator's claim that "according to their natures, [the girls] spread and grew. They were lonely; they were lively — and they had, *however unexplored and undefined*, musical gift, musical need and desire" (emphasis added, 15), a passage which echoes the description of Luisa and Mary Lavelle's encounter. In the mountains, when Mary's hymen has been broken and Juanito has reached orgasm, after a brief interval we are told that "the storm of feeling broke and took them again," and while there is no way of telling what kind of lovemaking is being explored, Mary certainly registers a change (see O'Brien *Mary* 311). However, given that there is no trace of any physical pleasure on her part, that her loss of virginity is painful, and that Juanito ejaculates inside her in full awareness of the danger of pregnancy, Mary's claim that he "knew how to be a lover" (ibid.) is testing, unless we substitute "lover" for "bullfighter" and read the encounter as a lesson in courage.

Simone de Beauvoir, discussing "Sexual Initiation" in a chapter of *The Second Sex*, claims of the rupture of the hymen in an archetypal heterosexual initiation that, for a woman, it marks a break between imagination and reality, and goes on: "By analogy with the training of a bull, Michel Leiris calls the nuptial bed 'the real thing' [or 'the moment of truth' in bullfighting]; for the virgin, indeed, this expression assumes its fullest and most fearsome sense" (401). In the words of anthropologist Margaret Mead, feminist agitation in the 1920s "was accompanied by an insistence on women's need for sexual climaxes comparable to men's, and the demand that women respond to men became a burdensome demand on them to behave like musical instruments rather than full human beings" (*Male* 23; see 269–270). The reification of orgasm may be problematic in other contexts, but given the sexual history of women, it is significant that many commentators agree that the importance of the clitoris was only "discovered" by the English speaking public at large in 1953, with the publication of Alfred Kinsey's *Sexual Behaviour in the Human Female*. What Mead referred to as "phallic athleticism" (*Male* 23) appears to have been the norm in heterosexual sexuality for most of the twentieth century (see the Hite Report of 1976), and it seems pointless to judge the sex scene in *Mary Lavelle* in terms of wishful thinking. What the novel can and does do is to undermine any idealistic notions through a subversive use of symbolism and careful wording; what the novel can and does do, is to show a young woman capable of making sexual choices and of taking her assertiveness as far as her knowledge and experience will allow.

Bullfight

"MISE-EN-SCÈNE" (SETTING THE SCENE)

In *Mary Lavelle*, suffering is stylized. The key point to the bullfight is that the experience is mediated by the "*mise-en-scène*" (see O'Brien *Spain* 139). A "newer self" emerges in Mary after going to a bullfight for the first time and facing its horror, a horror "made absolutely beautiful by a formula of fantastic peril," which is "more vivid with beauty and all beauty's anguish, more full of news of life's possible pain and senselessness and quixotry and barbarism and glory than anything ever before encountered by this girl" (O'Brien *Mary* 116). The encounter with art in *Mary Lavelle* is specifically linked to the sublime, as elaborated by Edmund Burke in 1757. The emotion (Burke calls it the "passion") caused by the sublime is astonishment, "that state of the soul, in which all its motions are suspended, with some degree of horror" (Burke 53). In *Mary Lavelle*, John describes the bullfight as "[b]urlesque, fantastic, savage" (116), and in *As Music and Splendour*, the revelation that a character's lover is a priest is summed up with "[t]he distortion, the grotesque, the inferno!" (O'Brien 342)—both outbursts are reminiscent of Stephen Gordon's "wrong, grotesque, unholy" love (Hall 199). In *The Land of Spices*, sex appears "vast or savage or gargoyled or insanely fantastical" (O'Brien 158). Burke discusses the "vastness of the sublime" in his *Philosophical Enquiry into the Sublime and the Beautiful* (124–5). O'Brien's description of the period 1934–1937 in Spain as "a death, or a *vast*, unpredictable birth" (emphasis added, *Spain* 36), and Milagros's description of the bullfight as "an immense thing" (*Mary* 140), are also allusions to the Burkean sublime.

Edmund Burke's crucial switch between beauty and the sublime in the hierarchical order — his essay amounts to a dethroning of beauty — is also interesting in a queer context, because, to Burke, beauty is aligned to the feminine, while the sublime is equated to the masculine. The use of the sublime in *Mary Lavelle* is in effect a queer move (whether we read Burke as misogynistic or homophilic is immaterial), knocking normative aesthetics off its pedestal and replacing it with gargoyles, savagery, and horror, all of which are (in the logic of the novel) embodied in the encounter between Juanito and Mary "grotesquely and harshly made one" (O'Brien 309). The novel turns the bull into a sacrificial virgin, tears replacing shed blood, and when John looks at Mary's face, "flung back against the moss, [he] saw her set teeth and quivering nostrils, beating eyelids, flowing, flowing tears. The curls were clammy on her forehead now, as on that day when she came into Luisa's drawing room from the bullfight" (308–9).

This monstrous face is the face of Europe, but it is also important here that the bullfight is, to the non–Spanish, emblematic of Spain. The link was popularized by D.H. Lawrence in his 1926 *The Plumed Serpent: Quetzalcoatl*, and by Ernest Hemingway in his novel of the same year, *The Sun Also Rises*, set in the Basque Country. Hemingway did much to associate Spain with bullfighting, but he had some special associations with the Basque Country, to the extent that his brother declared upon his death that his tombstone should have been inscribed "Here Lies a Basque Shepherd" (E. Jiménez 105; see also Barandiaran)—the traditional job for Basque emigrant men in the United States. Interestingly, Hemingway considered himself a disciple of Pío Baroja, a Basque writer from '98 and a self-confessed "individualist ... anarchist" (126). In 1937, the year of publication of *Farewell Spain*, another work of art was to use the bull as a prominent symbol linked to Spain and the civil war: Pablo Picasso's *Guernica*, the presentation card of the leftist Spanish Republic at the International Exhibition in Paris. On April 26, 1937, Gernika (*Guernica* is the Spanish spelling), a Basque market town a few miles away from Bilbo/Altorno, had been destroyed by the Nazis as an experiment in decimating an entire town from the air. Picasso had explored the bullfight in a series of allegorical paintings and poems since 1934 (see Klingsöhr-Leroy 86), and now he used the symbols of the bull and the wounded horse to mobilize Europe into responding to the shared threat of fascism. It may not be by chance, at this point in the civil war, that the bull in the top-left-hand corner of *Guernica* can be read in a number of ways: as protector, as a non-implicated bystander, or as the cause of suffering.

The bull is not associated to Basque iconography, with the notable exception of the prehistoric stone sculpture in the Basque Museum in Bilbo known as the "Mikeldi," dated between 600–400 BCE, which is generally believed to represent a bull. One of the effects of relying on bullfighting as a symbol is that this "Spanishizes" the Basque setting. Mary recalls that "Conlan had said 'Castile is good'" and "had compared it with the bullfight. Nevertheless that admiration was suspect and savage in anyone. Mary had never dared to analyse it in herself. Meantime in confusion of heart, and half hoping she would never have a chance to see it, she had waited for Castile" (O'Brien *Mary* 215–6). The strange language here may refer to Mary's impending illicit affair with Juanito, or to a suppressed lesbian longing (part of a subtextual narrative, with Luisa as Castile). Mary's reaction to Castile, like her going to the bullfight, is a "test," so she is relieved when she finds it to be "Heaven[ly]" (216).

The stylistic decision of equating Mary to a bull may have a comparable precedent in Emile Zola's *Nana,* in an episode where a horse named after the protagonist enters a race in what is presented and perceived (by the characters) as a metonymy. In the chapter, Zola creates an erotically charged comic aside, and it is interesting that "Corrida," the title of a chapter in *Mary Lavelle,* not only means "bullfight," but it is also Spanish slang for "reaching orgasm." However, by contrast with Zola, O'Brien's novel turns the scene into a *surrealist* vision where there are no clear conceptual contours, and, more importantly, it turns archetypal heterosexual initiation into a ritual of death. This is assisted by an impressively tight structural pattern. The chapter "The Good Basque Country," which describes the sexual encounter, opens with Juanito and Mary after he has found her in the Café Alemán, as they get into his car and drive through the mountains. While in the car, Mary tells him: "You're good at finding people.... This is the third time" (302). The number three is a talisman in *Mary Lavelle.* Don Pablo insists on the fact that Mary and Juanito have met three times (see 318), but also, his own spiraling towards death happens, we are told, in "three jerks" (326). Mary had danced with Juanito in the square for "three minutes" (219), but also, Agatha had lived by San Geronimo for three years, Mary and the girls went to Madrid for three days, Mary's bedroom and Luisa's drawing room have three windows, and so on. At another level, we have the triangle of an extramarital affair, and the "tripartite" lesbian bildungsroman of Nieves/Mary/Agatha. It may also be relevant, given O'Brien's fondness for exegesis, that in the gospels, in Paul's second letter to Corinthians, he refers to his exhortations as a "third" warning. First and foremost, however, the relevance of the number three to the novel is dictated by the bullfight, which is divided in three stages, known as the *tres tercios de la lidia* or "three thirds of the combat" (in Hemingway's translation; *Death* 96). The last *tercio* culminates in the killing of the bull, known as *el momento de la verdad,* "the moment of truth, or of reality" (see ibid., 174). As we will see, Kate O'Brien followed the three "acts" of the ceremony with the scrupulousness of classic drama.

Death in the Afternoon is perhaps the most comprehensive and detailed introduction to the bullfight published by that date, although a number of non–Spanish writers had discussed it before, while in Spain commentators like Mariano José de Larra in the nineteenth century and José Ortega y Gasset from 1929 onwards gave the ceremony historical and conceptual depth, before the encyclopedic study by José María de Cossío appeared in 1995–1998 (see Benítez 17–33). *Death in the Afternoon* includes full chapters on the stages of the bullfight, on the rearing and qualities of fighting bulls, and on the desirable skills in bullfighters, as well as a survey of techniques and styles illustrated by numerous photographs in an appendix. The book is also full of digressions, such as short stories, fictional exchanges in dialogue form, and autobiographical sketches, as well as in-jokes and outbursts deriding various people, customs, and cultures, with the cocky bravado that became Hemingway's trademark. We saw an example of a "digression" in his long reference to El Greco.

O'Brien never acknowledged her debt to Hemingway, though she admitted to liking his work with reservations in a 1937 review (see Walshe *Kate* 70). She insisted that her passion for bullfighting had been unmediated by literature, and her enthusiasm is beyond question: she once described the bullring in Madrid as "[a] contribution to human happiness" (*Spain* 141; see 38). *Mary Lavelle,* however, provides direct links to *Death in the Afternoon.* For example, the emphasis on death, in Hemingway's claim that the "pagan virtue" of pride "makes the bullfight[,] and true enjoyment of killing ... makes the great matador" (Hemingway 233; also echoed in A.L. Kennedy). Or in Agatha's pronouncement that Mary's first bullfight had been too good for her to possibly appreciate its subtleties, a statement borrowed verbatim from *Death in the Afternoon* (see O'Brien *Mary* 117), as is the claim that the bullfight is "indefensible" (see Hemingway *Death* 319 and O'Brien *Spain* 134–5). Another example is Hemingway's description of the bull as "the figure broken by the shock of the encounter" (*Death* 238), used by O'Brien to describe Mary in the sex scene.

The bullfight, then, is made of three *tercios* ("thirds"), or acts. As Hemingway puts it, they consist of a trial, a sentencing, and an execution (*Death* 98). Each of the three acts is clearly demarcated in *Mary Lavelle* in the progression of the romantic narrative, which is clearly cross-referenced with the bullfight scene in the novel — and as clearly informed by Hemingway's comments in his book. Juanito's appearances are structurally orchestrated to mirror the three acts of the bullfight. Let us consider them in turn.

The first part is known as the *suerte de varas* or "trial of the lances": "Act one is the act of the capes, the pics and the horses. In it the bull has the greatest opportunity to display his bravery or cowardice" (Hemingway *Death* 96). The attendants of the bullfighter begin by making a number of random passes on foot with their capes around the bull, in order for the matador to learn which moves are favored by the animal, so that the bull can be properly and safely tackled by him later on. Then the mounted horses are brought in, and when the bull invariably charges, the "lancer" expertly wounds the animal several times in order to weaken the bull and correct his tendency to horn to one side or the other. In the novel, this corresponds to the dancing in the Plaza San Martin (Saint Martin's square) in Altorno, at the end of "The Poetry Lesson" chapter. Given that the dance is observed by Don Jorge, who later attempts to blackmail Mary, perhaps the priest may be seen as "the picador," or lancer; although the music itself seems to wound her: "a tune rang through her as harshly as if played by a band at a bullfight — 'I met my love in Avalon'" (210). Unwanted suitors approach Mary as she watches the dancing, unable to take part, until the man destined for her suddenly appears.

> She leant against the tree, and looked at the figures moving in beauty through the violent depths of light. She knew the tune they were dancing to: "I met my love in Avalon...."
> Juanito found her under the tree [189].

The second stage, or "act," in the bullfight, is the *suerte de banderillas* or "trial of the sticks": "These are pairs of sticks about a yard long, seventy centimeters to be exact, with a harpoon-shaped steel point four centimeters long at one end. They are supposed to be placed, two at a time, in the humped muscle at the top of the bull's neck as he charges the man who holds them," Hemingway tells us, and explains: "They are designed to complete the work of slowing up the bull and regulating the carriage of his head which has been begun by the picadors: so that his attack will be slower, but surer and better directed" (Hemingway *Death* 96–97). In the novel, this corresponds to Mary wandering off from the Plaza Zocodover (Zocodover square) in Toledo, pestered by "touts and beggars" until Juanito reappears unexpectedly, in the chapter "A Hermitage."

> "Oh, go away, please! Leave me alone — I don't want any of you!"
> The touts and beggars laughed at her foreign Spanish and pressed still more about her....
> She put her hands across her eyes and gave herself up to a moment of darkness. The noise of the admiring touts fell away; there was a sudden cooling silence over her; she felt as if she sat in shadow. She opened her eyes and found that so she did. Juanito stood above her, having scattered the crowd [240].

The third stage of the bullfight culminates in the moment of the killing, which, as we know, corresponds in the novel to the sexual encounter. However, before the bull is killed there is a *faena*, or series of passes, with the *muleta* (the cloth placed on a sword) in preparation for the end. Most bullfighters, Hemingway points out with some regret, are not required to be consummate killers, because the public has grown to place increasing value on the *muleta* skill. "If the spectators know the matador is capable of executing a complete, consecutive series of passes with the *muleta* in which there will be valor, art, understanding and, above all, beauty and great emotion," Hemingways explains, "they will put up with mediocre work, cowardly work, disastrous work because they have the hope sooner or later of seeing the complete *faena*" (Hemingway *Death* 206). In the novel, this *muleta* work corresponds to the last conversation between Mary and her suitor, Agatha, the woman who understands the bullfight "like a matador" (according to someone who knows, the retired bullfighter Pepe, perhaps inspired by the famous Bilbaian bullfighter Castor Jaureguibeitia Ibarra, known as "Cocherito de Bilbao," who retired in 1919 — see Valdelande 27). Mary asks Agatha, "Why have you — liked me so much?" and her friend explains why, unflinchingly referring to "the sin of Sodom" (298).

> But she was reluctant too to leave Agatha, and in general dreaded going out from this place for the last time. Another farewell disposed of, another bit of Spain chopped off. She laid the money for her chocolate on the table, but still sat, weary, heavy-hearted....
> The café door opened and shut. There was a gentle step on the tiles. Mary looked up. It was he, Juanito [300].

The progression of the metaphorical bullfight up to "the moment of truth" in "The Good Basque Country" is more than a set of stage directions for the novel, because it is meant to mirror the psychological/emotional stages Mary goes through. As Hemingway puts it, "[a]side from the normal physical and mental stages the bull goes through in the ring, each individual bull changes his mental state all through the fight" (*Death* 150). The increasingly regular references to Mary's "tiredness" (physical, but also relevant to her struggle with her conscience) as the narrative progresses, are also akin to the progressive slowing down of the bull in the bullfight. As Hemingway explains, the states "that the bull goes through in the course of the fight ... are the natural progress of his fatigue if the fatigue has been properly induced" (148).

There are other "props" in the novel signaling parallels to the bullfight. For example, in Spanish both bull rings and town squares are described by using the same word, *plaza*, and O'Brien scrupulously places Mary in a plaza/square at the opening of the three relevant scenes in "The Poetry Lesson" and "A Hermitage," as well as in "The Good Basque Country," which begins with Juanito and Mary hurrying "through the dusk into a square where the black sports car was parked" (302). The bullfight is, of course, a public event, and at the three stages in the romantic narrative the lovers meet in non-private locations (a leafy square, a hermitage on a hill, a field), gradually closer to nature and to the uncontaminated purity of their primordial selves. "This is my own country," Juanito admits for the first time in the novel, as they reach the mountains. "This is the good Basque country of my people" (302). There is a blatant incongruence in this man proudly declaring his Basqueness when he is about to re-enact the fiesta, the epitome of postcard Spain and, to many Basque nationalists, an emblem of colonial cultural oppression. It is not by chance that Mary's reflections on Basque and Irish nationalism are meshed in her mind with "the wound of the bullfight" (128; see Mentxaka "Politics"). A remarkable title for a key chapter, "The Good Basque Country," with its ceremonial sex in a rural setting, is among other things a conservative, regressive re-enactment of a primitive ritual. The Basque anthropologist Joseba Zulaika has suggested that the notion of sacrifice is central to Basque culture, because of the double influence of Catholicism and Basque nationalism (see *Basque*), and perhaps that link alone makes the title of the chapter fitting.

THE "LAST ACT OF THE COMBAT" AND THE "MOMENT OF TRUTH"

The sex scene (and the romance plot in general) is a reversal of realist technique, so seamlessly conducted and crafted that it resembles a coin twirling in the air — each reader's unique flick of the hand will ultimately determine the outcome, but there are two separate and distinct events taking place at once: a sexual encounter and a bullfight. The result of this unorthodox coupling (of realism and surrealism, of human and beast) is also a textual hybrid. In the romance narrative, Juanito has no designs and no intention of making a sexual advance on Mary; he

merely wants to talk and spend some time with her before she leaves forever —
and perhaps attempt to make her stay. Conversely, in the romance narrative Mary
has not premeditated a sexual encounter and is grateful to spend some time with
her beloved before she returns (perhaps) to her pre-ordained life in Ireland. In
the allegorical narrative, however, Juanito the bullfighter and Mary the bull know
exactly what they are doing. The scene takes place in three hours, possibly to underline the fact that there are also three parts to the final stage of the bullfight, with
the bull *parado*, *levantado*, and *aplomado*. Following the long preparation of the
first acts, then, "The Good Basque Country" marks the final meeting of bull and
bullfighter. As they both know, this is a fight to the death, the moment of truth
("now they found courage to look at each other with deliberation," 303). The bullfighter is holding a "cape" ("he pulled rugs out of the car"—304) and knows where
he wants the bull ("come this way"—304). With his cape he attempts to direct the
bull to a certain spot, as the pass known as a *verónica* sometimes does ("He flung
the rugs under the tree"—305). The *verónica*, Hemingway explains, it is so called
"because the cape was originally grasped in the two hands in the manner in which
Saint Veronica is shown in religious paintings to have held the napkin with which
she wiped the face of Christ" (*Death* 459–60); the function of this pass is to root
the bull to the spot. The bull does not take this cue, and it is *levantado*—"risen,"
"on its feet," or "lofty" in bullfighting terms ("but she didn't sit down," *Mary*
304). The bull instead forces the bullfighter to come to where the bull is, in order
to charge ("She put her arms around him and pulled his head down for her kiss"—
304). He shakes himself away ("he moved, and murmured uneasily into her hair"—
305) and considers what to do ("He tilted his head back gently and searched her
face"—305). The bull takes its favored place and is rooted to that spot, *parado*—
"stopped" in bullfighting terms ("She dropped on her knees on the rug, and
held her arms to him. / 'Come here,' she said,"—304). The bullfighter is reluctant
to match her move, but appearing to accept the bull's terms apprehensively gets
closer and kneels by the bull ("He went on his knees beside her, but hesitatingly"—
305) to lure the bull towards him ("He still knelt motionless and without touching
her"—306). The bull has taken a favored spot, a *querencia*—"loving," "want," or
"fondness" in bullfighting terms (see O'Brien *Spain* 139)—and will not move from
its position close to the barrier ("She had moved a little from him, and leant against
the tree-trunk"—*Mary* 306). The bullfighter makes up his mind to go for the
killing ("I'm going to take you"—307), gets as close to the bull as he can, and
manages to get the bull in position, *aplomado*—"leaden," "exhausted" in bullfighting terms ("They clung together trembling. Juanito kissed her eyes and ears and
throat and though Mary burned to kiss him too, intuition told her to lie still awhile,
to let him love her.... He began to undress her, gently and kindly"—307–8). The
bullfighter kills the bull without hesitation by thrusting his sword in the precise
place ("He took her quickly and bravely. The pain made her cry out and writhe in
shock, but he held her hard against him and in great love compelled her to endure
it. He felt the sweat of pain break over all the silk of her body"—308).

In terms of lovemaking, Juanito's technique is rather poor, but in terms of bullfighting, the matador has responded to the bull's idiosyncrasies with the courage and skill required for the job. Mary, a strong, brave, and intelligent bull, is determined to "kill or be killed" there and then. Juanito may have dreams of a life together, but this bull will not go back to the *toril* to wait for a new encounter with another, less honorable bullfighter. In psychological terms, her *querencia*/desire/determination is unshakeable. Hemingway goes through some detail as to the possible course of action for a matador that cannot persuade a bull to leave a *querencia*, when all attempts have failed. "But if the matador, impatient, finally says, 'Alright, if he wants to die there let him die there,' and goes in to kill, that will probably be the last thing he will remember until he comes down out of the air with or without a horn wound" because "the bull will watch him as he comes in, will knock out the *muleta* and sword, and will catch the man every time"; while, if the bull doesn't leave his *querencia* "the matador is justified in killing the bull in any way that least exposes the man," that is, "*The thing to do is to kill him quickly, not well,* for a bull who knows how to use his horns and who cannot be made to leave his *querencia* is as dangerous for the man to come within range of as a rattlesnake and it is impossible to make a bullfight with" (emphasis added, *Death* 153). In this light, the fact that Juanito "took her quickly and bravely" acquires radically different connotations. This is the bullfighter's only option if he is to save his life. The danger posed by Mary the bull is a very real one, as Juanito himself intimates just before he attempts the killing: "You seem so terrifyingly beautiful, you're so artless and innocent and heavenly that I have fooled myself that you are the sort of myth that might ruin any man, however true, however virtuous!"; yet, Juanito wonders, "[I]s that so? Are you a fatal exception that makes splinters of everything normal?" (*Mary* 307). As a lover, Mary may appear resigned not to experience any pleasure to a ludicrous extent; for example: "though Mary burnt to kiss him too, intuition told her to lie still awhile" (307). However, in bullfighting terms this is not self-imposed passivity, rather it corresponds to the stage at which the bull is *parado*, a moment when, as Hemingway puts it: "The bull has no desire to play, only to kill" (*Death* 147). Nothing could show more clearly the gulf between the realist narrative and the surrealist transformation taking place before our eyes.

When the coupling is consummated, the scene divides again in two very different narratives. Hemingway explains that the work of an able bullfighter who becomes too arrogant in "the moment of truth" will end in "an anticlimax or a goring" (239; see also 234). And that may be just what happens in the novel, which refers to the death of Don Pablo as the "anticlimax" to Juanito and Mary's lovemaking (*Mary* 338). In another sense, Hemingway also explains, "the sword business" is always "a not particularly interesting anticlimax" (*Death* 234) to good *muleta* work, until one gets to know the peculiar difficulties and skills associated with the killing of the bull. In sexual terms, Juanito's quick "sword business" has the effect of undoing any allure he may have had up to that point. Hemingway further recollects of his first bullfights: "knowing nothing about it, I thought perhaps it was really an anticlimax and that the people who spoke and wrote highly of the killing of the bull in bullfighting were merely liars" (ibid., 234).

In *Farewell Spain*, Kate O'Brien highlights the performances of two famous bullfighters, Juan Belmonte and Ignacio Sánchez Mejías. According to Hemingway: "The increasing importance and demand for the style of cape work and work with the *muleta* ... was first invented, or perfected, by Juan Belmonte" (*Death* 175). Belmonte could be the model for the bullfighter Pronceda in *Mary Lavelle* (see *Mary* 187; *Spain* 133), who may be intended to mirror Agatha's temperament. We may therefore consider Agatha's gravity and self-containment, and Juanito's speed and bravery, as parallels of the two bullfighting styles hailed in the novel. One of the most distinctive features of the sex scene in *Mary Lavelle* is the fact that the lovers kneel facing each other and linger in that position. In *Farewell Spain*, O'Brien recalls seeing the bullfighter Mejías in Bilbo "on the Sunday before he got his last and fatal *cornada* [horn wound] in Coruña," in 1934, and she chooses to highlight the fact that "He took his bull kneeling," of immediate resonance to those who, having read *Mary Lavelle*, may remember the sex scene. Possibly laughing under her breath, O'Brien adds, "that's not particularly interesting to watch," although "for a man no longer young or quick it was tricky," and continues: "[H]e was so closely held between the *barrera* [barrier] and the horn that the 'fans' cried out imploring him to forbear. A swaggerer perhaps, but gay and disarming that afternoon" (*Spain* 204–5). In the travelogue, O'Brien protests that "Hemingway is very hard on Mejías" (*Spain* 204), but in fact Hemingway merely accused him of displaying his bravery (see *Death* 64), which is about the mildest criticism he bestows in the book, so this may be an excuse for O'Brien to mention them both. Also, Mejías did not die in La Coruña, but in the plaza of Manzanares, near Madrid, and given that his death was a national event, the fan that O'Brien was would have remembered if she had seen him the week before he was killed. Given her compulsive intertextuality, it wouldn't be beyond O'Brien to include a glaring error in her account in order to point to its fictional shadow image, connecting the travelogue and the novel as two joint hemispheres with reverse polarity, held together by the same force. In the novel, Juanito did, as we know, kneel by Mary, who had placed herself in a certain spot, leaning against the natural barrier of the tree, from where she drew her lover to her.

Why would O'Brien suggest Mejías as a model for Juanito? The main reason is likely to be the fact that Mejías died shortly after the performance she describes, just as the death of Don Pablo is the aftermath of "The Good Basque Country." But there is more to attract O'Brien's interest. A legend in his lifetime, Ignacio Sánchez Mejías (b. 1891, d. 1934) seemed to have a universal sex-appeal, with many commentators referring to his androgyny. He had an extremely close relationship with the (equally famous) bullfighter Joselito which we may describe as homosocial. Most relevantly, Mejías was also a writer and an intellectual, having produced a number of experimental plays, and having hosted the first meeting of the enormously influential group of poets that became known as the Generación del 27. The meeting was intended to celebrate the centenary of the poet Luis de Góngora, a gesture that symbolized their interest in a return to formalism, and often read as a reaction to the intellectualism of the Generación del 98 that preceded them (much as Juanito challenges Don Pablo's beliefs). Many of the members of the group were close to surrealism. Deeply affected by the death of Mejías, his friends the poets Rafael Alberti and Federico García Lorca wrote elegies that have become part of canonical literature.

Yet despite all this, the sex scene in *Mary Lavelle* is not a homage to Mejías' courage, nor a tribute to Hemingway's knowledge, nor even primarily a metaphor for the protagonist's seduction by Spain. "The moment of truth" in "The Good Basque Country" is both a realistically depicted queer heterosexual sexual encounter *and* a carefully crafted allegory of a lethal confrontation. It is in the blatant "staging" of the scene that the sexual/aesthetic freedom to rewrite an old script becomes apparent. If the sex scene is likened to a bullfight — and this is clear — who has survived the encounter? Not Juanito. Besides being the only one of the pair to have experienced the "little death" of orgasm, we learn that his double Don Pablo has been "mortally wounded" at exactly the same time, in the retrospectively narrated chapter "Anguish of the Breast," which follows "The Good Basque Country" in the novel: "Every time [Juanito] had met [Mary's] eyes in the last forty hours he had known that she was thinking, not hysterically, but in realistic pity and regret, of how his father had spent the hours of their stolen love in holding off death while he waited for his dallying son," and the lovers knew that this was "their love's fantastic, heavy anticlimax" (338). Mary is conferred a matador's cape in the next and final chapter, clearly indicating that she has graduated in Agency. She leaves Altorno/Bilbo with the cape on her lap, not in her trunk — to be kept ready at all times. She has earned it, having learned that there's only one thing to do with freedom, with life: "it must be faced" (140).

It is possible to read the scene as ascribing a momentous quasi-mythical quality to the archetypal heterosexual sexual initiation in terms of identity, in line with Martin Heidegger's famous equating of the moment of death (at the end of an individual's lifespan) to the moment of truth. It is also possible, however, to see "The Good Basque Country" chapter as an undermining of the emotional/psychological value often ascribed to loss of virginity in women. As we have seen, Hemingway points out that one of the main changes in modern bullfighting is "the pardoning of deficiency in killing of a matador who is an artist with the cape and *muleta*," to the extent that the bullfighter's performance immediately preceding the killing "has become almost as much a moment of truth as the killing ever was" (*Death* 175). In other words, in *Mary Lavelle* the sexual encounter may be a climax in terms of plot, perhaps even in terms of identity development, but it is not the peak in the romance narrative. Juanito's standing as romantic hero suffers if graded in terms of his final performance. It is in Juanito and Mary's falling in love, and in their parallel struggle with their consciences, where the value of their romantic pairing of equals (as bull and bullfighter) lies. General ignorance in sexual matters, decrepit notions of women's and men's roles, and an inordinate historical valuing of virginity, contribute to the sexual encounter in the novel coming across as a sordid affair. Some of the stylistic nuances in the chapter seem designed to disguise that fact, yet other features seem designed to acknowledge it. In a critical assessment of the scene, however, placing too much emphasis on Juanito's incompetence is unhelpful. Mary herself seeks what she expects to be an ordeal and undergoes it in fully compliant mode. For many women, loss of virginity is an event associated with misery, pain, and horror. The emphasis on pain in the scene doesn't do anything to dispel that notion.

Mary's expectations, her decisions, her experience, happen in a specific cultural and historical context. There is nothing "natural" about lovemaking, an activity that must be learned and is subject to cultural and historical frameworks. Even the biological potential for female orgasm is tied to social construction, as Margaret Mead showed when comparing the range of approaches to women's sexual pleasure in a number of cultures (see *Male* 203–209). In the sexually conservative climate of the 1930s in the West, virginity was required in marriageable women, and discussion of sexual matters was still circumscribed to the medical profession, with a pervading ignorance, particularly crippling women, being encouraged by the Catholic church in countries under its influence. Kate O'Brien set herself the difficult task of elevating the role of individual women — if they have no choice in the "how," they may still have a choice in the "when" (and the "with whom") — while idealizing the parity of the lovers as far as the text would allow and introducing a new element: the danger posed by an assertive woman to the emotional integrity of a man. In turning Mary from woman to fighting bull, O'Brien privileges temperament over knowledge and morality. After the moment of truth, of reality, Mary is the one who has a realistic plan; after the bloody ceremony, Mary is the one who, strikingly, *laughs* at *Juanito's* innocence (see 312). In a sense, neither lover is mortally wounded in the scene; rather, the final victim may just be the traditional romance narrative.

Four

Modernism

Introduction: Avant-garde

Kate O'Brien was an experimenter, and her work reflected the new approaches to fiction that were being tried out in her time. Modernism is linked by critics to artistic experimentation, which is in turn assumed to equate difficulty and, inevitably, elitism. O'Brien experimented with genres, structure, themes, voice, writing style. She chose to do so in a way that, by and large, only alienated one section of her potential readership: literary critics. Modernist experimentation has been understood in the narrowest possible terms, to the exclusion of genre, plot, theme, narratorial voice, subtext, the merging of artistic mediums, and the use of devices such as personification and allegory, and without taking account of "vernacular modernisms," Miriam Bratu Hansen's useful concept. On the other hand, a male-dominated academia prioritized male-authored texts, claiming that stylistic features were the only selection criteria, but the telling omissions from the curriculum only highlighted the internal contradictions of a politics of exclusion. Technically challenging works such as Virginia Woolf's *The Waves* (1931) and Djurna Barnes's *Nightwood* (1936), for example, were not studied until the 1980s. Modernism has long been the most respected area among scholars of literature. To highlight the modernist aspects of *Mary Lavelle* cannot be justified as an attempt to "upgrade" O'Brien's work, but it is a neglected and crucial task in its contextualization.

Kate O'Brien's popularity worked against her inclusion in the curriculum. The librarians in charge of the Kate O'Brien Papers in Limerick always tell their visitors about the film *Brief Encounter* (Dir. David Lean 1945), where the heroine pops into her local library to get "the new Kate O'Brien" which she has reserved, a reference that the audience at large was assumed to understand. In the film, the reference is a subtle indication of the "forbidden-love story" about to unfold, and it suggests that this Kate O'Brien fan has a framework for the ethical issues she will confront in the narrative. Declan Kiberd believes that "While it is true that O'Brien deployed some of the methods of popular romantic fiction, she spliced them with those of the art novel in a fashion which ensured that she could never make much money" (*Classics* 557). O'Brien's resistance to provide "sellable" novel titles that pleased her publishers, despite their pressure, may just be a case in point. For example, *The Anteroom* was originally titled *Triduum*, and *That Lady* was first *For One Sweet Grape* (she managed to retain it for the American edition) and later *Esa Señora* (see Hayes 27, 8). And yet, despite her lack of interest in marketability, on one occasion O'Brien herself answered the question of why she wrote what she wrote by laconically referring to "Pounds, Shillings and Pence" (quoted in Walshe "Note" 11).

According to Lorna Reynolds, *Without My Cloak* was the only best seller of O'Brien and *Mary Lavelle* "was never popular" (*Kate* 62). However, throughout her career she was popular *enough* to make a living, supplementing the income from book sales with journalism since the late 1930s. After 1950 (when O'Brien bought a house in the West of Ireland) both her income and her popularity steadily diminished and, as we know, she died in poverty and relative obscurity, having depended on the generosity of friends and family in her later years. By the 1970s all her books were out of print, and she had disappeared from the critical radar, only to make it back onto the shelves with the flourishing of feminist publishing in the next decade. Despite the uneven popularity of her work, O'Brien is constantly described as a "popular novelist," on account of her themes and style. Aligned to the "family saga" and the "romance" genres, part of the construction of O'Brien as popular by critics has to do with preconceptions of women's writing, and what critics see as her dependence on (rather than her subversion of) popular genres.

In 1946, Vivian Mercier described O'Brien as "perhaps the ablest practitioner of Romance in the English language" (quoted by Hayes 3). Her "idiosyncratic" approach to Romance has also been remarked. Anthony Roche, for example, referring to *The Anteroom*, describes the frustrated affair in the novel as "anything but the conventional romance it has sometimes been taken as, [given] the extent to which it challenges rather than indulges the romanticism with which it engages" ("Anteroom" 93). Elisabeth M. Hayes actually uses a quote from *Mary Lavelle* to make the same point, bringing in the novel's reference to "the mighty lie of Romantic passion" (see Hayes 39). Anne Fogarty claims that "Kate O'Brien's novels may be described as a fusion of the conventions of romance and realism," only to add that "[u]ncomfortably, they straddle these two modes" because "they ultimately refuse fully to accede to the rules of coherence and transparency which underwrite the structure of the *Bildungsroman* and of the romance novel," so that "by bringing the *Bildungsroman*, a literary genre which is a product of high culture, into contact with women's romance, a form of popular fiction, O'Brien creates an idiosyncratic literary space of her own" (emphasis in original, "Desire" 104). Declan Kiberd, following Fogarty, puts it in a slightly different way: "In the space she occupies between high and popular art, she opens up a zone of ambiguity in which an unprecedented knowledge may become possible" (*Classics* 567–8). One of the least acknowledged facts about O'Brien is her insistence in mixing genres and forms.

If *Farewell Spain* is a political travelogue and *The Anteroom* is a novel-play, *Mary Lavelle* is a documentary-autobiography-romance-anticapitalist novel, and these terms are not exhaustive. Trans-genre approaches were part of the experiments of modernist writers. Virginia Woolf's novel-essay *The Years*, T.S. Eliot's play-poem *The Wasteland*, or James Joyce's catechism-based chapter in *Ulysses* are just three examples, while Oscar Wilde's non-dramatic works provide earlier instances of the same restlessness with given form. The Generación del Noventayocho, a group O'Brien has much in common with as we have seen, also experimented with genres frequently. Arguably, most modernist texts included some merging of genres and forms

This willingness to "contaminate" the narrative space is reflected in, among other things, the "eclectic web of intertextual references" (Fogarty "Desire" 104) in Kate O'Brien's work. As Fogarty notes, "O'Brien's novels seem to draw indiscriminately *and willfully* on a self-constructed artistic canon, thereby ignoring any traditional separation of so-called high art from the domain of popular entertainment" (emphasis added, "Desire 104). *Mary Lavelle* includes references to *Don Quixote* and *Pepita Jimenez*, two novels that cross the divide between the traditional academic canon and the popular canon in Spanish literature; the English pastoral poem that is so crucial to the development of the romance narrative, and the records played by the Areavagas, are further examples. The mixture seems to me to be quite deliberate. O'Brien's own understanding of avant-garde may be illuminating in this context. In a lecture of 1966, she claimed that Wilde, Shaw, Yeats, Synge, O'Casey, Joyce, and Beckett were "sheer *Avant-Garde* unschooled Avant-Garde [sic]. Simply the thing itself—accidental. Individual—a new way of crying out loud" (emphasis in original). The work of those listed is the staple of the traditional academic canon, but O'Brien in fact opened her lecture by describing Douglas Hyde's translations of Irish language poetry as avant-garde and, later, among the then new-coming writers, she also listed the work of Edna O'Brien, more noted for its groundbreaking thematic concerns than for its technical experimentation. The inclusion of Douglas Hyde and Edna O'Brien here is a radical move. In the lecture, Kate O'Brien makes it clear that avant-garde is not just about style. According to her, Jean-Paul Sartre was for years "the leading European Avant-Gardiste (not in the *art* of writing, not at all, but as a moralist, and as a fearless censor of social thought, a director of society)." Sartre is "a *thinking* and dedicated Avant-Gardiste," comparable to Swift, O'Brien says: "In Swift, didn't Ireland produce an all-out Avant-Gardiste, whose anger and contempt for society were a new assault, but whose prose was also of a new, pristine mint?" (emphasis in original, ibid.). Sartre was a novelist as well as a philosopher, and the claim that his abilities as *writer* are "not at all" noteworthy effectively changes the goalposts of literary merit.

In an article of 1965 titled "Irish Writers and Europe," O'Brien clarified what she meant, by describing "writing to a high standard" as "non-parochial and free" (37). In a sense, O'Brien's redefinitions of *avant-gardism* and *high standards* make obsolete the distinction between schools or movements such as modernism and realism, bypassing the divide between genres, between styles, between translation and original work, between fiction and nonfiction. O'Brien is on the side of the new, of the groundbreaking, whatever shape it may take. O'Brien's lecture appears to contradict her endorsement of Walter Pater's aesthetics of "manifest non-utilitarianism" in *Farewell Spain* (13). Yet style may also be a qualifier to the avant-garde. It is often noted that she was among the first to enthusiastically receive the work of Samuel Beckett, in her review of *Murphy* in March 1938. The review highlights the effect of *Murphy* on certain readers, as aesthetic and intellectual stimulant, but it makes no claims to the book's "objective" value: "It truly is magnificent and a treasure — if you like it. Quite useless, quite idiotic, if you don't. It is a sweeping, bold record of an adventure in the soul; it is erudite, allusive, brilliant, impudent and rude" (quoted in Michael O'Toole "Writing" 132).

Opening an essay of 2004 titled "Regendering Modernism," Gerardine Meaney points out that between 1922 and 1960, "Irish fiction was dominated by an *avant-garde* writing elsewhere and the local dominance of the short story. Attention to the non-canonical fiction of women during the period, however, reveals a literature that exceeds this paradigm" (67). Discussing O'Brien's last novel, Meaney sees the possibility of modernist thematic concerns, even in the absence of modernist style ("Modernism" 81). The distinction is very useful, yet, regarding O'Brien, this is a false dichotomy. She was not just attentive to the intellectual avant-garde in general, but she paid particular attention to stylistic experimentation among her contemporaries (e.g., Proust, Joyce and Woolf). In *Mary Lavelle*, O'Brien included a number of references to Proust, in obsessively repeated mentions to the exhaustion and weariness of Mary and Pablo (see for example 248, 287, 289), as well as their equally obsessive investment in the role of memory (see also *Spain* 208; *My Ireland* 22, 36), and in the claim that Mary and Luisa felt an instant empathy because "Greek always recognizes Greek." *Sodom and Gomorrah* was published in 1922, the year of Mary's visit to Altorno. In a famous passage of Proust's novel, the narrator, prompted by the discovery that a gentleman of his acquaintance is in fact a woman, launches into a lengthy description of the homosexual "race of beings" (Proust 18), who form "a freemasonry far more extensive, more effective and less suspected than that of the lodges, for it rests on an identity of tastes, of habits, of dangers, of apprenticeship, of knowledge, of commerce and of vocabulary" (20–1); this is a freemasonry, the narrator continues, "in which even the members who do not wish to know one another at once recognize one another" (21). The reader of *Mary Lavelle* may wonder why would Mary and Luisa recognize each other, and the meditations of Proust's narrator, extended for several pages, offer the answer. In the words of Eve Sedgwick, Proust presents "*the spectacle of the closet as the truth of the homosexual*" (emphasis in original, *Epistemology* 231). But there are no closets in O'Brien, despite her investment in the idea of recognition. In *As Music and Splendour*, the opera divas Clarabelle and Luisa can see, through their Orpheo-and-Eurydice disguise, "their one true dress wherein they recognized each other," and so they are able to "sing as if their very singing was a kind of Greek, immortal light" (*Music* 110).

James Cahalan was the first to point out that Joyce's *Portrait of the Artist as a Young Man* is also "echoed at several points" by O'Brien in *The Land of Spices* (*Novel* 208, 217). I agree with Ann Owens Weekes, who believes that O'Brien mirrors Joyce "in a parodic female fashion," in a "deliberately revisionist treatment" (122, 123). O'Brien goes further than "echoing" Joyce, in that she actually imitates his style by using long and meandering sentences to capture Ana's thoughts, for example in the scene that reworks the "girl on the beach" scene, which had inspired Daedalus to develop an aesthetic theory: "Now, however, she saw Pilar in a new way. She became aware of her and of the moment on a plane of perception which was strange to her" and "saw her, it seemed, in isolation and in a new sphere, yet one made up of broken symbols from their common life and which took its light from the simplicity of shared associations"; to Ana, this "foolish school-girl" became "an exquisite challenge to creativeness; she saw Pilar as a glimpse, as if she were a line from a lost immortal; she saw her ironically, delightedly, as a motive in art" (O'Brien *Land* 271–2; see also the references to *Ulysses* in O'Brien *Wanderer* 59–60).

It is not the only time this occurs in Kate O'Brien. The relevance of Virginia Woolf's work to O'Brien's has not been explored, yet she was a major influence, and there are important and numerous intertextual references to her books in O'Brien. *Pray for the Wanderer* includes a description of Bloomsbury as "an esoteric entity" and what may well be a crude stab at Virginia's unconventional sexuality (217; see 139)—O'Brien's partner Margaret "Stephie" Stephens had been a secretary of Virginia Woolf's friend Maynard Keynes (Walshe "Irelands" 42), her partner E.M. Delafield and her friend Theodora Bosanquet had been published in the Woolfs' small press, and Kate herself had lived for a number of years in Gordon square in London, where the Woolfs and other people in their circle had lived. If in 1938 Kate O'Brien seems somewhat hostile to Virginia Woolf and the "Bloomsbury Group" she is associated with (Bloomsburyphobia became a sport for much of the twentieth century— see Marler), by 1953 O'Brien is paying homage to Woolf in one of her most daring and most misunderstood books. Just over a decade after Woolf's death, *The Flower of May* performs a curious experiment, by bringing together some of her more memorable creations, re-fictionalized. For example, the protagonist's mother, Julia, dying by a lighthouse (Mrs. Ramsay was based on Woolf's mother, Julia), a mermaid-like Fanny (same imagery as Rhoda), or a determined and eccentric aunt Eleanor (sounding like Eleanor Pargiter). *The Flower of May* mainly rewrites *To the Lighthouse* (Nicole O'Connor also detects links to *Orlando*— see Walshe *Kate* 123), while *Mrs. Dalloway* is revisited in O'Brien's last novel. In addition, *As Music and Splendour* also mimics Woolf's style at several points. For example, there is an unmistakeable reference to *The Waves* when the five old friends in O'Brien's novel sit down at a restaurant and "as moths fluttered between the dreaming faces" and "the street noises beyond the open door ebbed down to the singing of one child — the secret thoughts of four at least of the sippers of Frascati moved shadowily in ironic parallels" (*Music* 266). Four different interior monologues follow, each opening with the question "How will it be ... [here and now]?" (267 — also reminiscent of *The Years*). Certainly in these two examples about Joyce and Woolf (and perhaps less clearly in the links to Proust), O'Brien seems to be saying, and *showing*, that although she could have written a more experimental prose, she chose not to do so. Why then, pepper her narratives with these disruptive references to extreme examples of modernist experimentation? To borrow Bernard Smith's distinction in the visual arts, perhaps Kate O'Brien, rather than an innovator, was a "courier of the new" (323), bringing the reader of popular fiction into contact with the discoveries of the avant-garde.

O'Brien did not just insert high modernist fragments in her realist narratives, however. The whole of *The Land of Spices* can be seen as a response to Joyce's first novel, an attempt to provide a "Portrait of the Artist as a Young Woman." Similarly, the whole of *As Music and Splendour* can be seen as a response to *Mrs. Dalloway*, a lesbianization of the original text. Most revealingly, in *As Music and Splendour* the double of the autobiographical Clare, the composer Thomas Evans, seems partly devised to provide an explanation of O'Brien's technical choices throughout her career. Thomas may be partly modeled on T.S. Eliot (there is also an intriguing link to Cecil Day-Lewis — see Jordan "First Lady" 229), and perhaps even on Thomas Vaugham, the alchemist twin of the poet Henry Vaugham (who is relevant to *The Land of Spices*). Clare sings other people's compositions, interpreting them according to her individual taste, while Thomas is a composer himself, and his most radical piece, "Songs for Clare," is unmistakably modernist. The composition is allegedly inspired by a group of acacia trees they had both admired once, perhaps related to the acacia trees highlighted in Mary Lavelle's visit to Madrid (see *Mary* 228), but Clare sees the "twelve randomly worded songs" and wonders, "Where on earth are those poor little acacias?" The songs are breathtakingly complex in execution: "They were beautiful. They were difficult to get into outline at first; their design seemed arbitrary, and too firm and eccentric for the basic inspiration suggested in the dedication" (*Music* 348). Initially annoyed by "the arbitrariness of arrangement," which seems "arrogance being silly," Clare learns, "stumblingly, to find her way in their firm, clean structure" (348–9). The twelve songs, Clare realizes, are an idiosyncratic description of Rome on a given day, and an expression of "the contradictory and random-true emotions of an individual [Clare], to which Rome does not listen" (*Music* 348–9). Clare's analysis of Thomas's songs, like Anna's epiphany in *The Land of Spices*, is crucially placed at the very end of the novel, in a narrative turn that provides a conceptual and stylistic grand finale.

The "wandering Thomas" (*Music* 302)—clearly a reference to the autobiographic novelist Tom of *Pray for the wanderer*—is not so different from the developing artist Clare. "'I'm an actress—I'm a rogue and a vagabond,'" she says, and he replies, "'[Y]ou are becoming an interpreter of the world — in one medium'" (*Music* 99). In *As Music and Splendour*, artistic training is also related to sexual development, here suggested in a lesbian Clare—"to which Rome does not listen," and it is also in a context of sexual and emotional autonomy that the "performer" has an alter ego in the "composer." In the context of O'Brien's aesthetic allegiances as a writer, however, Clare (O'Brien's "realist" style) is the one who carries us through the novel, while Thomas (O'Brien's high modernism) is a secondary character, her shadow. Yet there is no getting over the fact that Clare and Thomas, as the novel puts it, are like "twins" (the idea is repeated throughout the text, starting at page 54). They are one and the same, like the two O'Briens.

Modernist Themes

SETTING

Mary Lavelle is the only O'Brien novel set in its entirety in an urban center, yet this is not deemed relevant in accounts of her work. The city is one of the main protagonists in *Mary Lavelle*, a book which is partly a documentary on life in Bilbo/Altorno in 1922. Altorno is characterized by its being "chaotic," which, Wanda Balzano noted in a paper of 2002, points to modernism, as does the very idea of narrative simultaneity, which is so important to the structure of O'Brien's novel ("Question"). Here is one example of urban effervescence:

> It was nearly eight o'clock. She paid her bill and walked out.
> She did not take the train, however. She turned into the racketing mazes of old Altorno. In Spain the clocks are not put on in summer and at this hour the town, shut in by its obliterated hills and velvety, dim-starred sky, was fiercely illumined and shadowed, through plane-trees, archways and shop windows, by torrents of white electric light. It was the noisiest of Spanish hours, the pleasure hour before supper, when girls paraded, five and six together, singing, when every café chair was filled and every beggar, shoeblack and seller of lottery tickets was crying out his trade. Tram-bells clanged excitedly, motor-horns sounded and policemen blew their whistles; evening papers were yelled on every corner, young men guffawed at the girls and tried to sing flamenco; the bands were tuning up in all the squares [*Mary* 187–8].

No other urban center plays as important a part in an O'Brien novel. A frequent traveler, she singled out Bilbo and Milan as the most overwhelming cities she had visited, in moral and aesthetic terms— she recalled being "disgusted" when walking through "Milan's very modern, industrialised suburbs" (*Ireland* 19). The specific "disgust" of O'Brien is with patent industrialization, thrown into relief by its surrounding capitalist display. Together with Bilbo and Milan, New York was also set up by O'Brien as a polar opposite to the visual and aural restraint of Irish cities and towns in her first novel, *Without My Cloak*. As we have seen, other literary visitors to New York experienced an immediate adverse reaction, and they translated the experience into modernist terms.

In this context, it is interesting that Mary likes Madrid instantly, whereas she has to "get to know" Altorno before she can appreciate its "inner beauty." Yet Bilbo/Altorno also has a small-town quality. Lavelle/O'Brien had a chance to experience it, by virtue of residing in the quaint suburb of Cabantes/Portugalete and by her regular visits to the city's café Alemán/Suizo, for example. This café, so important in the novel, was originally situated in the somewhat self-enclosed old quarter, a part of the city circled by a meander of the river and backed by mountains. A small, concentrated maze of narrow streets and tall buildings, this area of Bilbo/Altorno, known as "the seven streets" ("Zazpi Kale" or "Las Siete Calles"), remains the liveliest part of the city and today it still feels like a miniature town. As a woman born in Artekale (near where the original café Alemán was situated) recalled, in the 1930s and 1940s each street had its own character, so that Artekale street (in Basque, "the street in between"), for example, had a greater concentration of Basque speakers, its own co-op shop, and a majority of Basque nationalist households (Jone Mentxaka Ugalde, in conversation June 10, 2004).

In modernist accounts of city life, such as those in Woolf's *Mrs. Dalloway* and Joyce's *Ulysses*, the protagonists mirror the complexity of their surroundings in their inner being. It is not evident whether this happens by a process of osmosis, or if the intricacy of urban living is simply a useful metaphor for the convoluted turns of thought and feeling in the characters. What is clear in the account of Mary's acquaintance with Altorno/Bilbo is that she soon begins to perceive it as a place of possibility, of change, and this is a seductive prospect for her. It is not a coincidence that, as Mary grows to appreciate the inner beauty in her surroundings, she is "ready" to fall in love with Juanito, a driven, complex, "untidy" man, who is not "an Adonis" (175). The change doesn't take long, as we discover when Mary observes the city from Allera/Begoña, a hill in the old quarter, for the first time.

> "It's a filthy old town, Altorno," said O'Toole.
> "That's true," said Mary, in tired, unwary dreaminess.
> The river, twisting under mine-gashed hills, past furnaces, churches and coalyards to where Torcal and Cabantes waited, and at their elbows the sea; the smoke, the foundry frames, the yellow trams; the convents with grilled windows; sinking roofs of slums, the old brown campaniles and leafy plazas—Mary looked down with gentle eyes—
> "I believe you like the hole," said O'Toole [195].

The dominant feature in the landscape of Bilbo is the Ibailzabal (or Nervión), a perennially dirty river, busy with trading ships. This tidal river serves as a symbol of life in *Mary Lavelle*. Far from an idealized model of orderly motion towards a fateful destination, the river becomes a modernist vision of the self as site of exchange, of accumulation, of unpredictability.

> By living outwardly for long enough and with determination, all would be restored. A bad dream would vanish. A memory, a sensation which already sometimes seemed so unreal and fantastic that perhaps it was indeed only a dream, would be rubbed away, lost, misshapen by the persistent loading up and tossing about over its face of every kind of rag, bone, and bottle from the rest of life [O'Brien *Mary* 202].

INNER SELF

If Altorno/Bilbo is known for its blast furnaces (one of the most important, Altos Hornos, giving the fictional name to the city in the novel) and steel foundries, the narrator leaves no doubt as to the specific effect this industrial environment has, when Mary and Luisa are contrasted. Both equally beautiful, they differ in the fact that while Mary is unselfconscious to an extreme, Luisa is quite the opposite, "far too highly civilised to make a parade of civilisation" (151–2). Mary dresses simply, but Luisa's studied simplicity betrays "the true ring of *steel*" (emphasis added, 151). Yet Mary is not immune to another "civilising" force, the "ulcerat[ing]" effect of love, which forces her to remold herself internally: "Five days could change the perfectly well-known, the simple valley of oneself, into a place of circus and buffoonery, where nothing kept its stance or features for two consecutive seconds" (186). This is a reference to the local urbanization process since, in the nineteenth century, as we will discuss later in more detail, Bilbo/Altorno turned from a "valley" into a "circus." This industrialized city is therefore the ideal mise-en-scène and prompter to *the self in motion*, a key modernist preoccupation. Arguably, the main drive behind modernist topics and techniques was in fact the exploration/expression of the inner workings and mutability of the mind, a theme only partially explored in earlier fiction.

Faint suggestions of modernism have been made occasionally by other O'Brien critics (see Roche "Anteroom" 91; Kiberd *Classics* 562). Gerardine Meaney pointed out in a 1997 essay, with a conviction unmatched by any other critic, that Kate O'Brien's work "demands to be read, but rarely is read, as simultaneously but distinctly *Irish, modernist and feminist*" because "[t]he construction and re-definition of identity, the problematics of language and history for the feminine subject, and the relationship of sexuality to politics are recurrent factors in her work" (emphasis added, "Territory" 81). Every one of O'Brien's books, as we have seen, is laced with another modernist concern: sexuality. Works published in the same year as *Mary Lavelle*, such as Anaïs Nin's *House of Incest* and Djurna Barnes' *Nightwood*, clothed their illicit passions in technical challenges. O'Brien treated queer sexualities overtly — and then added a set of subtextual and allegoric tunneling. In *Mary Lavelle*, O'Brien's style may not *appear* to be consonant to that of her modernist contemporaries, but her themes certainly are.

For example, O'Brien often seeks to illustrate inner conflict/harmony and, to this end, she sometimes splits a character. This is an important technique in *Mary Lavelle*, although arguably it appears in its most extreme form in her last novel's doubling up of Clare and Thomas, which makes manifest the workings of internalized homophobia. The doubling up of characters has a long-standing tradition in literature. Otto Rank, for example, based his 1914 analysis of literary "doubling" on Freud's theory of narcissism, among other things linking paranoia and homosexuality. Eve Kosofsky Sedgwick (in her studies of 1980, 1985, and 1990) elaborated that link, identifying a group of novels that she describes as "paranoid Gothic," by which she means, as she summarized in 1990, "Romantic novels in which a male hero is in a close, usually murderous relation to another male figure, in some respects his 'double,' to whom he seems to be mentally transparent" (*Epistemology* 186). The use of "doubles," so often linked to canonical high modernist literature, was also familiar to the general public through popular film at the time. In Laurel and Hardy's 1933 film, *Twice Two*, the two actors play their usual characters as well as those characters' wives, while in *Our Relations*, for example, which opened the same year as *Mary Lavelle*, the "twins" of the respectable protagonists have the same personalities but different social selves (they are penniless sailors and womanizers). O'Brien herself highlighted the relevance of Laurel and Hardy, through her autobiographical Tom, a fan of the duo in *Pray for the Wanderer* (see 120). Clinical psychoanalysis was also familiar enough to audiences by 1938, for the Astaire and Rogers musical comedy *Carefree* to satirize it. O'Brien's punctual use of psychoanalytic terminology shows that she was somewhat acquainted with Freudian theory, which was so influential in the 1930s. However, her use of doubling to signal submerged sexuality incorporates, but also exceeds, the use of the method to signify narcissism, paranoia, the unconscious. Mary is truly very different from her double Agatha.

The voicing of a self-repressive impulse has continued to be used in homosexual bildungsromane. For example, in the 2000–1 season of the television series *ER*, the lesbian bildungsroman of Dr. Kerry Weaver was assisted by the introduction of a double, Maggie, a bipolar woman in denial about her condition. Another example is Monique Truong's novel of 2003, *The Book of Salt*, in which the protagonist (Gertrude Stein's cook) must finally silence the condemnatory voice of his father in his head: "Shut your mouth, Old Man, and let me finish. This is my story. I will tell it, and you will lie there mute" (196). In her last novel, Kate O'Brien borrowed the use of the double from Virginia Woolf's *Mrs. Dalloway*, with Clare as a "liberated" Clarissa and Thomas as Septimus, unable to process his homosexual feelings for his dead comrade, Evans. As we know, Clarissa and Septimus do not even meet in Woolf's novel. By contrast, the conflict between Clare Halvey and Thomas Evans is "brought out" onto the arena of the main text as an actual dialogue, which heightens the antagonism, the sense of inner dislocation. This self-conflicting relationship in *As Music and Splendour* is a variation on a theme, because Agatha and Mary may be considered to be the 1936 prototypes for Thomas and Clare, but *Mary Lavelle*'s subtext works on a different premise: Agatha is the woman Mary will become in 15 years' time, and their relationship is a figurative meeting of past/future selves. Mary is also in part a duplicate of Agnes in *The Anteroom*, but in a "quantum" sense (by which I mean part of a "multiplication" of selves reflecting different, mutually exclusive possibilities), with the earlier character offering an example of what Mary may have become, had she made different choices.

Lois Oppenheim claims that, in Samuel Beckett, "autotextuality, or the author's return to his own texts" is a constant occurrence, and that this "self-dialogue" is "as much deformative or detotalizing as constitutive. For it amounts to the endless undoing of every work posited as referent, the making of each a work-in-progress whose ultimate creation is forever thrown into question" (19). This perhaps "postmodern" method (see ibid., 18–21) is not the same as O'Brien's. For her, themes/plots/characters go back and forth, not forward. There is neither a totalizing nor a detotalizing impetus in her work. She is interested in how the subject comes into being (and at what cost), in many variations. If the autotextual, or intratextual, character of O'Brien's fictional doppelgangers—such as those in *Mary Lavelle*—proves one thing, it is that O'Brien is undoubtedly a modernist in her consistent preoccupation with psychology, and specifically with *the process* of identity formation and management.

Modernist Style

Stream of Consciousness

Kate O'Brien's use of point-of-view is worth considering. Declan Kiberd suggests that sometimes she seems to "object[t] to the modes of the realist novel which she cannot ultimately transcend" (*Classics* 562), and he goes on to claim that *The Anteroom* contains "brief" interior monologues "set within the consciousness of most of the major characters, so that the precedent set by *Ulysses* is honoured: but the device is so sparingly and so cautiously used ... as to constitute a regression to nineteenth-century modes" (562). Kiberd is discussing modernism in an Irish context, but it is important to keep in mind that the device of the interior monologue set within a consciousness was a precedent established by Dorothy Richardson and ultimately originated in the work of Henry James—in an Anglophone context. Elsewhere, the work of Fyodor Dostoevsky or Leopoldo Alas "Clarín," for example, is crucial to the development of the technique. *Mary Lavelle* is a novel in which little happens, and whatever does simply triggers a chain of reflections in the characters. It is not a plot-driven novel, but a thought-driven novel. Not coincidentally, O'Brien's favored narratorial point of view here is that of the modernists: third person free indirect style. Often claimed to have been invented by Jane Austen (one of Mary Lavelle's favorite authors; the Areavaga girls read and enjoy a copy of *Emma* belonging to Mary; see O'Brien *Mary* 178), the technique was adapted by modernists to provide access to the minds of characters without obvious mediation. This is the *dominant* mode in *Mary Lavelle*, which also includes full chapters of stream of consciousness: "Don Pablo" and "Anguish of the Breast." The fragments opening with structural introductions such as "Mary thought" (136) are in the minority, and most of the time we are confronted with undiluted reflections such as the following: "Well, she would be going home soon — away from this beginning of lies. That was well. She would be unhappy now with his [Juanito's] three sisters. Away from them it would be better; in Mellick there would be only John to deceive — or hurt. Only John" (255). The narrator's inserts, for the most part, supply information about the setting or the characters (see for example 217). Ostensibly irrelevant thought processes are allowed to flow, as in the following:

> Mary switched her thoughts with deliberation to the evening ahead of her. She must dine, she supposed, with Doña Cristina and Mademoiselle [after arriving in Madrid]. Depressing prospect. But as the meal would not be served until half-past ten, and as it was now not long after eight, perhaps she might go out — to a cinema, or to walk by the lake in the Retiro. Or perhaps she had better not. The two old ladies may be scandalised. Better stay in, write letters, and cause no trouble. She moved unhappily in her chair. She was really afraid of solitude nowadays, especially when it came swift on the heels of exhilaration. She wished she could go out again. How absurd a life! [225].

The chapter "Anguish of the Breast" charts the increasing agitation of Don Pablo: as he reflects on Mary's departure, begins to suspect she is having an affair with Juanito, and finally confirms his suspicions. This psychological progression is mirrored in stylistic terms, and the section moves from "traditional" narration ("Don Pablo sat and smoked on the stone bench of the terrace"— 315) to free indirect style ("Was he jealous and going crazy? Was he inventing the whole thing?"— 322) to direct rendering of thought ("Never mind"— 325).

ALLEGORY

In terms of narrative technique, then, *Mary Lavelle* has a strong investment in modernist techniques. As we saw earlier in the double narrative of the sex/bullfight scene, or in relation to the lesbian subtext, much depends on the reader's own priorities. The novel often presents simultaneous, sometimes contradictory, narrative strands, inviting the reader to *choose* one or the other, or both. In this context, it may be helpful to consider modernism as a "reading practice" as much as a literary practice (Gerardine Meaney, in conversation, February 14, 2007), which would also explain in part the failure of most critics to identify experimental/modernist/unorthodox technical and plot-related features in *Mary Lavelle*. Another reason for this failure may be that, at the level of language, the lyricism and grammatical obfuscation of the modernists do not play such important parts in this novel. When we encounter grammatical obfuscation, it is always an indication of subtext, not out of the sheer pleasure of word-play that one finds in other modernist texts.

In some ways, we can see the female characters in *Mary Lavelle* as representing different aesthetic approaches. Agatha is pure intellectual restlessness, Consuelo is all form and no substance, Mary's effortless beauty and outward simplicity hides complexity and intelligence, and the embodiment of agreeable modernity in the novel, Luisa, is sui generis because her mastery of fashion hides a passion for what is beyond the surface, and she is "bored by the flâneurs ... of fashionable Madrid" (162). Of the four women, Consuelo is derided, and Agatha and Luisa are admired by Mary but kept on the margins of the narrative. Mary may appear "a simpleton," but she is "a quite exceptional simpleton" (45). As a metaphor for the stylistic parameters of the text, this is as clear a statement as any. *Mary Lavelle* is all about reaching beyond the surface. In the same way, rather than word-play and linguistic experimentation as a source of pleasure and intellectual stimulation in itself, O'Brien is more interested in a layering of meanings. We could describe her as a "moralizing fabulist," the term she used to describe George Eliot in 1955. O'Brien was very interested in metaphor-based narratives, whether we refer to them as "fabled," "visionary" or "allegorical." Allegory and subtext were more suited to her aims and style than to those of other modernists. In fact, all her fiction suggests that she is primarily an allegorist.

As we have seen, allegory may be defined as realistically rendered elements presented in a non-realistic combination to illustrate a specific point or idea. We find the same in surrealism, with the difference that the juxtapositions appear random or absurd. The method transcends historical periods and artistic mediums. In painting, allegory is supposed to have reached a peak with Ambrogio Lorenzetti's Siena murals in the Renaissance, while William Blake (b. 1757, d. 1827) is the single artist most often linked to the method, but Modernism and allegory are particularly inter-related because of the modernist interest in the art of Medieval Europe, which was pronouncedly allegorical. Allegory has regularly beguiled modern artists whose production was not primarily allegoric. For example, O'Brien's contemporaries, the Irish painters Mary Swanzy, Sean Keating, and Beatrice Glenavy, may be perceived as stylistically irreconcilable, in that they are respectively cubist, realist, and surrealist, yet they all produced important allegorical works throughout their careers. In literature, contemporaries of Kate O'Brien such as Iris Murdoch and Sylvia Townsend Warner used the method. These two writers would appear to be even more difficult to classify than O'Brien; their often remarked "originality" is an indication of the critics' bewilderment. Of the three, perhaps Murdoch is the most extreme allegorist (although there is considerable variation in this prolific author). For example, it seems to me difficult — but not impossible — to read the 1963 *The Unicorn* as anything other than an existentialist metaphor for the construction of identity, or her Hiberno-English speaking Japanese Buddhist monks in the 1973 play *Three Arrows* as anything other than archetypes or symbols. Townsend Warner's 1938 *After the Death of Don Juan* is at least occasionally acknowledged by critics to be a political parable on fascism in Spain, while her *Summer Will Show*, published the same year as *Mary Lavelle*, continues to divide the critics: It was seen in 1990 as a "lesbian fantasy" by Terry Castle and in 1995 as a socialist realist novel by Janet Montefiore. Montefiore claims that these are "irreconcilable" readings (143), but I disagree — both readings are possible, simultaneously, a fact that links Warner to O'Brien and Murdoch.

O'Brien, Murdoch, and Townsend Warner shared a queer sensibility, and all three dealt with the topic of same-sex love in subtext and parable. As Graham Robb has noted, subterfuge and innuendo in gay writing were the "rhetorical equivalents of the inconveniences suffered by gay men and women in daily life: communicating with nods and winks, changing the loved one's gender for the purposes of conversation, pretending to share jokes about sexual deviance"; the literary equivalents of these strategies were radically different from allegory, which "could create a separate world in which whole dramas were acted out and even brought to satisfactory conclusions (215). Yet O'Brien, Murdoch, and Warner *also* dealt with homoeroticism explicitly, and we find queer strands in the plots of *As Music and Splendour*, *The Unicorn*, and *After the Death of Don Juan*, for example. These three writers were also politically committed to feminism and socialism; if O'Brien and Murdoch shared a passionate interest in the fate of Ireland as a nation (see Murdoch's 1965 *The Red and the Green*), O'Brien and Townsend Warner had a similar devotion to Spain that extended to the revolutionary upheavals in the country. Like they had done with sexuality, these writers approached politics not just explicitly, but also through political fables. Queer sexualities and politics being two touchy subjects, it is remarkable that these three writers favored allegory in their methodology, even though they were obviously able and willing to provide radical realist plots on the surface.

It is even more remarkable that a stylistic preference so crucial to their production is never seen to be on the cutting edge of technical innovation and, therefore, never seen in relation to modernism. Writers of O'Brien's generation deployed Henry James's undermining of plot, Fyodor Dostoevsky's use of the doppelganger, Oscar Wilde's subversion of classical logic, George Eliot's adoption of scientific ideas and terminology, and Franz Kafka's political use of parable, to give just five examples of technically radical approaches. The experiments of O'Brien, Murdoch, Townsend Warner, and others, should force us to reassess the relevance of nineteenth century avant-gardism to twentieth century literature and, conversely, force a reassessment of the narrow stylistic parameters ascribed to modernist writing.

Mixed Media: "Minor" Arts

"Mixed media" is a term from the visual arts which can be applied to Kate O'Brien's aesthetic practice in general and *Mary Lavelle* in particular. The term is normally used to convey the presence of a variety of materials in a single artwork. I use it here to refer to O'Brien's tendency, not merely to mention a number of arts and art mediums, but to borrow their distinctive qualities and language for her own purposes. By referring to intermedial elements as "mixed media," I also want to highlight the influence of the visual arts in modernist rethinking of themes and materials. This aspect of her work has also been neglected by critics. We can keep Kate O'Brien's radical appropriations of the language of the visual arts in a perpetual "Salon des Refusés," or we can use her experiments to rethink modernist intermediality. Literary modernism tends to be equated with high modernism. In the visual arts, it was also the critics who decided that abstraction and cubism were the apex of modern art (see Tom Wolfe's survey *The Painted Word*), even though those "schools" shared with dadaism, constructivism, expressionism, and surrealism an imperious desire for change, which deliberately crossed mediums. Surrealists, for example, developed collage and applied it to books, "subverting existing genres and literary forms" and recycling lesser forms of literature (Gille 130–1). Let us take a brief look at O'Brien's use of interior design, bullfighting, and dancing, as aesthetic languages.

Interior design is one of the "minor arts" which plays an important part in characterization in *Mary Lavelle*. Stepping into Luisa's drawing-room in Madrid offers Mary another new experience, as she "never before had set foot in a room which was the conscious expression of an isolated aesthetic sense" (232). Luisa's drawing-room, we are told, has been featured in *Vogue*—a "women's magazine" surveying the latest trends in fashion and décor, and therefore less worthy in terms of the aesthetic canon. It is for this reason, for example, that Oscar Wilde's work in *Woman's World* between 1887 and 1889 is rarely mentioned and has yet to be reprinted (it is even missing from the 2001 *The Complete Works of Oscar Wilde*). Elevating *Vogue*'s status as aesthetic referent cannot be dislodged from the fact that *Vogue* is only partially "mass culture," and that it represents in itself a mark of status, with its own distinctive politics. For example, a relatively recent article in the magazine, titled "Conflict of Interest," dealt with the "problem" faced by Israeli women trying to keep up with the latest fashions while inconvenient bombs may explode as they shop; the subheading of the article claiming that "shopping keeps Israeli women sane" (Grant 17). Despite recurrent signs of totalitarian dementia in "lifestyle" magazines such as *Vogue*, and despite claims that the lyric descriptions in the magazine-like Property pages of the *Irish Times* during the economic boom in Ireland were "pornography for the Irish Middle Classes" (McWilliams), borrowing the terms of interior design is a radically democratizing move in *Mary Lavelle*, because the experience of being in Luisa's drawing-room is comparable to Mary's acquaintance with the "masterpieces" in the Prado museum in the same chapter. Luisa's "easily beautiful" room is "deprecatory and gracious in its harnessing of baroque and First Empire to each other and to the sunlight, flowers and gaiety of immediate and happy human life," showing that she would "strain nothing, not even by the shadow of a hair her own pure taste" (232). In the context of O'Brien's use of "mixed media," the room is a metonymy of Luisa, to the extent that the setting represents the most insightful description of the character in the novel. Luisa's "well-disciplined sophistication," "passionate intelligence," and general restraint, in Mary's report (see O'Brien *Mary* 232–3), may stand for a certain modernist attitude, but her room also symbolizes a sense of self, a certain temperament, and a specific sexuality.

As we have seen, in *Mary Lavelle* bullfighting is as much a metaphor for a sexual encounter as the romance plot is an analogy for the bullfight. Ernest Hemingway claimed, "I know no modern sculpture, except Brancusi's, that is in any way equal of the modern sculpture of bullfighting. But it is an impermanent art as singing and the dance are." He goes on: "Suppose a painter's canvases disappeared with him and a writer's books were automatically destroyed at his death and only existed in the memory of those that had read them. That is what happens in bullfighting" (*Death* 99). This unwillingness to treat art mediums as isolated languages deaf to each other is something we find in *Mary Lavelle* where, at one point, Mary likens painting to poetry and the bullfight with the same ease as Hemingway: "She had reflected, standing before Rubens' 'Three Graces,' that she could no more have written *Kubla Khan* or explained how it was written than have painted this picture. Nor kill a bull as Pronceda did, or analyse his way of doing it" (*Mary* 227). The three "acts" of the romantic narrative in the novel link the bullfight consecutively to the "undervalued art" of dancing in a town square, to the "lost art" of Romanesque in a ruined hermitage, and to the art of lovemaking in a couple's first sexual encounter. When she attends her first bullfight, Mary learns "that emotion at its most crude can *by relation to a little art enchant, overwhelm, and seem eternal*— that is an awful lesson, most disconcerting to the gentle and orthodox" (emphasis added, 129); and she declares: "here was art in its least decent form, its least explainable or bearable. *But art, unconcerned and lawless*" (emphasis added, 117). As Lorna Reynolds points out, "Mary has had, in the bullfight, a revelation of the possible pain of life but also of its possible control through attitude, through the formalization, the distancing and patterning of art" (*Kate* 100). In other words, this is a loss of virginity regarding the aesthetic, and therefore related to the scene in *The Land of Spices* where Anna opens her eyes to Pilar, a school-mate from Lima, as "a motive in art" made of "broken symbols" (O'Brien *Land* 272, 271) the idea is presented in similar terms to Milagros's description of the bullfight, when she links it to "the greatest poetry" (O'Brien *Mary* 140), and sums it up as "death and horror presented theatrically and really, both at once" (140). When the bullfight is described in *Farewell Spain* as "a great art, a symbolical and most moving spectacle" (135), the passage contrasts this "great art" to foxhunting, which is to O'Brien merely a "pastime" (135) — perhaps a class judgment. O'Brien's militant attitude to aesthetic boundaries is generally concerned with undoing rank while avoiding uniformity; her method is to aggregate rather than segregate, as in Mary Lavelle's garland of great artists, prompted by a visit to El Prado: the painter Rubens, the poet Coleridge, and the bullfighter Pronceda.

Dancing in the squares plays a crucial part in the novel. "Formal" dancing in dancehalls or at private parties does not feature, consistently with O'Brien's interest in "ordinary people dancing" (*Self-Portrait*). Salon dance and elaborate choreographies held the interest of filmgoers around the time *Mary Lavelle* was published, with musicals such as the 1936 *Swing Time*, with the Astaire and Rogers team, giving a new spin to conventional romantic narratives. In *Mary Lavelle*, merely by listening to a record of a tango tune in the Areavaga sitting room, Mary suddenly "wanted to escape, to be at home. She wanted to be where she was mistress of herself, and not paid to sit demurely through the sociable whims of others, not paid to sit and suffer un-examinable tensions" (*Mary* 137). All doubts vanish when she later dances with Juanito in the town square. We are not told what kind of dance they engage in — the film version of the novel, *Talk of Angels*, plausibly presents the pair in a pasodoble (double-step), a relatively fast-tempoed, simple, and somewhat stifled popular dance in Spain at the time. Interestingly, the official hymn of the famous bullfighting appreciation society from Bilbo, "Club Cocherito," composed by bullring-band musician Federico Corto in the early twentieth century, was also a pasodoble (see Bacigalupe "Visita" 34). Much as in O'Brien's novel, dancing is a turning point in the emotional experience of the protagonist of Maura Laverty's *No More Than Human*. The scene takes place in 1924 at the Carnival Dance in the Ritz Hotel in Madrid, to where Irish governess Delia Skully has been taken by Mr. Robertson. The sudden appearance of the Spanish Rafael, the sherry, and the tango, prove an irresistible combination: "I had never known that dancing could be like that," she admits; "I, whose mother — and her mother before her — had never danced anything more languid or sensuous than a jig, found myself gliding and swaying and turning as if I had been born and bred in Buenos Aires" (47). Delia soon learns that different dance routines have different effects on her: The tango makes her "sentimental and yearning," while the pasodoble is "gay, blood-quickening" (48). Art, like eroticism, is not a set of practices or meanings, but *an experience*. To paraphrase Clive Bell, art, like sexuality, is a "significant experience." Love and sexuality are not just mediated by art, but equivalent to it. After the first confirmation that Juanito does indeed love her, Mary reflects:

> "Life was fantastic. One minute you were afraid to breathe for pain, the next you were dancing in the Plaza San Martín."
> "I have the poem," he said. "I'm trying to learn it."
> She thought of the bullfight suddenly, of how it ravished her memory. This too she would need to remember [190].

Dancing, poetry, and bullfighting, mentioned in rapid succession, have the intended effect of merging into one another.

Mixed Media: Architecture

SAN GERONIMO

Architecture is another art form crafted by Kate O'Brien into the characterization and plot of *Mary Lavelle* with striking results. For example, San Geronimo (Saint Jerome), a sixteenth century church that is "[o]ne of the few beauties of Altorno" (98), is a metonymy for Agatha Conlan. The austerity of her room and her book collection are reminiscent of Saint Jerome's, and her temperament and place in the world are akin to those of the building. Through Conlan's window, which overlooks the square and the church, Mary saw "the fountain and children playing about the old gentleman in the scene; saw, more veiled by the tops of plane-trees now, the church façade and tower; saw the rigid masts of ships and the wine-red mountain-side with evening light on it" (97). This chapter in the novel, stressing the importance of San Geronimo by adopting it as its title, is set in an actual square in Bilbo and San Geronimo is the main architectual feature there, the church of San Vicente. The "old gentleman" in the passage refers to the Basque romantic poet Antonio de Trueba (b. 1819 d. 1889); or rather, to the bronze sculpture of Trueba sitting on a wooden bench, placed on a block of Bizkaian marble (from Ereino/Ereño) in the middle of the square, a sculpture by Mariano Benlliure, paid for by popular subscription a few years after the poet's death. The most famous poems of the once-miner Trueba ecstatically described the Biscayan hills around Bilbo that are alluded to in the passage in *Mary Lavelle*. The church of San Vicente is also mentioned by O'Brien in *Farewell Spain* (which included a drawing of the church by Mary O'Neill): "nearer the river and in a quiet square of shivering leaves and tall, sad houses, there is the soaring, Renaissance porch of San Vicente. Very noble, very melancholy, much enhanced by plane-trees all about it" (*Spain* 208). This is an intertextual enhancement of the novel, which had explained that Agatha's face was "nobly planned" (*Mary* 85).

Earlier in the "San Geronimo" chapter, Mary's wanderings through the town had brought her to this very spot:

> The stroll had brought her at last from the luxury streets to this peaceful square where she was glad to sit awhile. She liked the great façade of the church. She noted the immense and sweeping height of the porch, and the faded, sweet colour of the buff stone, so different from the bright grey banks and clubs. She noticed that ornaments were gently scrolled and wrought on its aged surface, and how the bell-tower, soaring up against the background of the mountains, seemed beautiful and patient as they, and almost as old [74–75].

Seamlessly, this particular view prompts Mary's mind into reviewing her own perfect adaptation to her surroundings, a mark of good architecture, but here applied to an emigrant's cultural location after *she* has adapted to her surroundings: "She had begun to drink wine at dinner, and to dip churros in her chocolate; she had studied her map and accepted the vastness and regionalism of Spain, and understood already that the north is not the south; ... and might even smile at tourists" (75). But suddenly, "she felt an unexpected solemn movement in her heart; something like premonition took her, oppressing, puzzling.... It was as if what she looked on thus accidentally were ageing her, as if it were imposing knowledge," and "the weight stayed on her; her eyes remained stupidly fixed on the tall church and the plane-trees" (75–76). Renaissance Christian architecture may perhaps be considered, in terms of Basque art, as a foreign element, here perfectly adapted to its local environment — to the Basque mountains, and *not* to the banks and clubs (see earlier quote 74–5); and Lavelle's move away from the "luxury streets" into this peace and simplicity is a form of political retreat. The square and, particularly, the church building, also suggest a new home of the mind, a perhaps temporary spiritual refuge that, crucially, Mary will share with Agatha. It is not merely that the building is a metaphor; the metaphoric *language* used to express these ideas is itself borrowed from architecture.

ROMANESQUE

A pronounced interest in medieval art occasionally resurfaces in Kate O'Brien's work, as when she highlights the supposed medievalism of El Greco in *Farewell Spain* (see 146). She was particularly drawn to Romanesque architecture, an interest which has a political component, similar to Pre-Raphaelite medievalism, part of a search for emotion away from contemporary mechanistic approaches. There was a medievalizing impetus in much modernist art, from the 1913 publications of the painter and theorist Albert Gleizes in France, and continuing in the lectures of her disciple and collaborator Mainie Jellet (see S.B. Kennedy 36–8; and Arnold 70, 89, 100–10). In Ireland, early medieval Christianity was a regular referent across mediums, from Austin Clarke's poetry to Evie Hone's watercolors. Monastic communitarianism, simplicity, and nurturing of the arts, were nostalgically reclaimed as a mythic "Celtic Christianity" by Irish malcontents. On the one hand, Jellet believed that the revaluation of Celtic art "would give our art a national character" (quoted in Arnold 181). On the other, writers like Austin Clarke and Kate O'Brien hailed a communitarian and creative Celtic monasticism as "a kind of utopia" (O'Brien *Ireland* 25), suggesting Romanesque style as a referent for their own twentieth century political and aesthetic allegiances, anti-authoritarian and modernist (for Clarke, see Kiberd *Classics* 464). Romanesque is said to adopt a different way of representation — a symbolic, subjective mode ("spiritual"), opposed to the pursuit of realism ("materialistic") in the visual art of the Italian Renaissance (see Arnold 101). In *Farewell Spain*, Kate O'Brien claimed that Romanesque "appeals at once to human ideals, and intellectual human sympathy" (198). Mary Lavelle's unassuming beauty, her simplicity, and her distinctive Irishness (locatedness) are akin to those of a Romanesque temple. Her physical and temperamental traits symbolize a specific conception of the self, just as a Romanesque church represents a particular type of spirituality. Romanesque churches are dark, austere, and small; or rather, they are human-sized, as opposed to the gothic verticality, luminosity, and transcendence of human proportions. Built in an isolated spot, placed in a rural setting, Romanesque hermitages such as the one in *Mary Lavelle*, unlike the collective, urban, transcendental project that the gothic cathedral represents, are conductive to introspection, making the religious experience intimate and direct. A Romanesque space is likely to include non-naturalistic low relief sculpture and painting (with scenes from daily — lay — life and biblical stories), conveying religious notions through a clear symbolism that ordinary people can understand.

In the chapter "A Hermitage," where Mary and Juan visit a ruined Toledo hermitage, "a small, forgotten jewel of Romanesque," they find that "its only furniture was, on its southern wall, a low relief of gay, exulting angels. Their wings were chipped; their heaven directed trumpets almost worn away. Sunlight poured in on them through glassless windows and through a hole in the roof" (*Mary* 249). Don Pablo had said that these angels were "one of the most beautiful things in Spain," another link to La Belle, who sees them and declares: "Northern, and twelfth century. Really Christian. The Spain I like" (ibid.). O'Brien is concerned with presenting this Romanesque space as a symbolic location for love and politics. Mary and Juanito bring the hermitage to life by walking into its crumbling structure: Their love is a rekindling of a lost tradition, just as Juanito's political project is regenerative and restorative. Unfortunately, O'Brien's project is also racist and Muslim-phobic, which also contribute to shaping the novel in general and the meeting at Toledo in particular. The scene is also full of awkward and implausible dialogue, which should not be read in realist terms; it is *not* realism, but symbolism, in the manner of the non-naturalistic art of the Romanesque.

In the chapter of *Farewell Spain* titled "Romanesque and Neolithic," set in the region of Cantabria, O'Brien recounts her visit to the famous Colegiata building in Santillana del Mar, explaining that "it is '*romanico puro*' [pure Romanesque]," and proof that "functional rightness is beauty, beauty is functional rightness" (62). In the chapter, Kate O'Brien had just described a brawl between a group of leftist republicans, which she assumed to be anarcho-syndicalists, and a passing priest — with O'Brien at the ready to jump to protect him. At the end of her description of the Colegiata she sets up this incident (an example of the generalized unrest before the civil war), against the gentle, intellectual, individualist anarchism of a man she met at an earlier stage of her trip, Don Ángel (63). The wedging of idealized Romanesque between these two models of anarchist activism and ideology is no coincidence; Romanesque here provides a political topos. O'Brien was using architecture as political metaphor as late as 1969, in her "Long Distance" column for the *Irish Times*, where after discussing urban planning and architecture in Limerick, she claimed that the town's urban planning and its citizens were both characterized by "self control and by good manners," to which she added: "In an ugly world there is still the good anarchy of Ireland. If only Dublin were more aware of the importance of that quality" (quoted in Liddy ed. 34–5). This is more than a reference to the historical "Limerick commune" (sometimes referred to as the "Limerick Soviet"), it is itself an ideological operation (despite the fact that anarchism becomes a "quality" rather than a political movement). O'Brien seeks to counteract not only the commonplace equation of anarchy to chaos, but also the "other-worldly" perception of anarchist ideals, by firmly planting them within sight of ordinary people.

Mixed Media: Painting

Referents

References to painting pepper Kate O'Brien's work. They often appear as passing comments—in *My Ireland*, for example, where O'Brien points out that the "dazzling beauties" of Botticelli and Phidias are not to be found in real life (20). They also play a part in characterization when significant paintings grace private rooms—for example in *The Flower of May* Aunt Eleanor has a copy of Leonardo's *Virgin of the Rocks,* painted around 1508, and in *As Music and Splendour* Paddy owns a reproduction of Raphael's *The School of Athens*, painted between 1508 and 1511. In some instances, paintings are crucial aids in the articulation of emotion—for example in Anna Murphy's epiphany in *The Land of Spices*, where Pilar makes her think of the "battered volumes of old master reproductions" in the convent's library, and Anna recalls Mantegna and Giorgione, to finally liken her schoolmate to a young girl "eternally lifted off in joy" in a Goya painting (a reference to an actual painting), and thinking of Pilar as "something that life can be about, something with power to make life compose around it" (O'Brien *Land* 272—or on it; Pilar and "pillar" have the same spelling in Spanish). Many examples in O'Brien's work show her confidence in her knowledge of painting, sometimes bordering on arrogance, although arguably the assertiveness of art critics is a characteristic of the discipline that may come across as excessive to the lay person; we find examples in *English Diaries and Journals* (37) and *Farewell Spain* (141). But she has much of interest to say. For example, we have seen how important El Greco is to the conception of *Mary Lavelle*, and although he is sometimes considered a proto-modernist painter, as we have seen, or a proto-romantic, in *Farewell Spain* O'Brien insists that he is "much more related to the formal mediævalists" (146).

As Gerardine Meaney has noted, "[w]hile women have not figured prominently in the histories of Irish literary modernism, they were central to the development of modernism in the visual arts in Ireland" ("Modernism" 68). But these two worlds were far from separate. In Ireland, like elsewhere, modernist artists and writers shared family ties and social circles, and there were also links by training; Elizabeth Bowen and Rosamond Jacob, for example, went to art school before deciding to become novelists. Mainie Jellett's first public lecture, "Cubism and Subsequent Movements in Painting," was given to the Dublin Literary Society in 1926, and it emphasized the links between the avant-garde *in all art forms* (see Arnold 92). Kate O'Brien posed for a remarkable cubist portrait by Irish painter May Guinness, wearing the ceremonial robe and hat of a honorary degree conferred in maturity. Women's changing attitude to the arts canon is important in this context. When Mary visits the Prado Museum in 1922 and stands "awestruck and tremulous" (*Mary* 227) in front of Rubens's *Three Graces*, painted 1636–1638, she is changing history, because in Charlotte Brontë's novel of 1853 *Villette*, another governess abroad, Lucy Snowe, had stood *appalled* in front of Rubens's "army of ... fat women" (259) and had mocked the madonnas and whores by male painters in a Brussels museum. In the same novel, in the same chapter, Lucy's description of the theatrical performance of "Vashti" (inspired by French actor, Elisa Felix) had repositioned aesthetics, in a Burkean move, from beauty/feminine to the sublime/masculine. Charlotte Brontë remarked in a letter of 1851: "[Felix's] acting transfixed me with wonder, enchained me with interest, thrilled me with horror. The tremendous force with which she expresses the very worst passions in the strongest essence forms an exhibition as exciting *as the bull-fights of Spain*" because "[i]t is scarcely human nature that she shows you, it is something wilder and worse; the feelings and fury of a fiend" (emphasis added, quoted in Moglen 29–30). Jane Eyre and Lucy Snowe, it is rarely noted, are themselves skillful and original amateur visual artists, and their work presents women under a new light, just as their first person narratives do, "omit[ting] no harsh line, smooth[ing] away no displeasing irregularity" (Brontë *Jane* 161). As Christina Rossetti had lamented in a poem of 1896, woman was represented "[n]ot as she is, but as she fills his [the painter's] dream" (1027). To O'Brien, however, Rubens has an admirable "pagan gusto," so that his religious themes, as much as his "myths, allegories and radiant worldly portraits," are a vehicle for "[p]ure painting" (*Spain* 143–4), while Goya is a "historian, satirist, novelist, angry spectator of his own day who happened to be mainly a painter" (ibid., 144). To O'Brien, Velazquez is "perhaps *en masse* somewhat boring, just as El Greco is a shade fatiguing" (*Spain* 145). In 1914, a suffragette had attacked Velazquez's *Rockeby Venus*, a painting of around 1650, with a meat chopper, but a mere decade after the attack a new wind was blowing. In 1922, in the Prado Museum, Mary Lavelle allows herself to be intoxicated by "an air that was strange to her, blown in from abstract life, remote, impersonal, held in perspective" (227).

SYMBOLISM

The influence of painting in Kate O'Brien can be traced in her regular mentions to painters, schools, mediums, as well as to practices associated with the art form. For example, she compared writing to painting — impressionist, expressionist, abstract — in a number of occasions (see respectively *Teresa* 9, *Parlour* 9, *Self-Portrait*). Her "recycling" of artistic terms is more remarkable. For example, when Mary Lavelle arrives in Madrid, she feels that she is not "collected" enough to go to El Prado (224), making a breathtaking association between the individual self and the painstaking, slow construction of a canon. This is reminiscent of a crucial point in *The Land of Spices*, where Helen Archer recalled a memory "[i]n the stretched canvas of her eyelids" (158); what follows (a description of the famous "embrace of love" which outraged the censors) may perhaps suggest a surrealist panting or a scene by Bosch in the nightmarish scenario that Helen conjures up, but, even more strikingly, the turn of phrase clearly indicates that memory equates personal interpretation, and creativity; that it is, at least in part, a fiction.

Non-normative eroticism in *Mary Lavelle*, as we have seen, is partly signaled through El Greco. The novel links him to Castilla (see for example 216–7), which encourages the reading of the region as mythical place, as mythical *homosexual* haven. Mary later claims, "Indeed, would she but examine the superstitious delight she took in her sudden infatuation with Castile, she must see that it could only be the omen of trouble" (218). Not just trouble for Mary, one may add — her infatuation with a region associated with El Greco also means "trouble" for the heterosexual narrative. Sexuality, of any kind, is compared to painting at several points. For example, Mary's visit to El Prado is, like the bullfight, presented as parallel/mirror to the sexual encounter with Juanito, as suggested by her thinking: "There's something to be said ... for sudden, exhausting encounter. There's really something in being half-choked and stupefied. Ah, but if I were younger, if there were time [to learn]! And this is only *one* of the world's galleries!" (emphasis in original, 227–8). One way of reading this is that Mary regrets her lack of art/sexual education, and the museum/Juanito seems a good place to start. An appreciation of art is equated to eroticism elsewhere. For example, it is more than a coincidence that Mary's first sexual encounter will take place in a "field" — "prado" in the Spanish language.

We are also told, in the Madrid interlude, that "[Mary's] mind was hung with broken memories of paintings" (227). The sentence not only anticipates Mary as "broken San Sebastian," it also transforms Mary's mind into an exhibition space where academic/canonical images are displayed. She must absorb other people's "visions" of what she may be, before she can spurt out her own personality on the blank canvas of the self, in her own (artistically mediated) language. Tradition must be engaged with before one leaves it behind, after packing one's trunk with borrowed insights. Likewise, Mary's admired Rubens was notorious for his borrowings from the old masters: a turn of the brush here, or a torso there, or a shaft of light. Mary alludes to the freedom to wander and borrow, in terms suggestive of sexuality — she has an epiphany in El Prado which prompts her to reclaim her right to "wander ... from flower to flower of these immense fresh fields" (228).

PAINTERLINESS

In her 1927 novel *To the Lighthouse*, Virginia Woolf had dipped in and out of the fleeting consciousness of multiple characters to offer a post/impressionistic group portrait. In 1922, in *Ulysses*, James Joyce had color-coded each chapter. *Mary Lavelle* uses a host of techniques associated with the visual arts of the time. Jean Hangstrum's description of "painterliness" (she uses the term "pictorialism") in literature in her 1958 book *The Sister Acts* is summarized by Lois Oppenheim as follows:

> [T]he writing must, first, be translatable into or imaginable as a painting or sculpture; second, consist in [sic] visual detail "ordered in a picturable way"; third, involve a diminution of motion towards stasis [the concentration of action in a single moment of energy]; and fourth, limit meaning primarily to that which derives from the "*visibilia* present." Unconfined to school or method, it may relate to imitative or abstract, representational or symbolic art [124].

Kate O'Brien's novels show all of the above characteristics at many points. In *Mary Lavelle*, the color blue is used to make subtextual, intertextual, and autobiographical links. In O'Brien's fiction, blue is a signature mark, perhaps comparable to Dimitri Shostakovich's "signature notes" in his musical compositions. We find it as far back as her first novel, *Without My Cloak*, where Caroline's "lightning-blue" eyes were "stressed by the blue note of pattern in her grey gown and the blue-grey feather that curled on the brim of her bonnet" (41, 176). In *The Flower of May*, as Lillian is about to leave on her honeymoon, her mother looks at "her beautiful blue eyes flash oddly, shadowed and disturbed" (5), while Fanny remarks on the extraordinary "sapphire blue" eyes of Lucille (74; see 336). In *Mary Lavelle*, blue is combined with white to provide a link between Luisa, Agatha, Mary, and Nieves, as we can see in a number of key passages. For example, Mary describes Nieves as "[t]hin and dawdy in a 'middy' blouse and an old blue skirt, she looked an innocent fifteen-year-old. Her eyes were either grey or blue.... Her chief day-dream was that she was an English boy at Eton" (16). Similarly, Don Pablo describes Mary as "[a] girl in a pale blue cotton dress and tennis shoes, a girl with very white skin and a faint rose-flush on her cheeks," while "[h]er hair, of goldish brown, was curly and clung to her head like a Greek boy's. Her blue eyes, boyish too, androgynous, were wide and shy, but darkened by dark lashes and by shadows of fatigue" (66–67). At the hermitage, Mary is described by Juanito as follows: "Her short, unsettled curls stirred softly. The dark blue, careless clothes and composed, braced attitude of meditation gave her for the moment the non-voluptuous, introverted air of a boy" (248). Mary notes that Agatha "wore a shiny, threadbare navy blue suit and a white linen blouse demurely closed at the neck by a silver Tara brooch.... 'What beautiful eyes!' Mary thought. They were deep blue and full of light, with black brows arching delicately" (85), to later reflect that "[y]ou may take her for a boy just now" (117). In addition to their shared "masculine" potential, as these examples show, Nieves, Mary, and Agatha are clearly coded as blue-white. White and blue are also the colors of the Virgin Mary in Christian iconography (Gerardine Meaney in conversation December 4, 2006; see John Turpin on Marian imagery in Ireland), as signaled early on in the novel by the small religious statuette in Lavelle's room with the Holy Mary "in muslin dress and sapphire crown" (11). The novel may be presenting three subtextually linked virgins, a female trinity. But it is equally relevant that in *The Flower of May*, Fanny's blue chiffon dress is meant to emphasize her "mermaid quality" (O'Brien *Flower* 4). This is how O'Brien builds the text, by crisscrossing symbolic references, by accumulating undertones only discernible on a second reading/viewing.

Luisa is also coded blue and white (*Mary* 230, 233), like her drawing-room. When Mary enters it she herself looks "somewhat whiter, ... with bluish shadows stressing the innocent, blue gravity of her eyes," and "sculptured" curls clinging above her "snowy forehead" (246). However, Luisa's eyes are not blue, but gold, like Pilar's. When Mary first meets her, Pilar is wearing a "frock of pale blue linen fitted [which] became her well" (ibid.), but she realizes that "[t]he grey of her eyes never gleamed blue as did Nieves'" (17); in fact, Pilar "had lively eyes of so light a brown that they were almost gold" (16). She shares these not only with Luisa but also with Juanito, while we are told that Milagros, "grey-eyed and fourteen, was remarkable for detachment" (14). It seems clear to me that these interlinked color referents signal lesbianism (blue, and in the case of the young Nieves's blue-grey eyes, potential lesbianism) and bisexuality (gold). The same color-code is used in *As Music and Splendour* precisely to mark a continuity with *Mary Lavelle*'s subtext: Clarabelle has blue eyes, while Luisa Carriaga's are golden, matching Mary Lavelle and Luisa Areavaga's in order to merge their life stories as the earlier novel did not dare doing. Further, as we mentioned earlier, the "gleaming" blue eyes in Nieves, Mary, and Agatha suggest that this is the same person, at three stages of development — that is, *Mary Lavelle* appears to offer, in code, a miniature lesbian bildungsroman: from the off-key gender identity of a fifteen-year-old, to a twenty-three-year-old's first exercising of sexual assertiveness (a man to end all men), to a thirty-eight-year-old's acceptance of her own lesbianism.

Mixed Media: Film

SCRIPTS

Cinematographically speaking, there is much in O'Brien that is easily translated into film, including stories that revel in collective visual experiences (the bullfight, the Catholic mass, school performances, the opera) and psychological, dramatic plots that suit a certain kind of film (David Lean's *Brief Encounter* comes to mind). There have been a handful of film adaptations of

Kate O'Brien novels to date: the 1955 *For One Sweet Grape*, based on *That Lady* (see also Walshe *Kate* 108); the 1998 *Talk of Angels*, based on *Mary Lavelle*; as well as a television version of *The Anteroom*, in four parts, broadcast in Ireland in June 1981 (see Cawley 38). *The Land of Spices* was once next in line for adaptation to film and television, as scriptwriter Jackie Mills explained in a paper of 2003, but producers are intimidated by the novel's scope, even though the most perilous task according to Mills may in fact be casting, with Helen Archer easily turned, in the wrong hands, into "a drag queen" ("*Land*"). O'Brien wanted Garbo to play the princess of Eboli, other than not Olivia de Havilland (Walshe *Kate* 121). She found nothing to like in *For One Sweet Grape* and walked out of the cinema halfway through the film (see Hogan "Introduction [1985]" x–xi).

The adaptation of *Mary Lavelle* was made after O'Brien's death, following the discreet revival of her work in the late 1980s, and it aimed at an international mass audience. The playwright and poet Frank McGuinness wrote the original screenplay, which was remarkably faithful to the novel in spirit. In fact, it "improved" O'Brien's book in certain ways, for example by bringing the story up to 1936, by renaming Juan as "Francisco," or in the treatment of Agatha, who was somewhat unceremoniously dropped at the end of the novel, while in the script she secures a job as governess with the Areavagas, a perfectly measured gesture in the best tradition of courtly love. The strengths of McGuinness's script *as a version* of the novel are also its weaknesses: *Talk of Angels* is tighter and more coherent than *Mary Lavelle*, and his heroes are more consistent and likeable, but the rich slipperiness of O'Brien's writing did not survive the transition. McGuinness did, however, underline the novel's subtext about angels in his title, which takes up the greeting that introduces Agatha in the novel, and he also added a surreal touch of his own in the figure of an anonymous woman who accosts the Areavagas in the street, "the image of Picasso's Celestina," who seems to symbolize the impending madness of the Spanish Civil War, as the story is moved forward to 1936.

The adaptation of the novel onto the screen was fraught with problems because of the producers' changing priorities. They changed the original script by McGuinness without consulting him, and, as I mentioned, unaccountably set the story in Portugal during the Revolution of the Carnations. Unsurprisingly, McGuinness decided to pull out of the project — although the final script contained enough of the original material for his work to be acknowledged, and he is credited as co-writer of the script (Frank McGuinness in conversation, December 10, 2006). The first draft of a new script by Ann and Eduardo Guedes opened by indicating that, in the 1920s, "The Portuguese First Republic was in political and social turmoil, floundering from crisis to crisis. Republicans, monarchists, socialists and anarchists jostled for hearts and minds, and the threat of Fascism grew" (1). The androgynous Uma Thurman was originally cast in the title role. The production company Miramax was following its then recent box-office success of 1996 *The English Patient*, but *Talk of Angels* failed to become another popular blend of romance and politics (see Major), and the film was a flop. One of the interesting features of the final version is that it turns Don Pablo into a doctor and intellectual, which concurs with the biographical elements in the novel, as we will discuss later. It is also interesting that one of the books written by "Dr. Vicente" is shown in the film — its title, "La Contribución de Darwin y Marx al Progreso de la Humanidad" ("The Contribution of Darwin and Marx to the Progress of Humanity"), suggests that Vicente's Marxist sympathies contrast with his son's as Francisco is an anarchist sympathizer, and this tension is an exact reverse of the situation in the novel. As for the Basque context, it disappeared from both scripts — and from the screen.

Kate O'Brien was a keen cinema goer since childhood, when her "chief craze" was Pearl White, the star of the serial *The Perils of Pauline*, action films where the protagonist got into various scrapes and managed to escape by the end of each installment (see O'Brien *Parlour* 37). In O'Brien's novel *Pray for the Wanderer*, the autobiographical Tom is a novelist banned in Ireland who loves popular film (praising Stan and Ollie, and Chaplin; see 120). Tom borrows cinematic terms to explain that his job is not to moralize but to show "[t]hat life is so and so on *the screen of my closed eyelids*.... I give you life translated to my idiom" (emphasis added, ibid., 184). After her initial success as a playwright, O'Brien attempted to become a scriptwriter in the 1930s, a "natural progression" for many women as Alison Butler has pointed out (26), and O'Brien's scripts, dialogue-dependent and dominated by static indoor settings, seem indebted to drama. Kate O'Brien wrote at least two film scripts, *A Broken Song* and *Mary Magdalen*, and set one of her plays, *Gloria Gish*, amidst the emerging film industry in England. They show an interest in pushing thematic and visual boundaries. *A Broken Song* is a never-produced, undated screenplay, which perhaps could be dated 1931–2. The script, sent to a New York agent, is set in Munich, Paris, New York, and London, and tells the story of a young tenor born in Australia of Irish parents, who has repeated dream-like visions of a woman's face, in sequences that puncture the main narrative. *Mary Magdalen* is another never-produced, undated screenplay, possibly from the 1930s, which shows a greater proficiency in film techniques. It is a political and existentialist fable, centered on the Mary Magdalen from the Christian gospels as she takes the life-changing decision of following Jesus. The script has a contemporary feel, as if it had been accidentally set 1,900 years in the past, and it reads like the biography of a wealthy and well-educated flapper who pursues sexual promiscuity as a sort of ethical compulsion, out of a sense of duty to herself as a modern woman, without realizing that she is living in what Jean-Paul Sartre called "bad faith." The film has a sustained radicalism in vision, for example in the suggestion that the Virgin Mary and the whore of Magdala were in fact one and the same — and judging by the pages and content of the typescript at the National Library of Ireland, O'Brien may have been asked to change a perhaps too daring ending. *Gloria Gish* is an unproduced play, perhaps written in the early 1930s, set in

London possibly in the late 1920s or early 1930s, and offering a twentieth century rewrite of the legend of Helen of Troy in the story of Gladys, a beauty who is charmed away from her financier husband by a film producer who promises to turn her into a star, the next "Gloria Gish" (a composite of early film stars Gloria Swanson and Lillian Gish). In the play, Gladys is associated with Ealing, an area famous for its film studios, and perhaps the character itself is a commentary on the alluring vacuity of many film productions of the time.

In her fiction, Kate O'Brien was particularly interested in experimenting with film language, but she was a novelist borrowing film techniques, rather than a filmmaker manqué. In her novels, she is partial to panoramic and moving shots; we find them, for example, in the description of an upper middle class house interior in the 1938 *Pray for the Wanderer*, with the narrator's lens moving from object to object: "the wood fire, the Victorian sofa, pink flowers on the wall paper, the old brass cake stand" (Joan Ryan describes this as "photographic detail"; see 132, 127). Or we find it in the "cinematic" recollection of a painful discovery and an attempted escape in the 1942 *The Land of Spices* (Pine 95). By 1958, in her novel *As Music and Splendour*, a moving shot of a practice-room will seamlessly open the narrative, introducing the main theme of learning to sing/sin, and advancing the end of the book and the co-protagonist's tears after her lover sails away in the *Saint Catherine*. In the scene, the narrator's camera moves from "a glass door leading on to a dark passage," to "an oleograph of a young woman with a palm branch in her hand," to "a tuning fork on the shelf," and then shows how "[r]ain beat against a tall window" (O'Brien *Music* 1). This is economical, effective, *visual*.

In *Mary Lavelle*, chapters and scenes are conceived in visual terms, so that consecutive settings give information about inner states. There are many close-ups, the chapter "A Walk with Milagros" has the feel of a long moving shot, the chapters "Candles at Allera" and "San Geronimo" include the equivalent of panoramic shots, and the key scene in the "A Corrida" chapter is a summation of frames recorded with the coldness of a camera in documentary style, all the best to elicit a nonmediated emotional response. If Mary's final tears are comparable to a fade-out (Gerardine Meaney in conversation February 2005), the novel's "Prologue" is the equivalent of a voice-over by an all-seeing, all-knowing narrator. The opening and ending of the novel are marked by a visual repetition that would not have been out of place in a film: a governess's trunk opened at the border. One of the main features of the novel is the constant, even compulsive, use of flashbacks. Remembrance, and the deliberate fixing of an *image* in a store of memories, is one of the main themes of the novel; Mary's mantra is "I must remember this." It may be argued that flashback is not a specifically cinematic technique (see Eisenstein 4; K. Elliot 124), but other stylistic features in O'Brien's novel, such as zooming, moving shots, and lighting, are clearly indebted to film language. For example, Mary recalls a bullfight, in a way that resembles a tightly edited documentary film, when "the summery sweetness of scene and hour" recedes into the background because "a cloudy region of her mind was showing her other things: a boisterously running bull, a cape bunched up for a veronica, a blindfold horse, a drooped muleta, a matador's placating hand. Her head was full of the day's new images" (O'Brien *Mary* 120). Experiences are edited, creatively re-mastered, and finally projected in "a cloudy region of her mind." Memory does not quite work in this way—film does.

INFLUENCES

The climactic scene in *Mary Lavelle* merges words and film. It is through visual clues that Mary is presented as a bull and her reluctant lover as a bullfighter who will not survive the encounter. We have seen how, for example, the bullfighter's cape trying to lure the bull away from the wooden barrier later metamorphoses into the blanket that Juanito throws by the trunk that Mary leans on. In the cinematic montage of the novel, she is the perfect nemesis. It is possible that Kate O'Brien saw Cecil B. DeMille's silent film adaptation *Carmen*, released in 1915, where DeMille subtly linked the bullfight to the murder of the female protagonist by having the first as backdrop (happening unseen behind a wall) to the second. While DeMille is realist — the staginess notwithstanding — O'Brien is surrealist, and her mise-en-scène destabilizes the normativity of characterization and plot. Lumière cameramen had documented bullfight scenes as early as 1900, but the most relevant cinematic use of it was *Blood and Sand*, of 1922. This film offered a remarkable conjuction of queer talent, with Dorothy Arzher as editor (and perhaps director of the bullfight sequences— see Gaines 99), June Mathis as scriptwriter and Rudolph Valentino in the starring role (they had worked together in the Nazimova-produced *Camille* of 1921, the predecesor of the "all-gay" *Camille* of 1936). Valentino plays a bullfighter named Juan (his mother calls him Juanillo, or "Little John"), who is seduced away from his wife by an amoral wealthy woman looking for a thrill. It is likely that O'Brien saw this film and she may have been inspired by the climactic death of the bullfighter after he becomes "reckless" in the bullring, consumed by anger and guilt.

As we have seen, the bullfight shadow-play is not the only visually coded subtext in the novel, which triplicates a character through "her" striking blue eyes, to offer a lesbian bildungsroman. The very careful montage shows a young woman experimenting with her sexuality (Mary), the same woman in her thirties coming out as a lesbian (Agatha), and the same woman again as a transgender girl who longs to be a boy (Nieves). Like a cinema screen segmented in three, we see past, present, and future selves simultaneously. Some of these strategies are reminiscent of surrealist film, introduced in 1926 by the lesbian filmmaker Germaine Dulac's *The Seashell and the Clergyman*, and by Man Ray's Basque titled *Emak Bakia* ("Leave me alone," literally "Give me peace"). Dulac's film is a study in sexuality and repression, while Ray's offers an asexual and de-gendered "ballet," merging human figures and modernist architectural forms. It has been claimed that "[i]n relation to gender and sexuality ... the historical avant-garde was by and large as patriarchal, misogynist, and masculinist as the major trends in modernism" (Huyssen 204), but is this the case? A recent retrospective exhibition of dozens of surrealist women painters titled *Angels of Anarchy* certainly contradicts that notion (Manchester City Galleries, September 2009–January 2010; see also Penelope Rosemont's survey of 1998). The surrealist montage of *Mary Lavelle* was designed by a woman to represent a woman, as an exercise in empowerment and self-expression.

Mary Lavelle is indebted to another "school," German Expressionism, in its recurrent use of dramatic light and shadow effects. For example, when Mary meets her employer, Don Pablo, O'Brien explains: "Shadows and lines over-dramatised his face in the evening light, so that Mary felt his foreignness with exaggeration, even remotely with alarm" (O'Brien *Mary* 38). When she meets Juanito, "[t]he evening sun, pouring in at the landing window, lighted each very sweetly for the other, as with a fatal halo" (143), and when they meet again, in a square, "[s]he leant against the tree, and looked at the figures moving in beauty through the violent depths of light," and we are told that when Juanito found her, "[t]here was a white, hard light streaming in on her obliquely" (189). At another particularly cinematic point, the novel explains that Mary "could see Doña Consuelo's shadow reflected on the terrace from the window. And [Juanito's] passing shadow, with Nieves' as they danced" (185). The interplay of shade and light is a device O'Brien was to prioritize in *The Flower of May* to the extent that the structure of the book relies on it. This is a recurrent stylistic thread in *Mary Lavelle*, and there is no reason, *in writing*, for this investment on striking lighting effects and the heightened contrast between black and white popularized by German expressionist film before the advent of color or sound. In a unique way, the tactic allows O'Brien to recreate a certain mood, as well as to emphasize the *constructedness* of the narrative.

There are remarkable similarities between the 1926 film *Metropolis* and *Mary Lavelle*, in plot, characterization, imagery, and themes. In the underground tunnels of Metropolis, the prophet Maria preaches to the workers about impending apocalypse, and the ruler of the city, Master Joh, creates a robot replica of Maria to foil her movement; however, Joh's son and Maria fall in love, and the robot goes out of control causing a flood to run through Metropolis. Maria declares: "Between the brain that plans and the hands that build, there must be a mediator. It is the heart that must bring about an understanding between them," and as the film closes, Master Joh and a representative of the workers are forced to shake hands by Joh's son, the mediator. Not only do we find a correspondence in names, a similar triangle, a comparable use of character doubling to startling effect; not only do we have references to the "subterranean" source for the wealth of Altorno/Bilbo and an anti-capitalist apocalyptic allegory (to be discussed in the next chapter); we also have the revolutionary Juanito, an upper-class "mediator" between two ostensibly irreconcilable sectors of society. In addition, the newly restored version of *Metropolis* (2010) emphasized a homophilic narrative strand thanks to the recovery of some "lost" footage. It is in comparing Mary to Maria — and her robot double — that the link between the texts is most interesting. "Surrounded by children and neo–Christian symbols, the working girl Maria represents one type of idealized woman — virgin, Madonna, angel," located in a "subterranean feminized space," in Peter Ruppert's words (par. 12). And yet, the robot Maria is not an unqualified agent of evil, because despite the fact that "the machine-woman is a product of male industrial technology and male sexual fantasies, her actions indicate that she is also much more as she defies her male programming and changes from robot passivity to active cyborg aggression," in order to "transgre[ss] the boundaries that separate masters and slaves, capitalists and workers — boundaries on which patriarchal rule in Metropolis depends" so that she becomes "a figure for the possibility for radical social change" (Ruppert par. 10). That is, Maria prefigures Donna Haraway's 1999 famous metaphor of cyborg consciousness as a potential conduit/creator for socialist-feminist meaning. After her arrival in Altorno/Bilbo, Mary Lavelle imagines, and *hopes*, that during her term of employment she will be to everyone "a foreign and more or less satisfactory machine" (O'Brien *Mary* 37), a "tool" without personality, "something paid for to be used by them" (71— in *The Anteroom*, Agnes is a "dutiful machine" —158). Mary is the only person in the Areavaga household confident enough in her mastery of new technology to attempt to assemble a set of "contraptions," the latest novelty in the capital: a wireless set. Mary studies the "sheaves of printed instructions" and decides that it will have to wait until morning because "there's the aerial and the earth, you know" (156). The Areavagas are puzzled. Only Mary can understand the intricate idiom of "coils and wires" (155). Mary is the only one at home here. And what could be a more modern aspiration? Mary wants to be an efficient machine, to help assemble other machines. What could be more a more postmodern aspiration? Mary wants to assist the Areavagas, who are in many ways the opposite of herself, in their incorporation to the "integrated circuit" that the wireless represents. And, actually, what could be more timeless, more spiritual? To let go of the self, to connect heaven and earth. This Robot Mary surrenders to the city — she desires its impersonality, its relentless, directionless advance.

Kate O'Brien did not publicly admit the debt of her 1936 novel to German Expressionism (and the rural-urban schism of *Sunrise* and the duplications and lesbian undertones in *Vampyr* may have also touched Lavelle) and reserved her praise for French films produced around 1938, in an article of that year titled "Why the Rage for French Films?" in which she declared that the best place "to learn what cinema really is," is in films produced in France, and that it is the French who deserve most of the credit for the creation of this new art form, having led in other arts for over a hundred years ("Rage" 12). After discussing with admiration and a critical eye the work of filmmakers like Jean Renoir, Julien Duvivier, or Jacques Feyder, O'Brien traces what today we may call "cinematic elements" in earlier French literature and painting, and links them, not to a general interest in the visual, but to the new form of perception inaugurated by modernist art.

> The French mind has not so much learnt from Cezanne as accepted his announcement of the weight of significant beauty which can lie in a rumpled table-napkin, and a half-empty glass; with Flaubert it recognises quite unselfconsciously the melancholy potentialities of a cab in a rainy street; with de Maupassant it smiles at a fat little feminine hand on a café-table; with Matisse it is made attentive by canaries in a café or sunlight falling across a sofa.

O'Brien follows this by claiming that the French mind "finds the screen a good meeting place for the novelist's and the painter's perceptions—and *it is interested in having them assembled*, is interested in the *artist*'s flashlights on life" (ibid.). Assemblage was a characteristic modernist technique, and here she extends the notion of assembling objects/segments, into the joining of different perceptual modes, different mediums. Further, she italicizes the word *artist*, to de-emphasize the differences between painters, novelists. Even though film is destined to become the "sister art" of theater, O'Brien claims, the links between painting and the novel in fact run deeper, and cinema is a place "where certain functions of those two arts can be united, to re-create life in a new medium" (ibid.). She attempted such a fusion within her own fiction. Like the underground tunnels in Metropolis, *Mary Lavelle* itself is run through by a flood, of painterly, architectural, filmic, literary, documental, biographical, political, radical, baptismal currents. This modernist cyborg of a novel is part of the artistic avant-garde, not on a mission of destruction, but of regeneration.

FIVE

History

Spain and the Basque Country

BASQUE

With *Mary Lavelle*, Kate O'Brien's work walks out of the Irish drawing room and steps into Europe, becoming immersed in European politics and culture. Its first port of call is Euskal Herria, the Basque Country. Is it possible to do a post-colonial analysis of a post-colonial writer? Certainly. But what is the role of the post-colonial in the context of a region legally prevented from self-determination, in a situation which does not fit in with the traditional definition of colonization? And how is this reality articulated in O'Brien's work? Let us start (as is commonplace in Basque-Spanish political discourse) by considering language issues. *Mary Lavelle* is, after all, a novel about an Irish girl hired to teach English to the children of a Basque family.

In O'Brien novels, proficiency in European languages is not just a passport out of poverty (see *Music* 15–6) but also the aspiration of Irish characters with a European vocation. *The Flower of May* is perhaps an extreme example of this attitude — half of the novel (the "bright" part of the book) is "in French," even though the conversation is translated, while the other half (the "dark" half) is in English. This is the only O'Brien novel which remains out of print, and it would not be unreasonable for an enterprising publisher to bring out a bilingual edition (I should perhaps point out that I do not speak French myself). *The Flower of May* is concerned, after all, with the "chiaroscuro" of Europe (see O'Brien *Spain* 1). French is by far the most important European language in O'Brien's work, followed by Spanish and Italian. For Lucille and Fanny, and for Clare and Luisa, French is "their language together" (*Flower* 224; see *Music* 262). In *As Music and Splendour*, Rose tells Clare, "'We're getting to be such polyglots, darling, that soon we'll lose our identities completely'" (ibid.). But the opposite may just be true: Clare *Halvey*'s fragmented personality is evident in the fact that she is variously called "Chiara Alve," "Clara," "Clarabelle," "Reverend Mother," and "Eurydice" by her acquaintances— the names bestowed on her take the pulse of her relationship with the world. Irish plays a marginal role in *The Land of Spices*, as well as in *The Flower of May*, a novel which feasts on Hiberno-English through a problematic "almost stage–Irish" character, the servant Honoria (Reynolds *Kate* 88). There are songs in Welsh in *As Music and Splendour* (348) and risqué Flemish songs in *The Land of Spices* (141).

The degrees of "purity" of English and Spanish are a recurrent topic in *Mary Lavelle*, which is set in a city of "anglophiles" (*Mary* 130; *Spain* 213). In her first letter to Ireland, to Mother Liguori, Mary explains, "'The girls ... can speak some English, which is a relief, as no one else in the house or anywhere seems to speak anything but Spanish or Basque" (*Mary* 4). This is one of a handful of references to Euskera, the Basque language, in the novel. Pilar feels that her fondness for speaking Euskera (to the servants) requires justification, while Milagros clearly sees their first language as a contaminating influence that needs to be purged: "I beg of you don't learn any Spanish from Pilár," she tells her new governess, but Mary smiles "at [her] pomposity"; Mary can hear in the speech of the Areavaga girls "the high, insidious singing of the Cork accent. Miss Anita [the previous governess] must indeed have worn the green, and Mary Lavelle could only assume that she now brought to the Areavagas another kind of brogue. Poor Milagros, in love with purity!" (18; see also 206). The girl's pomposity is treated by O'Brien with her trademark irony, when Milagros later recalls a man who has been sexually molesting her, to make an astonishing declaration: "Personally, I find his dreadful [Andalucian] Spanish the most objectionable thing about him" (133–4; see also Mary's "purity" 153). The children's Cork accent is the legacy of the governess Anna Murphy (possibly a "guest starring" appearance from the co-protagonist of *The Land of Spices*— despite the accent). Mary's own accent is also substandard, "diseased," she feels, for a language teacher. When Luisa says, "How beautifully you speak.... So purely, and yet with that strange, faint nuance that simply is not in the English voice," Mary can only reply, "But that's a defect.... I feel very uneasy in case I pass it on to these children" (153). The Wexford-English of Conlan, the Dublin-English of O'Toole, and the Tipperary-English of Harty are richly textured in the novel. There are some beautiful examples of Hiberno-English, such as (Agatha to Mary) "It's jam for the stupid" or (Rosie to Agatha) "None of your transports!" The governesses are presented as a linguistic community, with a shared English which does not erase individuation — another opportunity taken by O'Brien to underline a major theme in the novel.

At another level, however, if English and Spanish stand in the same position in relation to Irish and Basque, O'Brien's treatment of the last two shows a narrow cosmopolitanism complicit with cultural imperialism. However, she is also sensitive enough to problematize her characters' linguistic baggage:

> "I shall never understand Spanish," said the governess as they left Jaime behind.
> "Perhaps not," said Milagros, "but that was Basque, Pilár [sic] has a bad habit of speaking Basque to the servants."
> "It's the only way of making sure they understand," said Pilár [18].

The Areavagas are not British functionaries in India, they are Basque men and women living in the Basque Country. Only Nieves shows some faint awareness of the absurdity of the situation: "'Milagros is a snob about the way people speak,' she said. 'She thinks that her own Castilian is the purest of Altorno'" (ibid.).

Sadly, there is as yet no translation of *Mary Lavelle* into Euskera, although there have been recent calls for it in the Basque press (see Tobar-Arbulu "Kate" and Mentxaka "Kate" [2009]). In a paper of 2002, Wanda Balzano suggested that the repressed Basque language in the novel operates as a symbol of Mary's repressed sexuality. Within the main narrative of forbidden heterosexual love, then, what Mary should/will get away from is the Spanish language as marker of normativity. Yet the novel does not encourage this reading. Mary's increasing fluency in Spanish (which occurs at implausible speed) is best read as symbolizing her fast-growing infatuation with Spain, mirrored in her infatuation with Juanito. It follows that if there is a code at play regarding the suppression of Euskera, it may perhaps be related to the necessity to abandon heteronormative inhibitions (the Spanish language) and access the submerged lesbian possibilities (the Basque language). There is a recent example of a comparable use of languages in relation to nationalist articulation and lesbianism, in the Catalan film of 2004 *Sevigné*, by Marta Balletbo-Coll. It may be also possible to read Juanito's Basqueness as the mark of Mary's un-utterable, forbidden, sexual attraction for him (by/for a queer heterosexual). However, Juanito never once speaks Euskera in the novel (it is an *implicit* assumption that this is the Areavagas' first language, but only his sisters use it in the book). In fact, if there is a symbolic sexual code here, Juanito's insistence that Mary should speak Spanish to him, which is clearly beyond her capabilities even though she is in principle willing (see "A Hermitage"), soon begins to feel like the machinery of heteronormative misogyny has just been spurred into action. Spanish may be the language of love (*Land* 173), but it is also the language of the empire.

What is, then, Mary's relationship with Euskera? Mary hears Basque spoken all around her in Altorno/Bilbo and notes with excitement that the names of Irish nationalists crop up in the otherwise unintelligible conversations of the locals. The text assumes every Basque speaker to be a Basque nationalist. This becomes (unintentionally) comical when we are presented with Juliana, a peasant, a Basque speaker, an "old woman, [and] a strong Basque nationalist" (217), a stereotypical lump of a woman who, by a strange orientalizing spell, is also a practiced palm reader (in the "Basque" style, we are told — 220, although palm reading is not associated with Basque culture), all of which attributes are conflated and confirmed by an allergic reaction to the Castilian landscape. Juliana's conversation with the girls turns, under Mary's gaze, into a "gay pantomime" (217).

Mary is not an exile in Bilbo (Reynolds *Kate* 99), and she is more than a visitor. Under the (re)definition of Basqueness sketched by the previous Basque regional government (in the "plan Ibarretxe"), linking citizenship to residency (see *Euskadiren* 4), Mary would be considered Basque. Should that label have been available to her, would she have entertained the notion? Unlikely. She is more in empathy with a Spanish-Castilian identity, within a European framework. Mary recalls the often repeated Northern European assumption that "Africa starts at the Pyrenees" and is indignant at the idea (O'Brien *Mary* 215). Nevertheless, given the positive references to the "Reconquista" in the novel and the travelogue, and the novel's investment on the cultural/gendered/emotional/sexual border of the hermitage in Toledo, it would appear that O'Brien simply shifts the "African" border halfway down the peninsula. The "Reconquista" (the "reconquest") was the term used by Christian Spain to refer to the military campaign to expel Muslims from the Iberian peninsula. Toledo was conquered by Christians in 1085, the first important city of Al-Andalus (the Muslim state in the peninsula) to be taken over.

Mary Lavelle is the first of Kate O'Brien's books to be concerned with Spain and the Basque Country as integral parts of Europe. Spain was to play a crucial role in her output. In addition to *Farewell Spain*, another two books would be concerned with Spanish history: the novel *That Lady* and the biography *Teresa of Avila*. Spanish characters are central to *As Music and Splendour* and to her last, unfinished novel, *Constancy*. The Basque Country would not play a part in any book after *Mary Lavelle*, with the exception of *Farewell Spain*, although two token inclusions are interesting. A minor character in *As Music and Splendour*, the opera singer Manuel Arrez, is introduced as "a Basque from Pamplona" (245). This is a political statement. Nafarroa/Navarre, of which Iruina/Pamplona is the capital city, is a semi-autonomous region in the Spanish state claimed by Basque nationalists, who make up a minority in the population of Navarre. Manuel Arrez's Basqueness is therefore an endorsement of Basque nationalism's historical claim. The statement is more interesting than the character itself, a stereotypical Basque figure — a glutton and a singer (the equivalent of the alcoholic, verbose stage–Irish), and perhaps related to the shopkeeper Pepe Valdez in *Mary Lavelle* (see *Mary* 27).

In *That Lady*, another minor character, the daughter of the protagonist Ana de Mendoza, is given a Spanish name which incorporates a Basque suffix, "Anichu" (the Spanish spelling for "Anitxu," meaning "little Ana" in Basque), a telling feature in the context of this sparsely populated political allegory. The name suggests that the Basque Country embodies, in a physically smaller version, the antifascist politics of (the Castilian/Spanish) Ana. This is a striking move not just because, according to this reading, the Basque Country may be read as attached to/originated *in* Spain, but because it is also embodied in a child (most unusual in relation to what's often described as "the oldest culture in Europe"), indicating that she is the promise of the future at a symbolic level, destined to take over her mother's role. Another interesting feature in *That Lady* is the inclusion of a historical Basque woman in the list of "significant women in the world" that the proto-feminist Antonio recites to an ignorant Ana: "Margaret of Navarre, Elisabeth of England, Mother Teresa, the Princess of Eboli" (187). Queen Marguerite, who was born in Angulême (France), was the author of *The Heptameron,* a collection of erotic tales in the French language, from 1559, that may be considered the earliest example of Basque queer (heterosexual) literature.

Discussing *Mary Lavelle,* Gerardine Meaney perceptively pointed out in 1997 that:

> One of the most interesting aspects of the novel is its assertion that feminine sexuality is political, is indeed the key to a different politics and another history. Mary's "adultery" is a rejection of an Ireland which has not fulfilled the promise of independence. Moreover it is crucial to the novel's engagement with the political future of Spain and of Europe as a whole. In the novel's concern with Ireland's relation to a broader European culture and politics, it marks both the integration of the new Ireland into that culture and the difference that remains. Moreover, both national and international identity is posited from the margins, through relation to the Basques, not the old colonizer or major centres of Europe. Since that relationship is, here and elsewhere, explored in terms of a feminine protagonist, O'Brien's fiction offers an unusually explicit account of the relationship between gender and territoriality and a putting into question of "the nation space" produced by such a relationship ["Territory" 90–1].

With the exception of Gerardine Meaney and Wanda Balzano, critics have *ignored* the fact that *Mary Lavelle* is set in the Basque Country, is immersed in Basque history, culture, and politics, and is populated by Basque characters. Maribel de Foley's declaration that "the novel is set in Spain and ... the majority of the characters are Spanish" ("Country" 26), typifying the critics' approach, is all the more lethal in its matter-of-factness. Critics *choose* to sail through *Mary Lavelle*'s obfuscation of national issues as if through "a halcyon sea," and they inevitably fail to reach the battered Cantabric coast.

In 1935, Kate O'Brien was writing for an audience that knew little about Spain and even less about the Basque Country, and many of the political and artistic decisions that affected the composition of the novel relied on a highly problematic manipulation of her subject matter. *Mary Lavelle* is littered with more or less subtle distortions. All the characters in the novel who are not Irish or English, with one exception (Luisa), are Basque, yet they are referred to as being Spanish. Not only that, but we are told, for example, that Milagros was "patriotic as any Spaniard" (228). This is reminiscent of a passage in *Farewell Spain,* where O'Brien's description of a Galizian city, Santiago, includes what in a different context would be seen as a gross provocation from a right-wing propagandist: "men are Spanish here...," she declares (79). It is a paradox that *Mary Lavelle,* a novel that sprung from a writer's intimate knowledge and love of the Basque Country, would apply itself to the task of obliterating Basque uniqueness, in a book that elevates individuality and diversity to a sacramental status.

THE "SPAINS"

Mary thinks, again and again, that Altorno is "not a bit like my idea of Spain" (*Mary* 6). She is puzzled when she arrives, because in 24 hours she has not seen "anything Spanish that reminded her of Spain," and her confusion deepens as she gets to know this "unlooked-for Spain" (39, 74). We are told that Mary reads avidly as many books as she can find on Spain, and Ford, Washington Irving, Gautier, and Borrow are listed (see 215, 223). O'Brien mentions them again in *Farewell Spain*, with the addition of Salvador de Madariaga, whose book *Spain* had been published in London in 1930. It is not a coincidence that Madariaga describes El Cid as a northern hero, a "herald" and "a free lance" (Mary has a reproduction of the Cid's trunk in her room), that he emphasizes that in Spain the individual "becomes the standard of all life" or that his chapter on industry and commerce in *Spain* describes Bilbo as "the centre of the world-famous iron ores, in which the *Altos Hornos de Vizcaya* have developed a flourishing industry" (Madariaga 29, 36, 165). There is a constant in O'Brien: How much she knows as an author remains a private matter, how much she tells to her reader becomes a *creative* decision, and how much this matters in her intertextual dance suggests a source of anxiety as much as empowerment. Her research is not that crucial — she had lived in Bilbo herself and she had returned on numerous occasions. O'Brien knew far more about Basque history, culture, and politics than she allowed *Mary Lavelle* to show.

Simultaneously, the text makes it impossible to understand the Areavagas, or Altorno, or Mary's love for either, if we evacuate the fact that they are Basque. Juanito, like his father, believes that the only conceivable direction for a progressive government/system to take is to warrant autonomy to the different regions of "the Spains." The Basque Country is "my own country," Juanito declares (302), while Mary dreams of "perpetual self-government" (27), the demand of Basque nationalists in 1922, and 1936, as Kate O'Brien was well aware. But Basque aspirations are loose threads in a Spanish whirlwind. The centralism of the novel's ideology seems blind to its own flamboyant localism. Nowhere in Spain is like Altorno — indeed, nowhere *in the Basque Country* is like Bilbo either — yet a Castilian barrenness (read spiritual purity) must cover all irregular features like a veil.

Mary falls in love with Juanito's "irregular, erratic face" (i.e., non–Spanish) (175) and haphazard appearance, the signs, ultimately, that he has failed to convince in his Spanish impersonation. Yet, to the novel, he is a symbol of Spain: "In the brief weeks of her acquaintance with Spain she had fallen day by day — she saw that now — a little more and a little more in love with it. This love had, timidly, fed curiosity, and curiosity, humoured somewhat, had fuelled love" (214). Mary's supposed political innocence is contradicted in the little we glean of her past allegiances and current interests. In Ireland, she has been involved in assisting the operations of the Irish Republican Army in such a capacity as to make her liable to imprisonment (see 25). In the Basque Country, to where she has arrived following a suggestion from her former history teacher to land in the house of a historian, Don Pablo Areavaga, Mary has been attentively following political developments and has familiarized herself (presumably through the press, as she is an avid newspaper reader?) with the nationalist movement. In a moment reminiscent of Fanny Price's reference to slavery in Jane Austen's 1814 *Mansfield Park* (see Austen 165–6), Mary blurts out:

> "Do you then sympathise with the nationalist ambitions of the Catalans and the Basques?" she asked Luisa.
> The other raised her brows.
> "You take an interest in our intricate affairs?" she said with surprise. "Your question is difficult. The kings of Castile have been kings of all the Spains for a very long time. Myself I cling to the old tradition, but Juanito says my clinging is of no importance!" She laughed very prettily. "He says that some form of federated autonomies will have to be conceded. And Juanito belongs to the future" [152].

Later on, in passing, Mary compares her infatuation with Juanito to an infatuation with Michael Collins (218). Again, her experience of Irish history is only articulated obliquely. The important links between Irish and Basque nationalism are casually overheard in the market, when Mary is "amused" by mentions to Arthur Griffith and Patrick Pearse through the "oration" (a deliberate O'Brienism) of a Basque nationalist (128). Clearly, the novel is also intent on silencing Irish nationalism, and any inkling of a related colonial context in Bilbo is to be sidestepped with a ballerina's soft touch. But the references are there, and it seems more than a coincidence that both Collins and Griffith died in 1922; in fact, Mary meets Juanito in August, the month Collins was killed (see Foley's emphasis in fn.5 *Pasiones* 251). O'Brien had an "allergy" to orthodox nationalism, predating her being targeted by de Valera's censors. Like other Irish people, she loved "an Ireland of the spirit, an island without Border or politics," which was as true as any other version, "for," as Winifred Letts put it in 1933, "a country has many moods" (8–9).

Arguably, the de-emphasizing of Basqueness in the characters works to the detriment of their force as political beings. *Mary Lavelle* presents alternative ways of being Basque. For example, Don Pablo is a "matter-of-fact" anarchist, "a loather of institutions" and of violence, who would have empathized with the sentiments of the Basque anarchist collective that declared in 1986: "What is the use of fighting for a country which doesn't need borders to exist, in order to build another country which can exist by virtue of its borders[?] It is merely an aesthetic issue" (Legasse et al. 35 — my translation). Juanito is the antithesis or idealism, lawyer (see *Mary* 63), but he is also a federalist and hopes to create a socialist confederation of regions and nations that will facilitate their self-government. This brings together the two political strands in the novel, socialism and nationalism, but the reader is left to work out the connections by herself.

Early on in the novel, Mary explains that "she had studied her map and accepted the vastness and regionalism of Spain, and understood already that the north is not the south" (*Mary* 75). The statement could not be more purposefully vague. Later, in Madrid, she refers to the Basque Country as "the northern coast" (215) or "the north" (239, 254). Every one of the other "Spains," however, is also obliterated in the clean slate of the Castilian sky. There is one exception, Andalucia, which is dealt with in *Mary Lavelle* with inexcusable viciousness. There is seemingly no irony in the trendy Areavagas listening to records of "cante hondo," heard by Mary in the immigrants' slums that sustain the lifestyle of Altorno's "great"; these impoverished people are disposable and their culture a prop. The only villain in the novel is also the only *Andalucían* (but see 75): "Andalucian Don Jorge" is referred to as "the Andalucian priest," the "Andalucian music master," "the Andalucian man" with his "Andalucian jokes," "the filthy Andalucian," and so on (13, 173, 198, 174, 132, 324). It is not the only instance in O'Brien's work. In *That Lady*, for example, prejudice contaminates Ana de Mendoza's impression of Mateo Vasquez, Secretary of State: "The Princess of Eboli did not like the Andalusian accent. / 'He is very likely a Moor,' she thought flippantly" (*Lady* 11). The "flippancy" could have been balanced by her beloved servant Bernardina, but even this affectionate and loyal woman is, her mistress "jokes," "a lazy Andalusian" (160).

This "tactic" (repeated in the vilification of Germans in *The Flower of May*, for example), in *Mary Lavelle*, is part of the scaffolding of Kate O'Brien's promotion of Castile, a project which, as we have seen, she shared with a generation of intellectuals. *That Lady* shamelessly pushes this agenda to the forefront: Ana de Mendoza, considering "the kingdoms of Spain," is disappointed with the king's decision to set the capital in Madrid and not in Toledo or Avila (with its "pure Castilian style"), in the same region, but she nevertheless agrees "[t]hat Castile and the centre should rule the rest was obvious" (186). Even Ana's act of defiance, the core of the novel, is described by the protagonist as "one small service for Castilian good sense before I die" (296), while O'Brien herself opens *Teresa of Avila* by referring to "the civilised world — in which Spain, *Castilian Spain*, played a leading part" (emphasis added, 17). It is unsurprising that, in 2007, following on the footsteps of Kate O'Brien for a television program, Irish historian Margaret McCurtain declared when approaching Avila that she felt she was "travelling to the soul of Spain" (*Time* RTE).

In this context, the main problem to the cohesiveness of *Mary Lavelle* is that the allegorical plot demands that the Basque Country impersonate Spain, which it could never do. Hence the silences, the displacements, the energy spent in keeping all those knives rotating in the air. The novel risks all to ensure that this illicit, inevitable embrace (between Europe/Ireland and Spain) takes place — the ritual purging (of the Basque Country) is a prerequisite to conjure up a "fantastic" Spain (see 202). *Mary Lavelle*'s pressing concern is to publicize and make intelligible the momentous instauration of a radical leftist government in Spain. In her most political novel, at her most utopian, Kate O'Brien barely manages to contain a second political agenda that threatens to contaminate her priorities. It is at least a mark of honesty that the shadow is allowed to loom over.

Altorno/Bilbo

BILBO, LIBERAL TOWN

Karin Eva Zettl believes, accurately in my opinion, that *Mary Lavelle* can be considered a historical novel, "in the sense that a certain period of historical time divides the narrated time from the time of narration. Kate O'Brien looks back from her present into a historical past and there is a constant tension between the two time levels" ("Kate" 13–4). As we will see, the history of Bilbo plays an important part in *Mary Lavelle*, a novel that relies on an interplay between past and present, heritage and self-invention. When Mary arrived, the city had become a laboratory of identities—the result of a particular trajectory.

Bilbo has a reputation as a liberal town. In 1874, it heroically resisted a siege by conservative Carlist troops for 125 days, and the "liberation" of Bilbo on May 2 was commemorated for decades afterwards. On account of its resistance to Carlism, Bilbo became known as "la ciudad invicta," "the unconquered city" (see O'Brien *Spain* 202). Nationalism located itself at an ideological border between the Liberal bourgeoisie of the city and the Carlist rural poor. The Basque had lived in the area since prehistory (see Jose Miguel de Barandiaran, in Ugalde 19), while Euskera was not of Indo-European origin and appeared to be unrelated to any known language, which prompted some commentators to suggest that Basques were in fact the original natives of Europe (for a recent example of this claim, see Hamel and Vennemann). Collective entitlement was often rationalized in proportion to uniqueness and antiquity. The Basque region (meaning the area with a Basque-speaking population) was divided in the 19th century as it is now, between Spain and France, and it can be argued that the main Basque Nationalist claim is first and foremost the right to a border — with all that this implies in cultural and economic terms. The only "national" geographical border of any significance before the launch of Basque nationalism in 1893, is woven into Basque folklore: the Malato Tree ("Arbol de Malato"), an ancient tree that stood south of the Basque Country on the limit with Castile, and in which trunk the Basques stuck their swords after expelling invading armies, a gesture which exemplified a disinterest in retribution or expansion. In the Bilbo of the nineteenth and twentieth centuries, the potential demarcation of the Basque land was, in a fundamental sense, antithetical to the liberal agenda and repugnant to industrial capitalism.

The Carlist/Liberal divide is crucial to understand the city — and the country — Mary Lavelle steps into in 1922. A famous poem by the Bilbaian Javier de

Bengoechea sums it up: "I live in a demure / Inner Bilbo besieged / By the Nean-
derthal Basque / My place is that of the artist / With one grandfather Liberal /
And one grandfather Carlist" (quoted in Sota *Bilbao* 11— my translation). The
crux of the conflict was the local charts ("Lege Zaharra" or "Fueros"), which
were regulated by a number of proto-parliaments ("Lege Biltzarrak" or "Juntas") since at least 1053 in the case of Biscay, where the famous gatherings under
a sacred oak in the town of Gernika ("Guernica") became a symbol of the
Basque right to self-government.

In *Mary Lavelle*, the (Irish and Basque) lovers' first private meeting takes
place in a hermitage south of Toledo, an area which once marked the contested
limit of Christian and Muslim Europe. Queen Isabella was queen of Castile when
her husband inherited the crown of Aragon, which created a political and military
entity of unprecedented strength in the Iberian Peninsula. In 1492, Isabella and
Fernando, known as "the Catholic Monarchs," launched a successful offensive
against the Arab kingdom of Granada, which put an end to partial Muslim rule
in Spain and allowed the crown of Castile to assemble under one crown all the
territories that would become known as Spain, with the exception of the Kingdom
of Navarre, which would be incorporated in 1515 (by 1016 the entire Basque
Country was included in the Kingdom of Navarre). Isabella and Fernando, like
subsequent monarchs, respected local charts and gave special privileges to certain
regions. For example, they granted all Biscayans the staus of "noble," with legal
immunity in certain circumstances (for some views on this controversial issue,
see Ugalde 144–147).

But the charts were abolished on four different occasions in the nineteenth
century, a crucial issue in the development of the Carlist Wars (from 1833 to
1939 and from 1872 to 1876), which initially broke out between followers of
Doña Isabel (with her mother Maria Cristina as regent) and Don Carlos, both
of whom had a claim to the Spanish throne. In the Basque Country the conflict
acquired the character of a civil war. The Carlists defended tradition, including
respect for the Basque charts, while the Liberals were associated with progressive
politics of a French hue. This historical background, alluded to in O'Brien's
novel, is essential to understand the ideology of Don Pablo, who feels at home
in liberal Bilbo, but was "sick of the self-deceptiveness and inertia of Liberalism
in Spain" (*Mary* 49, 61), and it may have informed specific elements in the
novel. For example, it is interesting that Tomás de Zumalacarregui, an enormously popular Carlist military leader, seen by many as a supporter of Basque
independence (see Ugalde 171–2), died in June 1835 after being *wounded* in
Begoña/Allera during the siege of Bilbo in the First Carlist War.

The Carlist Wars became part of the mythology attached to the historical
Basque struggle for self-determination, not just in the Basque Country, but in
revolutionary Europe, with William Wordsworth penning his 1810 poem "The
Oak of Guernica" (838–9), a declaration of support for Basque independence,
as a response to the Carlist conflict. In 1897, the Basque writer and philosopher

Miguel de Unamuno had published a historical novel documenting the last Carlist siege of Bilbo, *Paz en la Guerra* ("Peace in War"), and he was justified in claiming, in the 1923 edition prologue, that the book was still relevant (123). The impact of the Carlist conflict on Basque society and culture cannot be overstated, as is evident in Unamuno's further (and characteristically immodest) claim: "This is not a novel, it's a people" (124). Carlism was to shape Basque politics to come. The Carlist slogan "God, King, and Charts" ("Dios, Rey, y Fueros" in Spanish), would be adapted by the founder of Basque Nationalism, Sabino Arana Goiri, by simply eliminating the reference to the Spanish monarchy, to read "God and Charts" ("Jaunkoikoa eta Lege-Zaharra" in Euskera, commonly abreviated to JEL), as Arana explained at the launch of the movement *in Begoña/Allera*, on June 3, 1893.

Kate O'Brien devoted a long paragraph of *Farewell Spain* to explain the relevance of Carlism to Bilbo, defining its supporters as "upholders of conservatism, oppression and the divine right of kings," explaining that distinctions between "a 'Carlista' or a 'Cristino'" among neighbors were still common in 1923, and going on to make the striking (from a Basque point of view, absurd) claim that Fascist troops are "the twentieth-century Carlists" (201–2). It is true that some Carlists in Navarre provided support for the 1937 military rising, but this is an example of O'Brien's perilous tendency to promote her political views by buttressing them with anything and everything that comes her way. One is reminded of the association of Cromwell with progressive politics, outside Ireland, which simply makes no sense from within the Irish experience. The *Farewell Spain* paragraph concludes with a prophecy, which sadly will not be realized: "Bilbao may indeed have to face another siege," O'Brien says, "but she is used to winning them" (202).

BILBO, INDUSTRIAL CITY

Bilbo may have been liberal, but its liberal businessmen were also chartists. Biscayan charts established that only Biscayans could register ownership of local mines, an unusual legal circumstance (rescinded by 1841— see Montero *Mineros* 39) which allowed the concentration of wealth in local hands, contributing to the creation of a Biscayan oligarchy. The decisive mining boom in Bilbo took place in the late nineteenth century, but local foundries were already known throughout Europe in Shakespeare's time, as we can see in *The Merry Wives of Windsor* and *Henry V*, where we find references to "Bilbo"—a type of iron manacles made in the city (see Woodworth 107). An archaic term by the twentieth century, "Bilbo" was fittingly used to name the protagonist of J.R.R. Tolkien's medieval-inspired saga *The Lord of the Rings*, written in 1937 and 1954–5 partly as a response to the rise of fascism. In 1782, the Irish traveler William Bowles had claimed a common ancestry for Ireland and the Basque Country in his *Introduction to Natural History*; the book also discussed the busy port in Bilbo, remarking on the independent spirit and physical strength of women workers there (see Mesa "Usos" 52–3). Industrialization gave the cityscape a distinct look, perceptively discussed in a 2007 book by Irish journalist and writer Paddy Woodworth, who, like his contemporary Mark Kurlansky, has a remarkable empathy with the Basques. Woodworth quotes anthropologist Joseba Zulaika, who explains that Bilbo used to "wear its ugliness like a badge of honour"; then he offers his own view of the city, declaring that even in the early 1980s, it "could still seem like a film set for a fascist Hades, designed by some deeply depressed expressionist" (Woodworth 116).

Often in *Mary Lavelle*, we get a glimpse of the "wine-red hill[s]" around Altorno/Bilbo, "craggy" and "sinister hills, deep-scarred and shadowy," because they are full of iron mines (O'Brien *Mary* 69, 6, 73). The mines in Bilbo were mostly open-air operations rather than tunneling, which affected the landscape in this unique way. As Manuel Montero points out, the invention of the Bessemer method to produce steel, in 1855, was crucial to the boom, because the method required non-phosphoric iron, and the Biscayan mines were not only rich in that type of mineral, but they also had the advantage of being close to a big and relatively modern port for shipping (see *Mineros* 19–20). Iron from Bilbo began to be exported to British blast furnaces first, then to France, Belgium, and Germany. In the next 50 years, "the geographic and human landscape" of Biscay was transformed; the left bank was lined with "blackening ovens, suspended trains, mineral washing points," while "the expansion of numerous towns in the area and the emergence of a working class linked to the exploitation of the mines" were to change "[Basque] history," and the sudden influx of capital would facilitate "the total insertion of the province [of Biscay] in the ambit of industrial capitalism" (*Mineros* 20 — my translation).

Shortly after her arrival, Mary learns of the "iron mines from which most of the rich people round here get their money" (O'Brien *Mary* 7). Mines and blast furnaces are a source of imagery for O'Brien, as they had been for Vicente Blasco Ibáñez in his 1904 novel, *El Intruso*, a portrait of the fractured Bilbaian society at the turn of the century, protagonized by a Dr. Aresti (another version of Enrique Areilza, "Don Pablo," as we will see later). Areavaga reflects on his marriage: "Explosions of temper against trifles, hot, high moments about exciting nothings, ... sparks which seemed always to generate a renewal of passion in him..." (O'Brien *Mary* 57). Using remarkably similar language, Aresti says, "No, I am not a liberal; I am a man of my time" and explains that "I am a Jacobean; I want to be an inquisitor, reversed, you understand? a man [sic] who dreams *of violence, of iron and fire, the only remedies to wipe his land clean of the misery of the past*" (emphasis added, Ibáñez 138).

The high furnaces and mines of Bilbo seemed destined to be the site of literal, not metaphoric, revolution. Socialism was growing fast in the Basque Country at the turn of the twentieth century. The appalling working and living conditions of immigrants encouraged the development of socialist activism on a scale unprecedented in the Basque Country or the Spanish state, as shown by the historical General Strike of 1890. The activist Facundo Perezagua arrived from Madrid to publicize socialism among the workers; Tomás Meabe was to abandon his nationalist beliefs, to become editor of the *La Lucha de Clases* ("Class Struggle") journal, and to set up "Juventudes Socialistas" ("Socialist Youth"; an organization renouncing to violence, religion, alcohol) in Bilbo in 1904. And the conservatives were also radicalizing — a Basque-Irish man, Pedro Eguillor y Atteridge, a gourmet and intellectual, "was cooking the Bilbaian recipe of proto-fascism" ("prefalangismo") (Sota 18). Many Basque internationalists came to politics through the direct experience of the brutality and the poverty endured by miners at the turn of the century. Dolores Ibarruri, "la Pasionaria," was one of them. Born in 1895 in the mining village of Gallarta, in the outskirts of Bilbo, of miner parents, she would gain enormous fame as an inspiring orator in the 1930s, always dressed in black and wearing rope-soled shoes, and would go on to become a key figure in the communist movement, as a "cool and calculating" politician (Preston "Pasionaria" 317; see 286). Around the corner from Portugalete/Cabantes, at about the same time as Mary Lavelle was being introduced to communist ideas by Juanito, the young woman who was to become Secretary General of the Spanish Communist Party was penning her first articles for *El Minero Vizcaino* ("The Biscayan Miner" newspaper).

A contemporary, Indalecio Prieto, although born in Asturias, spent most of his life in the Basque Country. He grew up in absolute poverty in Bilbo, where he educated himself and built the basis for his remarkable political career with the Socialist Party, launched after moving to Madrid in 1917. Paul Preston claims that "one of the objectives of General Primo de Rivera's coup of 13 September 1923 was to silence Prieto" ("Life" 242). It didn't work. When the Dictator Primo de Rivera turned the socialist union UGT into the official/compulsory union in Spain (while making the anarchist union CNT illegal), Prieto was vocally against collaboration with the regime, but his life-long rival in the party, Francisco Largo Caballero, opted for an alliance. Prieto remained a dynamo on the left. According to Preston, Prieto "did more than any other individual to create the Second Republic, to sustain it in power, to defend it in war and, in exile and old age, to continue working for the re-establishment of democracy in Spain" (ibid., 235). Prieto was a reformist rather than a revolutionary, and he was convinced that working class organizations had to work in tandem with bourgeois Republicans, a central idea in *Mary Lavelle.*

Meanwhile, the impact of Irish independence was enormous in the Basque Country, although the initial public reactions to the Easter Rising were not auspicious. *Euzkadi* (the old nationalist spelling of "Euskadi," the Basque Country), the official newspaper of the Basque Nationalist movement published in Bilbo, because of its anti–German and pro–British stance during the European war, condemned the Irish rebellion. At the same time, the ultraconservative and

anti–Basquist Bilbo newspaper *La Gaceta del Norte*, because of its pro–German
and anti–British stance, hailed the Irish rebellion with enthusiasm (see Espinosa
53, 55).

As José María Lorenzo Espinosa has documented, within the Basque
nationalist movement there were many that highlighted the absurdity of their
official line, and the numbers and determination of these dissenters grew fast.
A particularly hostile article on Roger Casement, published in *Euzkadi* at the
end of August 1916, shortly after his execution, prompted serious protests
within the ranks of the movement, demanding that the editor step down (see
Espinosa 56). Those who were actively seeking changes were younger nationalists, from organizations such as the mountaineering group Eusko Gaztedija
("Basque Youth"), which was in fact a political organization surreptitiously creating an unofficial "army" of Basque militants (see Espinosa 151–6). A more
radical segment of Basque nationalism continued to grow in numbers and visibility, culminating in 1930 in the creation of EAE/ANV (Eusko Abertzale
Ekintza–Accion Nacionalista Vasca, "Basque Nationalist Action"), a laic, eth-
nic-nationalist, and independentist organization (see the 2005 study of Eduardo
Renobales). The EAJ/PNV (Eusko Alderdi Jeltzailea–Partido Nacionalista Vasco,
"Basque Nationalist Party") was at the time, by contrast, Catholic, defending
a racial claim to Basque distinctiveness, and pursuing reformist and moderate
aims.

In 1922, Sinn Feinn member Martin O'Daily gave a series of lectures in
Bilbo, an event organized by the leader of "Basque Youth" Eli Gallastegui. One
of these lectures described the activities of the Irish nationalist women's association Cumann na mBan. In the discussion that followed, at Gallastegui's insti-
gation, "a group of fifty women, with Karmele Errazti on the lead, decided to
second the initiative, which in such a spontaneous fashion resulted in the creation a few days later of Emakume Abertzale Batza" (Espinosa 65). The group,
called "Union of Basque Patriot Women," although not specifically feminist
(see Espinosa 66), was to become a formidable militant organization, promoting
a degree of political involvement in women that was previously unseen in the
nationalist movement.

After the end of the dictatorship of Primo de Rivera in 1932, the organization EUSKERIN, funded in Bilbo, sought to strengthen the connections
between Euskadi/the Basque Country and Erin/Ireland, with the specific objective of helping Ireland overcome the commercial veto by the UK between 1932
and 1935 (see Espinosa 59). Also in 1932, the regrouping of Basque nationalist
forces would result, among other things, in the celebration of the first ever
Aberri Eguna (Day of the Basque Homeland), an event promoting the independence of the Basque Country, which would be organized annually on Easter
Sunday, a day chosen for three reasons: It was the day in which the founder of
Basque Nationalism, Sabino Arana y Goiri, had the first "revelation" of the new
ideology, it was a day of fitting religious symbolism, and it was "a way of paying

tribute to the Irish of 1916, to make up for the previous attitude of official Basque nationalism" (Espinosa 62).

Mary Lavelle includes few references to nationalist agitation — and none to socialist activism. The very visible suffering of maimed beggars is duly noted by the protagonist of the novel; it is a counterpoint to the ostentatious wealth of the city's bourgeoisie. But there is no dwelling in the horrors of poverty, and for a reason — O'Brien's socialist heroes are middle and upper class, trapped in dilemmas of moral (not physical or psychological) survival. Mary's rope-soled shoes and Pablo's black clothing exemplify their austerity, but, given their class, there are limitations to a political gesture that doubles up as individual signature.

In the Bilbo/Altorno of 1922, the majority of immigrants live in slums. Mary Lavelle describes her first impression of the city: "Outside the station she had found a very showy street of offices and shops" and "in the distance huddled heaps of slums, and the brown tower of a crumbling church; around the whole, red, sinister hills, deep-scarred and shadowy; above an undramatic pale blue sky" (O'Brien *Mary* 73). In a gorgeous intratextual duet, standing in the exact reverse spot to also highlight the sharp contrast between foreground and background, Kate O'Brien recalls in *Farewell Spain* that these slums were "awful in their stillness and despair" with their "crumbling Renaissance church, ... the dilapidated girl at the brothel door; boys, pale and stooped, coming up the lane from their shift; a little way off heavily loaded trolleys rattling down the hill," while far away one could see, in the valley, "the pricking light of Bilbao, outlines of banks and moving ships, softly sounding horns of Hispano-Suizas [cars]" (205).

The slums, O'Brien also explains, are "savage and shameless in poverty, but very gay on Sundays, with ... young men and women, shining and neat, crowding on to the train to go and dance at a *verbena* [a public dance] in Santurce" (emphasis in original, *Spain* 213). This makes the contrast to their everyday lives all the more horrifying. The rest of the week, from the very same commuters' train, the landscape becomes mechanized, and the workforce dehumanized. The train "ran by the river and through the premises of the most famous foundries — the 'Vizcaya,' the 'Altos Hornos,' the 'Santa Ana' — where the great fires never went out and where half-naked men moved like unreal creatures through glare and darkness" (Ibid.), O'Brien explains, giving her reader a clue to identify the name "Altorno."

Vicente Blasco Ibáñez's *El Intruso*, like *Mary Lavelle*, takes its protagonist to a number of emblematic places — the birthplace of Ignacio Loyola is one, a high furnace is another. *El Intruso* includes a detailed description of the process by which iron ore is turned into iron, but Ibáñez's focus is on working conditions — the book is an activist novel seeking to denounce the inhumanity of mines and factories, with the furnaces reminding the protagonist "of the fiery idols that boiled, in their bellies, in repugnant holocaust, their human victims"

(Ibáñez 162 — my translation). In the early twentieth century, many novels by Ibáñez were popularized through Europe and the United States in films targeting audiences eager for political commentary. The protagonist of *El Intruso*, Dr. Aresti, observes how a worker pokes the mouth of the blast furnace, covered in refractive soil, until "a river of dark red, as if blood from a bull, ran sparkling onto the ground" (Ibáñez 163 — my translation). This debris (known as the "escoria") that precedes the spurting liquid iron resembles a deep cut, gushing ceremonial blood, in a process technically referred to as "bleeding" ("sangrar"). *El Intruso* describes the furnace workers "moving like lizards between rivers of fire, tightened, blackened just as mummies" and going about "nearly naked, with long pieces of leather over their copper bodies, like Egyptian slaves occupied on a mysterious rite. Their limbs were exposed to the sparks of the iron, which flew in particles of burning scratch. Some showed the scars of horrible burns" (163 — my translation).

A number of films produced around the year of the publication of *Mary Lavelle* dealt with industrial processes. The 1936 science fiction film *Things to Come* showed a future where mining operations would be done by machines alone, which represented the supreme example of progress. Charlie Chaplin's *Modern Times*, of 1936, offered, in the factory scene, the most iconic image of the dehumanization associated with industrial capitalism: an unstoppable conveyor-belt set which was stylized, trimmed to a near-two-dimensional clarity, because critical commentary was prioritized over realism. Two other feature films with a central romantic narrative linked gender adjustments to an industrial process presented in documentary form: the 1937 *God's Country and the Woman*, to the timber industry, and the 1936 *Major Barbara*, to blast furnaces. It would have been implausible for Mary (and impossible for O'Brien) to offer any details of the workings of mines or factories in the city in 1922. Arguably, the limited mobility of the female protagonist in *Mary Lavelle* encouraged the creation of narrative strands that went *inwards*.

Euskera seems to be "underground," as we see in the Areavaga mansion, where "[t]he gentle servant-maids [who] smiled benevolently on [Mary]" and moved around "noiselessly," were "girls from the mountains and were believed to understand Castilian only when it was spoken very slowly and simply"; this allows the Areavagas to say "what they pleased to each other in pure and rapid Spanish, eating the while with industry" (*Mary* 69, 42). In the early twentieth century, Biscayan women outside Bilbo only learned Spanish out of necessity if they became servants to Spanish-speaking families (as the centenarian Bitori Ugalde Arrien, who had left her village to live in "Old Altorno" in the 1920s, explained; in conversation June 10, 2004). The Areavagas speak *"with industry"* and through industry, and the scene — those noiseless Basque servants orbiting around the dining table of the Spanish-speaking bourgeois Areavagas—can easily be read as a metaphor for the transformation of Basque "iron" into Spanish "steel."

At another level, the inexorable transformation of mineral in the neighboring foundries is a sure sign that, in Bilbo, the natural world of feelings must be beaten into submission, domesticated, civilized. When Mary arrives in Altorno, she is an undisturbed valley about to be dynamited; her entrails will be scooped out, her resources loaded into trains and taken away, her vague dreams turned into liquid fire, her doubts set into cold metal.

BILBO, CAPITALIST METROPOLIS

On her first visit to Bilbo's city center, Mary observes that the hills, "which met her eyes in every direction beyond the ornate buildings were not opulent at all ... and yet she knew they were the fertile womb of limousines, French hats and platinum rings" (O'Brien *Mary* 74). Pablo follows "three generations of culture and public service.... As shipowners and ironfounders his family had been among the earliest and most enduring builders of Altorno's industrial greatness" (49). A character in Unamuno's *Paz en la Guerra* explains: "Even if us Bilbaians would turn Carlist, Bilbo would continue to be Liberal, or it would stop being Bilbo.... Without liberalism it is impossible to trade, and without trade, our people are inconceivable" (quoted by Montero in *California* 35–6 — my translation). Many Irish immigrants had contributed considerably to the trade networks of the Basque Country: leather craftsmen from the late seventeenth century onwards, as well as Catholic priests and monks escaping persecution, many of whom settled in Begoña/Allera (see Bilbao [sic] 36, 107). The Irish were known as "chiguris," a term used in local legal documents in the eighteenth century (see ibid., 110). Irish immigrants in Bilbo created dynasties like the Archer family, from Thomas Archer's arrival in the mid-seventeenth century onwards, and already in the first decades of the eighteenth century part of "the elite of Bilbaian retail businesses," later making important contributions to cultural and scientific circles (ibid., 44; see 141, 146). By the late nineteenth century, Bilbo had become a commerical hub and a trading port, as well as a banking center, all thanks to the exploitation of the local mines (as well as exports of Castilian wool), in a boom that had benefited from some unusual circumstances.

A modernization process began in the period of peace between the Carlist wars. Owners of small foundries invested in new technology and expanded their facilities. The company Ybarra Hermanos (Ybarra Brothers), for example, had purchased a foundry in 1827, it owned some iron mines and conducted some limited trade, but in 1846 Ybarra went on to build the first modern siderurgical installations in Bilbo and, in 1882, their original factory was turned into the most emblematic blast furnace in the city: Altos Hornos de Bilbao. As we have seen, this is the furnace that lends its name to Altorno — and provides O'Brien's novel with a recurrent metaphor of forceful inner transformation.

In the 1870s some enterprising Bilbaians were hoping to turn the area into "the California of Iron" (see Montero *California* 13). As Lavelle puts it mimicking the mining process, the wealth of Altorno was "always growing at that time, always deepening, inexhaustibly available" (O'Brien *Mary* 49). But no one could have anticipated the economic boom in the region after the end of the last Carlist war, with the building of a host of massive iron factories between 1888 and 1892. As Manuel Montero has documented, the huge profits from the mining industry exceeded the volume of capital that the local bourgeoisie was accustomed to, and the fever of financial speculation that followed was decisive in turning Bilbo into the "bank-encrusted" city (O'Brien *Ireland* 19) it had become by the 1920s.

In one of the great social vistas from *Farewell Spain*, a knowledgable, perceptive, and politically committed Kate O'Brien discusses the busy industries and port in Bilbo, and explains that "French, Belgian, English and German exploiters have had their lucky dip at this source of wealth.... But the Spanish [sic] bourgeoisie has done very well for itself, by all appearances[,] and has been more than a match for the helpful foreigners" (202–3). On the year when Spain lost its last important colony in the Cuban War of Independence, Bilbaian investors had a first moment of "euphoria" (Montero *California* 23), and the banking boom that lasted between 1898 and 1901 created an entirely new financial structure in the city, with shipbuilding, blast furnaces, electricity supplies, insurance companies, and overseas trade all feeding each other (we should note that Mary's fiancé John is waiting to inherit his uncle's shipping business in order to get married).

Parallel to these developments, as Manuel Montero points out, another decisive change began to take shape, when some industrialists began to get involved in politics. In 1886, mine owner Victor Chávarri, for example, was elected deputy for Balmaseda, a district that encompassed the mining towns and the industrialized left bank in Bilbo. The trend would increase, to the extent that by the elections of 1893, six out of eight deputies and senators representing Biscay in the Spanish parliament had important financial interests in the local mining industry and trade (see ibid., 30–34). One of them was the industrialist Francisco Martínez Rodas, who appears in *Mary Lavelle*, as we will see later, as Jerónimo Parajo, Don Pablo's father-in-law.

It may seem striking that voters would entrust representation to their bosses. Universal male suffrage had been introduced in 1890, but elections were democratic in name only; rigged elections were the norm, coercion was widespread, and an enormous amount of votes were bought and sold. In 1891 in the Biscayan town of Berango, for example, a vote was priced at 50 pesetas, the equivalent of a three-week salary for a worker (Montero *California* 31). In a Spanish context, there was nothing unique about electoral corruption or about financiers positioning themselves in key places of political influence; what was unusual about Biscay (apart from the fact that Biscayan elections tended not to reflect the trends in Spain) was that businessmen, rather than making alliances with professional politicians to influence policies, entered the political arena *themselves*. As Montero points out, the myth of a Liberal Bilbo was dissolving fast (ibid., 31, 35).

In 1893, worried about the Spanish government's move towards easing restrictions on imports, a number of industrialists from Bilbo set up the Liga Vizcaina de Productores "Biscayan Producers League" as a pressure group to prevent the influx of cheaper foreign goods and services into Spain. They also developed an ideology to safeguard profits, their own brand of Protectionism. It provided the "conceptual baggage" of "the *Spanish nationalism* which would later constitute the main mark of identity of the political position of the Biscayan oligarchy" (emphasis in original, Montero *California* 38). It was this group of Basque bourgeois who coined the slogan "Spain for the Spanish!" (see ibid., 38, 43), a striking historical fact that evidences that capitalism is blind to irony and can absorb any contradiction.

The Parable of Altorno

The notion of a capitalist hub is not something Kate O'Brien deals with for the first time in *Mary Lavelle*. As we have seen, during a trip to New York in *Without My Cloak*, Denis discovers that everyone in the city ("from 46 Street to Merchants") seems obsessed with money, their favorite topic of conversation (see 385). Although he tries to tell himself that "the clambering, clattering, impressive and ridiculous town all round him [is] as insignificant as Ballyhooley," he is "impressionable," and feels "curiosity, fear, amusement, wonder, delight, disgust" (384). Mary Lavelle could have said the same about Altorno/Bilbo, and it is relevant that, like Denis, she is a visitor from a part of Ireland yet to be transformed by industrialization. In New York, Denis hears of "the new alchemy—petroleum" (385); in Altorno/Bilbo, iron is "the raw wealth which founded this glossy splendour" (O'Brien *Mary* 74). They make it possible for capitalism to emerge in all its glittering glory, turning communitarian, compassionate, generous impulses into a hardly visible substratum. Moneyed men are the "demigods" in New York, because "gold was its first principle and holy grail" (*Cloak* 385, 386), and also in Lavelle's new home, where wealth "was naturally, after God, Althorno's god" (*Mary* 49). Cities play an important part in many O'Brien novels. The sunny, peaceful Venice appeases the soul, while Brussels has a small-town quality that feels like home to the visitor. One can pick and choose in Rome's gregariousness. New York and Bilbo, by contrast, are a slap on the face for the gentle minded.

In Vicente Blasco Ibáñez's *El Intruso*, the protagonist describes Bilbo as beautiful, but "with the beauty of a well kept cemetery" (172). As we have seen, in her first trip to the city center, Mary notes the "pretentious[ness]" and "self-indulgence," and realizes that the "showy" appears side by side with the "shabby" (73). The showy and the shabby are married in Altorno—quite literally, since Juanito and Don Pablo, both described as "shabby," have married pretentious, rich women. We have seen how Mary had underlined the contrast between the "bright grey banks and clubs" and the "faded, sweet colour of the buff stone" of San Geromino/San Vicente, which matched the "old" mountains behind the church (O'Brien *Mary* 76). She had felt "as if what she looked on thus accidentally were ageing her" (ibid.). The building transubstantiates into Mary, who seems to become as old as the Basque mountains, detaching herself from the *new* banks and clubs. This links Mary to land and nation, severs her from modernity and capitalism.

In scenes such as these, the book seems to offer a *subtle* comment on the harms of industrial capitalism. At another level, however, the angelic Mary fulfills a symbolic role as messenger of doom, transforming the novel itself into a warning/announcement of impending apocalyptic collapse. It is tempting to see *Mary Lavelle* as a premonition, if not of a violent revolution to come, at least of the Spanish Civil War. Although the social unrest witnessed by O'Brien during her visits to Spain and the Basque Country in 1934 and 1935 certainly played a part in the conception of the novel, O'Brien herself insisted on her ignorance, at the time of writing *Mary Lavelle*, of what was to come: "One did not know that summer — or indeed, God forgive us, even when one returned in the next — that one was in at a death, or a vast, unpredictable birth" (*Spain* 36).

The apocalyptic subtext to *Mary Lavelle* is not primarily concerned with war or ideology, but with industrial capitalism as a system bound to implode. We have seen how, in *Without My Cloak*, Denis arrives in New York and thinks of the "warnings of a hundred fallen empires" (386). In *Mary Lavelle*, as we have seen, wealth is "Altorno's God" (49), and the text suggests a double link to two biblical versions of divine threat of destruction: the story of "Sodom and Gomorrah" (Genesis 19; see *Jerusalem* 38–39) and the story of "The Golden Calf and the Renewal of the Covenant" (Exodus 32–34; see *Jerusalem* 122–126). According to the first, apocalypse is a certainty, and Pablo Areavaga (who survives in his son) is the modern Lot who will be spared, redeemed by his anarchism. According to the second, apocalypse shall be averted, after the people repent from their sins and mend their ways.

When Mary reports Don Jorge's sexual harassment, Don Pablo says, "I believe I am more angry for the insult to you — for you are after all a sort of guest in Spain — than for the cruel cheapening of my daughters" (O'Brien *Mary* 174). This is an astonishing declaration, rather implausible, except for the fact that it represents the exact same attitude of Lot in the bible, who had offered his daughters to the mob in order to protect his guests, the angelic messengers of doom. Considering how regularly the tale of Sodom has been used by some Christians to malign homosexuals, O'Brien's version is an activist gesture. It is a merciless rewrite, with the Sodomites transformed into a heterosexual Catholic priest who is a child molester.

As for the other story, the golden calf was a false idol, cast after melting the golden jewelry worn by Israelite men and women (the furnaces of Altorno, connected to the "showiness" of its citizens), when their trust in their leader

Moses had been undermined by his disappearance on Mount Sinai (Don Pablo's defeatism and his "retreat" into celibacy). However, Moses returns (Juanito as the new Don Pablo), bringing with him a new covenant from Yahveh (his state socialism model), which persuades the Israelites to continue in their march towards the promised land, preceded by an angel (Mary and *Mary Lavelle*) who will clear the way by disposing of their enemies.

There is a related biblical reference in *Farewell Spain*, where O'Brien referred to the ominous signs she saw in the Bilbao of 1922: "everywhere— about [the war in] Morocco, about Basque Nationalism, about agrarian and foundry troubles, about all Bilbao's thousand woes—writing on the wall. Always plenty of writing on the wall. But no one seemed to read it" (*Spain* 216). The reference is to the Book of Daniel, which recounted the offences and excesses of King Nebuchadnezzar of Babylon and his son Belshazzar, who praised idols and forced others to do the same under threat of being "thrown into the burning fiery furnace" (Daniel 3:6; 5:4—*Jerusalem* 1472, 1480). In *Mary Lavelle*, Pablo had realized that he had cast his wife into a "symbol," an "ideal," an insubstantial idol (57); in a parallel course, he had loved "Spain," and his youthful energy had "burnt upward to be used by her" (54). In the Book of Daniel, during a royal feast a ghostly hand suddenly appeared and wrote four words on the wall in an unknown language, "mene mene teqel parsin" (sounding as foreign to the European ear as Euskera would have been to O'Brien). Daniel translated the signs, prophesizing an end to the king's rule *and* to the oppression of the Jewish people (see Daniel 5:26–28—*Jerusalem* 1481).

Later in the biblical account, an angel told Daniel of the history to come, speaking of "a time of great distress, unparalleled since nations first came into existence," but promising that "your own people will be spared—all those whose names are found written in the Book" (Daniel 12:1—*Jerusalem* 1492). Hence, we can look at the apocalyptic subtext of *Mary Lavelle* as an expression of wrath, but we can also see it as a salvational gesture—O'Brien's attempt to rescue the things and people she loved, from oblivion, by placing their names in the Book of Life. We can think of Mary as a "recording angel"— a figure transcending time, whose task is to keep a record of, rather than actively engage in, history (see Sucksmith's notes to Collins 607). Or, we can think of Mary as another kind of angel, as, in Luce Irigaray's phrase, a "messenge[r] of ethics" (13; note that Agnes is likened to Daniel in *The Anteroom* 114).

Or we can think of Mary as an active force for change, perhaps as a new Girolamo Savonarola, the agent of the fall of the Florentine "bourgeoisie" in the fifteenth century (with the Medicis as the original "banking emporium"), who persistently foretold deluge and damnation. Like him, Mary also has an ally (her own count Juan Pico de la Mirandola) in the austere, educated upper-class Don Pablo/Juanito. Renaissance Florence was sometimes referred to as "the new Sodom" by those critical of the supposed lassitude towards homosexuality in the city-state, and Savonarola's regeneration campaign ably mixed political and moral issues.

Sodom is of course still primarily linked to homosexuality, thanks to the homophobic operations of the Catholic church and its official reading of the biblical story, when the "sin of Sodom" was in fact lack of hospitality. Michael Warner has shown that the sixteenth century Puritans of the Great Migration to America saw England as Sodom and linked the biblical myth, not to sexual deviance, but primarily to "national judgment" and the idea of an entire society "in need of saving" ("Sodom" 331, 332). The Marquis de Sade is perhaps best known for *Hundred and Twenty Days of Sodom* (written around 1782 and a favorite of the French surrealists, who hailed Sade as the epitome of anti-establishment and freedom), but one of his non-pornographic books, *Aline and Valcour*, published in 1795, is more interesting in our context. In an episode, Zamé, the prophet and ruler of the utopian kingdom of Tamoé, tells his French guest, "You do not wish to have beggars! Do not accumulate in the capital the streams of gold flooding in from your provinces"; Zamé advises the abolition of money and the redistribution of resources, prophesizing that, as it had happened with Semiramis, in Greece, in Atate, "[y]our modern Babylon will crumble away ... exhausted by the embellishment of this new Sodom, [it] will be swallowed up, like her, beneath its gilded ruins" (Sade 85–86).

Sade claimed to have written the book before, and therefore anticipating, the French Revolution, although this is dubious (see Crosland 86–87). In 1922–1923, when Kate O'Brien had lived in Bilbo, when Mary the angel was announcing impending doom, there had been a crucial event following her departure: the coup d'état of General Miguel Primo de Rivera on September 13, 1923. Catherine Byron is the only critic to have linked *Mary Lavelle* to the coup, in an unpublished essay of 2003, noting that in the novel Mary "finds herself involved with political activists who will organize resistance to Primo de Rivera's dictatorship" (see "Changes"). His coup is the catastrophe prophesized by the book. The apocalyptic subtext of the "Parable of Altorno" in *Mary Lavelle* was no doubt incorporated by O'Brien into the novel in the awareness that the world she had described and Mary had experienced had collapsed in 1923.

In the narrator's prologue, as we have seen, there is a reference to the Spanish "revolution" of 1931 (*Mary* xvii). In that year, the people of Spain rose against the regime, and King Alfonso XIII, who had legitimized the dictator's rule, was driven out of the country. Primo de Rivera had left Spain in January 1930, and the King had appointed another general in his place, but August saw the "San Sebastian Pact," a secret agreement of Republicans to overthrow the regime, at a meeting which took place in the Basque city of Donosti or San Sebastian. The Republic was declared, and the country's first attempt at democracy began. To suggest, as *Mary Lavelle* does, that the dictatorship represented some sort of divine retribution (by the god of History) for the social irresponsibility of the upper and middle classes in the city of Altorno/ Bilbo, is transparently problematic, and it is perhaps for that reason that the parable is kept under wraps and in the margin. It was the poorest segments of the population who suffered most with the new regime. Anarchists and Basque nationalists were also favored targets of Miguel Primo de Rivera. Any form of dissent was banished — sometimes literally, as when Unamuno was forced into exile. Capitalism did not come to a halt, it continued flourishing within a new form of Spanish totalitarianism. Franco was to learn Primo de Rivera's lessons well.

The Local

If a subtext of *Mary Lavelle* is concerned with the possible imminent collapse of an "empire" (see O'Brien *Cloak* 386), the text also documents and celebrates the vibrant culture of Bilbo. One of Kate O'Brien's strategies is to survey a number of sites of cultural production, by which I mean social activities linked to specific spaces. We will consider them in turn: sports, church-going, dancing, the ferry, the "paseo," the café, and cuisine.

SPORTS

A ritual that is part sport part artistic performance, the bullfight, as we have seen, is central to the novel. The bullring of *Vista Alegre* ("Cheerful View" in Spanish), built in 1882 and destroyed by a fire in 1961, had room for 12,000 people. The same artistic experience is shared by the upper, middle, and working classes, in the circular set up of the bullring — although some seats are more expensive than others, and attendance is used to mark the coming of age of the daughters of the aristocracy, like Milagros, who will be among "Altorno's debutantes" the following year (O'Brien *Mary* 42). Mary herself refers to the experience in coming-of-age terms. She has reasserted her independence from her fiancé (John disapproves of the sport), only after she has made friends of her own (she goes with Agatha), and has secured an income (she pays for her own ticket) — so the bullfight marks for Mary a sexual, social, and economic entrance into adulthood.

The first time we meet the governesses in the Café Alemán, they are discussing the soccer match at the weekend. Futbol (football) is the sport most readily associated with Bilbo, a city notorious for its devotion to the local team, the Atlético de Bilbao (Bilbo Athletic). Fans have their own unique cheer, "Alirón!" which according to legend is a corruption of "All iron!" shouted at the port during ship loads, by the English who introduced the sport in Biscay.

The famous local soccer arena, San Mamés, was religiously filled up with aficionados every Sunday, which gained it the nickname of "The Cathedral" ("la catedral"). Discussing the Sunday match inthe novel, Keogh points out that "[t]he colony was there *en masse*" (italics in original, 86), and the interest of the governesses on the "local celebrities" in attendance rather than the match itself shows better than anything how little they have adapted to their host city. Their conversation leaves no doubt about how passionate Bilbaians are about the sport, in the remark that, as usual, they "[n]early lynched [the referee]" (86). Characteristically, Agatha Conlan's second sentence in the book already indicates that she takes the sport seriously and that she attentively reads soccer match reviews in the newspapers (see 86–7).

Culturally, the bullfight, soccer, and tennis (the Areavagas have a tennis court in their back garden) were once imports. The Basque sport of pilota or Jai Alai ("the great festival") is only mentioned in some throwaway sentences in the novel. Pilota or pelota (Spanish for "ball") is listed among the local pastimes/idiosyncrasies by Mary (see *Mary* 128). In *Farewell Spain*, O'Brien explains that the game is "of the Pyrenees" (206), which can be seen either as some complicated syntactic maneuvring to avoid referring to "the Basque Country," or as an acknowledgment that there is a Basque French Country that breaches this "natural" frontier. After discussing the bullfights in Bilbo for two pages in the travelogue, O'Brien stops: "But why drag in this controversial bloodiness? Bilbao has other amusements than *corridas*. You can see the Basque *pelota* game played there at its best" (*Spain* 206), she says, before discussing the sport in some detail.

We find a metaphorical use of Pilota, in the Basque filmmaker Julio Medem's 2003 documentary on Basque Politics, titled *Basque Handball: The Skin Against the Stone (Pelota Vasca)*. In *Mary Lavelle*, pilota is subtly integrated by O'Brien into a scene where Mary and Agatha converse sitting on a bench in Allera/Begoña. As the two women tentatively give and seek information from each other, children play pilota in the background, taking turns to throw the ball "against the black wall of a house" near by (*Mary* 196), reacting to each other's subsequent move. When Mary asks Agatha if she, like other governesses, hopes to get married, one of the players misses the ball and the game stops (see 207).

Church-Going

In the scene just mentioned, the children play pilota while "[t]wo nuns walked up and down saying their rosary" (O'Brien *Mary* 196). Presenting these contiguous activities in the same sentence has the striking effect of likening the rosary to a game, perhaps even a sport (conversely, it spiritualizes pilota — Olatz González Abrisketa describes Basque handball as "a ritual, an aesthetics," in a book of that title). Church attendance and related Catholic rituals play an important part in the narrative, as they do in the life of the inhabitants of Altorno/Bilbo. The most important church in the city is in Allera/Begoña, and it honors a particular statue of the Virgin Mary as patron of Biscay, the "lady Mary" of Begoña or "Begoinako Andra Mari," referred to simply as "Begoña" by the locals (see O'Brien *Spain* 208). It is interesting that, from the late seventeenth century to the early nineteenth, a group of Irish Dominican friars settled by Begoña, where they ran a hospice, promoted Catholicism among protestant immigrants, and worked as translators and interpreters (see Bilbao 107).

In addition to the popular Begoña, there are numerous other churches in Bilbo/Altorno, such as Mary Lavelle's (and Kate O'Brien's) favorite San Geronimo/San Vicente, famous among Bilbaians for a variety of cultural and historic reasons (see Urriz "San Vicente" 7). Among other things, San Vicente houses the remains of Antonio de Trueba, who wrote about the Biscayan hills with proto-nationalist ardour, and who left us, together with stories set in Castile and the Basque Country, and a novel on El Cid, an account of the mythical Basque military leader born in Ireland and known as "jaun zuria" ("the white lord").

Another important location in *Mary Lavelle* is San Martin square, which in reality represents the area known as El Arenal ("The Sandy Stretch" in Spanish), where we find the church of San Nicolás ("Saint Martin" may refer to Martin de Porres, who remains so popular in Ireland that a magazine is devoted to his cult; Martin was born in Lima in 1579 as the illegitimate child of an upper-class Spanish man and a freed black slave). Catholic doctrine requires the attendance to weekly mass on Sundays and feast days; only the very pious attend mass daily, like Agatha, who stitches altar cloths in her spare time, and who is a "connoisseur" of churches—despite living across San Geronimo, she walks to the Carmelite church every morning, because she rates its atmosphere above the rest.

Pilgrimages are also part of Catholic practice of the time, and it is significant that Mary and Juanito begin their affair after traveling to see the ruins of a Romanesque hermitage in Toledo, although this is not a formal pilgrimage. In 1922, the governess Rosie O'Toole informs Mary that the latest trend in religious traveling among Bilbaians is a visit to a Basque French town, where "Saint Joseph has taken to lifting his eyebrows at the people of Zara, if you please" (*Mary* 80). Zara, situated just over the border, is also of historical significance, as the Basque on both sides rebelled against the imposition of the Spanish-French frontier between Navarre and Basse Navarre in 1765, and many of Zara's inhabitants were deported as a result (see Ugalde 159).

There is a pious Bilbo and an anti-clerical one. One Sunday, in October 1903, both sides collided in the city center and a day of violent riots ensued—an incident described in the closing pages of Vicente Blasco Ibáñez's *El Intruso* (see Montero "Prólogo" 31–33). In the Bilbo of *Mary Lavelle*, however, even socialists are believers.

DANCING IN THE SQUARE

As we know, dancing plays an important part in *Mary Lavelle*. The dance scene in Plaza San Martín/the Arenal is, like the bullfight, structurally and stylistically linked to the sex scene with Juanito. Mary Lavelle's unrealistic expectations of the Basque Country are summarized in her outburst: "[W]here were the castanets and the flowers in the hair?" (*Mary* 74). Flamenco is traditional of Audalucía but, unfortunatley, ignorance of regional/national diversity in the Iberian peninsula was and remains prevalent outside Spain, while the relentless promotion of stereotypes continues. The 1959 film *Thunder in the Sun*, for example, a romantic western about a group of Basque-French emigrants in the United States, full of jaw-dropping fantasies about Basque culture, opened with a scene set in the Basque Country with the female protagonist dancing flamenco on a table.

Kate O'Brien once claimed that she got inspiration from "ordinary people dancing," to add that "all novels are hidden in that phrase, that idea, of ordinary people trying to be happy, trying to enjoy themselves" (*Self Portrait*— my transcript). In Bilbo/Altorno, the public open-air dances (known as "verbenas" in Spanish) were more popular than bullfights because, being free, they were favored by the working class. Don Jorge reminds Mary that "a young lady of your class" should not attend a public dance (O'Brien *Mary* 199; see 189), yet the governess can't help but return to the "shadowy squares" (see 126, 127, 156, 187), where, after the daily "commotion" at eight o'clock, "workboys in overalls danced, very gravely and beautifully, with their red-mouthed girls.... [N]owhere, she believed, could everyday dancing be made to seem so noble as by the common people of Spain" (188). Mary "had wondered *what it would be like to be one of them*, to dance in that raucous music, over the uneven earth, in and out of the shadowing trees" (emphasis added, 188–9), but she felt she could do nothing but lean against a tree, in an uneasy border, and look "at the figures moving in beauty through the violent depths of light" (189).

The public dance is, despite its participative character and its celebration of bodily pleasure, a carefully demarcated heteronormative ritual. Men and women are as identifiable as light and shade, and a girl must be asked to dance by the male who will guide her steps (see Michael Dyer's 1993 analysis of gender roles and dancing). In this scene of O'Brien's novel, a number of men approach Mary, but she feels she "ha[s] to refuse" (O'Brien *Mary* 189). When Juanito makes a surprise appearance, Mary forgets her qualms, and they dance to the tune of "I Met My Love in Avalon," so that she becomes "one of them" by the grace of this egalitarian champion, this philosopher knight. In Malory's version of the Arthuriad, Lancelot returns to his native France to avert conflict, sailing to the Basque town of Baiona/Bayonne — near Biarritz — with his followers (see Malory 497), but it is already too late, and his journey only precipitates the fall of Camelot. In the dance scene, Juanito/Lancelot says: "'I'm going to Biarritz....

I'm on my way. The car is there by the river'" (*Mary* 189). In terms of the use of space, dancing in a square has some of the stylized unpredictability of the "dance" in the bullring. Mary, dancing upon the "uneven earth" (189), has entered a new way of being, where each step brings uncertainty and danger.

TAKING THE FERRY

Altorno/Bilbo aristocrats attend private dances, while the working class goes to the public dances in the squares, but there are many opportunities for mixing in this small, somewhat crammed city. The ferry is one of them. The ferries—known as "gasolinos" in Bilbo/Altorno at the time—took passengers back and forth at about 12 different "station" points. These boats, as Iñaki Uriarte points out, are part of the "heritage, cultural memory, and identity" of the tidal river (36), which is to say, of the city of Bilbo. There are no bridges joining the two banks in the last stretch of the river before it meets the sea in Cabantes/Portugalete, and Mary Lavelle will regularly take a ferry with her charges, who attend private lessons and visit their friends on the right bank, in the bourgeois enclave across the water in Neguri. In the Belle Époque, Neguri (a neologism meaning "winter town" in Basque) successfully attracted the wealthier inhabitants of the city, who settled in what Manuel Montero has called "the English dream of the Bilbaian bourgeoisie" (*California* 17), a gardentown with suitable services: golf course, horse-track, tennis courts, and spa. In *Mary Lavelle*, "Casa Pilar" was unfashionably built overlooking the sea and the fishing harbor, on the left bank, as a permanent residence, a generation earlier; the house was "[a]bout a hundred years old ... but [Pablo] only bought it when he was married in 1896" (2; see 59). In actuality, the mansion that inspired the setting of the novel, known as "El Salto" and now demolished, had also been built by a nouveau riche, Martinez de Rodas, in 1890, and it had also, like the house of the Areavagas, started a trend.

The gasolino is one of the first things to catch Mary's attention when she arrives into the house. The ferry is preparing to leave for Torcal with "[c]lerky old men, and laden peasant women, a cavalry officer, two ladies in beautiful organdie, two or three priests, many errand boys, many children and beggars. Tankards, baskets of fish, a dog, and an old man with a mule"(O'Brien *Mary* 37). Mary watches the loading up — "It was difficult, it was amusing"— until she hears approaching steps: "She glanced around, and saw an elderly-seeming man in black" (ibid.). It is Don Pablo, and the loading up of the boat is a perfect introduction to a man of utopian leanings, whose political aims are perceived by many to be an "unmanageable" project. Mary has just witnessed a momentary abolition of class privilege, cheerfully undertaken.

Soon after arriving in Altorno/Bilbo, Mary had been surprised by the ease with which "the postman [sat] down for a chat with the master of the house" (*Mary* 123), but Jaime and Pablo are not alone in this disregard for class. When

Old Chaco and his mule arrive to the pier as usual, to get the ferry, "every passenger, however well-dressed, however preoccupied, was taking a part in getting the two squeezed in" (122). To Mary, this proves that the Basque/the Spanish are "[a] reasonable, realistic people, who in the midst of violent social wrongs and gluttonies, their own and their neighbours', yet hold each other's routine rights and day-to-day dilemmas most matter-of-factly in respect," so that "bootcleaner and yachtsman, waiter and marquis" can still "walk and talk together exactly as whim takes them" and remain "self-conscious of his own especial social eminence" (ibid.). These people always know "the value to each man of his ego, his pride, and his opinions," and they are always "simple in personal contacts—in that much, a hopelessly aristocratic people, and doomed, therefore, in a world which has outstripped the aristocratic principle" (*Mary* 123). Several points in the scene are echoed in *Farewell Spain*, for example, in the claim that "the people [in Spain] are natural aristocrats, which means that they are profoundly democratic" (*Spain* 224). Mary carries on with her reflections, which for the first time include some political awareness, wondering about "democrats, communists, or what you will," only to catch herself thinking. "Mary smiled. To reflect thus, to generalise, was new to her, and she knew that she could never order such confused impressions so as to present them in decent form" (*Mary* 123). There is an "order" to her thoughts, just as there is a logic to the mismatch of the ferry's cargo, but it can't be uttered, or made decent. It represents anarchism, communism, socialism in practice.

There is another layer of symbolism too. When Mary "hurr[ied] down to the ferry *stage*," she saw that "[t]he *scene* wore its usual evening beauty," and admitted to herself that "Milagros' talk of the bullfight—so *theatrical*—had jarred her nerves. The moment of truth. How could truth lie, for any decent person, in mere *parade* of self, in the infliction of a deadly wound?" (140–1). Sitting in the crowded ferry, as if in an opera pit, Mary confessed that "[s]he felt alien, dejected, *out of tune*. Almost as if she had been injured by this innocent place, as if it sought to wound her" (emphasis added throughout, 142). When the chapter comes to a close, "she heard all three voices raised above the general landing din cries of rapture and astonishment: / 'Juanito! Juanito!'" (143), and this is our introduction to Don Pablo's son. The ferry scene also anticipates the sexual encounter; with the "untuned" Mary unable to join in, this "rapture and astonishment" is the climactic end to the musical interlude that is the ferry trip.

GOING FOR A WALK

The "paseo," the habit of taking a leisurely walk, is another favorite pastime in Altorno/Bilbo. Characters take paseos in many Kate O'Brien novels, but it is mostly the aimless walk of foreign visitors getting to know a city; Venice in *The Flower of May*, for example. Even in that novel, as in *Pray for the Wanderer*, going for a "drive" (to the other side of the country, as the case may be) is of greater significance to the narrative than walking. In her description of Madrid in *Farewell Spain*, O'Brien refers to the "Spanish mania for the *paseo*, that sociable, frivolous, indeterminate and adventuring stroll" (*Spain* 164; see also 196–7). Mary goes for "a walk with Milagros," and again the focus on this activity in the chapter of that title is perfectly fitted to the girl's "discursive" conversation and temperament. "One afternoon she walked with Milagros along the cliff path of Torcal" (130), we are told. With the effectiveness of a feature film, the "visual" framework — in this case the slow movement forward, by the edge of a cliff — reinforces the dialogue and the "progression" of the protagonist. The chapter exemplifies O'Brien's style, in her modernist disregard for eventful narratives and her emphasis on internal change. Nothing "happens" in this scene, *except* that Mary is slowly forced to admit to herself that every one of her beliefs is open to question.

A Sunday paseo in town (often following weekly attendance to mass) has connotations of display and sociability rather than exercise, and is perhaps most accurately described as a middle-class affair. Hill walking, arguably less class-bound, is something of an institution in the Basque Country. A satisfactory plan for a leisure day with friends or family is to walk up a chosen hill or mountain (or sets of mountains), admire the view, have a picnic, and return, perhaps through a different route. In *Mary Lavelle*, some "serious exercise" is included in the daily routine of the Areavaga girls, such as "a long walk into the mountains, a scramble among the rocks of the wild shore, or a row across the bay to a cove beyond Torcal, where they had a bathing hut" (70). However, as we have seen, formal mountaineering groups had long been established in Bilbo/Altorno by the 1920s, often as a nationalist strategy to have a pool of committed youths that could be turned into a militia at a moment's notice (see Espinosa 151–6). We could say, then, that walking, and exercise, are in a continuum from the revolutionary to the conservative.

Traditional walk-trails within the city include an occasional visit to Begoña/Allera, "up on a hill, up many steps, a goodish walk" (O'Brien *Spain* 208). The church is located in a settlement known as Santutxu ("little saint" in Basque, after a small holy statue kept in a hermitage of 1737 which no longer exists— see Baza "Santutxu" 5), which only became legally incorporated into Bilbo in 1925. This is a place where one can't fail to notice the view, or to philosophize. A passage in *Farewell Spain* describing the view from Begoña reads like a revised version of William Wordsworth's "Composed Upon Westminster's Bridge, September 3, 1802," where the "ships, towers, domes, theatres" (727) of the poem are distinctly deglamourized when considering a city that is now wide awake: "from outside [Begoña] there is a wide and complex view of all Bilbao, all its activities, successes and distresses, all that it might have been and all that it is, its furnaces, slums, ships and villas, its spires and bull-ring and winding river" (*Spain* 208). O'Brien adds, memorably, that "López de Haro founded [Bilbo] well beside the mobile river and between the breasts of hills" (ibid.). In the novel, during a pause in her conversation with Agatha in Allera/Begoña, Mary too looks down on the city: "[She] set herself to examine, as if for a memory test, the indentifiable landmarks of the town. She looked for the Plaza San Martín," where she had danced with Juanito, and then "searched like a busy child for the Cabantes [train] station, the Jesuit church, the park"; soon, she realizes that her survey is a tactic "to smother panic — just to keep piling irrelevancies over it with steady industry — bury it in a good-sized rubbish-heap" (*Mary* 201–2). Mary, in "piling irrelevancies" over her troubles "with steady industry" is reproducing, adopting, the city's own behavior.

In the scene, Mary is positioned at a "border" between the mountains and the city, respectively the natural and the unnatural, the moral and the immoral, sitting by Agatha and thinking of Juanito (the obfuscation of natural/unnatural here is, as always in O'Brien, quite deliberate). If we take into account Mary's rural background (in both senses of the word), the bench at Allera/Begoña is looking at the future. With her back to the shrine of Begoña, her back to the church, Mary acknowledges the pull of the unstoppable urban mayhem. This border space may also be seen to stand between Basque nationalism on the one hand and internationalism on the other; and perhaps it is also useful to recall the contrast between the factory as Marxist emblem of class oppression, and the enduring anarchist interest in self-sufficient rural communities. What is important is that the setting of each scene in the book, and Mary's physical position in it, are inseparable from our understanding of her internal state. Whether she is static or moving aimlessly, she steadily follows an invisible trail of conceptual set designs laid out for her in the novel.

GOING TO THE CAFÉ, READING NEWSPAPERS, DEBATING

This is also clear in *Mary Lavelle*'s responsiveness to the café culture characteristic of Altorno/Bilbo, which is given pre-eminence in the governesses' use of the Café Alemán as a meeting place. Other cafés are also mentioned, such as Don Pablo's favorite Café del Río (see *Mary* 66), where he actually spends his last hours reading a newspaper. The reading of newspapers was in the 1920s an important part of everyday life in Altorno/Bilbo — it remains so in the Basque Country and Spain, where press journalism is generally of a high standard and plays an important political role. Mary had been spurred into learning Spanish by "the illiterate insolence of most of the misses towards that language" (106). We are told that "[a]s respite from a few dull classic novels which she bought at random, she formed the habit of skimming over the newspapers, guessing her way through this paragraph of that," and "this superficial reading, making the immediate life of Spain more real to her, became attractive as Spain grew more attractive," so, like her friend Agatha, "[s]he grew addicted to the newspapers" (*Mary* 106–7).

Reading the newspaper and going to the café are symbiotic activities in the Bilbo of the time, and one of the favorite activities of the locals—a more sober affair than that described in the Weil/Brecht song "The Old Bilbao." In O'Brien's novel, we see how Mary "bought an evening paper and went into a cake-shop in the Alameda San Tomás. She pulled off her hat, drank coffee and read about a bullfight in Valencia," observing a bunch of English engineers who "offered each other Gold Flakes and out-of-date *Daily Mails*" (*Mary* 187). Taking her cue from Agatha, Mary smokes *Favoritos*, the strong and cheap tobacco—of the type known as "black tobacco"—favored by the working class, and often reads *El Debate* in the café. *El Debate*, mentioned on a number of occasions, was an actual newspaper at the time, known for its progressive politics, unlike the *Daily Mail*. O'Brien consistently changed or disguised local referents in the novel, yet she retained the title of *El Debate*, perhaps because the word exemplifies democratic practice. Meaningful conversation can be understood as the materialization of a utopian space, as a practice based on respect, responsiveness, and cooperation, which is necessarily both resistant to pre-mapping and open-ended. There is a contrast between Mary's official language-teaching methods, which rely on memorization of canonical texts, and the unofficial learning *as exchange*, through philosophical discussions encouraged by Milagros in her faltering English, debates which are, *for Mary*, "in general educative in exactitude" (139). As Joseph Kupfer points out, this kind of teaching can also be understood as an aesthetic experience, given that "questioning generates thought that reaches past itself" (16).

A passion for debate is characteristic of Bilbo/Altorno, and numerous tertulias—informal debating groups—in the city continue meeting up today. The model for Don Pablo, Dr. Areilza, was in fact the founder of the most famous tertulia in Bilbo, which took place weekly in the Café Lion d'Or. Intellectuals and artists from Bilbo regularly met there, playing hosts to visitors from the rest of the Basque Country and Spain to discuss art, economy, philosophy, and politics. When Vicente Blasco Ibáñez arrived in town to research local culture for his novel *El Intruso*, Enrique Areilza took him to a tertulia in the Café Boulevard, in the old quarter. A meeting point for Liberals, Carlists, radicals, intellectuals, and bohemians, it is no wonder that the letters *C.B.*, engraved on the bowls which held the sugar cubes, were fondly referred to by customers as "Convivencia Bilbaina," "Bilbaian Coexistence" (Bacigalupe "Adios" 36). The beautiful art-deco Café Boulevard, located in El Arenal/San Martin since 1876, was a "franchise" of the Café Suizo ("Swiss Café"), in the Plaza Nueva (or Azoka Barria, in the old quarter), also "famous for its tertulias," until its closure in 1945 (Baza "Tradición" 4). The café was famous for another reason, as Juanjo Molinero, director of the Pâtisseries Guild in Bilbo explains, because Bilbo was "the first town [in the world], on record, where the fusion between the patisserie and the café takes place," thanks to two Swiss entrepreneurs, Matossi and Franconi, who resettled in Bilbo and around 1814 took over a café in the Plaza Nueva, followed by another which they named Café Suizo and which they later linked to a contiguous pâtisserie on the other side of the building, in Correo street, known as La Suiza (the Swedish, in the feminine) (quoted in Díez 28). This café is the meeting point of the governesses in *Mary Lavelle*. In the third chapter, Mary offers to buy a cake for Agatha and Rose to celebrate her first visit to the café. In 1922, governesses regularly met in the Café Suizo/Alemán on Correo Street, on Thursdays and Saturdays; mainly Irish, they were not in speaking terms with the small colony of German "misses," who gathered separately, according to José María Areilza, because of the lingering hostility after World War I ("Mary" 227). It is significant that O'Brien chose to rename this real café the Alemán ("the German"), stigmatizing the governesses as a group. Freedom of speech was *sine qua non* to tertulias, and the policing of behavior, dress, and opinion among the governesses in the novel functions as a negative photographic image of the radical cultural site that cafés embodied in the city.

EATING AND DRINKING

In the Bilbo/Altorno of 1922, there were four distinctive commercial-public spaces: the "cantina" (cantine), where workers bought their groceries on credit; the "taberna" (bar), where workers, peasants, and artisans met after their shift for a glass of wine and a light meal; the "café," where semi-professional and professional workers met for coffee or chocolate; and the "txakoli" (a winehouse), where mixed groups of people drank the local txakoli wine while enjoying local dishes in the outskirts of the city. Bilbo tabernas and cafés were primarily meeting places; in them, "numerous social initiatives were forged and the seeds of political and activist actions were even grown on occasion" (Haramburu Altuna 254). The foundational meeting of the Basque Nationalist Party, at which its founder Sabino Arana first read a manifesto for national regeneration, took place in the txakoli of Larrazabal, in the hill of Begoña/Allera, in 1883. Most of the guests (including the man who inspired Don Pablo, as we will see later) were upper class, yet rather than one of the newly fashionable restaurants of French inspiration, a txakoli was chosen for the event because, as Luis Aramburu Altuna points out, the txakoli in Begoña/Allera was "a mythic culinary space," and Arana's ideology was "a construct where the rural becomes paradigmatic, and the exaltation of the home-grown becomes the medium to reach the perfection to be found in that which is natural and simple by contrast to the complex and heterogeneous" (257 — my translation).

Mary's ordering of hot chocolate instead of coffee in the Café Alemán is an indication that her palate, like her mind, has tuned itself to the local. It was a Basque company of imports (the "Real Compañía Guipuzcoana de Navegación de Caracas") that first thought of the lucrative possibilities of Venezuelan cocoa beans and promoted the drinking of chocolate in Europe in the eighteenth century. Some of the Jewish people expelled from Spain in 1492 had settled just over the French border, in the Basque town of Bayonne, and their descendants would become world-famous for the exquisite quality of the chocolate they produced. The protagonists of *As Music and Splendour* drink chocolate in a posh pâtisserie in Paris in 1887 (32), but around the same time Bilbo workers were including it in their breakfast, and the drink remains popular today.

The gastronomy of the Basque Country is nowadays a tourist attraction, and the interest in food may be said to amount to religious devotion among the Basque — particularly after the impact of nouveau cuisine in the 1970s, although this has long been perceived to be a region of gourmets, or gluttons, depending on the source. In her first letter to John, Mary explains that "[t]he food is awfully nice, but you are expected to eat more than is humanly possible" (*Mary* 9). The stereotypical Basque character included by O'Brien in *As Music and Splendour*, Manuel Arrez, is, rather predictably, obsessed with food. So is Mr. Basterra, the Basque cork merchant that first employs the governess protagonist of Maura Laverty's *No More Than Human* (see 10): "Meals were very important to Señor Basterra. I never saw anything like that man's appetite. He would eat enough of one course to do four turf-cutters and then attack the next course like a man who has been on hunger-strike for a week" (10).

As Luis Haramburu Altuna points out, cooking is "not neutral or devoid of significance, rather, gastronomy includes a conjunction of cultural elements that denote an affiliation to diverse spheres and groups" (257 — my translation). There is an interesting "divergence" between *Farewell Spain* and *Mary Lavelle*, in the praise of the local txakoli wine in the travelogue, and its absence from the novel, with the beverages in the Areavaga household being nonindigenous to the Basque Country (such as Madeira — see *Mary* 68), as one would expect of a pretentious bourgeoisie imitating upper-class Spanish and French custom. However, the "bread soup" that Milagros craves (41) is still today considered the working-class dish par excellence. Milagros describes herself as an anarchist, and perhaps her taste in food is meant to match her politics as a hat would.

Olives (from southern Spain), figs, and pickled tuna are unelaborated, rather ordinary foodstuffs on the Areavaga table. One of the advantages of governessing, Agatha explains, is that "you drink Valdepeñas [wine] and eat turron and walnuts" (206), but two out of three of these items are also available to the working class. Equally, the salt-cod that Mary sees hanging in the working-class shops would have been enjoyed by poor and rich alike — it is the main ingredient for the most famous Biscayan (and perhaps Basque) dish, cooked in a red pepper sauce. By the time she travels to Madrid and is offered a "real English tea" by Luisa as a very special treat, Mary needs to be reminded that the teapot should be heated, and then just about manages a sip. It is not merely that she is nervous in Juanito's presence, but it is also as if the very makeup of her body has changed to acclimatize to her host country. She has just attended a bullfight with Milagros and, somehow, one ritual overrides another. Pilar teases her governess, "Why, Miss Maria, ... you're so Spanish already that you've forgotten how to make tea?" while Milagros declares that "the bull-fight had been terribly moving, and might she please have chocolate?" (233–4). Arguably, the imperialist tinge or the class-bound ceremony of "real English tea" are not what Mary fails to be enthusiastic about, but rather the generic "foreignness" of the custom. If this assessment is accurate, it follows that three months in Altorno/Bilbo have been sufficient to produce a thorough Basque-Spaniard, with the additional optional ingredient of xenophobic scruples.

CONCLUSION

The carefully chosen sites of cultural production in *Mary Lavelle* reflect an important part of real daily life in the city. These specific activities also allow a certain "traffic" between class boundaries. Discussing the options open to foreign "misses" with Mary, Agatha points that Rosie can never marry one of the foreign engineers in the city, because she is "a nobody"; she belongs to no set, because "we [governesses] have never been graded. We come out here with the good old Irish small-town notion that we're 'ladies'—and then by degrees we discover we're—nothing" (204). From the start, Mary had realized that her "place" was a "No Man's Land," but "she liked, as she had expected to, its neutrality, its twilight" (69). Mary is "not graded," so she can buy books in the working class stalls in the afternoon and listen to imported records in the evening.

The comprehensiveness of the novel's rendering of the city as it was in 1922 and the astonishing precision of the authenticating detail—to the extent, for example, of giving the *precise* situation of Agatha's balcony in an *actual* house in a *real* square in Bilbo/Altorno—demonstrate that *Mary Lavelle* was intended as a transgeneric experiment, as both fiction and quasi-photographic documentary survey. Arguably, however, realism is not the best measure of O'Brien's skill—which may lie in her ability to write fiction like a poet. When Mary invites her new friends at the café to have a cake, Rose tells Agatha to "'give the kid the pleasure of seeing you eat something!'" to which she replies, "'How could that sight give her pleasure?'" just before turning to Mary and asking, "'What do you think of Altorno, Miss Lavelle?'" For no apparent reason, Mary feels shy, but responds, "'The town is rather ugly, I suppose'" (*Mary* 91). Such an ordinary exchange is turned inside out by the fact that Agatha, as Mary had noted a few minutes earlier (see 85), is not pretty. In a later scene, in Allera, after Mary reflects that the view of Altorno was "untidy and worth contemplating"; then she turns around to Agatha, who is sitting beside her, and thinks, "'How beautiful the creature can seem!'" (*Mary* 196, 210). By all accounts, the city of Bilbo *was ugly* in 1922, only beautifying itself after 2000, in the wake of the building of the Guggenheim modern art museum. Agatha is also ugly, or rather, not beautiful in the usual sense. The tough and temperamental Conlan, with her heart of gold, her matter-of-factness, her knowledgeability, her uncompromising attitude, her unremitting energy, her austerity, her unintentional elegance ... represents a striking yet truthful portrait of Bilbo.

It is an interesting exercise to read back Mary's first description of Agatha, as a portrait, not of a woman, but of a city. As the president of the Bilbaian professional women's association "Asociación Mujer XXI" put it, responding to a journalist's question on the importance of fashion to local women, the Bilbaian woman has "the internal elegance of the woman who knows what she wants" (Rodríguez 24). Agatha Conlan is breathtaking in her courage and her openness to the new. In addition, her "look" is encoded. Agatha wears blue — the color favored locally to the extent that the town developed a popular shade known as "Bilbo blue," while Bilbaians consider navy blue to be quintessentially elegant. Agatha's mouth is "mobile" — the very word used to describe the Nervión river in *Farewell Spain* (see *Mary* 85). Her face is nobly planned, and San Vicente is "[v]ery noble, very melancholy," just as Bilbo itself, "a queer, melancholy town" (*Spain* 208, 211; see 201). If Agatha is resilient and uncompromising, occasionally showing a "cold mockery" in her eyes (*Mary* 86), so is Bilbo: "Her sober face is unrelenting, almost a judgement" (*Spain* 203). Agatha has as much a claim to represent Bilbo, as the Bilbo-born Pablo and Juan. If Mary is "careless" with her clothes and Agatha is "untid[y]," Juanito and Pablo are also "untidy," even shabby (ibid., 248, 85, 145, 38). Juanito also shares a "pockmarked face" with the city (*Spain* 24); his "irregular, erratic face" is not unlike Agatha's, while Pablo "was not good looking in the accepted sense" (*Mary* 175, 51). Yet all four, like Altorno, "can seem" beautiful, and both are full of "passions just under the skin" (*Spain* 210).

Six

Biography:
Enrique Areilza
(1860–1926)

Introduction

Kate O'Brien based some of her fictional characters on actual people, leaving aside the historical Ana de Mendoza of *That Lady.* For example, the character of Henry Archer in *The Land of Spices* has indications of being partly based on Henry Vaughan and perhaps partly on another metaphysical poet of the seventeenth century, George Herbert (see Rambuss for the homoerotics of the group). Critics have failed to notice that the novel includes a full, detailed biography of Archer, carefully woven into the narrative, and he is never considered as a rounded, complex character, but as prompter of plot. In *As Music and Splendour*, for example, it has been suggested that Clare may be a portrait of Margaret Lydon and Luisa may be based on Kate O'Brien's friend Violet Pickering (Fehan 122; see *Music* 141). O'Brien's interest in biography is beyond question, given that she wrote two strictly biographical works, *Presentation Parlour* and *Teresa of Avila*, as well as a series of biographical sketches in *English Diaries and Journals.*

Reading *Mary Lavelle*, it is surprising how much space is given to a secondary character which seems tangential: Don Pablo Areavaga. A full chapter is devoted to his biography and family history, as well as to an exposition of his political beliefs and evolution. We know that Kate O'Brien based *Mary Lavelle* on her own experiences during 1922–1923 in Bilbo, where she worked as a private live-in tutor for the Areilzas, a family that was to play an important role in Basque and Spanish culture and politics for many years. The head of the household, Enrique Areilza (b. 1860 d. 1926), was the model for the character of Don Pablo. He was one of the most remarkable European intellectuals and reformers of the late nineteenth and early twentieth century. O'Brien taught English literature to his children, José María and Eloisa. According to José María, *Mary Lavelle* was "set upon the stage of my adolescence, described with remarkable skill and realism and presenting many characters, half real and half fictional, built of fragments from life and ingredients from fiction" ("Mary" 228 — my translation — Dr. Areilza was also identified as the source of Pablo by Mary O'Neill in 1985 and Lorna Reynolds in 1987). He later listed the characters in the novel which were realistically drawn from real life: "nearly all my family, my father, my mother and my sister, were portrayed under different names, and with variations of character and circumstances, of course" ("Kate" 38). Enrique Areilza went into Don Pablo, Emilia Rodas (countess of Rodas) into Consuelo, and it is likely that Eloisa was transformed into the most relevant of the three Areavaga sisters, the fourteen-year-old Milagros. José María later insisted that none of his own personality went into the Areavaga son, Juanito, adducing that, after all, he was a thirteen-year-old at the time (ibid., 39). Ultimately, both Milagros and Juanito are presented in the novel as "reflections" or "duplicates" of their father, and it is the personality of Don Pablo/Enrique that dominates the novel.

Kate O'Brien was not the only writer fascinated by the personality of Enrique Areilza. The measure of his effect is the extraordinary fact of his direct implication in the composition of the three most important novels about Bilbo written to date: Miguel de Unamuno's *Paz en la Guerra*, Vicente Blasco Ibáñez's *El Intruso*, and Kate O'Brien's *Mary Lavelle*. All three can be considered historical novels, and the last two actually included a prominent character based on Enrique Areilza. Miguel de Unamuno (often referred to as "Don Miguel" by acquaintances and commentators) visited his life-long friend Enrique while he researched *Paz en la Guerra*, a book devised, as we have seen, to be a record of the last Carlist war in Bilbo, of which Enrique was an expert (see J.M. Areilza "Introducción" 222–3 and "Libros"; also, Enrique worked in Triano, where the Carlist pretender had set up camp during the final siege of Bilbo and near the site of the crucial battle of Somorrostro in 1874). It is interesting that, in *Paz en la Guerra*, the age of the co-protagonist plays the same symbolic function as in *Mary Lavelle*: "Pedro Antonio Iturriondo was born with the [liberal] constitution, in the year [eighteen hundred and] twelve" (Unamuno *Paz* 126).

Blasco Ibáñez also visited Areilza when researching for his description of the miners' working conditions in the city, and his political analysis of the emerging socialism and its clashes with the Basque bourgeoisie in *El Intruso*, protagonized by one Dr. Aresti. The choice of name Aresti/Areavaga/Areilza ensured that the biographical link would be recognized. As for the biographical details themselves, the available biographies and essays on Enrique Areilza are to be taken with caution; his son is not always reliable, while other biographers are inconsistent or neglectful with their sources. The descriptions in the novels are obviously to be considered as *approximations* to his character, but no actual biographical sketch of the doctor has conveyed the quality of his presence with the vividness of the narrative portraits. Here is an early description of Enrique Areilza/Pablo Areavaga in *Mary Lavelle*, showing how O'Brien's intelligent, precise brushstrokes, simultaneously delineate for the reader Don Pablo's appearance and the state of his soul (see also *Mary* 48, 51; J.M. Areilza "Introducción" 33–4):

He gave Mary an impression of great weariness. Though neither tall nor fleshy he suggested that his frame was a bothersome load. He had broad, sagging shoulders and a heavy, greying head. His eyebrows bushed somewhat wildly over far-sunk, heavily lidded eyes. His nose was a broad, strong promontory and his long smile showed two rows of teeth so even and white as to be startling. His chin had a shadowy, unshaven look and his black clothes, untidied by cigarette ash, hung too loosely on him. Shadows and lines overdramatised his face in the evening light, so that Mary felt his foreignness with exaggeration, even remotely with alarm [O'Brien *Mary* 38].

One thing the sketch doesn't mention is that Enrique Areilza had some physical resemblance (judging by photographs and portraits) to Arthur Griffith.

The present chapter deals with the personality, the "political beliefs" (see *Mary* 159), and the accomplishments of Enrique Areilza, elucidating the accuracy and relevance of his portrait in *Mary Lavelle* and other books, in order to highlight the fact that, despite critical neglect, he was a major (perhaps the main) influence on Kate O'Brien's thinking and aesthetics.

Dr. Areilza

Enrique Areilza is still remembered in Bilbo as "Doctor Areilza." In fact, one of the main streets in the city carries that name to this day — a remarkable feat, since very few names of important streets have survived the changing priorities of successive local governments in Bilbo. In addition to the "Doctor Areilza Boulevard" (Alameda Doctor Areilza), there are three public monuments in Bilbo marking his contribution to improving the standards of health care. An eminent surgeon, Areilza gained some notoriety in his lifetime for his use of new technologies and practices. For example, he was one of the first surgeons in Spain to experiment with trepanations as part of surgical treatment of head trauma. Rarely mentioned, but no less remarkable, he was also a pioneer in the use of hypnosis, which he employed particularly in the rehabilitation of post-trauma patients, an unorthodox treatment method which caused the spread of popular yet apocryphal stories on his superhuman powers (see J.M. Areilza "Introducción" 21). It seems that some people refused to play cards with Areilza on the basis that he had the ability to manipulate his playmates' minds. On one occasion, he successfully ordered a passerby (a former patient) to fall asleep on the spot, to the astonishment of his friends (see Ortiz 109 — it happened during a walking trip to Anboto, the mountain believed to be the home of the most powerful creature in Basque mythology, Mari). Dr. Areilza was said to have abandoned the use of hypnosis after an unspecified incident with a patient that greatly alarmed him (see ibid.).

Areilza was also particularly interested in skin transplants, the rehabilitation of physically and mentally injured patients, and preventive medicine, but it was in the field of emergency medicine where he made his name. His surgery in the Miners' Hospital of Triano was furnished with the latest available technologies, acquired by himself in the research trips he undertook every summer through continental Europe (see Ortiz 85–121; J.M. Areilza "Introducción"). The local government had employed Dr. Areilza in 1881 to set up medical facilities around the mining area of Triano, were horrific accidents due to the appalling working practices in the mines were an everyday occurrence. Fresh from college, after specializing in surgery in Paris, Enrique was a brilliant student without any experience. At this time, by all accounts, Triano was like a war zone (as Dr. Areilza himself often remarked — see J.M. Areilza "Introducción" 20–21): disposable emigrant workers living in the most inhumane conditions and working strenuously for a pittance, routinely suffered fatal or severely disabling injuries in explosions, crashes, and landslides. Dr. Areilza set up a number of emergency posts in the area and did his best to provide a modern and efficient service in the main hospital.

Only four years after his appointment, when he was 25 years of age, a cholera epidemic broke out in the neighboring provinces, and Dr. Areilza seems to have been instrumental in stopping it from spreading to Triano— and from there to Bilbo (see Ortiz 110). The epidemic had one tangible positive result: the mining companies introduced reforms geared towards improving hygiene by offering more adequate facilities to the workers (see ibid., 117–8). Dr. Areilza stayed as director of Triano for 20 years, completely devoted to his work, constantly improving the service in the hospital, and becoming, not just a renowned figure in emergency medicine among his colleagues, but a respected bourgeois worker among the working class. Dr. Areilza was employed by the Association of Mine Administrators (Asociación de Patronos Mineros), and they relied on his reports when making decisions on health issues, which often had political consequences (see ibid., 102). He was uncompromising, for example presenting to the Association a report aimed at improving sanitary conditions and nutrition for the miners— insisting on the fact that higher salaries were the only way to improve their health; unsurprisingly, he was ignored (see ibid., 98).

Enrique Areilza followed the developing trade union movement with interest and was often invited to speak in workers' centers about health issues. The doctor never wasted an opportunity for social commentary. For example, he gave a paper on January 9, 1898, entitled "Physical Work" ("El Trabajo Muscular"), at the Bilbaian Workers' Federations Center (Centro de Federaciones Obreras de Bilbo), and he opened the paper with the claim that the traditional division between intellectual and physical work was a fallacy: "[T]his division, origin of numerous social errors, I consider it to be arbitrary and lacking of any scientific basis, because it assumes two organs as closely related as muscles and brain to be functioning in isolation and independently from each other" (see ibid., 197–8 — my translation). Areilza went on to say that the jobs performed by the wood-carver, the writer, the journalist, and the surgeon are not so different from each other in this respect, given that they all require the conjunction of muscular movement with intellectual capability. Areilza then proceeded to list different muscles and discuss their behavior and their relation to nutrition. The paper may have been jargon-free, which was appropriate for an uneducated audience, but there was no dumbing down of the conceptual framework; as an expert on the area commented in 1967, Areilza's description and classification of muscles as shown in this paper was *fifty* years ahead of the advancements in the field (see ibid., 199).

His versatility was also remarkable. He gave papers on biology and philosophy of science, links between low salaries and deficient nutrition, a new method to asses typhus contaminated water, or a number of natural remedies for complaints associated with mountaineering (see Ortiz 193, 199–204, 213–4). Dr. Areilza was not afraid of controversy either, as shown by the fact that when the famous Dr. Gregorio Marañón came to give a paper in Bilbo in 1925, titled "Sexual Ethics" ("Ética del Sexo"; see J.M. Areilza "Recuerdos" 113), his being in disfavor with the Dictator Primo de Rivera meant that no one wanted to be associated with Marañón by introducing him — no one except Areilza, that is.

The two men became friends after this, and it was Marañón who was summoned to Enrique's deathbed in an attempt to save his life (see Ortiz 76). For many years, Dr. Areilza suffered from heart problems (a "soplo systólico"), which he attributed to a hypertrophy of the left ventricle, believing that it was caused by his devotion to mountaineering. In *Mary Lavelle*, Don Pablo dies of angina pectoris, a fitting creative decision given that he is suffering from "anguish of the heart" (the title of the chapter) over Juanito's affair with Mary. Although there was a basis for this turn of events in Areilza's medical history, as O'Brien was possibly aware, this was not in fact the cause of his death. Feeling unwell after returning from a walking trip in Portugal in May 1926, he was eventually diagnosed with glomerulonefritis (see Ortiz 75). He died in the early hours of June 14, 1926. *Mary Lavelle* marked the anniversary of his death ten years later.

When Mary Lovelle looks at the slums across the river from Allera (and when Kate O'Brien looks at them in *Farewell Spain*), she is looking at the place where Enrique was born — San Francisco Street, a stone's throw from Old Altorno/Bilbo Zaharra. Enrique's uncle was a surgeon with a practice in San Francisco, a street which also had a famous convent, perhaps because it was "on the way from Bilbo to Balmaseda, the route of access to Castile which was part of the Santiago Way" pilgrimage route (Montalbán *Doctor* 45), joining the Galizian north-west to continental Europe. There were two more convents nearby, including the one that Agatha Conlan had been tempted to join. In the novel, the street is renamed the "Callejón de los Sastres," "Tailors' Alley" (O'Brien *Mary* 59), but in fact, in the nineteenth century, the area gradually became associated with prostitution, an association maintained throughout the twentieth century (see Romano 28). Enrique's grandfather, followed by his father, had owned the second biggest forge in the province of Biscay, near the increasingly exploited "mines of Miravilla, which, together with those in and around Triano, would sing the funeral mass for the old forges" (Montalbán *Doctor* 20 — my translation).

As director of the Miners' Hospital in Triano, Enrique Areilza's reputation had grown fast, and visitors from all over Spain had arrived to learn the innovative techniques of the doctor — and to see firsthand the new social landscape in the mining area. In 1897 he was summoned to Donosti (San Sebastian) to assist the Spanish president Antonio Cánovas del Castillo, who had been shot by the Italian anarchist Angiolillo, but Cánovas did not survive. Having opened a private surgery in 1888, Enrique Areilza left the directorship of Triano in 1890, although he continued to work there twice a week without remuneration (see Ortiz 118–21). Between 1918 and 1926, he was appointed director of the Basurto Civil Hospital, another post he undertook renouncing a salary, according to his son (J.M. Areilza "Introducción" 31); his biographer Manuel Vitoria Ortiz suggests that "on repeated occasions, he destined his salary, of 7,500 pesetas [a year], to matters requiring attention in the institution" (Ortiz 138), which was chronically under-funded.

There was no Faculty of Medicine in Bilbo (or the Basque Country, after illustrious precedents such as the University of Oinati/Oñate, which had opened in 1542), and Dr. Areilza supported the compaign to open one, after overcoming his reservations about a project in danger of becoming "a convenience-store for degrees" (quoted in Ortiz 134). He was passionate about education, however, and he turned the Basurto Hospital into a teaching hospital, organized regular conferences for medical students, and donated his extensive medical library to the center (see ibid., 64, 137–8). Dr. Areilza's biographer Josu Montalbán suggests that he promoted the development of a faculty, perhaps even lobbying the queen, and that Primo de Rivera refused the creation of the faculty after Enrique Areilza had turned down his invitation to become lord major of Portugalete/Cabantes (on lobbying, see *Doctor* 175, 126; on the dictator, see 75, 121). Areilza would not see a faculty in his lifetime — it was to be created by the regional Basque government in 1936, dismantled with the fascist victory in the Civil War three years later, and only reopened in the 1960s.

Educational projects are a constant in Dr. Areilza's biography. He attempted to open a School and Workshop for the Temporary and Permanently Disabled (Escuela de Tullidos y Lisiados; projected in 1912, it was finally inaugurated in 1926). He was instrumental in the creation of the Bilbaian Ateneum (Ateneo Bilbaino), which he saw as a first step towards the creation of a public university in the city (see Ortiz 229 — the Universidad de Deusto had been opened in Bilbo in 1896 by the Jesuits). He was also a member of the Academy of Medical Sciences (Academia de Ciencias Médicas) since its foundation in Bilbo in 1895 and became Academy president between 1897 and 1898, encouraging and increasing debates (see ibid., 69). Also, he regularly taught to a group of miners at one of the Workers' Colleges (Ateneos Obreros) in Gallarta, the mining area (ibid., 56). At the time there were numerous cultural associations, set up by Bilbaian bourgeoisie with some link to the mining industry, which operated near the miners' slums and aimed at educating the miner population.

Areilza apparently referred to this unofficial network as "Gallarta University" (see ibid., 221; but see J.M. Areilza "Introducción" 215). His friend Pedro Giménez Ilundain was a businessman and an intellectual who had set up a literary tertulia in Gallarta, which Enrique attended until Pedro's relocation to Paris in 1898 brought the meetings to an end. In a letter of 1902 to Ilundain, the doctor explained:

> Here in Bilbo the logorrhoea continues. There is nothing anymore but orators and conferences everywhere. The bourgeois feels himself to be full of compassion and good before the workers and pretends to be fraternally disposed towards [them] with the charitable work of teaching to him who does not know. The socialist, on the other hand, gradually washes off some of his dirt and stench and wants to hang around with the intellectual gentlemen pretending to be posh, a lover of culture, and most of all not to be the baby-eater that those up above had imagined he was [Ortiz 222 — my translation; see E. Areilza *Epistolario* 75–6].

Dr. Areilza was instrumental in the setting up of the Gorliz Sanatorium in 1919, a groundbreaking preventive treatment center for children of the poorest backgrounds at-risk of tuberculosis, which was endemic and often fatal at the time. He seems to have been the first to suggest the opening of such a center (see Ortiz 64). In 1907 he had been commissioned by the local government to direct a medical team to research possible approaches to prevent tuberculosis, and it was after visiting a number of relevant centers in France, Belgium, Holland, Germany, England, Switzerland, and Italy that the proposal for a sanatorium was put forward (their report was published in 1921— see ibid.). The main inspiration for Gorliz Sanatorium came from a similar institution in Becks, France, but Gorliz seems to have been the first health center ever to combine talasotherapy and heliotherapy (see Ortiz 180); that is, sea-water baths and sun-bathing, supplemented by a special diet, as a therapeutic treatment. The institution, catering to "all poor children in Biscay" (ibid.), became an international referent in preventive medicine, and Areilza became as associated with Gorliz in the popular imagination as he had been with Triano. It is symptomatic that the sanatorium attempted to place a monument in his homage at its door, but when Enrique Areilza heard the news he opposed it so vehemently that an empty plinth stood in the approved location for many years— until Areilza's death, when a bust of the doctor by the sculptor Moisés Huerta was finally placed on the pedestal (ibid., 64, 78).

In 1920, Dr. Areilza was temporarily drafted (perhaps after suggesting the project himself) to set up medical facilities during the Moroccan War, and he set up a Disinfection Center in Melilla (see J.M. Areilza "Introducción" 31–2; Ortiz 64). In 1921, he became director of the Military Hospital in Las Arenas, again without remuneration, according to his son (J.M. Areilza "Introducción" 32). In April 1922, just before Kate O'Brien became the English tutor of his children, Areilza added further responsibilitiesto to his busy schedule when he accepted the invitation to become director/manager of the newly opened Provincial Hospital in Areeta/Las Arenas ("Playablanca" in *Mary Lavelle*), set up to treat the returned soldiers wounded in the Moroccan War. Despite all this activity and accomplishments, the only trace of Dr. Areilza's voluntary work and his link to charitable institutions in *Mary Lavelle* is Pablo's commitment to the "Areavaga Working Men's College," as well as a reference to some other unspecified charitable activities.

Enrique was also a dedicated mountaineer. He often repeated to his children: "If man loses touch with the natural world around him, he becomes stupefied in a jungle of artifice" (quoted in Ortiz 73 — my translation). In *Mary Lavelle*, we are told of Don Pablo that "he knew the bay and the mountains with a long sweet tenderness which he liked to foster in his children" (O'Brien *Mary* 53). The "sugared-water" that the children drink when they return from their walks with Lavelle is an old remedy used by mountaineers to prevent muscular aches and pains. The excursions undertaken by Enrique and his friends often classed as cultural events as much as sporting activities. The list of the people who joined him in walks and mountaineering trips includes some of the most important writers and artists of the time, such as Pío Baroja, Darío de Regoyos, Ignacio Zuloaga, and Manuel Losada (see J.M. Areilza "Introducción" 224). His son recalled that he often repeated "There is no landscape without history" (ibid., 25), and pointed out that "what really fascinated him [Enrique] were the treks in which the aim was to locate a forgotten monastery, a tucked away church, an ignored battlefield, the burial place of a historical character, or a work of art about to perish" (ibid., 25–26; see Ortiz 258–9 — my translation); in another occasion, his son gave "a ruined Romanic church" as example of one of Enrique's typical destinations (J.M. Areilza "Introducción" 175). There is a trace of this in *Mary Lavelle*, in Don Pablo's appreciation for the derelict Hermitage of the Holy Angels south of Toledo and his recommendation to Juanito that he visit the site.

In fact, many of Enrique's walking trips took place in Castile, one of his favorite destinations. In a published essay of 1917 on his mountaineering experiences on the Sierra de Gredos, he referred to "old Castile, craddle of the [my] Spanish homeland" ("Gredos," reprinted in J.M. Areilza "Introducción" 226 — "la vieja Castilla, germen de la patria"). Mountaineering was a new pastime at the end of the nineteenth century, and a group of leisurely walkers in remote areas often caused surprise on the locals. A famous incident took place during Dr. Areilza's trip to the Monastery of Silos with some friends, when the group was taken for a gang of robbers who were terrorizing the region, and they were surrounded and "captured" by the townsfolk (Ortiz 260; see J.M. Areilza "Introducción" 227–8). Manuel Vitoria Ortiz explains that the incident was widely reported in the press, drawing attention to the monastery as a cultural traveler's potential destination, when at the time, the beauty and historical significance of Silos was not appreciated by the public at large.

At the time, "cultural trips" to "local" destinations were largely unheard of as a form of leisure. Areilza's excursions often took place during the course of a few days, with a 25-day walking trip to Asturias marking a particularly long trek, but more regularly the doctor would undertake short excursions within Biscay or the Basque Country (the geography of which he was believed to know like the back of his hand). He appears to have been involved in the founding of the Basque-Navarrean Mountaineering Association (Federación Vasco-Navarra de Montañismo), a pioneering group in both sporting and cultural terms. Often, he would just walk the hills around his house in Portugalete and, more often still, he would take to the city's walking areas in the popular "paseos." His devotion to walking managed to merge many of his interests: the company of his friends, the visit to forgotten historical sites, and political and philosophical discussions. He used to walk in the Paseo Volantín in the mornings, on the right bank of the river, often discussing some topic of interest with a friend such as Miguel de Unamuno if he was around (see Ortiz 280). Something of this errant philosophizing went into the *Mary Lavelle* chapter "A Walk with Milagros."

Enrique's various commitments and passions, as difficult to reconcile as they may seem to us, were concerted with the ease of muscle, bone, and joint. His son, who was 16 when Enrique died, described him as follows:

> What I remember of him, in the first place, is the enormous dedication that he gave to his work as a doctor. He left early every day to get to his sanatorium, returned rarely for lunch, and came back in the evening, carrying many newspapers and books, Spanish and foreign. Still he locked himself up in the library and consulted volumes, filing cabinets, specialized journals for a couple of hours and sometimes until dawn ["Doctor" 295–6 — my translation].

Unamuno recalled, after Areilza's death, that he had once "said to [me], that only disinterested work, work as religion, can console us from being born to die" (quoted in J.M. Areilza "Doctor" 302). In the period covered in *Mary Lavelle*, Enrique/Pablo's professional life was hectic, which makes the fact that O'Brien chose not to portray him as a doctor somewhat puzzling. Judging by his published letters, Dr. Areilza constantly referred to his medical experience to make analogies on the most diverse topics. Don Pablo describes love as "the malady" (*Mary* 51), but it is Juanito's tendency to use medical metaphors in his political analysis that is the most clear "residue" of this aspect of the life of Dr. Areilza in the novel:

> In argument he [Juanito] often took analogies from physiology to clarify his belief — but, in fact, he didn't care a snap for analogies. He simply saw that Spain's aching need was for the ruthless establishment in every cranny of the peninsula of justice, order, health and knowledge. Knowledge above all. And the only relatively quick way to such a goal was by an antiseptic scouring out of all precedented establishments, and the enforcing of the main principles and practices of Communism. But the Communistic theory, he would say, could be no more than a means to the truly vital creature — never, never, in any bearable world, an end. Desperate diseases need desperate remedies, and Spain was desperately ill [*Mary* 160].

Juanito is a lawyer, yet not once in the novel does he resort to the language associated with his profession. It is interesting that O'Brien herself often uses medical metaphors. In *Farewell Spain*, for example, she sees in El Greco an impetus "[t]o narrow and enfever — if you like, to infect — inspiration, however individualistically" (146); it is even possible that she was paraphrasing Enrique.

The profession of Enrique Areilza gives us yet another indication that Kate O'Brien's second novel was partly an "anteroom" to *Mary Lavelle*. As we have seen, the character of Dr. Curran, doubled in Vincent (O'Brien's "staging" ensures that they face each other a number of times as if in a mirror), is a precursor of Don Pablo. In Euskera, the Basque language, the root *aran* means "currant or plum," and it is possible that during O'Brien's visit, Enrique Areilza gave this as the origin of his name (Ortiz suggests instead the toponomic *aritza* or *aretza*, "the oak" — 305). A man much disillusioned, "William Curran had always been clear in his views about women. Every inch a doctor, he deplored the mischief which the amorous instinct had done and continued to do to the human race"; and he was persuaded that "[t]he sane thing was to despise [love], since you could never kill it" (*Anteroom* 55). Yet the "amorous instinct" infects the implicitly celibate doctor: "In something as superb as ecstasy then he realised that this girl ... had become the unique and mighty hunger of his life" (ibid., 56–7). Dr. Curran, much like Don Pablo in the later novel, attempts to keep himself in check — because, "What hope had he that Agnes Mulqueen would marry him?" (*Anteroom* 57) — then surrenders to his feelings, and ends up feeling defeated. Even before that experience, however, Curran already had "a cold sense of the futility of life, its brevity and sadness. 'We are helpless,' he thought" (53).

To Enrique Areilza there were no insurmountable problems, surgical or social. It was as a doctor that he was best known, and his close connections to people from remarkably diverse political positions were in part a consequence of his determination to improve standards of health care. "I think that in Spain we already have an excess of preachers of Regeneration," Enrique declared in a letter. "There is however a scarcity of activists ["actores"], of ethical people ["hombres de buena conducta"], capable of marching ahead to the redeeming ideal, unconcerned about sacrificing their own interests or their ambitions" (quoted in Montalbán *Doctor* 140 — my translation). Dr. Areilza was a man of action, although in later life his energies seemed somewhat depleted; in the words of his friend, the writer Ramiro de Maeztu, "He looked sad in his last years" (quoted in J.M. Areilza "Introducción" 248). His first commitment had been to the poor. At his funeral in 1926, Bilbo witnessed an extraordinary procession headed by his coffin, which was carried on the shoulders of miners. This unprecedented and unrepeated gesture of popular homage to a member of the Biscayan upper classes is perhaps the most indicative of the extent to which Dr. Areilza made a mark among his contemporaries.

He had an omnivorous approach to knowledge — for example, the first original editions of Freud and Proust were to be found in Areilza's library (in addition to his bilingual upbringing in Spanish and Basque, Areilza spoke French, German, English, and Italian), together with volumes on eastern philosophy, histories of the Carlist wars, and a host of other topics. He shared with his friend Miguel Unamuno the temperament of the Generación of 98, as both Kate O'Brien and later his biographer Manuel Vitoria Ortiz noted (see O'Brien *Mary* 60–1; Ortiz 257–262). It is not implausible that it was in fact Enrique's enthusiasm for Castile that initially inspired the group to adopt the region as an icon of the regenerative power of austerity.

A mover and shaker in intellectual circles, Enrique Areilza's contribution to the cultural life of Bilbo can perhaps also be seen as an extension of his professional endeavors, in that he pioneered a cultural regeneration of vast repercussions. In *Mary Lavelle*, we learn that Pablo was welcome in clubs and cafés because "he was full of life, made good jokes and liked good talk, sailed and swam well and was a good mountaineer. He read in all directions without prejudice; was critical, gay and a sharpshooter" (51). On more than one occasion, *El Debate* newspaper published pieces inspired by Enrique's views (see Montalbán *Doctor* 174); Enrique and his friends tried to keep up with cultural and philosophical publications in Europe, and they regularly selected essays, arranging for their Spanish translation and their publication in local papers and journals. During his time in Triano, Areilza founded a tertulia, an informal discussion group, named "The Harmony" ("La Armonía"), in the hostel in which he lived, run by Angela Arrien (see J.M. Areilza "Introducción" 25). Later, he founded another tertulia in town, which seems to have started in the Café Suizo (the Café Alemán of *Mary Lavelle*), then moved to the Café García, and finally settled in the Café Lion d'Or (J.M. Areilza "Doctor" 111). As we have mentioned, the tertulias of the Lion d'Or attracted the Basque and Spanish intellectual and artistic luminaries of the period. Any time there was a cultural or political event of note, the audience would swell up to debate or listen in the Lion d'Or, and it seems that many an article and editorial in newspapers such as the conservative *El Pueblo Vasco* ("Basque People") was directly inspired by the discussions in the café; if Unamuno was in town, and particularly if the doctor was at the café, the discussions were eagerly anticipated (see Montalbán *Doctor* 142). It appears that Enrique chose the topics for discussion, but only acted as moderator on occasion (see ibid. 141). José Carlos Mainer identifies a Bilbaian School (Escuela de Bilbao), an intellectual group with a politically conservative and specifically Catholic outlook, in which he includes the attendants at the Lion d'Or (see Sota *Bilbao* 64), but any such picture with Enrique Areilza in it must surely be complicated by his very presence.

The debates at the Lion d'Or resulted in the setting up of the Association of Basque Artists (Asociación de Artistas Vascos), as well as the Bilbaian Atheneo (Ateneo Bilbaino). The groundbreaking journal *Hermes — Revista del País Vasco* (*Hermes — Journal of the Basque Country*) was also gestated in the Lion d'Or. Published from 1917 to 1922, *Hermes* was a showcase for the most relevant Basque and Spanish thinkers of the time, also publishing work by, for example,

Ezra Pound and T.S. Eliot. It is likely that during Kate O'Brien's stay in the Areilza household in 1922–1923, she came across issues of the journal, and it can be speculated that this may have been in part the inspiration for the novel's references to "heavenly messengers" (principally the "angelic" Don Pablo, Juanito, Mary, Agatha, and Luisa)—the role of Hermes in Greek mythology. *Hermes* has been associated with the Generation of 1914 or Novecentismo, and the orbit of influence of the Spanish philosopher Ortega y Gasset (see Urriz 15). The journal is generally hailed as a remarkable and unique project in a Basque — and possibly Spanish — context, because it gave a joint platform to people from different political persuasions, from the far left to the far right, although some consider the editorial policy to be more conservative than popular perception would suggest (Luis de Guezala in conversation January 2, 2007). *Mary Lavelle*'s theme of the need for regenerative changes in Spanish political organization may also be seen to be linked to Enrique Areilza's interests in a broad sense.

According to his biographer Manuel Vitoria Ortiz (a medical doctor himself), as a scientist Dr. Areilza's knowledge had limitations, but in his writings he was "grave to the point of cruelty in order not to fill in any gap in knowledge with pure ornament"— and his published papers, along with his letters, are beautiful examples of articulate and imaginative yet direct, even stark, engagement with a broad variety of issues (Ortiz 272); as one obituary put it: "A less pompous and solemn man was never seen on this earth" (quoted in Alfau "Prólogo" 236). A medicine compendium that he carefully researched for decades lies unfinished and unpublished (see Ortiz 271–2), but his life's work was fruitful elsewhere: in his far-reaching transformation of health care in Bilbo, and in his contribution to the cultural and political life of the city.

At the Bilbaian Ateneo in 1925, when he gave the introductory speech for Dr. Marañón, who as we mentioned was blacklisted by the dictatorship, Enrique Areilza took the opportunity to remind the audience of the role of the doctor in the sixteenth century, when medicine "had to incorporate itself to the integral culture of its time, establishing intimate contact with philosophy, with morality, with art"; this was the time which saw the emergence "in the Spanish horizon" of "some types of double stars of philosopher-doctors, politician-doctors, moralist-doctors, etc., rounded always with a distilled writing style, acquired though a deep knowledge of classical languages" (quoted in J.M. Areilza "Introducción" 235; Ortiz 272 — my translation). Undoubtedly, Dr. Areilza himself brought that tradition into the twentieth century.

Beliefs

RELIGION

Enrique Areilza's beliefs, political and religious, are a contentious issue. Our main source of information is a selection of his letters, published in 1964.

The editor, his son José María, later admitted to have "softened" some of his father's assertions (see Ortiz Alfau "Palabras" 8), and it is likely that a number of these "interventions" sought to make Dr. Areilza appear less radical and less unpious. One thing that comes across clearly in the surviving correspondence is that Enrique Areilza was just as fond of medical metaphors as Kate O'Brien's William Curran and Juanito Areavaga. Another is that Dr. Areilza revered rationalism and was, at least for a period, openly hostile to organized religion. Upon hearing that his friend Miguel de Unamuno had converted to Catholicism after a rather vocal atheist period, he had written to him in 1897:

> It has now been made public your new evolution towards Damascus (Catholicism), and I remind you of it because the newspaper *La Avanzada* [*The Avantgarde*] has dealt with the matter. It appears that you have not been able to avoid the dominant epidemic in the civilized world and have chosen instead to petrify your protoplasm once and for all, jumping from the period of indifferent mobility, without going through the vital stage of differentiation, into a final phase of stability, close to the border of the final rest, or the absolute if you wish…. It would be regrettable if you would launch a frontal attack on all non-believers; [sic] and falling on the opposite extreme would ignore the value of human intelligence in understanding the universe. I am convinced that this is an essentially material faculty with which it is impossible to comprehend the harmony and above all the infinite goodness which governs every-thing in existence. But with it the soul is tuned, feelings turn more delicate and pure, and it even helps us glimpse, by exclusion, the greatness of that which is beyond its reach. That there are other ways of reaching the absolute outside reason? I am nearly ready to believe it, although I would not unequivocally endorse it; but you can be certain that those ways are not exclusively available to Catholicism, or even Chris-tianity [Enrique Areilza "Letter to Miguel de Unamuno, 20 May 1897" *Epistolario* 45–46 — my translation].

Enrique goes on to recommend caution, discretion, and humility to Unamuno, although with a forcefulness that does not attempt to disguise his own anger:

> Now that you lay on the bosom of a cult to sheepishness, endure this advice from a friend who cares somewhat for you. Never vent in public the intimate thoughts that assail and mortify you, if you doubt them and produce them solely in order to satisfy yourself. Self-consolation is a good thing, but it is not very charitable to inoculate in others the virus of paradox. I tell you this because you are practically responsible for a number of brain dislocations in some of our friends who used to live under a reflected light and now lay in darkness with the change in cerebral illumination. I suppose they will eventually thrive under the new lighting system, but meanwhile they are living in deep confusion [ibid., 46].

Enrique Areilza's point about reason's inability to comprehend the absolute makes him a man of his time. In Areilza's time "modernist" was used to describe a person who believed that God was not the object of science because God was beyond reason. This was referred to as "the modernist view," and it inspired irate documents from the head of the Catholic Church (Pio X's 1898 "PAS-CENDI" and "Lamentabili sane"), as well as innumerable essays, manifestos, and debates instigated by supporters (see Ortiz 288; Enrique refers to the posi-tion in his letters, see 110). It is worth stressing the fact that educated people of

Enrique's generation were the first ones to leave the Christian church en masse, encouraged by Charles Darwin's theory of evolution, which was seen to be incompatible with church teachings.

Two of Dr. Areilza's aunts had joined the French cloistered order of the Sisters of Charity of Refuge (Caridad del Refugio), one of them becoming mother superior in their monastery at Begoña (Allera in *Mary Lavelle*), where Enrique visited them every Sunday as a child — a scenario reminiscent of O'Brien's own experiences as retold in *Presentation Parlour*. By all accounts, the atmosphere Enrique grew up in was one of strict Catholic form and devotion. According to his biographer Manuel Vitoria Ortiz, Enrique's religious beliefs began to "cool down" when he was a college student in Valladolid, possibly because of his acquaintance with a priest who regularly and publicly broke his vows (33; see 32). Enrique's readings on Buddhism and Daoism are highlighted by Ortiz as an important step in his evolution towards atheism (see ibid., 38, 285). Again according to Ortiz, Areilza lost his faith during his time in Paris, although he continued practicing as a Catholic, stopping only after taking up his job in Triano, while in later life he began to practice again, though without faith (see ibid., 285, 287, 291).

Dr. Areilza counted devout Catholics among his friends and was on very cordial terms with the Siervas de Jesús (Servants of Jesus), a Catholic order of nuns on which he relied to manage and service many of his medical centers (he was the first person to place such responsibility in the relatively new order). He was, however, by all accounts outspoken, and his views on religion did widen the gap between Dr. Areilza and his mother, as he recalled after her death in 1901, in a letter to his friend Ilundain. "There was between her and myself, the abyss of religion; of that Catholic religion which, exaggerated, dislocates and breaks up so many human sentiments," he explained, "and no matter how much and how deeply we loved each other, I have never ever had with her a word of humility or sheepishness in this area" (E. Areilza *Epistolario* 65 — my translation). Reflecting on her death, Enrique exclaims, "I wish I could have prayed!" (66).

El Intruso presents Enrique Areilza as a very vocal nonbeliever. The title of the novel refers to Jesuitism, an unseen intruder, pervading and corrupting everything. "They [Jesuits] are like microbes," Dr. Aresti explains, "which amount to nothing in themselves, yet can cause an epidemic" (Ibáñez 132). Unlike Kate O'Brien's Areavaga/Areilza, who hangs on to Christianity as a useful structuring system, Aresti/Areilza has no room for Christian values. "Man did not want to base his morals anymore on the unknown, on God, benevolent or terrifying ghost of the childhood of humankind," Aresti says, "Neither could he tolerate Christian morality, based on resignation and self-denial. That morality had been nothing but the art of mutilating life under the pretext of protecting its highest forms, that is, the spiritual ones" (ibid., 255 — my translation).

It is disconcerting that all available biographical sources on Enrique seem to disagree on the point of his views on religion. The doctor was an outspoken atheist according to a famous contemporary, the founder of Basque nationalism, Sabino Arana, as we will see later. José María Areilza suggested that his father's broad interests had been misinterpreted: "What I remember of his life was a normal and serene religious practice. Regularly performing his Catholic duties, [he was a] passionate reader of apologetic or theological novelties" (J.M. Areilza "Introducción" 37; see 34). Yet the doctor's own references to religious practice in to his surviving correspondence are consistently dismissive. For example, writing to his friend Ilundain around 1897–1898, after ascribing Unamuno's conversion to loneliness, Enrique explained: "I have repeated the experience of attending sermons and holy celebrations in order to distract myself from personal upsets and, believe me, the poor brain lets itself be remolded without much resistance when the heart has weakened" (E. Areilza *Epistolario* 49 — my translation). In another letter, from 1898, discussing a bout of religious fervor in Spain at the time of the Cuban war, Enrique declared that the Catholic religion "has paralyzed the will of the people making them fall into the slumber of those who believe the only useful labor is that which serves to reach the afterlife" (E. Areilza *Epistolario* 53 — my translation).

José María Areilza, in a further effort to counteract Dr. Areilza's reputation, explained that when asked about his atheism Enrique referred to a tapeworm which, lodged in the body, may regrow after being severed, thanks to the Bilbaian atmosphere (see J.M. Areilza "Introducción" 37; Enrique's parable was retold by his friend Ramiro de Maeztu and is reproduced in Montalbán *Doctor* 72–3). It must have been evident even to the devout Catholic José María Areilza that the anecdote was far from an exonerating statement.

In 1902, writing to Ilundain, Areilza explains that he is beginning to suspect that Tolstoy has truly "no religious spirit; he is an oriental protestant.... I mistrust any religiosity capable of being expressed, and I mistrust even more those who could not be religious, if they were to be forbidden preaching" (E. Areilza *Epistolario* 79). In 1906, in a letter to the same friend, the doctor declares that "[t]he so-called religious sentiment is neither error nor malady.... It is as natural as the secretion of a gland, as positive as the certainty granted by the proposition that two plus two are four," part of an "internal sensibility" which cannot be demonstrated but only experienced (ibid. 130). In this context, it is interesting that the goodness of Dr. Areilza inspired a devotion bordering on the religious. An article published in Bilbo in 1926 quoted a local woman who, upon hearing that he was dying, expressed her sorrow by saying, "After God, Doctor Areilza" (quoted in Ortiz 81).

From Enrique's *Epistolario*, dealing with the period 1894–1925 (an incomplete record, of mainly two correspondents), it seems to me beyond doubt that he has nothing but contempt for organized religion, in particular Catholicism. Pablo Areavaga had declared that "a system of faith was essential ... indeed perhaps the only essential system" (O'Brien *Mary* 61). In a letter of 1904, Enrique did claim that religion and politics are very similar because both are "historical processes," originating when various groups are persuaded of their own righteousness, and all aim at social change, being "similar in their beliefs and their procedures" (E. Areilza *Epistolario* 97). From his letters, it seems equally clear that he does not believe in God (the God of the Abrahamic religions) or the afterlife. He is particularly interested in Buddhism, a godless system of thought, and seems to believe in a universal life-principle similar to the Atman of Advaita Vedanta Hinduism or to the Dao (Tao) of Daoism. In a number of occasions, he makes a sharp distinction between religions on the one hand and the religious impulse, spirituality, on the other. Writing to his friend Pedro Giménez Ilundain on the topic, in 1906, Areilza says:

> And what rewards, you wonder, do I gather from investigating the existence of a hidden sprite if I don't intend to sate my thirst in it? Infinite ones! It is the religious fire which like a perfume penetrates in the soul and is a tonic for human endeavours and a tranquilizer for our pain. Anyone who has felt it is forever comforted." To know its reality is to be forever hopeful. Despair is impossible when one is certain of escaping human suffering by jumping into the abyss of the unique, universal, eternal, I [E. Areilza *Epistolario* 134 — my translation].

SOCIALISM

The tradition of the "good doctor" is a staple in literature; the work of Anton Chekhov and Pío Baroja, both of whom had been doctors before becoming writers, provides some well known examples. Many doctors played important roles in radical politics in the nineteenth century, from Louis Blanqui in France and José Rizal in the Philippines, to the Irish anti-slavery activist and pioneering surgeon James Barry (later revealed to have been a woman). The novel *A Girl Among the Anarchists*, discussed in an earlier chapter, also makes the point that the anarchist cause seems to attract a disproportionate number of doctors (see Meredith 69).

There is no consensus on the political ideology favored by Enrique Areilza. Both *El Intruso* and *Mary Lavelle*, as we know, emphasized his socialism. Vicente Blasco Ibáñez's novel certainly aimed at provocation, and the play version (surprisingly, a comedy) opened in Bilbo in 1907 in a theatre surrounded by police guards who expected that its political content would rouse riotous violence, but after a warm and pacific reception, the play was canceled within days due to the public's lack of interest (see Bacigalupe "Intruso" 38). Regarding the "original" Luis Aresti himself, whatever the extent of his support for the socialist cause, the propagandist politics of *El Intruso* rather annoyed Areilza, who dismissed the Aresti character as an interested manipulation (see E. Areilza *Epistolario* 223).

It is likely that Kate O'Brien was aware of this portrait of her former employer, and it is even possible that part of her impetus in writing *Mary Lavelle* was the desire to set the record straight. For example, in her emphasis on the fact that "[c]ertainly he was no Communist" or in the assertions that Don Pablo considered Christianity to be "the only learned religion" and that he actually believed in a "difficult creed of anarchy and faith" (O'Brien *Mary* 61) — while his son is also a "Christian communist" of sorts (see ibid., 160–1). The Christian anarchist Leo Tolstoy was one of Enrique Areilza's favorite writers, but as we have seen Aresti is one of "us heathen," even if he considers Jesus to have been "a great poet of morality" (Ibáñez 253, 257).

One thing that O'Brien's portrait of Areilza cannot be accused of is lack of clarity on the strength and validity of his anarchist beliefs. Enrique Areilza's son once claimed of his father, "He was not — I have said it before — a political man" ("Doctor" 295). One is reminded of Leonard Woolf's similar disclaimer of 1967 about his wife: "Virginia was the least political animal since Aristotle invented the definition" (27). It was possibly based on the same premise: Political ideologies and movements outside the party system, such as feminism and anarchism, simply do not count. Some Bilbo intellectuals liked to think of their city as "the Athens of the North" (see J.M. Areilza "Siglo" 140; Sota "Bilbao" 64), but they did not want to be told that the Basque *pólis* also relied on a silenced sex and a slave class. José María recalled that "my father used to describe, in the tertulia [of the café Lion d'Or], how those first semi-clandestine meetings took place in [the mining area of] Gallarta, with Facundo Perezagua as the main speaker," but, José María adds, the doctor "always remained impartial in the workers' disputes, and had friends both among the bourgeoisie of the city and among the leaders of the nascent socialism" (J.M. Areilza "Doctor" 111 — my translation).

After his death, his friend, the socialist politician Indalecio Prieto, equated the doctor's lifelong work to a political commitment: "Wherever Doctor Areilza went, he was always researching and reforming, always revolutionizing" (quoted in J.M. Areilza "Introducción" 329; Ortiz 78 — my translation). Ramiro de Maeztu claimed that "[t]here was in him a governing and organizing capacity which the nation did not take advantage of" (quoted in J.M. Areilza "Introducción" 248). The tertulia founded by Enrique Areilza in the Lion d'Or became synonymous with tolerance, but in its last period it also provided a budding ground for a number of young men of fascist leanings, who would later play important roles in the ideological grounding, instauration, and maintenance of the Francoist dictatorship, such as Rafael Sánchez Mazas (co-founder of the key fascist organization Falange), Pedro Mourlane Michelena, or Dr. Areilza's own son, José María Areilza (see Sota "Retrato" 31).

Was Enrique Areilza an anarchist, as *Mary Lavelle* claims? Astonishingly for such a public figure, the available scholarship does not elucidate this point. His known references to anarchism were not hostile, at a time when anarchists were being targeted. For example, he regretted Unamuno's move away from anarchism in the early 1900s (see E. Areilza *Epistolario* 105), and, discussing the political climate in his letter of 1902 to Ilundain, already quoted, he referred to "...the government, which has one hoof on the Vatican and wants to place the other one on [socialist leader] Pablo Iglesias. And all because of Spain's fear: the anarchist. It is most curious to see the governor and Perezagua linking arms, arresting and jailing anarchists"; and added: "If the beginning of progress is the dislocation of existing things, we may as well think that we are on our way towards it, because they are dislocating" (quoted in Ortiz 222; see E. Areilza *Epistolario* 76 — my translation).

Kate O'Brien insists that the doctor was an individualist anarchist; Vicente Blasco Ibáñez suggests he was a socialist, perhaps a communist, perhaps a Marxist. In a letter of 1898 Enrique shows both distaste and admiration for Marx: "I can understand Tolstoy or Jesus Christ, but I can not understand Marx preaching morality," because "the motives which inspired his brain to signal the rotten pillar which served as the base of society, were [in] a brain dominated by envy of other philosophers greater than him" (51). José Fernández de la Sota ("Retrato" 23) and Manuel Vitoria Ortiz (279), reproducing José María Areilza's claims, state that the doctor was a Maurist. Antonio Maura was leader of the Spanish Conservatives for a number of years; as Minister of Internal Affairs in 1902, and then President from 1905 to 1910, he directed his efforts at eliminating political corruption. Maura believed in a "revolution from above," a phrase that he made famous, based on the notion of a morally unblemished elite as main agent of progress. It has been claimed (a suggestion perhaps instigated by José María Areilza) that around 1909 Maura had offered Enrique Areilza the post of president of the Conservative Party in Biscay but that he had declined (see Ortiz 279; a parallel story claims that Maura failed to persuade Enrique's brother, the reputed lawyer and fanatically religious Lorenzo Areilza, to join his political team in Madrid — see ibid., 23).

According to José María Areilza, Enrique Areilza was closest to Maurism than to any other contemporary political movement, perhaps, he says, because it offered a "true radicalism"; José María claims that his father was "a Platonic follower [of Maura], without detriment to his intimate Basquist devotion" ("Prólogo" 38 — my translation; see 27). Judging by Enrique's correspondence, it seems clear that the doctor did admire Maura's abilities as orator, as well as his work ethic, but I am not persuaded by José María Areilza's argument, echoed by Manuel Victoria Ortiz in his biography (see Ortiz 267). Although a comment in one of his letters *does* suggest some conservative sympathies: "They got me the card and named me part of the junta" of "a conservative committee" (E. Areilza *Epistolario* 169). Ortiz is rather emphatic on what Dr. Areilza *was not*: a Carlist, a monarchist, a socialist (see 175). Similarly, de la Sota states, "Despite his acute sensibility to social issues, Doctor Areilza could not be a socialist. He wasn't one, just as he wasn't a nationalist, despite his considerable passion for everything related to the Basque Country" ("Retrato" 23). Socialism can be used sometimes as an umbrella term, as I have done here on occasion, but it was a distinctive movement in its own right too. Dr. Areilza was often critical, in his private letters, of socialist leadership and their political aims (not socialist ideas), in the context of the organized political entity that was the Socialist Party. For example, in a letter of 1901 to his friend Ilundain:

Socialists do little progress in Spain because of their faulty strategies: they are determined to fight to the death with republicans and libertarians [anarchists] and they
are lacking in intellectual weight, they are burdened with suspicion towards those
whose hands are callous-free and on the other hand they continue holding on tightly
to the Marxist rule, excommunicating with anathemas those shades which, in greater
or smaller measure, vary from their doctrine-like catechism. Without a doubt Le
Bon, in his psychology of masses and races, is right when he states that in Spain
whenever there is a change of party or type of government, all that is changed is *a
name (un mot)*. The socialists are blood relations of Torquemada and they are the
modern intolerants [emphasis in original, E. Areilza *Epistolario* 71–2 — my transla-
tion].

Josu Montalbán, a socialist representative in a local council in Biscay (as
well as a medical doctor), claims in a recent biography of Enrique Areilza that
it is not possible to establish "a clear political position" in his correspondence
(144), although after his appointment in Triano he was clearly "in the avant
garde of all the social, sindical, and workers' movements which would be developed in years to come," and in fact, according to Montalbán, the establishment
of socialist organizations in the area from 1888 onwards "allowed Areilza to let
go of some of his concerns" and become the "critical conscience" stinging the
money-thirsty mine-owners (89, 96). Montalbán suggests that the doctor was
"a rebellious liberal" (144). It seems clear to me that he sympathized with socialist and nationalist ideas, but he did not agree with the political programs of the
parties which represented them, and I think it is plausible that he was in fact,
as O'Brien suggests, an individualist anti-authoritarian, or, at the very least,
someone sympathetic to anarchism.

I see Enrique in the Felipe of *Constancy*, where we are told that "Felipe is
nearly an anarchist — anarchism is pure good sense" (O'Brien 10). The same
idea is expounded in Milagros's talk with Mary as they walk by the cliff in Tor-
cal/Algorta: "You see, [my father] thinks exactly as I do, that any political
organization, no matter what, is most offensive. An insult to life, he says," in
one of his articles, because "he is intellectually an anarchist. So am I, of course.
It's the only possible thing for an intelligent person to be. But," Milagros continues, "unless you can have perfect anarchy, father would say, I think, that it's
better to dodge organisation as much as possible — even at a terrible price"
(O'Brien *Mary* 135). Milagros is partly a mouthpiece for Pablo's/Enrique's
beliefs, but she is also a fearless and independent thinker — and a remarkable
portrait of Enrique's daughter, Eloisa Areilza, as a young woman. Surprisingly,
given the portrait of Milagros, Eloisa went on to marry a prominent fascist,
Julio de Escauriza e Ipiña.

Perhaps the doctor's egalitarian sympathies may be seen to inform his
habits. By all accounts the doctor had nothing but contempt for titles, wealth,
and status. His austere appearance was often remarked, and he was remembered
as a "man in black" by those who knew him (see J.M. Areilza "Introducción"
34). Also, he never accepted the title of count given him by marriage (see

Montalbán *Doctor* 136). On one occasion, his son declared Dr. Areilza's indifference to money to be "bordering on the pathological" (J.M. Areilza "Introduction" 231), although José María Areilza's own priorities clearly differed from his—for example, José María pointed out without irony that his mother, the countess of Rodas, was "known as Emilia Rodas by her closest friends" (ibid., 28; see also "Doctor" 295). Although this can be nothing but speculation, Kate O'Brien may have transferred the early ambition of the young José María Areilza onto the fictional Pilar, who is disliked outright by Mary (see *Mary* 3, 8). As an adult, José María's prose was often weighted down by ungrammatical pretentiousness (although he was given the highest honor in Spanish philological circles, a seat at the Royal Academy of the Spanish Language), and he regularly used the title of Count of Motrico. A sympathetic commentator, in an article commemorating the centenary of José María's birth in the conservative Basque paper *El Correo Español*, opened the piece by wondering, "Was there ever anyone so refined?" (Cortázar 40). As we can see below, *Mary Lavelle* explains that Don Pablo's father had married "into the lesser nobility" (50), when in fact it had been Enrique/Pablo who had married a (second generation) countess, even though he was by all accounts not interested in titles. Dr. Areilza was, however, a wealthy man, a fact transferred into his portrait in *Mary Lavelle*; as I have argued earlier, this increases the impact of Pablo's political views, in much the same way as Mary's beauty highlights her contempt for physical appearance.

Mary Lavelle gives a family background for Areavaga/Areilza which frames him as an educated bourgeois with a conscience:

> Pablo's father, Don Juan, had been a grave and studious man. Before he took his place in business he conformed with an Areavaga tradition and went to Salamanca to read law. In due time he married into the lesser nobility. His wife was intelligent and even saintly and their family life austere and quiet. They lived in a huge cold house of dark stone which had been since 1800 the Areavaga mansion. They were scrupulous in observing the dignities and obligations of their position and though simple in personal tastes they were socially generous and practised both ceremony and charity [49–50].

Enrique's mother Ramona Arregui Olabarrieta was notorious for her extremely strict devotion to Catholic ritual (see for example Ortiz 284), and Enrique did grow up in a big house; it seems to have been a two-story house, with the ground floor in use as a forge and with grapevines and a vegetable garden in the backyard, built around 1760 in San Francisco street (not a "mansión," but a "casona" in Spanish; Montalbán 21; see J.M. Areilza "Introducción" 14; but see the illustration in E. Areilza *Epistolario* 42). Other than that, the passage is pure fiction. There was no Areilza/Areavaga tradition of sending the males to study law. In reality, the doctor's ancestors were smiths, milliners, and peasants, and Enrique's father, Julián Areilza y Hurtado de Saracho, a smith reputed as a veterinarian, had died when Enrique was seven years old, leaving the family in a precarious financial situation. Enrique Areilza's mother, with the financial assistance of her brother-in-law, Miguel Areilza, managed to offer a university education to her sons (by moving the household to Valladolid). Enrique studied medicine, and his brother Lorenzo law; their sister Raimunda helped out in the house until she married and moved to the Philippines with her husband, to run a business owned by his family in what was then a Spanish colony (see Ortiz 23). After Enrique's graduation, it was his uncle Miguel who financed the doctor's further studies in Paris (see J.M. Areilza "Introducción" 15–19). In the context of the idealistic and idealized portrait of Don Pablo/Enrique in *Mary Lavelle*, it is interesting that Dr. Areilza did admire an enterprising attitude, claiming in 1898 that the Catholic religion "has encouraged laziness, mother of all our ills, killing the ideal of daily ambitions, the ideal of wealth, sole base of all progress," which has been replaced "with the Christian resignation manifested of old in the soup-kitchens of convents, and today in the baby-gruel of permanent-contract-mania" (E. Areilza *Epistolario* 53 — my translation). Emilia Rodas owned a number of mines (a number of women did in Biscay), and Enrique seems to have invested in the shipping industry (see ibid., 188, 190).

The Don Pablo of *Mary Lavelle* inherited the legacy of an industrial magnate, his father Don Juan, but, like Enrique Areilza, he took a different path — a historian in the novel, a doctor in reality. In Areavaga, this represented in itself a betrayal to his class, although his father had already presented the signs of a rudimentary egalitarian conscience with a libertarian tinge. Don Juan, "a rich man with a conscience," was "convinced to the last drop of his blood of the absolute dominion of personality over system," while his son Pablo "inherited his conscience, intellect and individualism, but took from his mother's saintliness a handful of poetic fire" (O'Brien *Mary* 50). Don Juan's philanthropy would "generate" Pablo's Christian anarchism, which in turn would "evolve" into Juanito's brand of Marxism — a state communism "very different from Lenin's," insisting on the original Marxist emphasis on a temporary "slave state" seeking its own end (see 169–72). Kate O'Brien thus presents, to her readers of 1936, a symbolic genealogy of radicalism, a progression flaunting its "naturalness" in an extremely problematic way. The years immediately preceding the Spanish Civil War were, for those committed to leftist politics, a time for answers, demanding workable, practical solutions, and through *Mary Lavelle*'s mixture of mysticism, materialism, poetry, and politics, and its innocent-seeming manipulation of historical and biographical facts, O'Brien regurgitated a plain plan in order to contribute to that pressing need.

CARLISM

The English anthropologist Rodney Gallop, writing in 1930, claimed that the Basque have a "[d]eep rooted sense of continuity" regarding tradition and the ancestors; this prompts Gallop to declare: "There is no more conservative race on the face of the earth" (60). One of the most striking features of *Mary Lavelle* is the fact that, in addition to a full biography of the secondary character Don Pablo, the novel offers a miniature biography of his father, Don Juan. Such a digression serves no obvious purpose to the narrative, although, as we will see later, it follows an internal logic related to the autobiographical strand of the story. The wealth of the Areilza family was partly due to the enterprising abilities of Enrique's *father-in-law,* Francisco Martínez Rodas, a banker and mine-owner with his own transport fleet. The intensity of the exploitation of mines in and around Bilbo fluctuated, but its highest point was achieved in 1899, shortly after Martínez Rodas had decided to invest heavily in the mining industry. His sudden success was unparalleled, and in a couple of years he had either created or taken control of several important companies in a variety of sectors, following an investment policy described as "spectacular" (Montero *Mineros* 305; see 304–10). This has been suggested as the reason why he was granted the title of Count of Rodas, when he was the main figure in Biscayan (and Basque) economy, at the peak of his career in 1901 (ibid., 306). Just as suddenly, the financial crack of July of that year put an end to his empire.

When most Basque industrialists entered politics in order to protect their financial interests, Martínez Rodas was a unique example of a man with a political career already underway before his business interests developed (ibid., 305): a deputy in the Spanish parliament since 1893, he became a senator in 1896. His political career had been itself preceded by an equally illustrious military career, with Martínez Rodas obtaining a high rank in the Carlist war on the side of the liberals (lieutenant, according to his grandson, or colonel, according to Manuel Montero). In *Mary Lavelle*, O'Brien turned Francisco Martínez Rodas into Jerónimo Parajo, owner of the company "Herónimo [sic] Parajo and Sons." By keeping a Spanish surname for him, O'Brien signaled the fact that Martínez Rodas had been born outside the Basque Country, in Huesca.

Remarkably, *Mary Lavelle* transfers some of the biographical information from Martínez Rodas to the family line of the Areavagas, who are shipowners and ironfounders committed to the liberal cause (see O'Brien *Mary* 49). Kate O'Brien wanted to create a contrast between the superficiality of the Parajos and the intellectual weight and progressive politics of the Areavagas. We have seen that Enrique Areilza came from a decidedly Carlist family, which in the Basque Country meant a commitment to proto-nationalist and conservative ideas. His mother, Ramona Arregi, had acted as a spy for the Carlist faction during the second Carlist war, carrying at least one letter to an insurgent military leader sent by her brother-in-law, Miguel Areilza, who became a lieutenant colonel and field marshal with the Carlists (see J.M. Areilza "Doctor" 294, "Introducción" 16). Miguel funded doctor Areilza's education, and in his will left his sword to Enrique, his favorite nephew (see J.M. Areilza "Introducción" 15–19). However, as we have seen, Emilia/Consuelo's father, Francisco Martínez

Rodas, had fought with the liberal army in the second Carlist war. The non–Carlist, liberal background of Don Pablo is pure fiction; biographical details in *Mary Lavelle* are therefore distorted in a specific way, seeking to emphasize a non–Basque nationalist and a progressist background for Don Pablo Areavaga.

The historical background of the Carlist wars, alluded to in *Mary Lavelle*, is, unlike surnames, essential to understand the personality of Don Pablo, who feels at home in the liberal Bilbo (see O'Brien *Mary* 49). Enrique Areilza's published letters make it clear that he was very critical of Carlism. As Manuel Vitoria Ortiz points out, the childhood of both Areilza and Unamuno was marked by the siege of Bilbo by Carlist troops in 1874 — while their contemporary and friend Pío Baroja, who grew up in the Basque province of Gipuzkoa, also saw the city of Donosti (San Sebastian) bombed by the Carlists (see Ortiz 257). According to Ortiz, this experience was crucial in gestating what became known as the Generation of 98, which as we have seen was characterized by having a sizable Basque contingent among its ranks: "To all of them sends Carlist Spain the message of its inconsistency; to all of them shows the sad vacuum in its body and the lack of historical horizons that encourages no hopefulness whatsoever" (257). Paddy Woodworth, discussing the final abolition of the Basque charts in 1878, also remarks on nationalist references to the "catastrophic yet ultimately regenerative impact [of that loss] on national consciousness," offering "a curiously parallel sentiment to Spanish perceptions of the 'Disaster' of 1898" (31). Ortiz, in his biography of Enrique Areilza, attempts to elucidate how his views are consonant with the 98 group, in a section titled "Encounter with Spain: Enrique Areilza 'a man of ninety-eight'" (257–268).

Dr. Areilza's son played a prominent part in a very different project for the regeneration of Spain. After the instauration of the Republic in 1931, José María Areilza began his political career by founding the Monarchic Youth association (Juventud Monárquica) in Bilbo, standing in elections for the far-right Renovation party (Renovación [Española]) after co-founding and leading its Biscayan branch and quickly building a profile in fascist circles. He published in the official journal of the fascist JONS (Juntas de Ofensiva Nacional Sindicalista, "Juntas for a National-Sindicalist Offensive"), an organization that he attempted to bring together with the similarly inspired "Falange" (J.M. Areilza anticipated Franco, who at the beginning of the dictatorship joined the two groups and turned them into the only party that was legal in Spain for 40 years). "Falange" was funded by the son of the dictator general Miguel Primo de Rivera, the lawyer José Antonio Primo de Rivera, ideologue and martyr of the fascist cause. J.M. Areilza may also have been close to an ultra-conservative Catholic party, the CEDA, Confederación Española de Derechas Autónomas ("Spanish Confederation of the Autonomous Right-wing Associations"; see Sota "Retrato" 24; Anasagasti disagrees— see 55). José María Areilza did a good job of positioning himself during the Republic, and, after fascist troops took control of Bilbo in 1937, he became the first fascist lord mayor of the city practically by self-appointment (see Anasagasti 133). He took his post with a venomous public speech, still remembered, in which he encouraged — in a context of widespread summary executions throughout the city — the extermination of all Basque nationalist "rats," and praised Spain's "only true friends": Hitler and Mussolini (see J.M. Areilza "Discurso" 218–9). José María went on to join the Spanish State Council, after which he represented the regime as ambassador in Argentina, the United States, and France. In 1968, José María Areilza coined the term "la derecha civilizada" ("the civilized right") to describe a "modern, updated" conservatism to which he subscribed at the time (quoted in Anasagasti 296), and he is often credited for his contribution to the democratization of Spain after Franco's death in 1975. But many saw José María Areilza as "a convert to Democracy" (ibid., 308), an opportunist who failed in his main objective: becoming Spanish Premier (see ibid., 287–91, 309–12). Juanito Areavaga is, literally, the son Enrique never had. Enrique Areilza had little tolerance for Spanish patriotism; consider, for example, his comments on Unamuno's new political turn in 1899: "Of Unamuno I don't even want to talk because he is growing more Spanishized each day, even though he claims to be an independent spirit free from the ghosts of party-politics" (E. Areilza *Epistolario* 56 — my translation). In *Mary Lavelle*, Pablo hopes that Juanito may become "one of Spain's great men," and José María Areilza turned out to be one of the "great men" in the history of Spanish fascism.

It is remarkable that, despite being on opposite sides of the political spectrum, Kate O'Brien and Jose María Areilza were always extraordinarily kind to each other. There is an anecdote related to José María's politics that is worth mentioning here, as it adds further historical relevance to *Mary Lavelle*. The headquarters of the Basque Nationalist Party were (and remain) situated by the church of San Vicente/San Geronimo, on the place where Sabino Arana Goiri was born, in the same square where Agatha lives in the novel, by the same garden where she declares her love for Mary, and near the bench where Mary herself first reflects on the "wild adventure" of her new freedom "to be Mary Lavelle" (O'Brien *Mary* 72). Whether O'Brien was aware of the relevance of this location in political terms or not, we do not know, but it is certainly possible that she privileged a space associated with nationalism when choosing a setting for Agatha and Mary's experiments in self-government. In the days preceding the military uprising in July 1937, José María Areilza had been meeting with other prominent fascists in Bilbo; they had been informed of the plans and, according to José María, he was hoping to be able to persuade the Basque Nationalist Party to join them in support of the uprising; again according to him, his attempts at contacting the party's leaders failed, and after spending the night of Saturday, July 18 listening to the updates of the fascist progress on the radio in a house near San Vicente, Areilza went to the seven o'clock mass in the neighboring church. There, to his surprise, he met the full contingent of the leadership of the Basque Nationalist Party, headed by José Antonio

Aguirre (who was also from Portugalete/Cabantes and knew the Areilzas) who would become the first president of the Basque government in the period of autonomy, independence, and later, exile. The Nationalists had clearly spent the night discussing the events and were now ready to publicly take sides with the leftist Republic in the war (see J.M. Areilza "Aguirre" 342–3). They had already supported the leftist coalition in the elections; in fact, a Basque Nationalist envoy to the Vatican in January 1936 had attempted to persuade the pope to remain neutral regarding Basque aspirations, and had tried to reason with Cardinal Pizzardo, who insisted that they support the right in a Spanish general election which represented, as he put it, a "fight between Christ and Lenin" (Anasagasti 92).

The staunchly Catholic and essentially conservative Basque Nationalist Party supported the left in exchange for the Republican government's promise of self-determination. That decision changed not only the fate of the Basque Country in the conflict and the dictatorship, but the shape of Basque politics forever. Across the aisle inside San Vicente, two Christian positions met in freedom for the last time. During the 40 years of Franco's dictatorship, the resistance would fruitfully bring together people of disparate beliefs and ideas in the underground struggle against fascism in Bilbo (as the Basque Nationalist activist Juan Mentxaka San Nicolás, "Menchaca," told me in numerous conversations throughout the 1980s). Kate O'Brien's Don Pablo had anticipated that future by showing what was seemingly impossible: that a person could be Catholic, anarchist, and Basque.

BASQUE NATIONALISM

The birth of Basque nationalism is regularly marked on June 3, 1893, the date in which the famous "Larrazabal Address" by Sabino Arana Goiri (b. 1865 d. 1903) took place in the outskirts of Bilbo. Enrique Areilza played a key role in facilitating the event, although, astonishingly, this has not received attention from commentators (see Jemein 1935, Arantzadi 1935, Larronde 1977, Atienza 1979, Guezala 1995). Sabino Arana Goiri had published *Biscay for its Independence* (*Bizkaya por su Independencia*) in 1892, a collection of four previously published essays defending the Basque right to self-determination. Enrique Areilza and Ramón de la Sota were so fascinated by Arana's views that they decided to invite him to an informal dinner to learn more. The encounter was to take place in a txakoli — a local eatery — in Begoña, in the outskirts of Bilbo (as we know, renamed "Allera" in *Mary Lavelle*). Enrique was in fact unable to attend, but a surviving letter from Sabino Arana Goiri, quoted below, makes it clear that the two friends organized the event. The address was printed shortly after, including a list of those in attendance and those absent.

A number of other people were formally invited to attend the informal dinner ("apari-merienda") at Larrazabal, some by the organizers, some by the guest. Most of the men in attendance, including de la Sota and another friend of Enrique, the painter Adolfo Guiard, were "euskalerriako" ("from the Euskal Herria"), that is, liberal Basque Chartists or non–Carlist Chartists, from the "Basqueland" ("Euskal Herria") association, who were dissatisfied with its leadership (see González de Durana "Guiard" 12). As we have seen, Chartism had concentrated on defending the ancient laws of the land. At the "Larrazabal Address," Arana explained that he had come to the realization that Chartism was obsolete, and that the Basque Country (he referred to Biscay but implicitly sought to extend those rights to the Basque Country) should not be satisfied with retaining some autonomy within a Spanish state but should become independent. He accused Basque Chartists of being complicit with Spanish attempts at eradicating Basque culture, something exacerbated by what he saw as the "invasion" of non–Basque immigrants to the mining area of Bilbo. Arana described a new political movement that would rest on two pillars—God, and Charters—Jaungoikoa eta Lege Zaharra (JEL). As we saw earlier, this is a variation of the Carlist motto, "God, King, and Charters." The motto is echoed by Kate O'Brien in *Mary Lavelle*, with a subtle and telling variation: "*The Church, the King, and the Family* made up the immovable rock upon which the Parajos had managed to clamber for Consuelo to be born there, most native of its natives" (emphasis added, *Mary* 58).

In a letter of 1897, Arana recalled the events at Larrazabal:

> When *Biscay for its Independence* appeared, my close friends communicated to me that certain individuals had liked it so much, that they thought of honoring me with a feast. Those individuals were: leading, Sota and Areilza, doctor, famous surgeon, atheist who has no qualms in declaring his ideas before anyone, and for that reason known as such by all; followers, a number of old conspicuous members of the *Euskalerria* [Basquist party], who had followed Sota when he left. The invitation got to me; I agreed: because the doctrine I predicated was new, the new party could not be made up of other than converts; it was necessary to assume good faith in those who came. The dinner took place in Larrazabal, the Begoña farmhouse. Koldobika came with me. The hosts were joined unknowingly by some personal acquaintances of mine. Areilza, absent, due to engagements [Arana Goiri 162–3 — my translation].

The dinner ended in a brawl, with Basque-chartists threatening to attack Arana, so outraged they were with his accusation that they defended Spanish interests ("Españolismo").

It seems incomprehensible that no attempt has yet been made to investigate the gestation of such a crucial event in Basque history. Enrique Areilza's son, José María, was predictably determined to minimize his father's interest in Basque nationalism, yet his claim that the doctor had been invited to the event (rather than organizing it) in his memoirs of his father may have been a genuine error. Inexplicably, however, José María's account also claims, against all evidence, that his father attended the event. In an essay of 1997, José María Areilza claims that Arana had been a patient of the doctor, giving this as the reason why his father "knew him well," and continues: "One day he received an invitation from him [from Arana] to attend a light supper in a farmhouse in the outskirts of Bilbo" where he was to make a public statement, and Enrique "attended moved by curiosity to discover with surprise that before the small group of diners, the host read nothing other than the programme of a new political doctrine to be known as Basque nationalism," summed up in JEL, which José María describes as a "primitive motto" ("Doctor" 295).

José María Areilza's incomplete and inaccurate account may be disappointing, but even commentators from the Basque Nationalist Party, such as Iñaki Anasagasti, in his biography of the Areilza family, have failed to assess Enrique Areilza's role in organizing the event (see Anasagasti 24–5). Ultimately, neither *El Intruso* nor *Mary Lavelle* offer any relevant insight on the subject. The socialist agenda prioritized by Blasco Ibáñez and O'Brien, and the latter's determination to construct an idealized image of Spain, required the relegation of Areilza's sense of his own Basque identity to the margins. It would have been a complex project, as both novels chose to pay homage to Bilbo, which was as atypical a Basque setting as Enrique Areilza himself was unorthodox. We know that the "Basque question" is referred to as an aside in *Mary Lavelle*, and yet, when it is mentioned, the implications are vast. For example, as we have seen, when the aristocratic Luisa suggests that the Irish treaty was a mistake, the "ignorant" Mary shocks her by asking, "Do you then sympathise with the nationalist ambitions of the Catalans and the Basques?" (152).

Enrique Areilza's love of the Basque Country and his interest in Basque nationalism are beyond question — as we can see in his surviving letters. He advised Basquists on occasion on the best way to promote Basque events, and he regularly complained about the historic falsifications of Nationalists, precisely because he was passionate about Basque history (see for example E. Areilza *Epistolario* 77, 138). He hated those who blindly followed Arana's doctrines (158) as much as those who bought Karl Marx wholesale (96) and in fact claimed that both ideologies were united by their obsession with wealth (98). Enrique hated even more any Basque commentators who fueled anti–Basquist propaganda: "I don't know where do all these pro–Madrilian [madrileñizantes] types get their hatred for anything which may give glory and renown to the country where they were born" (128). But he did not concur with the aims of what had rapidly become an orthodox nationalist *party*; referring to the JEL motto and discussing Japanese culture in 1904, Enrique declared that in Japan they "still love their King, their Homeland, and their Race, three old relics [antiguallas], even though it had seemed that the Tolstoyan infection had ordered them to back off" (101— my translation).

In letters from the first decade of the twentieth century, Enrique Areilza's main argument with Basque nationalism is its obsession with legalist, rather than cultural, aims: "In reality the nationalist or purely Basque ideal is still in a pronounced embryonic phase to enter the complexities of the political arena and it shouldn't have emerged yet from literature, science, the recovery of the language and customs, etc." (158), and it was far too early for it to develop "an intellectual tone" (146) or "form its left-wing current" (159 — represented by Pepe Orueta among others; see 75, 83, 84). If by 1903 he was claiming that Basque Nationalists "had lost for me the interest they had in their early times" (92), in 1907 he was saying that "this unreflective heat of the pioneers which was indispensable in the beginning, will undoubtedly yield soon because young people are almost all Basquephiles and among them there are emerging intelligent youths who are fond of learning" (158).

According to Enrique's biographer Manuel Vitoria Ortiz, the main discrepancy between Areilza and Unamuno was Unamuno's anti–Basque attitude, or as Ortiz puts it, the novelist's "Spanishizing Basqueness" (245). Unamuno's evolution from a scholar of Basque linguistics to a vocal proponent of the abandonment of the Basque language in favor of Castilian Spanish was documented by Martin de Ugalde in 1966. His position is worth considering briefly as an example of the complicated allegiances of people in Areilza's immediate circle, although bearing in mind that provocation was a Unamunian trademark. After many years away from Bilbo, teaching in Salamanca, Unamuno had been invited to address his native city at a festival in 1901. Before that date, the philosopher sent a copy of the speech to Enrique Areilza asking for his opinion; the doctor recommended to make revisions and soften the tone, but his friend ignored him. The central idea in Unamuno's speech was that Euskera, under threat from the Spanish language, should be allowed to die. He caused the ire of many and was coldly received in the city for years to come. Dr. Areilza's sad conclusion after the performance, in a letter to a common friend, was that "Beyond doubt Don Miguel has not come to this world to love or to be loved" (71). Four years later, Enrique told a Basque Nationalist friend, the anthropologist Telesforo de Aranzadi, that "the thing which I have always found *disgustingly repulsive* ["hediondamente repugnante"] is to flatter the sentiments of those who hate the [Basque] country, supporting a thesis which not even he [Unamuno] believes or gives a toss about" (emphasis in original, 108; see also 119).

After the (unsurprisingly) hostile reaction in the Basque Country, Unamuno claimed he had been misunderstood. He had not meant to dismiss Basque culture or Basque identity, he said, and went on to declare that the Basques had to take over Spain, culturally speaking, and that the adoption of the Spanish language was paramount to achieve a "Basquization of Spain"; Basques should demand, "not that we be allowed to govern ourselves, but that we want to govern everyone else, because we are the most capable to do it well" (quoted in Ortiz 245–6 — my translation). It was hard to take Unamuno seriously, but he did insist on this point with unusual energy: "I believe that we Basques have been the ones who have better felt and understood Castile, and I won't be seen to be lying after considering Zuloaga's paintings and Baroja's novels" (quoted in ibid., 246). "To be Basque," he declared, "is to be even more Spanish" (ibid.).

As Kate O'Brien's novel documents, in the Areilza household the Basque language was mainly used to communicate with the servants. We do not know how often the doctor used Euskera or what value he placed on it. We do know that the Gorliz Sanatorium management provisos, which he drafted in 1921, states that it was a requirement for doctors and chaplains to speak Euskera in order to best communicate with patients (see Ortiz 188). This clause is a rare example of an official *document* which made provision for the needs of Basque speakers at the time, a general concern of the doctor, as his letters attest (see E. Areilza *Epistolario* 138).

Enrique Areilza's biographer Ortiz devotes some pages to elucidate the doctor's allegiance to the Basque Country (his "Vasquismo" — see Ortiz 262) which suggest his "evolution" from an enthusiastic phase of support of the Nationalist cause, to a cooling down, followed by hostility. Ortiz begins with a letter sent to a friend from Vienna and dated March 4, 1894, in which Enrique Areilza reports having witnessed police repression of Nationalists in Prague: "believe me if I tell you that I felt the urge to sing the [Basque anthem] 'Gernikako' in the main square of Prague, and to shout 'Long live Basqueland! Down with foreign influence!'" (quoted in ibid., 265 — my translation). "Gernikako Arbola" ("The Tree of Gernika") was a famous song written in 1853 by (the Carlist) José María Iparragirre to celebrate self-determination and democracy: " spread your seeds all over / a world that needs you so / we worship you old oak tree / symbol of holy law" (my translation). Basque anarchists like Manuel Chiapuso were also fond of this unofficial Basque anthem (see 294–6). Beyond question, José María Areilza's final assessment of his father as "a great Bilbaian man and a great Spanish man" ("Introducción" 234) is hopelessly inadequate. And the elision of Basqueness in that statement has, somewhat strikingly, the same effect as the disappearing act performed by Kate O'Brien in *Mary Lavelle,* a novel set in "the north of Spain" and concerned with someone who may be "one of Spain's great men" (*Mary* 49, 61).

Love, Sexuality, Family Matters

The sexual and gender politics in *Mary Lavelle* are in fact interwoven with the parallel strands of nationalism and socialism. Don Pablo is a political mongrel, in addition to being a sexual one. He struggles against the Spanish side of his character, just as he fights to keep his unorthodox sexuality in check. As we have seen, the sight of the androgynous Mary, who looks "like a Greek bo[y]" (*Mary* 67), stirs and disturbs Don Pablo in a way that he must have recognized, as he is familiar with the work of Havelock Ellis. Enrique Areilza's library included the German editions of the work of Sigmund Freud, and Areilza was no doubt acquainted with his essay of 1911 on Dr. Schreber — the first time Freud conducted his analysis on someone unrelated to his practice, by studying the doctor's own account of 1903 *Memories of My Nervous Illness.* Freud saw the cause of Dr. Schreber's mental illness in repressed homosexuality. It may not be a coincidence that Kate O'Brien renamed Enrique as Pablo (Paul), also the name of Dr. Daniel Paul Schreber. More significant is the link to the Christian Saint Paul (b. 10 d. 67), reputed with introducing Christianity to Spain, who has often been considered an example of repressed homosexuality, as pointed out by José Manuel Enríquez in a 1978 essay published in an anarchist collection (see 110–116; see also McNeill). Saint Paul linked Greece/paganism to homosexuality, and his Letters to the Corinthians set out the model for moral condemnation of homosexuality which was to be followed by the Catholic church into the twenty-first century. Saint Paul's admission that he had an ongoing struggle with a "thorn of the flesh" (2 Cor. 12:7), a statement following his discussion on same-sex sexual contact (including one of the earliest references to lesbianism), can certainly be seen as a suggestion of repressed homosexuality. O'Brien was undoubtedly aware of the connection, because she paraphrased Paul's Letter to the Corinthians in a passage of *Teresa of Avila*, where she implied that the Spanish saint was lesbian, before suggesting that Teresa had repressed her attraction to women. If we see Don Pablo as a repressed homosexual Christian, this may serve as a further example of O'Brien's complex and radical use of cross-referencing.

Pablo "had been schooled at the Escorial and afterwards at Salamanca, where, somewhat to his father's disappointment, he had read not law but modern history," after which "he travelled to France and England on a voyage of undefined intellectual exploration and after an absence abroad of eighteen months returned to Altorno passionately glad to be in Spain again. He looked forward to life ... with a true enthusiasm" (O'Brien *Mary* 51). Areilza in fact studied medicine in Valladolid (a town less familiar to O'Brien's readers than Salamanca), and although he lived in Paris between 1879 and 1880 to continue his studies, I have found no evidence of his traveling to England before this time. He spoke and read English, however, as we have seen. Like *Mary Lavelle*, *El Intruso* also summarizes the family background and youth of the doctor, to the extent of mentioning an uncle by the name of Don Juan (in fact Areilza's uncle Don Miguel) who had financed his studies in France. Both novels are, in different ways, remarkably accurate in their biographical details and surprisingly consonant in their tracing of the emotional trajectory of Areilza. By the time Mary meets Pablo, his youthful enthusiasm is all but gone; Juanito, we are told, is "the recreation of his youth," but Don Pablo was a "much disappointed man" (O'Brien *Mary* 144).

His wife, however, is no less disappointed. Consuelo and Pablo can be compared to the beautiful Caroline and her lawyer husband, Jim, in *Without My Cloak*, with erotic needs that are impossible to reconcile and sharing a life without intimacy. All that Caroline had dreamed of was "to be loved in the sun as much as the dark, to be laughed at and teased and companioned in the day, to be shouted at and quarrelled with and called soft names, to see her beauty brighten her husband's eyes unfurtively at sudden meeting, to be loved naturally"; but instead of that, she is "snatched in the night and bowed to respectfully by day," so that her nerves are "frayed to tatters from loathing of a man's desire, from disturbance and frustration of her senses" (173). Jim is, in the words of the "connoisseur of love and passion" Eddy, "no more than a beast in the country of love" (ibid.). It is not inconceivable that one of the reasons why Mary could not envision a life with Juanito is that, for all his charm and passion, he is sexually selfish and unimaginative, and incapable of showing tenderness. Juanito is contented with the facts that his wife "loved him and ... gave him sensual peace," and following the same irony-free trail of thought, he equates marriage, for a woman, to a job paid for in "bed [and] board" (*Mary* 166).

Mary Lavelle's lengthy description of Pablo/Enrique's background opens by stating that "Pablo Areavaga y Galdéz, now in his forty-ninth year, had married in his twenty-fourth, as lately his son had done. His marriage had been fortunate in that it was a love match and yet entirely satisfactory to his own family as well as to his bride's the Parajos" (48). If O'Brien states that marriage had been a "good move" for the two families involved (49), *El Intruso* clearly indicates that Aresti's marriage had been arranged. Both biographical portraits insist on the fact that Areilza was in love at the time of his marriage, but O'Brien raises doubts about the nature of his feelings by ambiguous references to "faith," "adjustment to adult routine," and "[t]he malady" of love (O'Brien *Mary* 51).

Dr. Areilza, a single man at 45, was a "confirmed bachelor," a "character classification" which, according to Eve Kosofsky Sedgwidck, "came into currency" halfway through Victorian times, "a type that for some men both narrowed the venue, and at the same time startlingly desexualized the question, of male sexual choice" (*Epistemology* 189). The bachelor, according to Sedgwick, was "a figure of the nineteenth-century metropolis" (193) associated to intellectual pursuits. It is interesting that Enrique Areilza surprised everyone by marrying the 25-year-old Emilia Rodas in 1905 when he was 45, and equally interesting that this is one of the biographical details that O'Brien decided to change when she wrote the novel, which makes no reference to the age gap. Also, the Areilzas had two children, while the Areavagas have five (one of whom dies at a young age, as with Vincent and Marie Rose in *The Anteroom*—but see the emphasis on the first two in *Mary* 51).

Enrique Areilza met Emilia Arana y Mendiola, Condesa de Rodas, when she became his patient, as she was suffering from a disease affecting her lungs (see J.M. Areilza "Introducción" 28, 60; Ortiz 60). Rumor had it that she was the one to propose marriage, but it was perhaps his friends who spread the rumor, as they seem to have been without exception shocked by the news, to the point that many did not believe the marriage had taken place (due to her mother's illness the ceremony was a small, private affair) (see J.M. Areilza "Introducción" 63 and Montalbán *Doctor* 136). It does not seem to have been a happy union. It is worth noting that José María Areilza dealt with his parents' marriage in a grand total of three lines, in two memoirs of his father totaling 38 pages (see "Doctor" 295 and "Introducción" 28; see also 31). *El Intruso* and

Mary Lavelle present a somber picture of a marriage that, under its exemplary surface, is a failure (O'Brien *Mary* 51–2). The personal circumstances of Dr. O'Byrne in *The Last of Summer*, although clearly he is a very different character from Don Pablo, have much in common with his (see O'Brien *Summer* 65). Enrique Areilza himself, when asked the reason for his late marriage, used to answer that "a tuber does not grow until it is really and truly buried" (quoted in Ortiz 63 — my translation). Pablo, however, "was no middle-aged fidget with a sexual grievance. He was a Spanish realist, a serious, domesticated man who loved his children and was honourably devoted to his wife" (O'Brien *Mary* 52).

By the time Mary meets him, Pablo has abandoned the *ideal* that launched him into married life, and has "withdraw[n]" into celibacy (57, 62). Sex and politics appear to be interchangeable at various points in the "Don Pablo" chapter. For example, as we have seen, the narrator explains that Pablo "loved Spain with a quite simple mysticism, and all his energies when he was young burnt outward to be used by her" (54). Don Pablo and Doña Consuelo represent the state of the nation: two irreconcilable visions of Spain that remain interlocked, initially out of pure inertia, and later through precarious self-control (see the comparison to the Bourbons on 47). "[T]hus the years of rage began, the years of hatred" (58), we read of the marital breakdown in the novel. Don Pablo may seem a self-contained political anomaly in an essentially romantic tale, and yet he provides the reader with a blueprint to reread the novel in terms of gender and sexual politics *linked* to a subtext of nationalist aspirations, the ineffectuality of the ruling class, and the emasculation of leftist intellectuals. The barely suppressed tension in the Areavaga household may enact the fractures of a divided city, nation, and state. And in turn, Mary Lavelle's choices may make her an outcast after her return to Ireland, the self-sacrificing martyr (see 309) of another front guard: a sexually liberated woman.

Throughout the "Don Pablo" chapter, the word *nature* is compulsively repeated. It appears in various contexts, but always, when not overtly ironic, is a means to problematize given assumptions. Don Pablo's seemingly "unnatural" attraction for a "Greek boy" and the references to El Greco can, as we have seen, be effortlessly read as attempts at queering the male(s) in the novel, perhaps in order to suggest a suppressed homoerotic tendency. It is interesting that *El Intruso*, which refers to homosexuality explicitly in another context, also suggests at several points that Aresti/Areilza has an unusually keen appreciation of male beauty (see for example 64, 80, 82). But what are we to make of the fact that, in *Mary Lavelle*, Luisa may well be read as a version of Consuelo/Emilia, a duplication equivalent to that of Juan and Pablo? Luisa de Maraval may have also been inspired by Madam Laval, a refined French millionaire who spent her summers in Areeta-Las Arenas/Playablanca in the early twentieth century and was notorious in the "Nautic Club" for preferring the company of men and favoring masculine pursuits such as playing billiards, something which caused admiration among some aristocratic women in Bilbo (see Mesa

"Mujeres" 17; for billiard-playing women, see *Mary* 164, Foley *Pasiones* 192). In view of the lesbian subtext, the biographical link suggests that Emilia may have been susceptible to homoerotic feelings, but all we know (through fictional portraits) is that her passion for Enrique may have cooled down, and that she may have become pronouncedly religious in later years.

Many acquaintances of Dr. Areilza remarked on his shyness. Many others referred to "repression" as an important factor in his life. The fascist intellectual Pedro Mourlane Michelena, for example, claimed that "Don Enrique took pleasure in imposing law to enthusiasm as if to a peak of disorder. He learnt from his youth onwards to repress himself and freeze that fire with which he forged his temperament"; this meant that "[h]e kept a close and incessant watch on himself and was shy with tenderness, as if it meant a clandestine complicity. Modesty and good taste were the prickles with which he protected the charming repertoire of his mistrusting reserve" (quoted in Ortiz 78 — my translation). But even his biographer, Manuel Vitoria Ortiz, remarked on Areilza's reserve and felt compelled to clarify that the young Areilza was attractive to women, and that his social retirement during his years at Triano had been a "voluntary cloistering" (59; see 272). A number of commentators refer to his shyness, despite his tough exterior. There certainly seemed to be a profound loneliness in Enrique Areilza in those early years in Triano, despite his busy schedule, his many friends, and his fondness for debate. At the death of his mother, in 1901, he wrote that: "I ... alone nearly always through life, and now truly alone, completely, because it [has] ended for me the only disinterested love [in my life, and] I won't be able to find consolation for my grief either in the future, or high above" (quoted in Ortiz 287–8 — my translation).

I have found no suggestion of latent or actual homosexuality or bisexuality in records of the life of Dr. Areilza. Although it is clear that the most meaningful part of his life developed in homosocial contexts, this would have been typical for a man of his time, class, and education. Areilza, Aresti, and Areavaga are in fact unorthodox in that they treat women close to them in equal terms. *El Intruso* is a novel which highlights the oppression of women, by the morality and piety of the church, by the practice of arranged marriages among the bourgeoisie, and by the resort to prostitution among the working class (see Montero "Prólogo" 18–20); yet the novel also shows that Aresti/Areilza is unique among his contemporaries in that he hopes for, and attempts to establish, some parity in his relationship with his wife.

Unamuno's letter of 1926 to the newly widowed Emilia Rodas bordered on acknowledging a passion for Areilza, with the philosopher suggesting he envied their years together. "I loved him, the way we know how to love over there, and he loved me. He gave me the most exquisite proofs of his affection and today I feel that they have torn him out from a place deep inside myself," Unamuno writes. "And to you, my lady and my friend, what else can I say? I wish for myself the source of consolation at your disposal. All I ask of you is that sometimes you may join the remembrance of he who was your life's companion, to the memory of this your friend" (quoted in J.M. Areilza "Prólogo" 228 — my translation).

Of Enrique's sexuality, we know that he abandoned a resolute bachelor-hood for a marriage that disappointed him, facts which amount to little without any other information. In his published letters, he refers a number of times to homosexuality and lesbianism as a matter of course, sometimes, but not always, to belittle someone (see 55, 62, 67). In *Farewell Spain*, Kate O'Brien recalls "a certain cultured elderly Spaniard" (211) alarmed at her reading Jacinto Benavente during her stay in Bilbo, apparently because of Benavente's homo-sexuality, and the man could well be Don Pablo (that is, Enrique), described in *Mary Lavelle* as "elderly-seeming" (37), in a deliberate intratextual link.

Don Pablo, as we have seen, has a book by Havelock Ellis in his bedroom as well as, among others, an unidentified volume by Proust. It is likely that Areilza owned a copy of Ellis's book on inversion, given that his library included well over 6,000 books (see Areilza "Introducción" 224), and he was widely read in scientific, cultural, anthropological, and historical matters as well as poetry and fiction. Areilza was "passionate about Proust," according to his son (ibid., 230), and given that he regularly received by post the latest French and German publications, it is not inconceivable that Proust's *Sodom and Gomorrah*, which deals with "inversion" with unprecedented honesty and which was first pub-lished in 1922, arrived in the Areilza household during O'Brien's stay. This may have inspired O'Brien's decision to weave a series of references to that novel into *Mary Lavelle*, as well as into the Bilbo section of *Farewell Spain*.

Wherever his erotic and emotional interests lay, Enrique Areilza, at least judging by the wide circle of his friends, was the epitome of open-mindedness. In *El Intruso*, Aresti/Areilza refuses to morally condemn a man whose behavior is seen as sinful, an attitude repeatedly found in *Mary Lavelle*. The man, Aresti's cousin, is having an extra-marital affair, and Aresti's reaction could have been ascribed to Dr. Curran in *The Anteroom*, to Don Pablo in *Mary Lavelle*, and possibly also to their original model, Dr. Areilza: "If the affair gave his cousin some happiness, he did well in continuing it. Life is sad, and man's ability con-sists in gladdening it, in illuminating with brilliant colours the grey contours of his existence"; the woman loved his cousin, "but even if love did not exist, it was the same in the end. The important thing was to believe oneself loved. In the world one lives of illusion and lies, and the greatest tragedy is to open one's eyes" (Ibáñez 129 — my translation).

In the chapter on "Don Pablo" in *Mary Lavelle*, the preoccupation with religion, sexuality, and politics provides a framework for the novel. Pablo/Enrique's life-journey, as retraced in *Mary Lavelle*, becomes something more than a portrait of a truly fascinating man, it becomes a call to abandon ruling principles, *archai*, and follow nature. The personality and the views of Enrique Areilza also offer a framework for Kate O'Brien's opinionated, politically com-mitted, always independent spirit. Like his namesake Henry Archer, Enrique

Areilza was a "Socrates of ... suburb[ia]" (O'Brien *Land* 143). Enrique may have "fed and loaded [the] mind" of Kate (ibid. 147). The doctor may have also provided the novelist with a model for spiritual agnosticism and individualist anarchism, for austerity and detachment, which O'Brien may have used to develop her own general views of Bilbo and the Basque Country, which she then extended to Spain, and which became important to her own thinking. It seems likely to me that Kate O'Brien was introduced to the noventayocho movement, to anarchist projects, and to an interest in Spanish culture and history, through her meeting with Enrique Areilza. His ways, and his opinions on many areas, made an impact on all those who knew him. Consider the following: his respect for religious feeling despite his outspoken atheism and his understanding of Europe as essentially "Christian"; his interest in the regeneration of Spain, his love of Castile, and his devotion to cultural travelling; his passionate arguments, striking use of words, and reliance on metaphors in writing; his egalitarianism, mistrust of party politics, and contempt for status and wealth; his various spiritual "homes" — the Basque Country, Europe, and Spain; his irony; and perhaps also his deep sense of loneliness. Do they not sound familiar?

Seven

Autobiography:
Kate O'Brien
(1922–1923, 1935–1936)

Autobiography and Kate O'Brien

"Proust has taught us that the memories we sit down to, that we select and seek, are false" (O'Brien, "UCD" 6); in other words, they are fiction. In 1955, Enrique Areilza's son, José María, was ambassador for the Francoist regime in the United States, when he received a letter from Kate O'Brien. Referring to the time she lived in Bilbo, O'Brien told him: "My short stay in your family home is printed indelibly in my memory. That period was so important for me that I used it to write *an almost autobiographical novel* called *Mary Lavelle*" (emphasis added, quoted in J.M. Areilza "Kate" 38). This autobiographical input is, I will argue, crucial to the themes and style of the novel. A focus on authorial intention has been devalued in literary criticism, after the introduction of doubts on the subject's cohesiveness in the late twentieth century. The turn was signaled in 1968 by Roland Barthes's announcement of the death of the author as primary source of meaning, an "act of political bravado" (to borrow from Sedgwick on Foucault, *Epystemology* 9) equivalent to Friedrich Nietzsche's pronouncement on the death of God in 1882. According to the poststructuralist view, meaning is constituted through language, which is inherently unstable and multivalent and is articulated through a number of historically determined discourses. This position invalidates the reification of the author, but conversely it enables a new understanding of language as accessible tool for re-signification, however ultimately unstable. "Kate O'Brien" may be a phantom partly constructed by critics and partly by O'Brien herself, but there is a productive line of inquiry in discerning some of the ways in which she re-figured her own experiences through language. That is, autobiographical readings of O'Brien's work have a place in literary criticism if they open up a text. O'Brien treated personal memories as malleable material, and considering the distortion of that material as presented in *Mary Lavelle* gives the reader a deeper understanding of the novel as an exercise in creativity.

There has been a renewed interest in life-writing as fiction of the self, partly thanks to a groundbreaking study of 1972 by James Olney, *Metaphors of Self*, partly thanks to the collective effort of feminist criticism to recover texts by women previously shunned by canon-makers, but a new approach to biographical output was a generalized concern of writers and readers at the time of composition of *Mary Lavelle*. Hermione Lee's comment on Virginia Woolf is equally applicable to O'Brien: "In her lifetime, psychoanalysis, wars, social changes and the reaction against nineteenth-century habits of mind meant a revolution in biography and memoir-writing" (*Woolf* 9).

In *Mary Lavelle* and *Teresa of Avila*, O'Brien echoes Augustine's influential *Confessions*, written in 397–398 C.E., in which he recalled his youth in Carthage in the fourth century, giving himself to lawlessness and lust before embracing Christianity. He tells of his being "in love with loving," discusses the pull of male friendships towards the "foul lustfulness" of Sodom, and regrets a godless youth when he (T.S. Eliot must have taken note) "became to myself a barren land" (Augustine 32, 33, 31). Leaving the *Confessions* aside, the first relevant autobiographies in Europe were written by women, from the early fifteen century memoirs of Leonor López de Córdoba and Margery Kempe, to the seventeenth century memoirs of the Duchess of Newcastle, Julian of Norwich, Anne Bradsheet, and Teresa de Jesus and, in the Americas, Sor Juana Inés de la Cruz and Sor Josefa Francisca del Castillo. The Basque cross-dresser and adventurer Katalin de Erauso, who became famous as "the ensign nun" in the seventeenth century, is a particularly interesting example, because the account of her life is a mixture of memoir and fictional autobiography, and its influence has endured (see Velasco). Ángel Esteban, discussing Erauso, has pointed to the relevance of the role of women in the development of the autobiographical fiction genre, which is striking given the inordinate restrictions placed on their crossing from the private to the public sphere (54–56).

It has often been argued that it was through autobiographical publications that the novel was developed, yet autobiographical novels have been derided by orthodox criticism, arguably because the link between this popular genre and women is seen in a context of merging fact and fiction as an infantile, amateurish practice. The upsurge of feminist biography in the 1970s did much to counteract that view, but life-writing remains outside the canon. Katie Donovan explained in 1988 that "[o]ne factor that critics tend to highlight in the work of both Kate O'Brien and [Mary] Lavin is the autobiographical nature of their fiction. This is usually proffered as a limitation for which they should be forgiven. However," as Donovan points out, "their contemporary male writers, for all their artifice, draw on the same source" (*Writers* 19).

Recording experience and recovering accounts have been particular concerns of feminists. Life-writing was also crucial to another collective largely written out of history, that of people seeking to obtain or offer expressions of same-sex love and desire. This was reflected in an interest in memoirs and letters, as well as in the production of self-fictionalizing accounts. For example, Radcliffe Hall's *The Well of Loneliness* may not be autobiographical fiction in a strict sense, but rather the expression of the life that the author would have liked for herself (see Barker 215). James Olney has claimed that "autobiography is the least complicated of writing performances" ("Autobiography" 3). That may be true at the purely technical level of writing, but it is no doubt inaccurate when we consider the genre's operation on subjectivity. When autobiography meets fiction, "complications" multiply.

Modernist writers of Kate O'Brien's generation conducted a number of experiments in autobiography which transformed the genre. Colette's *Claudine* novels (1900, 1901, 1902, 1903), Dorothy Richardson's *Pilgrimage* (1915–1935), James Joyce's *Portrait of the Artist as a Young Man* (1914–1915), Gertrude Stein's *The Autobiography of Alice B. Toklas* (1933), or Henry Miller's *Black Spring* (1936) are some examples. This interest is consonant with modernist interrogations of the "self in motion." Among the modernists there was a perhaps contradictory interest in "recording" the self, and in revising what "the self" may signify. In the sense that it attempted to represent or "capture" subjectivity, modernist art can be seen as a furthering of the realist project. We can consider at least some modernists as realists focusing on previously unexplored areas of experience, such as consciousness or sexuality. Even those who overtly opposed the realist model of representation, such as the surrealists, were in fact attempting to bring the real lived experience of irrationality (in dreams, violence, desire, chance, imagination) into the picture. Interestingly, the surrealists created a form of testimonial collage-publication, a new type of autobiography perhaps, bringing together letters, photographs, and drawings. As Vincent Gille explains, the surrealist author believed in "the obligation to speak frankly and in the first person. Inner experience was gradually developed (in the photographic sense of the word), and the prime concern was veracity," so that "surrealist texts can be seen as *documents* (they could almost be called 'reports'). They are indissociable from the experiences that gave rise to them, and reconstitute the substance and almost palpable aura of those experiences" (emphasis in original, 127).

With the increased interest in writing the self, came a preoccupation, or a fascination, with self-exposure. The tension between public and private was particularly resonant for women writers, who had repeatedly visited this theme in fiction, according to Dorothy Mermin in her 1993 study, *Godiva's Ride*. The threats and rewards of exposure were even more present for queer writers. In her *Epistemology of the Closet*, Eve Kosofsky Sedgwick has analyzed the pervading influence of concealment around sexuality in twentieth century Western culture. Kate O'Brien's reticence to discuss her private life in public has been noted by Emma Donoghue and Eibhear Walshe, with Paul Smith recalling that she was fond of pointing out that "[i]t is considered a political and social sin in Russia to print news about anybody's personal life" (104). Nevertheless, O'Brien was an avid reader of memoirs and published letters, and she was not herself averse to speculating in print about the ostensibly private matter of other people's sexual preferences. For example, as I have argued, her book on Teresa of Avila is an important but unacknowledged example of lesbian historiography, where O'Brien shows what a close reading of a self-censored testimony can yield. Teresa, her biographer explains, "is not explicit in her writings about the particular 'pastimes of the senses' to which she confesses her long addiction, but we may take her cool word for it that she knew as well what she talked of in their regard as she did in other contexts"; O'Brien goes on to specify that Teresa "was never a scarlet sinner, a Mary Magdalen," and adds that even though Teresa "read *The Confessions of Saint Augustine* with marked understanding and appreciation — 'seemed to see myself in them' — we can be certain that she ... could never have had any such acquaintance with sensual pleasures as the Bishop of Hippo allowed himself in his youth." O'Brien concludes that:

> Probably, like Saint Augustine, Teresa was, at her most tempted, always more in love with love than with any fellow creature; she suggests of herself that she was moody and restless in attachments. Yet she formed many of them, and chiefly with women, whose devotion, as her active years were to prove, she could always and effortlessly command [Teresa 43–44].

Another book by Kate O'Brien, the 1943 survey *English Diaries and Journals*, is in fact, overall, a "mass outing" of a number of intellectuals and writers (Pepys is dismissed as a "bor[e]" before the true detective work on the bookshelves can begin —18). It was written for a gay audience able to pick up her innuendo, as indicated by the original cover of the book, with a design of the Zodiac, one of the code signals for "Uranians." Despite the confidence often displayed by Kate O'Brien, there are indications that exposure remained an important concern for her. For example, she declared in 1963: "James Joyce is my man. Here is a writer who tells the truth about himself. It is almost impossible to tell the truth" ("Art" 46; it is an unacknowledged quote by Barbillion, see O'Brien *Diaries* 46). *Mary Lavelle* represented an attempt to tell the truth. Before it met the censorship of the Publications Act in Ireland, this "truth" had to negotiate O'Brien's own filters.

Michael Sprinker describes autobiography as "the inquiry of the self into its own origin and history" (342). It may not be a coincidence that Kate O'Brien was writing *Mary Lavelle* in the same year that saw the publication of *The Last Puritan: A Memoir in the Form of a Novel*, by the Spanish-American George Santayana, who remained one of her favorite thinkers throughout her life. O'Brien quoted from it in 1962, discussing the power of the unconscious to collect impressions ("UCD" 9). Reynolds, at one time O'Brien's partner, recalled of her last visits to her: "I used to urge her ... to write her autobiography — but in a sense this was stupid of me. She had already said what she wanted to say about her life in her novels, however obliquely" (*Kate* 133). Critics have implied or stated that all the protagonists of O'Brien's novels are in fact self-portraits. For example, according to Reynolds, Matt Costello "is clearly a persona of the author" (*Kate* 105, see 79; see also Reynolds "Women" 20), while Clare Boylan has declared that "*The Land of Spices* is Kate O'Brien's most autobiographical work" (ix), and similar comments recur in critical accounts. John Jordan pointed out discreetly that "[t]he most important influences in Kate's youth ... may have been her convent upbringing, her spell as a governess in Spain in the twenties, and her unsuccessful marriage. How she alchemized these influences is part of her achievement" ("Kate" [1976] 233). Vivian Mercier had made the same claim in 1946, listing "a convent upbringing, great beauty, and a marriage that lasted only a year" to conclude that "[i]f art is a product of neurosis, then we need search no further for the weapons which supplied the psychological wound and made Kate O'Brien into a chronicler of frustrated or sinful passion" (quoted in Cawley 3; Mercier 88).

Kate O'Brien's self-writing is not circumscribed to her fiction. In a paper of 2007, Anne Jamison pointed that not only is *Presentation Parlour* a "semi-autobiographical text," but also *My Ireland* can be considered a "pseudo-auto-biography"—although Jamison surprisingly failed to mention the nonfiction book by O'Brien which is most clearly concerned with personal experience: *Farewell Spain*. Jamison perceptively noted O'Brien's "dual, contradictory impulse" to record or document her life and to eliminate personal documents or hide autobiographical information, given that her surviving papers, for example, are "very self-conscious about their eventual destination."

Bilbo, 1922–1923

Kate O'Brien's visit to Bilbo is the single most repeated incident in autobiographical accounts by the novelist. She gave at least two lectures recalling her experiences there, she spoke of that time at length in a television documentary on her life, and she devoted to Bilbo the penultimate chapter of *Farewell Spain*, which marked the end of her sentimental journey through the country. This chapter, titled "Mainly Personal," provides a number of hints to the way her memories were incorporated into *Mary Lavelle*, even though the novel is never mentioned in the travelogue. As we have seen, there are numerous examples of these "clues"—it is worth looking at some of them again. In the travelogue, O'Brien declares: "I see now, looking down from Begoña towards the bridge and the Arenal where I search for my own ghost, that I was pleased, in my roots, with the unexpected Spain I had found" (*Spain* 211; in the novel, it is Mary Lavelle who sits at Begoña/Allera, looks down on the city, and reflects on her fate after "replanting" her roots—*Mary* 105). In *Farewell Spain*, we are told that "I remember the ships swinging up and down the Nervión [river]— I watched them from my window" (212); while Mary watches the ships from her window in the novel. In the travelogue, O'Brien also tells us that "I remember sitting often by San Vicente which I liked to look at and found very lovely" (215). In the novel it is Mary who sits in the square facing San Vicente/San Geronimo, which is also the view from Agatha's window.

There is more. In *Farewell Spain*, O'Brien discusses bullfights in some detail, referring to Hemingway's views on two occasions (204–5), while as we have seen the novel bases both the bullfight scene and the sex scene on Hemingway's descriptions in *Death in the Afternoon*. The travelogue gives a detailed account of the Carlist wars in the Basque Country, which would be part of the family background of the Areavagas in the novel. The travelogue indirectly refers to Proust—"[u]p there [in Begoña] is perhaps a good place from which to consider *le temps perdu*" (*Spain* 208)—a recurrent reference in the novel. In *Farewell Spain*, O'Brien comments on the conspicuous political graffiti, the "writing on the wall" (208), pointing to the apocalyptic subtext to her novel. In the travelogue, she also mentions having bought, read, and discussed *Don Quixote* in 1922 (see 212), the main characters from which would be remodeled in the quixotic Agatha and her sidekick Rosie in *Mary Lavelle*. "I liked to watch the dancing too at night in the squares, under the harsh lights, among the clipped plane-trees. Very beautiful and deliberate modern dancing" (215–6), O'Brien explains in *Farewell Spain*, repeating the main details from the dancing scene in the novel. In the travelogue, she also recalls the commuters' train that used to take her from the city center to Portugalete/Cabantes "through the premises of the most famous foundries—the 'Vizcaya,' the 'Altos Hornos,' the 'Santa Ana'—where the great fires never went out" (212), thus giving to her readers the origin of her fictional name, "Altorno." The next and last section of *Farewell Spain* opens with O'Brien in Irun, about to leave Spain (if not the Basque Country) on the train: an exact replica of the ending of *Mary Lavelle*.

Farewell Spain looks back at *Mary Lavelle*, just as *Mary Lavelle* was also a "return" to 1922. "I remember" is compulsively repeated in the Basque chapter of the travelogue, a counterpoint to the recurrent "I must remember this" in the novel. Yet, at the close of the Basque chapter, O'Brien presents herself as someone stubbornly, perhaps over-emphatically, self-effacing. "It will be seen that sitting up here near Our Lady or Begoña I have remembered nothing much, nothing of great general or personal interest from that lost year," O'Brien says, to add: "But I see now that, though smudgy, it was a more indelible year for me than many. I am glad to have had it, and glad to sit here again with its unimpressive memories" (*Spain* 216–7). This "lost year," with its "unimpressive memories," would see her first steps towards becoming a writer, inspire several novels, and prompt a host of references scattered through her work.

In *Farewell Spain*, Kate O'Brien points out, "in that winter [1922–1923] I began to attempt dramatic writing" (*Spain* 209), which seems to have started with "a fancy piece about the Cantabrian mountains and Charlemagne's Roland—though what I thought Roland was doing so far west of Roncesvalles I can't imagine"; she explains that "I got the idea of it when crossing the Puente Isabella [now "Arenal" Bridge] in torrential rain. So improbable is inspiration!" (*Spain* 210). Roncesvalles, in the Pyrenees, was the site of a battle between Basque forces and an invading French army in 778 (and again in 824), an event which inspired the *Chanson de Roland* (where the Basques were transmuted into an Arab army) and is often considered to be the first example of the Basque Country acting as a political entity. It is noteworthy that the first tentative steps in Kate O'Brien's career as fiction writer should be linked thus to the beginning of the Basque nation.

Much of the information on Bilbo included in the travelogue failed to be transposed into the novel: Descriptions of the city's slums and references to the municipal art gallery are missing from *Mary Lavelle*, as are mentions to Basque history, to Basque sports, to similarities between Ireland and the Basque Country in landscape and temperament. The discarded information pertained by and large to specifically Basque references, "explained" in the novel's attempt to present Bilbo as a generic Spanish location (although *Villette* uses the same strategy with Brussels partly to safeguard the author's privacy), and it is relevant that the Basque chapter in *Farewell Spain* in fact opens with a description of Castile, the region of Spain which took "precedence" as a symbol of the Spanish character in the novel. Conversely, there are a number of elements crucial to the novel that the account in *Farewell Spain* fails to mention: the Areilza family, for example.

The precise dates of Kate O'Brien's visit are also missing. How long was she in Bilbo? In a lecture of 1972, she explained that she had traveled there at "the end of August" ("Talk" [1]). In *Farewell Spain* she claims: "I lived and earned a living there for nearly a year when I was young and Alphonse XIII was still a merry monarch. (Actually Primo de Rivera pulled off his military *coup* and assumed dictatorship in that year — but I did not see that happen. I had just gone home)" (201). "That year" would suggest 1923, the time of the military coup, but in the travelogue O'Brien also mentions crossing the Basque Bidasoa river, in the Spanish-French border, in August, and having stayed in Bilbo in "the winter of 1922–23" (ibid. 209; see 212). Further confusing matters, José María Areilza claims that O'Brien left Bilbo *after*, and not before, Primo de Rivera's coup ("Mary" 227), while Iñaki Anasagasti, referring to a text by J.M. Areilza, gives "a year and a half" (26). According to John Jordan, who was writing while O'Brien was still alive and clearly using his friend as the main source of information, she spent ten months in Bilbo ("First Lady" 228), while Eibhear Walshe's biography states at one point that she stayed for "seven months or so" and later gives "eight months" (*Kate* 30, 31). In *Mary Lavelle*, Mary spends the summer in Altorno, that is, four months, from June to October (see *Mary* 288); Mary meets Juanito two months after her arrival, and they dance in the square in the last week of August; she goes to Madrid on the third week of September and celebrates her birthday there; they spend the night on the field on October 14, and Pablo dies the following day (see *Mary* 146, 214, 222, 336).

Kate O'Brien was 25 years old — Mary is 22 — when she traveled to Bilbo, while she was 38 years old — the same as Agatha — when she was writing the novel. Eibhear Walshe has noted that this is not the only correspondence in age between O'Brien and some of her most important characters, since she was as old as Helen Archer, Ana de Mendoza, and Eleanor Delahunt at the time of composition of the novels in which they appear (in conversation, July 2006; see also Walshe *Kate* 84, 123). Not only did O'Brien describe *Mary Lavelle* as a "nearly autobiographical novel," also José María Areilza, in his essay on the book, treats Mary Lavelle and Kate O'Brien as if they were the same person:

> Of Mary Lavelle I learned literary English at 13 [sic]. She was a young Irish woman of 25, tall and slender, with an athletic body, who walked in big strides, she had black hair, cut garçon style, her face was of very pale complexion and with a Greek profile, and her eyes, big, grey, looked around with an inquisitive air. She arrived in my parents' house in 1922, to spend a year there and learn Castilian Spanish, while my sister and I improved on our meagre vocabulary in the British language [sic]. She had in her room, which overlooked the mouth of the tidal river in Bilbo, a mass of books on English literature, together with an English-Spanish dictionary....
>
> She liked observing the Sunday dances in the square around the kiosk, where the band and the txistu players took turns, that is, there was a succession of *agarrao* [formal dancing between couples] and folk dances. She used to say she had never seen anything as merry as those crowded and popular dances. On Thursday or Saturday she used to go to Bilbo and meet up, in the Café Suizo of Correo street, with a considerable number of "misses," Irish in the main, who kept an interminable tertulia [debate] on issues related to their profession. There was also in that time a group of German *fräuleins*, but the European war, still fresh in memory, split the trade in two incompatible groups.
>
> Mary Lavelle used to lock herself up some evenings in her boudoir until supper time and allowed me to come in so that she could share her secret. She wanted to be a writer, a novelist, perhaps a playwright [emphasis in original, "Mary" 226–7 — my translation].

There are a number of other sources for information on how O'Brien's experiences in Bilbo were transferred to *Mary Lavelle*. In a lecture of 1972, for example, she recounts her overnight train trip from Paris to Bilbo in 1922, recalling that she took the trip with a rather posh friend and that her carriage was full of Basque people. In the middle of a heat wave in late August, the train stopped before Donosti (San Sebastian) for a few hours, and a worker at the station offered the hospitality of his home to the exhausted O'Brien and her companion. This gesture deeply moved her and coloured all her future impressions of "Spain." It is telling that the Basque setting to this crucial experience was obliterated from her account: "I know that I gave my heart to Spain in that vast, white kitchen that morning. I fell in love, and for ever, with all the austerity, the space, and the goodwill" ("Talk"). O'Brien's documentary for Irish television, *Self-Portrait*, retells the decision to travel to the Basque Country and her first experiences. I have attempted to record in writing O'Brien' speech in the film, including her hesitations and changes of pace:

> [S]o I came back to London [after the foreign pages in the *Manchester Guardian* folded], and I taught in a school in Hamstead, primary school, for about two terms. I didn't care for that and I went, from that, rather quickly, to Spain, again, to teach, but to teach in a house, to teach a boy and his sister English literature. He was a very

brilliant boy, and he wanted to be taught well, so I had to work hard, but I liked the life very much. A most intelligent pupil, and I found the peace and carefree routines of the life suited me well and helped me to think, and I altogether thought there was something to be said for that, and I got very much interested in … Spain in general, reading the papers and getting to know Spain, but I used to think sometimes on our walks up those Biscayan hills that what, how, Charlotte Brontë loathed the governess' life and what marvelous books she wrote on that theme and how she hated it, but that I disagreed with her I would have liked it especially in Spain I, I liked the, that year [sic]. But I didn't stay — personal events brought me back to London, and then for a time I was going from job to job looking, looking for freelance journalism … [*Self Portrait* transcript].

In the 1962 book, *My Ireland*, she likened her first impressions of Bilbo to her first visit to Milan:

The city of Spain that I first walked about in was Bilbao; and that was when I was very young and thought of Spain, I daresay, in terms of the opera *Carmen*. I cannot remember now if I was much taken aback, but I hope that I did get somehow hold of the idea that I had much to learn. And many years later when at last I got to Italy I had on my first afternoon to find my way through Milan, under blistering heat through Milan's very modern, industrialised suburbs. I remember that then I *was* surprised, not to say disgusted.

Ireland, being poor — as poor as Spain perhaps? — has no Bank-encrusted Bilbao to show the stranger, nor any tycoon-driven and rip-roaring Milan. For neither Dublin nor Belfast is temperamentally or materially endowed for such presentation [emphasis in original, 19].

Interestingly, if she claims here that her memories of her first impression of Bilbo were fuzzed, there was no uncertainty in a lecture she gave the following year, where as we will see she recalled having found Bilbo "very shocking" (quoted in Reynolds *Kate* 37). But a bond with Spain had been established. "Ten years later [after 1922] I returned as an ordinary traveler — and then I think that for most of the summers of 33, 34, 35 — until the Spanish War broke out in July 1936" ("Art" 7). She explains in another piece: "I used to fool about the cities of Castile. Taking my time and spending little money. I was fascinated and very happy" (ibid.). Judging by some of the photographs in the Limerick archive, Kate O'Brien may have returned to Portugalete/Cabantes in 1957. But O'Brien's final assessment of her time in Bilbo may just be in *Constancy*, the novel left unfinished at her death, where we find this remarkable self-portrait:

Treasa, who had been of the Doctor's household for twelve or more years — as house-maid, parlourmaid, tutor, secretary, shopper, friend — was a natural intellectual from the chief of the Aran islands. To the happy accident of the coming to their home and finding that she liked to live with them all the Doherty children owed their excellent Irish; for Treasa never opened her lips in any other language if she could help it. When she came to the Dohertys she was shy and unlettered, but life in Galway had made a kind of intellectual of her — so she was now a "character," a bookworm, a fanatic and a feminist. She was handsome and tall. Old Annie sometimes muttered to herself that the creature might go so far as to have her eye on the doctor, if you please. And that wouldn't do at all at all [35].

Beliefs

IRISH EUROPEAN, CATHOLIC AGNOSTIC

Kate O'Brien's political formation arguably began in UCD, where she arrived as an undergraduate to study English and French in the autumn of 1916. "Those were terrible years," she recalled, "all over the world, of course, the first World War was raging in Europe, terribly, and Ireland was in great uproar after, upset after, 1916, and in the throws of the really last final struggle for independence" (*Self Portrait* transcript). O'Brien explained that in college "I became almost overnight a lazy and sceptical student," and described her new friends as "an education" (ibid.). Women were relatively new to university, but, as Lorna Reynolds put it, there was not "a single, simple colleen among them" ("Women" 25). The colonial past of the Irish Republic meant a specific relationship to the world, one that assumed interconnectedness and accessibility. As Reynolds points out, "[g]oing to England after graduation was the common route for "every ambitious person with no clear career-pattern ahead of them," and O'Brien was "a born traveller," but also, Reynolds explains: "Young people sometimes today forget that she was born a British subject. Ireland then was still part of the British Empire, to every part of which the citizen was free to travel. She never felt herself an exile in Europe or Britain" (*Kate* 188). It is interesting to note Desmond Hogan's comment that "[a]n American writers' directory of the 1940s tells us that on Kate's visit to the United States in the late forties she was without an Irish accent" ("Introduction" [1985] vii).

Elsewhere, Reynolds remarks that "Europe, of which Ireland formed a part, shared a common market of ideas and culture, [Kate O'Brien] often pointed out, long before any economic alliance thought of it" ("Artist" 59–60). O'Brien's literary referents are European (see Magnus), and her view of Ireland was emphatically European (see for example M. Cronin 141). She may not have been orthodox in her devotion to Ireland, and the state reminded her of it on two occasions, but, as John Jordan recalls, she loved Ireland deeply, even if "in judgment ... she was consistently unsentimental" ("Talent" 231). In the words of Anthony Roche, "Kate O'Brien is at one with the other writers of the 1930s in writing about and diagnosing the failure of a revolution, the betrayal of the promise of Ireland to gain a full and meaningful independence" ("Anteroom" 95). She did herself refer to a "schizophrenic" Ireland of conflicting priorities and views (O'Brien *Ireland* 15). O'Brien had a horror of insularity both as a politics and as a state of mind, and on one occasion, in a lecture of 1966, defined good writing as "non-parochial and free." If a displacement of nationalist significance is characteristic of O'Brien, she occasionally referred to her Irish background as distinctive and valuable. We find a curious example of this in her discussion of the bullfight in *Farewell Spain*, where she refers to "that English sensitiveness to the feelings of animals which, I freely confess, runs more thinly in me, a mere Irishwoman" (*Spain* 137). Later in the book, commenting on a man who complained about "Bilbao's mud, and passions just under the skin," she put it down to the fact that he "is English — and I am Irish." She explained: "Mud was an ordinary matter in Ireland when I was young, and passions— so long as they be not sexual — are our familiars. So that the two things that fell new [sic] and raw on him were, I suppose, the two of all others which I took for granted and found homelike [in Bilbo]" (ibid., 210).

As Michael O'Toole pointed out, "Kate O'Brien's understanding of Irish convent life was ... unrivalled among writers" ("Foreword" 4). Catholic morality, and its concomitant guilt and hypocrisy, run through all her fiction. In *Mary Lavelle*, they are the main obstacle to the protagonist's development. Nevertheless, O'Brien conceived of Christianity as a cultural European commonality informing ethics, yet strikingly devoid of its religious content. That is, a belief in God or the afterlife plays no part in lived Christianity, which is presented in her work as a system that regulates society and culture. Lorna Reynolds claims that "[p]robably" Matt Costello's views coincide with Kate O'Brien's, and brings in a quote from *Pray for the Wanderer*: "his greatest faith was personal liberty — a faith that had finally driven him out of the Church, but which made it impossible for him to find any resting place in contemporary life" (quoted by Reynolds *Kate* 37)— Don Pablo could have said the same. "[O'Brien] herself, as she tells us in a fragment of autobiography, 'lost the faith,' as we say, while she was still at school"; Reynolds also explains: "intellectually she became estranged from Catholicism but emotionally she remained attached to it. She was, as long as I knew her, an agnostic, but a 'Catholic agnostic,' as the Dublin saying goes, and she died reconciled with the Church. (*Kate* 118). O'Brien herself did not publicly and explicitly refer to her agnosticism or atheism (see Walshe *Kate* 106–7), but she suggested on a number of occasions that she had lost her faith while living as a boarder in the Limerick school run by French nuns portrayed in *The Land of Spices*. For example, there is much distress over the young Fanny Morrow's lack of faith in *The Flower of May*, while in *Pray for the Wanderer* Matt Costelloe declares, "I was a doubter ... and an exerciser of private judgement, long before I was confirmed" (O'Brien *Pray* 190). With discretion, O'Brien did occasionally acknowledge the possibility of life outside a religious system, as in her off-handed comment in *My Ireland* referring to "whatever your faith or non-faith" (27).

I have discussed earlier the relevance of Christian anarchism to O'Brein's work, and her use of Romanesque to articulate feelings and ideas. Kate O'Brien was also particularly interested in Celtic monasticism, something she shared with other modernists, and with many artists committed to leftist politics. In her representations of religious communities and individuals there is a general impetus towards "agnostification," and a converse spiritualization of her laic, pagan, or agnostic characters (see Mentxaka "Catholic — Agnostic"). We have also seen how her Catholic background has determined the critical reception of her work in Ireland. O'Brien tends to balance out her critique of Christian morality as a repressive force with a parallel emphasis on the usefulness of Christian values and culture. I have to agree with Sharon Tighe-Mooney's claim that, "[d]espite O'Brien's affirmed agnosticism, there is a sense that she envied those who had faith" ("Sexuality" 131).

SPAIN

Christianity also played an important part in Kate O'Brien's "recuperation" of Spain as an integral part of Europe. Lorna Reynolds recalled: "She had no interest in, in fact, an active dislike of Moorish Spain. She used to get quite angry with me when I would argue that one could not dismiss the Arab contribution to Spain out of hand.... Christian Spain was what concerned her" ("Image" 105). In *Mary Lavelle*, the (striking) fact that the eldest of the Areavaga sisters, destined to become a pillar of society, is "dark, the darkest of the family" (8) is likely to be an O'Brien's marker for a visceral dislike, in line with her description of Andalucians as "brown," her claim that Arabs "imperilled and infected, but did not dominate" Spanish judgment, and her description of Franco as a "moor" (*Spain* 87, 183).

The consequences of O'Brien's opposition to Francoism have yet to be elucidated. Mary O'Neill stated that *Farewell Spain* "was banned in Franco's Spain, and Kate O'Brien herself was forbidden entry to Spain until after 1957" (xii–xiii). O'Brien had declared in a talk she gave in 1972: "I've never been *persona grata* with the Franco Government. It's the only feather in my cap that all my works were long ago totally banned in Spain — and so remain." Many intellectuals were declared "persona non grata" by the new Spanish regime. Some were glad to stay away until Franco's death in protest, such as Sylvia Townsend Warner, while others returned when the restrictions eased, such as Ernest Hemingway. O'Brien went through some trouble to explain her reasons for wishing to return in the context of a boycott to the regime, claiming that "I have never been able to feel like that — so renunciatory" (in her 1972 lecture). After interviewing O'Brien in 1971, John Jordan reported:

> As regards the title of the travel book [*Farewell Spain*], it is *not* to be taken as an overt comment on the issues of the Civil War. She would have gone back to Spain had she had a sponsor. To jump forward a decade, when she did try to return back to Spain in 1947, she was refused entry on the grounds that Generalissimo [sic] Franco had taken issue with her treatment of Philip II in her novel *That Lady* (1946). Eventually, with the intervention of the Irish ambassador to Spain ("who had to tell a lot of lies— I was a Reformed Character, a High-Class Convent Girl") she returned to Spain in 1957. Since then she has returned off and on to Madrid, and her beloved Avila, birthplace of her special, if not quite orthodox cult, Santa Tèrésa [sic] (she published a little book on the saint in 1951) [emphasis in original, "First Lady" 229].

Jordan is clearly quoting O'Brien here, and there have been doubts about her claims (see Walshe 75). As we have seen, Marisol Morales Ladrón and Ute Mittermaier have put the debate to rest with their archival research, confirming the banning of *Mary Lavelle* in Spain. No other O'Brien book was banned, although the 1943 translation of *The Last of Summer* was censored (see Morales 65–6 for censor's report). As Morales has documented, *Without My Cloak* and *The Ante-Room* appeared in Spanish in 1943, followed by *That Lady* in 1946. However, no requests for publication were filed for any other books, including *Farewell Spain* (ibid. 64, 68–9). Further, Marisol Morales Ladrón has shown that there is so far no evidence that Kate O'Brien was ever banned from entering Spain, and casts doubts on the reliability of O'Brien as a source of information given that her claim that all her books had been banned in Spain is clearly innacurate (ibid. 70). Critics' assumptions, and the challenges of archival research, are summarized in Mittermaier's doctoral thesis:

> O'Brien's claim in a lecture in March 1972 that she was never "persona grata with the Franco government" and that "it [was] the only feather in [her] cap that all [her] works [had] been long ago banned in Spain" (Canterbury lecture, 4) was clearly wrong. But so is Walshe's contention that "her work was freely available in Spain" and that "[t]he only form of censorship recorded was that permission was refused for the book jacket of *Without My Cloak* on the grounds of immorality!" (*Writing*, 75). In fact, permission to translate *Mary Lavelle* was denied on 7 January 1944, without any reasons being specified (Archivo General de Administración de Alcalá de Henares, expediente no. 8102–43). Moreover, the translation of *The Last of Summer* (*Final de verano* in Spanish) was only authorised on 15 June 1943 on condition that all "immoral" as well as all critical statements on Hitler and Nazi-Germany would be excised or paraphrased (ibid., expediente no. 3852–43). It is likely that Sheila Quinn, whom Walshe acknowledges as his source for information on censorship of O'Brien's oeuvre in Spain (cf. *Writing*, 75), failed to locate the relevant files for *Mary Lavelle* and *The Last of Summer* because the search for entries on O'Brien in the databases recording censorship files at the Archivo General de Administración de Alcalá de Henares using the correct spelling of the novelist's surname only yields five results, while other versions, such as "O Brien" or "Brien," return another seven results. I am very grateful to Alberto Lázaro Lafuente and Marisol Morales Ladrón from the University of Alcalá for alerting me to the Spanish censors' habitual inconsistency in spelling English and Irish names.

There are still many unanswered questions, particularly regarding O'Brien's visa applications to Spain. As Morales has discovered, there are a number of relevant files in the National Archive of Ireland which are vetoed to researchers, while other catalogued files are simply missing (see 69–70). It has been suggested by Joseba Felix Tobar-Arbulu that J.M. Areilza, because of his prominence in the Francoist regime, may have had something to do with O'Brien's banning of entry, but I do not believe that to be the case ("Kate"). Jose María Areilza is not always a reliable source of information, that is true; suffice to say that he gave three very different accounts of his first reading of *Mary Lavelle* (see "Mary" 228; "Kate" 38; and a letter to O'Brien dated May 26, 1952). Speaking at the "Kate O'Brien Weekend" Areilza declared that "stupidly" O'Brien had been barred entry in Spain ("Kate" 39), and it seems to me that his most likely source was O'Brien herself. There is a typed letter (on official paper from the Spanish government) by J.M. Areilza to "Dear Miss Kitty" [O'Brien] in the

Limerick archive, dated May 13, 1960, opening with, "It was great to have heard from you again after all these years!" and, after some introductory remarks, "[a]s to your request, I am writing today to the Head of the Cultural Relations Office in our Ministry of Foreign Affairs, to see whether we can do something about it," and adds, "[i]t will take some weeks before I get a reply, but I assure you that I will do everything in my power to see that something is done." J.M. Areilza's discreet omission of the nature of O'Brien's request, and her decision to keep the letter (she kept only a handful), indicates it was a sensitive issue — whether it had to do with a permanent visa, a publication, or something else, I have not been able to ascertain.

To complicate matters further (or to bring into play a clue which way prove to be decisive), "the former ambassador of Ireland in Spain during the 1950s, Dr. Michael Rynne," who may have been instrumental in lifting the ban, if there was one, "was a relative of O'Brien" (Morales 68). However, Marisol Morales Ladrón has found no evidence of his intervention. In the "Kate O'Brien Papers" in Limerick, there is an official *Spanish visa* stamped on one of O'Brien's surviving passports, dated September 9, 1957, and a stamp by the border officials dated September 14, 1957, but she entered Spain through the Basque town of Irun before that date, on September 2, 1954, as an official stamp indicates on the same passport. As Cinta Ramblado noted in a paper of 2005, a meeting with the prominent Francoist minister Manuel Fraga, marked in Kate O'Brien's pocket diary, may have been related to the visa ("Kate"). The visa secured by O'Brien in 1957 may have been a temporary one, and even though she had managed at least once to cross the border without adequate documentation, it would have been wise to obtain proper permits, because the fascist regime in Spain saw any irregularity as a threat and had no qualms about using violence. It seems clear that O'Brien over-dramatized her barring, but I see no reason to doubt that her visa was denied a number of times after 1947, possibly even for a decade until 1957, when she managed, either through Areilza, the Irish ambassador, or both, to return to Spain by legal means.

A comparatively minor mystery is the history of *Mary Lavelle*'s Spanish translation. Although I have not managed to find evidence to support or disclaim this point, it seems to me likely that José María Areilza was involved in the publication of the Spanish version of the novel in 1990. A year earlier, speaking at the "Kate O'Brien Weekend," he finished his paper by saying: "it is very possible that the book could be translated as it is a very interesting social and literary landscape of Biscay in the early twenties. If this takes place I will let you know" ("Kate" 41). This suggests that he was himself involved in arranging for a Spanish version to be produced, in which case it would not be surprising if he contacted Maribel Butler de Foley, then lecturer in Spanish at University College Dublin, who was to become the eventual translator, in what was to be her first ever translation project (see de Foley "Novels" 143). She produced a remarkably faithful version of the novel. But the tidiness washed away honed terms, turns, and subtextual hummings.

ANARCHISM

Kate O'Brien's political views were characterized by a deep dislike of political institutions, activist organizations, and dogmatic political movements. Despite the muted references to Basque Nationalism in *Mary Lavelle*, O'Brien was well aware of its relevance (see O'Neill's discussion of Gernika and the Basque Country, "Introduction" xiii–xiv). In a lecture of 1963, for example, she recalled: "Bilbao was and is a dark and formidable town—full of frowning banks and counting houses, with a great dirty river, and terrible poverty, terrible slums. A centre of great concentrated wealth and also indeed the heart of the Basque Nationalism movement." She adds that Bilbo is "[a] city of strong individuals and much character.... Here certainly was not any Spain an idle girl might have dreamt up— but I found it very interesting—and very shocking" (7; quoted in Reynolds *Kate* 37). In 1922, Kate O'Brien visited a "Batzoki," a Basque Nationalist meeting place, and was moved when she discovered that a photograph of the Irish nationalist Terence McSweeny (or MacSwiney), who had died in a hunger strike, hung on the wall (see J.M. Areilza "Kate" 35–6). The death of McSweeny had a profound impact on her, as she recalled in her documentary *Self-Portrait*, yet this is one of her experiences in the Bilbo of 1922 that O'Brien did not transfer to *Mary Lavelle*. Kate O'Brien implicitly distinguishes between the right to self-determination and nationalism; only the first gets her nihil obstat. In *Farewell Spain*, she is explicit about her political views—this is her favored outcome to the situation in 1937: "with time and luck the Peninsula will perhaps resolve itself into a loosely-linked federation of small, democratic states, all governed for external purposes from a centre, but internally run on regional, distributive principles" (224).

Kate O'Brien's attitude to "distributive principles" is also complex. Mary O'Neill, in her introduction to *Farewell Spain*, explains that "[i]n 1936 the common political attitude in Western Europe was *vaguely left wing*, and even could be said to favour the theory that the hope of political and social progress in the future *might lie in communism*" (emphasis added, xiii). Despite her cautiousness (see also Dalsimer 35), O'Neill's comments are still a welcome exception to the depoliticized landscape of O'Brien Studies. In O'Brien's essay "As to University Life," of 1955, she vividly recalled, in her student days, having "Communism explained to me, by the golden-haired, contemptuous and impatient David Sears" (7). Yet, in *Farewell Spain*, O'Brien was emphatic: "I am not a communist" (*Spain* 123). In the travelogue, she objected to the Marxist version of communism, by way of an analogy with religion: "If I dissent from communists in the matter of this Spanish war, my quarrel is mainly with non–Spanish doctrinaires who have 'got' communism in the all-surrendering way in which adults sometimes 'get' religion," sincerely believing "that history can be sufficiently understood, and its lesson applied, through the materialistic conception" (O'Brien 123). It is interesting to compare the passage with Enrique Areilza's often repeated complaints about socialists who "continue holding on tightly to the Marxist rule, excommunicating with anathemas those shades which, in greater or smaller measure, vary from their doctrine-like catechism" (E. Areilza *Epistolario* 72). Reading *Farewell Spain* there is no question about O'Brien's solidarity with the communist cause, just as there is no question about her determination not to endorse state communism.

> [L]oathe manifest Communism as you please, point to Stalin and say: "What is he but a rampant Fascist bully?["] — dread even as I do the Communistic insult to individualism and spiritual freedom — it is yet true that, at its most dubious and depressing, the root inspiration of Communism is simply the old, old generosity and decency of a few of the world's saints. "From each according to his ability to each according to his need." That is the corner-stone of Communism, however misguidedly practising Communists may seem to build on it [221–2].

This is reminiscent of a point in *El Intruso*, where Aresti claims that solidarity "had always been the way of martyrs and geniuses" (Ibáñez 253 — my translation).

In the travelogue, Kate O'Brien introduces Don Ángel, a lighthouse keeper and "a saint" (34), and then proceeds to expound his views:

> The anarchical idea startles no sober Spaniard. And as Don Angél [sic] talked on, of decentralisation, of the elimination of authority and its symbols, of the great offences of Lenin, of the significance of any one man, and the splendour and freedom of death, I kept thinking of Chesterton, the Catholic, and of how one may believe in anarchy, as in Catholicism, because it is impossible. As a man may be a fool in Christ, he may be a fool in his brother, and if mad for the love of God, so also mad for the love of man. *Credo quia absurdum* is a tautological axiom. You do not believe in Fascism. You see it and it is difficult to be as mystical about it as the old gentleman was who, looking at a giraffe, protested his disbelief in it. You can like Fascism if that is the kind of thing you like. But you needn't exert your self to believe in it. Nor, for the same reason, need you believe in Communism. But, as Don Angél said, no one has seen the Kingdom of God. No human agency has demonstrated it. Therefore it may be believed in [emphasis in original, *Spain* 34–35].

Kate O'Brien's stated or implied positions must always be taken with caution. In *Presentation Parlour*, she declared that she was "never much interested in political deviations and always concerned as to persons and their private decisions" (33). Again, in an interview with Jordan, she declared, "I have always been a-political" ("First Lady" 228). O'Brien was beyond question politically committed, and her disclaimers (both of which happen within a discussion of Irish history) are perhaps best read as opposing "political action," in the sense of opposing participation in the parliamentary party-system. We find several references to anarchism in O'Brien's work, all positive, with the exception of her criticism of anarchist-syndicalism in *Farewell Spain*, in a context that praises anarchist individualism by contrast to it. Historically, there was a tension between these two currents in anarchism, and Spanish anarcho-syndicalism had an important reformist trend personified in Angel Pestaña, as George Woodcock discusses in *Anarchism: A History of Libertarian Ideas and Movements*, an excellent study of 1962 (see 17–9; 349–358). O'Brien's general emphasis on individual rights and actions, as opposed to mass movements, is consonant with the libertarian individualist tradition on the left. She referred several times, both in fiction and nonfiction, to an anarchist "temperament," which she associated with Spain as a whole. This was (and is) a widespread assumption among anarchists, emphasized by historians of the movement. In a lecture of 1971, discussing student agitation in Spain, O'Brien declared that "this great wave of *anarchical or individual upheaval* was to me characteristic of the Spain I had known — and I saw life and vitality in it all, and a kind of relation to youth all over Europe" (emphasis added, 6–7). O'Brien invalidates any superficial application of "anarchy" as a synonym of "chaos" by specifically referring to "a wave of anarchical or *individual* upheaval" in the quote; her understanding of anarchism as radical individualism is of course debatable, but the equation is clear, as is the positive tone. On another occasion, she remembers her "fellow" UCD students, "poets and anarchists" heckling proceedings at the Abbey theater between 1917 and 1919 ("'That's William Yeats!'" 3).

In *Farewell Spain,* Kate O'Brien reserves her highest praise for anarchism (see for example 33, 35, 223). Upon hearing "an English chap" warn the tourists that the Spanish Civil Guard "are the only people now standing between Spain and absolute anarchy," in a rare outburst, O'Brien exclaims: "Good God! The Civil Guard has indeed a long tradition of loyalty to the top dog, and of ruthless courage in defending him and attacking his enemies" (*Spain* 32). But O'Brien is as horrified by something else: "'[A]bsolute anarchy'— oh my friend ... don't you know that that impossible condition of life would be Heaven — Heaven on earth?" (ibid., 33).

In my view, Kate O'Brien's main political interest, at least in the 1936–1937 period, lay in anarchism, specifically individualist anarchism as opposed to anarcho-syndicalism or anarcho-communism, although she shows signs, particularly in *Mary Lavelle*, of considerable ideological flexibility. Individuality was a personal obsession of O'Brien, who praised this trait in artists and intellectuals, and occasionally ascribed it to a whole culture (Basque, Spanish, Irish). Her claim, in *Farewell Spain*, that Spaniards are "astoundingly individualistic and inclined to meditation and mysticism" may well be a generalization derived from Enrique Areilza and supplemented by her research on Teresa of Avila (224). In the 1960s, she was still using "individualist" and "anarchist" as positive, complimentary terms (see O'Neill xix, Liddy 34–5). Pablo, Juan, and Milagros are individualists. Pablo and Milagros declare themselves to be anarchists, but Juanito's dream of a communist state, which is clearly presented as a desirable (if not without its problems) option in the novel, may be the ultimate anathema for "purist" anarchists. In the political parable that is *Mary Lavelle*, it is crucial that, in the end, Mary *leaves* Juanito. However, as we have seen, a leftist centralized state was also a short-term objective reluctantly embraced by the "reformist" sections of the anarchist movement in the elections that put a radical leftist government in power in 1936, and some anarchists entered the cabinet created after the fascist uprising. Some libertarians agreed to compromise.

O'Brien is at one with Orwell, who felt that the "Spanish anarchist tinge" would make state-socialism tolerable (*Homage* 84). Orwell's conclusion that the conflict at the heart of the Spanish revolution of 1936 was "effectively anarchism vs. communism" (ibid., 97) was made in hindsight, after, as Mary O'Neill noted, he had had "to flee from Spain in escape from communists fighting for the same cause" (O'Neill xiii). *Mary Lavelle* presents anarchists (Pablo and Mila), state-communists (Juanito), and their sympathizers (Mary) willing at least to listen to each other. *Farewell Spain*, written the following year at a different historical juncture, supports the leftist *parliamentary* Popular Front, with a (relative) generosity and open-mindedness that accommodates a variety of views that needed each other to survive.

It is my argument that Kate O'Brien was closest to anarchism, at least during the period around the Spanish revolution and the Spanish Civil War. Her appraisal of anarchism does not appear clear-cut, but neither can her views on Irish identity or her investment on Christianity be aligned to a given, orthodox position. O'Brien's thinking is consistent in one sense only: It resists simplification. Nevertheless, it is important to keep in mind that anarchism has been erased from Western public discourse, and the difficulties in assessing O'Brien's politics are partly owed to our own historical perspective. Even in Spain, which saw "the last and largest of the world's major anarchist movements" (Woodcock 374), a full assessment of the impact of anarchism is yet to be made, and it is only in the last few years that the younger segment of the general public has begun to become aware of the historical contribution of the movement.

It is interesting to contrast Kate O'Brien's views with her behavior. Lorna Reynolds described her as an "aristocrat" (*Kate* 28) in attitude, something corroborated by John Jordan ("Talent" 231). It may seem revealing that, in *Kate O'Brien: Self-Portrait*, O'Brien herself devoted a considerable amount of reel-time to an outline of her comfortable upbringing, opening with the statement: "We were well-off. Father was a wealthy man"; yet in the same program she also pointed to the financial difficulties after the death of her father, which prevented her from pursuing her childhood dream of becoming a doctor. O'Brien's one-time friend Paul Smith declared that "seldom, except in sentimental moments, could she stand the sight of a working class radical," to add, "I don't think it ever occurred to her, or to any of her generation, that the working classes were anything but people who had less money than you had" (101, 102). Be that as it may, one of the most damaging silences in O'Brien scholarship has been the refusal or inability to consider the full range of her politics, which should include, but not be reduced to, her sexual politics.

"Mainly Personal"

The line between personal and private perhaps fluctuates in every artist, but in Kate O'Brien this is a tidal stream, because her fiction relied so much, and so obviously, on her life experience. In *Metaphors of Self* James Olney defines autobiography as "both imitation and creation of the self" (49; quoted in Cuddihy 53). At 38, O'Brien reinvented herself in *Mary Lavelle.* Perhaps queer writers have a more acute sense of the relevance of personal history. Some of her contemporaries chose to document their sexual histories and, remarkably, they produced their memoirs, not at the end of their lives, but while they were comparatively young. Vita Sackville-West wrote the account published as *Portrait of a Marriage* at 28, Maurice Sachs wrote *The Witches' Sabbath* at 32, and Valentine Ackland wrote *For Sylvia* at 42. The opportunity to reinvent — rather than record — history is taken up in a higher or lesser degree by *all* memoir writers, in the sense that choosing what events to recollect and the order in which they are to be presented are creative decisions; an interesting example is Lillian Hellman, who "produced" a lesbian past in the 1974 *Pentimento*. In *Mary Lavelle* we are dealing with an autobiographical fiction rather than a fictional autobiography, and this is more than a change in inflection. O'Brien chose not to write her memoirs, although she wrote a handful of sketches of her childhood, some of which were incorporated into *My Ireland* (these sketches have been persistently and inaccurately described as "O'Brien's Memoirs").

There is a deliberate interplay between the personal information that can be gleaned from her fiction and her nonfiction. An interesting case in point is her treatment of a sexual molestation incident. As we have seen, Kate O'Brien wrote an unpublished short story, "Manná," dealing with a six-year-old girl's visit to a shop and her ambivalent response to the shop-attendant's sexual assault. Eibhear Walshe says that the story has the feel of a real incident from O'Brien's childhood (*Kate* 12). But it is more than a "feel" — O'Brien herself had left a clue about the factual basis of the story in *My Ireland*, where she refers to a setting of her own childhood that concurs with that of "Manná," and the careful wording of the mention seems an invitation to intratextual reading. In addition, the story is an extremely rare case in O'Brien's unpublished papers at the Limerick archive where she indicates on the first page that she copyrighted the story, and her desire to acknowledge authorship beyond doubt is relevant. It seems to me that "Manná" is not just autobiographical but that O'Brien wished for this to be known. Unless viewed in this context, as having a personal import, other references to children as sources of erotic/aesthetic pleasure in her nonfiction (in 1937 and 1943) look out of kilter, because O'Brien seems to be making a point by bringing them to the forefront and treating them in a matter-of-fact manner — there is a bravado in her directness (see *Spain* 87, *Diaries* 42).

As Emma Donoghue explained in 1993, "during her life and after it, Kate O'Brien, her family, biographers, critics, and friends all colluded to keep her in the closet. Not so much by covering up her bonds with women, as by denying that those partnerships were of any *relevance* to her work" (emphasis in original, "Order" 37). O'Brien's lesbianism was openly discussed at length for the first time by Eibhear Walshe in his biography (see Walshe *Kate* 46–9). He framed the discussion within the definition of lesbianism offered by Lillian Faderman in her 1985 *Surpassing the Love of Men*, a definition which (problematically) displaces sexual behavior. Walshe discussed O'Brien's sexual history far more directly and comprehensively in his article "Invisible Irelands" (see also "Chaps"). We have moved on from the days when careful evidence had to be gathered to suggest that Kate O'Brien "had at least one lesbian affair," through a "Private Conversation with Mr. and Mrs. Henry Boylan," editors of the *Dictionary of Irish Biography* of 1978 (Cawley 11); but as recently as 2007 I was still given information on O'Brien's sexuality by someone who felt he could not publish it (and the information is not used in this book). It has taken decades and the determination of many scholars, but it is now possible at last to speak of O'Brien's lesbianism and its relevance. After such emphatic silencing, it may seem perverse to focus on O'Brien's experiences as heterosexual or bisexual woman and how these were translated into *Mary Lavelle*. Yet one of the most interesting aspects of this novel as autobiography is precisely the tension between honoring the past and asserting the power of the present to rewrite that past. In 1936, O'Brien was by all accounts living as a lesbian, by which I mean having adopted a sexuality exclusively oriented towards women. Although we do not possess direct documental evidence as to her self-identification, the testimonies of those close to her suggest that she saw herself as lesbian. Yet in *Mary Lavelle*, Kate O'Brien revisited her experiences of 1922, possibly including her falling in love with a man and a description of her own heterosexual sexual initiation. There is certainly no direct statement from O'Brien that may corroborate or refute this point, just as there is no direct statement by her on her politics, her religious beliefs, or her love life after the end of her marriage. There are, however, a number of characteristically veiled suggestions from a number of sources that shed some light on what O'Brien attempted to do in this novel, and why.

How accurate a self-portrait is *Mary Lavelle*? Desmond Hogan retold an incident included in Lorna Reynolds's *Portrait*, which he says, "prepares us for the heroine of *Mary Lavelle*": Before going to Washington in 1921, O'Brien taught at a London school, where "Kate's beauty and graciousness made such an impact on the girls she was teaching that a mother traipsed to the convent to see what was astir, to be met at the door by a nun who declared, 'Well the fact is the beloved is very beautiful'" ("Introduction" [1985] viii). As we have seen, José María chose to remark on O'Brien's beauty, androgyny, and "Greek" profile, and confirmed that, during her stay in Bilbo, the governess "had a boyfriend with whom she kept up an intense correspondence, and who was a journalist with the London-based *Observer*" ("Mary" 227)—an echo of the letter-writing to John that takes up much of Mary's time in the novel. Another subtle indication of an autobiographical approach is offered by Mary's eyes, which recall the famous Thornhill eyes in the mother's side in O'Brien's family. Reynolds described the "blazing blue eyes" of the Thornhills as "extraordinary deep-set eyes [which] remind one of archaic Greek statues" (*Kate* 28, 29), and it is this unusually bright blue that O'Brien deliberately gives to Nieves, Mary, and Agatha. If, as I have argued, there is a lesbian bildungsroman hidden here, presented in the form of a triple portrait, it is equally valid to assume that the "progression" of the tomboy Nieves into the androgynous Mary and of Mary into the sexually unorthodox Agatha is a miniature autobiography of Kate O'Brien herself.

Crucially, as Wanda Balzano has noted, *agaton* is the Greek word meaning "good and beautiful" (beautiful because good), which offers yet another indication that Lavelle and Conlan are very closely linked, indeed ("Question"). In *Mary Lavelle*, there is no need to give precise details on Agatha Conlan's life, as they do not advance the narrative or deepen our understanding of the themes in the novel in any obvious way. Information on Conlan seems often an addenda, disrupting the flow of the text. For example, we are told of Conlan: "She came out here from some village in County Wexford when she was twenty-one, and she's been here since. She's thirty-eight now" (*Mary* 84). As we have seen, the ages are close enough to O'Brien's similar life-pattern to be noticeable: 25 on arrival, 38 at the time of writing. A sudden change in style is particularly noticeable in the following conversation, where Mary seems a brash young journalist interviewing a suitably eccentric older international celebrity: Agatha/Kate. In a way, the entire passage, full of otherwise irrelevant "data," reads like an in-joke, with veiled references to O'Brien's own background, which she expected would be picked up by those who knew her well. For example, the name "Kildalgan" is reminiscent of the hometown of her mother's people, Kilfinane. As importantly, Mary Lavelle was born in Kilbeggan (see 6), far too close a spelling to Agatha's town to make sense except as an attempt to approximate the two women. In fact what began in Kilbeggan may be seen to have a "finis" in Kilfinane:

> "When you were a kid did you loathe life?"
> "Oh, I suppose not. I can't remember. There was nothing very terrible. We were poor and my father was a martinet, but my mother was nice. She died just before I came to Spain. Father's dead now and my sister is married at home. Two of my brothers died in the war, and the youngest is in New Zealand."
> "What was it like at home?"
> "Kildalgan? A deadly little town — very pretty. Woods, I remember, and streams. My father was a bank manager and I suppose he had a fair salary, but we seemed to be very poor."
> "You ought to go back to see your sister."
> "Her? Good God! She married a frightful man who kept a public-house. He was twenty years older than her too. There was a most awful family rumpus" [207–8].

In the fictionalized 1922 of the novel, we have Mary/Kate talking with the person she will become by 1935. Yet this radical disruption of the timeline works both ways, since it is in fact the 38-year-old O'Brien/Conlan who is recording what happened on that crucial year of her youth. The author points several times to the complications of this double look back and forth, and it is with a touch of irony that Agatha extracts one promise from Mary: "Don't ever come back.... Don't ever come looking for me in the Alemán again" (297; also 298). It is also possible to see Luisa as a further duplicate of Kate O'Brien, the yin to Agatha's yang, given the author's creative use of names and the fact that she was Christened Kathleen Louie O'Brien.

It is beyond question that the main text presents a heterosexual love affair, coherent, self-contained. Although there is no incontrovertible evidence to support the claim, it seems absolutely crystal clear to me that O'Brien based the main narrative in the novel, including the affair of the protagonist with a married man in the Basque Country, on her own experiences in 1922. John Jordan said in 1973 that both *Farewell Spain* and *Mary Lavelle* "mirrored [O'Brien's] Spanish experience" (emphasis added, "First Lady" 228). Lorna Reynolds described *Mary Lavelle* as "her third work, *the theme of which belongs in the purely private sphere* and deals with the *psycho-sexual* development of a young Irish girl, the heroine, Mary Lavelle" (emphasis added, "Image" 181). One way of interpreting that statement is as a suggestion that O'Brien was dealing with "private," personal matters in the novel, specifically relating to her own "psycho-sexual" development. The sexual initiation of the protagonist of the novel, then, could be seen to be based on an actual experience. In a 1972 lecture, O'Brien did claim that in Bilbo, in 1922, "I was very green, a bright Irish green" and referred to "my belated and lazy immaturity of that time, which kept me very much 'in the moon,' as we used to say when we were children," which left her with a tendency to be slow in reacting, "which I have not outgrown. I believe I never understand things until about ten years after they have happened. The present tense is rarely indicative to me" (*Spain* 209–10). O'Brien's repeated references to her innocence at the time may themselves be intended as a link to Mary's sexual inexperience (see also the phrasing in Jordan "Kate" [1987] 237).

Should we take the novel's main narrative as autobiographical evidence, it would appear that if Kate O'Brien fell in love with a married man in the Basque Country, she loved wholeheartedly and was loved in return. The man who had an affair with O'Brien in 1922 and inspired the character of Juanito, *if* such a thing did happen, must have been someone remarkable, and a relatively public figure — if the portrait is in any way accurate. There is no information on record of any young man of his characteristics having played a part in O'Brien's life at that time. But there is internal evidence that the character of Juanito was in fact a duplicate of another character in the novel, Don Pablo, who is unquestionably a considerably faithful and detailed portrait of an actual man O'Brien knew well, Enrique Areilza. It seems likely to me that in *Mary Lavelle* Kate O'Brien set up a careful, deliberate doubling which allowed her, by creating an imaginary younger version of Dr. Areilza, to recall — or at the very least, to suggest — her affair with him in 1922. As we have seen, there are numerous indications of this doubling in the text; we find a remarkable example when the older Areavaga/Areilza has an intimation that the affair between Juanito and Mary is inevitable, and he claims, in a telling (yet otherwise absurd) turn of phrase: "She would be his *since* Juanito, so much loved and understood of him, was not only his flesh but spiritually him enhanced, corrected" (emphasis added, *Mary* 321). Indeed, Juanito can be seen as the "enhanced and corrected" version of the old and disillusioned Enrique Areilza, and his late passion for the young O'Brien may have seemed a temporal restoration of his youthful energy (J.M. Areilza, who celebrated his fourteenth birthday in August 1922, emphatically disclaimed that Juanito had anything to do with himself — see "Kate" 39; Montalbán, in a recent article, is not so sure — see "Kate" 10 — but I disagree). The doubling is made evident in the passage that describes the first telling glance between Mary and Juanito in the novel:

> These two were to know each other hereafter, and to arrive at their knowledge in reluctance, grief and protestation....
>
> Mary saw a light-limbed and heavy-shouldered young man, who wore his clothes and his dark hair untidily, as did his father; who had, though in young health, his father's pallor and tragically sculpted strong-set facial bones. The searching sun showed eyes more innocently opened than Don Pablo's and with more light and gold in them. Young eyes, but meditative and poetic, set in a questioning uplifted face.
>
> He saw, but less defensively, that which two months ago his father had beheld through half-closed, elderly, reluctant eyes. A slender girl, in tennis shoes and cotton dress, a girl with lightly curled short locks, with slender neck and sweetly springing virgin breasts; Greek-headed, with grave features and white skin.... [T]he blueness of her eyes which had already startled him, was veiled, but he noticed that they were blue-shadowed, and that for all her grace and youth, for all the unconscious arrogance of fatal beauty, she was a little weary in this moment, a little lonely and off guard [O'Brien *Mary* 145–6].

To reconstruct an episode of Kate O'Brien's life for which there is no evidence other than a fictional account is obviously fraught with problems (it must be said that given the circumstances, there "should" be no evidence). If Kate O'Brien retold the story of her first love affair, with the doctor Enrique Areilza, in her fiction, we do have at least two accounts of the same incident, in that *The Anteroom*, as we have discussed, seems to be also based on O'Brien's time in Bilbo. If this is the case, *The Anteroom* may provide a version of what could have happened if the decisions made would have been different, together with a fantasy of financial, emotional, and sexual self-sufficiency in the character of Agnes/Kate. It is impossible to demarcate conclusively which details are fictional and which factual in the earlier novel, but some information given (otherwise unnecessary to the plot) may even pinpoint the precise time at which the affair began with the Doctor — four months after her arrival: "So, for four months and more of his acquaintance with the Mulqueens" Doctor Curran "had stoked and steadied his soul, until at last one night," when, "[i]n something as superb as ecstasy then he realised that this girl with whom he held sad and friendly conversation on four or five mornings of each week, had become the unique and mighty hunger of his life" (*Anteroom* 49). It may be significant that "four months" is also the time Mary spends in Altorno, so that perhaps this was meant to mark a symbolic "break" in O'Brien's life. In *Distinguished Villa*, Gwen reveals she is pregnant four months after the opening of the story. It is also interesting, given that Saint Martin is the fictitious name of the square where Lavelle and Areavaga dance, that Saint Martin de Porres (as we have seen, a very popular saint in Ireland) is celebrated on November 3 — Agatha's mention of a "martinet" father is worth recalling here. Despite O'Brien's claim in the RTE documentary of 1962 that she did not plan her novels carefully, all her fiction (up to the surviving chapter sketch for *Constancy*) shows the very careful attention she gave to the use of dates. For example, Mary celebrates her birthday in Madrid just as the affair with Juanito tentatively begins (another pertinent use of symbolism); O'Brien's own birthday fell on December 3, and in the light of the novel this may be taken to suggest that a possible liaison may have begun (perhaps tentatively) at this time.

In his recent biography of Enrique Areilza, Josu Montalbán states that *Without My Cloak* is unmistakably set in the Areilza home in Portugalete and that this is also the case with Kate O'Brien's first play, *Distinguished Villa* (see *Doctor* 162, 164). Strikingly, however, Montalbán seems uncertain about the autobiographical content of *Mary Lavelle* (162). He claims that during O'Brien's stay, the doctor showed her the left bank and the mines, took her to the tertulia of the Lion d'Or, and even created another tertulia for the misses in the café Suizo (see 161–2), but this could be speculation, in a biography which includes several fictional scenes and numerous flights of fancy. Montalbán also suggests, subtly but unmistakeably, that Enrique was a great influence on Kate, and perhaps something more, and that she may have been forced to leave Portugalete for some unknown reason related to her stay (162). Josu Montalbán's identification of "El Salto's" central role in Kate O'Brien's first two important works invites us to reread all others with the Areilza household in mind. It is not difficult to see the "El Salto" mansion and its inhabitants in the Flemish "Villa des Glycines" in *The Flower of May*, and detect traces of Dr. Areilza in the Dr. O'Curry of the same novel (another suggestive name). We may also see "El Salto" in "Waterpark House," to where the "shabby" Angèle arrives one late summer day in *The Last of Summer* (O'Brien 3), and in the suburban "Rue Saint Isidore No. 4" in *The Land of Spices*.

Once the limitations in suggesting facts by way of assessing fiction have been acknowledged, it is worth insisting that, if Kate O'Brien had an affair with Dr. Areilza while working as a governess for his family, it is not extraordinary that she turned this experience into a plot for a novel, or a series of novels. In the transformation of her specific circumstances O'Brien had an illustrious predecessor in Charlotte Brontë's autobiographical works *The Professor*, *Jane Eyre*, and *Villette*. Traditional scholarship of which O'Brien was no doubt aware read these three novels as fictionalizations of the author's own experiences in a foreign country, including her falling in love with an "unavailable" man. But no legitimizing precedent was required by O'Brien for such an experiment. Writers rework experience, and their own lives are often the main quarry for malleable material. The doubling of the male lead in *Mary Lavelle* leaves Don Pablo Areavaga/Juanito/Enrique Areilza, the "master" bullfighter, agonizing after the sexual encounter with the bull, Mary. This alternative ending (perhaps linked to the violence "done to" the male leads in *Jane Eyre* and *Villette*), if taken in the context of a rewrite of an actual episode in the author's life, would seem to amount to an act of revenge. Discussing Mary's beauty in Madrid, Milagros makes the extraordinary claim: "Why, father would, quite innocently, die for you, I think, and so, I suspect, would Juanito!" (O'Brien *Mary* 229). Of course, the statement merely prepares the reader for the *subtextual* goring of Mary's lover at the end of the novel. The plot turn may be summed up in the chorus of a popular waltz by Mario Cavagnaro in Spanish: "Give me back my love, so I can kill it." Perhaps the deaths of Vincent in *The Anteroom* and Natty in *Distinguished Villa* can be seen in the same light. Emma Donoghue, in an essay discussing physical affection in Kate O'Brien's work, summarizes *Distinguished Villa* as follows: "Natty's refined wife refuses him kisses on the pretext that it is Sunday. It is hardly surprising when he spends a night with a prostitute, then cuts his throat" ("Embraces" 17). This is a melodramatic form of closure that is not repeated in Kate O'Brien's work after 1936 (if we exclude the death of Henry Archer of natural causes in *The Land of Spices*), arguably because she finally "exorcised" the past in *Mary Lavelle*. In my view, the novel's fictionalization of biographical and autobiographical detail is less about settling a score than about producing a definitive record of a certain event in O'Brien's life. Let us not forget that the primary narrative in the novel involves a young woman's decision to initiate an illicit affair — not the undoing of the affair. In *Mary Lavelle*, the *idealized* portrait of Enrique Areilza is less striking, in autobiographical terms, than *the decision* to provide a full biography of this Basque surgeon and intellectual, framed within an equally idealized family background to the man and his ancestors, occupying an entire chapter in the novel. It cannot be stressed enough how irrelevant this is to the development of the overall narrative, or, indeed, to the internal development of the protagonist. No doubt Dr. Areilza was a fascinating person, but if we take into account the complex doubling, the symbolism, and the subtexts we have been referring to, a different explanation emerges.

I would like to argue that *Mary Lavelle*, as portrait of a man and a woman at a point in time, and as record of an event, may have been intended in part as a form of legacy. The persistent rumor that Kate O'Brien had an illegitimate child has yet to be settled one way or the other (see Walshe *Kate* 36–7). O'Brien's friend John Jordan, who had nothing to gain from the news, publicly declared in 1988 to have verified O'Brien's maternity. It happened at the "Kate O'Brien Weekend," and Jordan claimed to have the information "on a very good authority, as it has been confirmed by a Dominican friar," interviewed by himself, in a monastery, in France (as recalled by Louise C. Callaghan in a paper of 2003; Callaghan incorporated this information into her play about O'Brien, *Find the Lady*, of 2003). Since then, Kate O'Brien's surviving relatives have persistently denied that she ever had a child or, another persistent rumor, that this child had been raised by O'Brien's sister, Nance O'Mara. The child in question, Peter O'Mara, was adopted, by admission of the family. A portrait of Peter with Kate O'Brien was reproduced by Lorna Reynolds in her biography of the author, and given Reynolds's ability to broach any problematic topic in subtle ways, this particular choice of photograph may be telling. The same photograph was included by Reynolds in an article of 1990, with the caption "Kate O'Brien felt at home in Limerick relaxing with Peter O'Mara" ("Place" 34). This is not as significant as the fact that Kate O'Brien herself kept a considerable number of photographs of Peter, which survived many successive purges in her personal archive and have made it into the Kate O'Brien Papers in Limerick University. It may be relevant to mention at this point that I had no interest *whatsoever* in the controversy until I saw this collection of photographs, which I felt made it impossible not to consider the possibility of O'Brien's maternity and its implications.

Whether Peter was Kate O'Brien's son or not, the possibility that she had a child that she had to give up for adoption may elucidate some features in her work. O'Brien may have made oblique references to a "lost" child throughout her work, beginning with her first book, the family saga *Without My Cloak*, a title taken from Shakespeare's Sonnet 34, and an image which was once interpreted by scholars as a coded reference to an illegitimate child (see Hayes 5). This surely allows another reading of the poem's significance to O'Brien's life in the light of the sonnet's emphasis on "disgrace," "grief," and "loss"; without forgetting that the other key image in the sonnet is a medical metaphor about the incurability of loss and sadness (in Katherine Duncan-Jones's edition — Shakespeare 178–9). It is possible that the title *Without My Cloak* (otherwise of no major significance to the story) was the last remnant of the "huge chunk" that was eliminated from the novel, as John Jordan recalls: "Kate once told me that the book was originally much longer, that 'certain material had been cut.' I did not press her on the nature of the 'certain material'" ("Kate" [1976] 234). In a subsequent article, Jordan quoted O'Brien as saying that the novel had been "purged" ("Kate" [1987] 237), and it seems possible that a subplot of illegitimacy in the novel was the target of the purge — with the published version showing traces of a suggested but undeveloped subplot. As we have seen, much of the "Denis and Christina" plot lends itself to be read as an appendix to Mary Lavelle's break-up with Juanito. Perhaps it may also relate to O'Brien's hypothetical bearing of an illegitimate child following her time in Bilbo. The cloak of the title ostensibly refers to a cape owned by Denis, which is lost by him at the same time as he looses Christina. Despite the social, cultural, and financial distance between them, Christina believes that Denis's love is real and that his offer of eternal love (and marriage) is genuine. Her thoughts on the page are not unlike the thoughts of Mary Lavelle. "She believed that. It was odd, considering the lawlessness with which he had taken her, that Christina should have been so sure of the will and power of this boy to cleave to her," but she is nevertheless right in feeling that "[p]rofligacy was not what she would have to fear, any more than she feared, so far as he was concerned, the difference in their stations" (*Cloak* 325). Different "stations" and "lawlessness" are two turns of phrase that suggest that O'Brien's sketches for a portrait of the older, wealthier, married Enrique Areilza in Pablo/Juanito, had not begun with *The Anteroom*'s Currant/Vincent, but with Denis in her first novel (Denis is 19 when the affair begins—see *Cloak* 324).

After Christina has been shipped out of the country by concerned relatives and Denis finds her in New York, as we have seen, the lovers have their final parting. Christina improvises a lie to end the relationship when Denis presses her to marry him: She claims that she has promised to marry another man, and when the incredulous Denis asks who this may be, "bravely fulfilling her lie," she gives the name of her employer, Emil Pahren, a "commonplace, elderly Swiss" (416, 417). It seems more than a coincidence that O'Brien went on to marry the Dutch Gustav Renier after her sudden departure from the Basque Country. *Mary Lavelle*'s Juanito/Mary/John could well be another version of the triangular relationship between Denis/Christina/Emil and perhaps also Gustav/Kate/Enrique. In addition to Emil Pahren, Gustav Johannes Petrus Renier (his full name) is likely to have been the inspiration for Mary Lavelle's fiancé, John. Eibhear Walshe suggests Renier was the model for Henry Archer in *The Land of Spices* (*Kate* 33), but in fact Henry's striking fondness for medical metaphors points to Enrique again. If the Emil/Christina relationship is based on Gustav and (the perhaps "Christ-like") O'Brien, it would certainly be entirely O'Brien-esque to revert the original factual details, so that a young lover is given up by Christina in order to marry her employer, whereas in fact the abandoned lover may be the elderly (and married) employer, Areilza, and the prospect groom a young man, Renier. Also of significance is O'Brien's choice of name for Emil Pahren, perhaps another oblique link to the remarkably similar sounding "Enri Are," the half-rhyme being suggestive of a partial portrait. But the ostensible link between the male suitors in *The Anteroom* and *Mary Lavelle* that are extraneous to the narrative is between Pahren and John McCurtain, as the "emergency exits" available to the female protagonists, who are "trapped" in an unviable relationship with their lovers, Denis Considine and Juanito Areavaga (see *Cloak* 417). *Without My Cloak* makes the suggestion that pregnancy has prompted Christina to marry in haste (see 418). Bearing in mind that, unlike Mary and Juanito, the pair of lovers in *Without My Cloak* are actually free to marry, the gratuitous reference to illegitimacy looks totally out of place. There is another possible real-life source for an illegitimacy plot, in the biography of Kate O'Brien's partner at the time when she was writing *Without My Cloak*, Margaret Stephie Stephens (to whom she dedicated the book, and who is mentioned, together with her daughter Ruth, in *Farewell Spain*). Stephens had raised her daughter alone; she never married, although she changed her name to pretend she had (Walshe "Irelands" 42). The subplot in the novel, however, suggests a different direction for Christina. According to Eibhear Walshe, "In [*Without My Cloak*], Eddy, the homosexual brother living away in London, is the character nearest to Kate herself" (*Kate* 52). I do not wish to refute, but to amend that claim, by suggesting that Eddy may well be the closest character to O'Brien as she was in 1932, but in the character of Christina, she may well have portrayed herself as she had been ten years before — and it is worth recalling here again O'Brien's statement that she required "about ten years" to understand anything that had happened to her (*Spain* 210). It seems to me that the same autobiographical doubling was to be repeated in *Mary Lavelle*, with Agatha=Eddie=1932/5 O'Brien, standing side by side with Mary=Christina=1922 O'Brien. It is not by chance that in her last, unfinished novel, we find a character referred to as "la belle Christine" (*Constancy* [1]).

Without My Cloak is set in the nineteenth century. At one time, illegitimacy was a traumatic and shaming event, and rarely the best option. It has been historically tied in to gendered expectations, with women carrying the burden of social punishment. My own great-grandmother was a foundling. This is, to me, a fact without moral connotations of any kind. As an author, Kate O'Brien was not interested in pretending that babies always land on a soft cushion. She made a career of speaking the unspeakable. In *Distinguished Villa*, Kate O'Brien's first play (and first substantial work of literature), which opened in 1926, the librarian Frances is a lodger in the house of the pretentious Mabel Hemworth and her sensitive and passionate husband, Natty. Frances "looks about twenty-eight and is slim and tall," has a pale face which "is leanly cut in noble boyish lines," and who favors "boyis[h]," somewhat "bohemian" clothes (18–9). She sounds like Mary Lavelle — and like Kate O'Brien. Another young woman in the play, Mabel's sister, the 21-year-old typist Gwendolyn, is "[e]xquisite to look at" and "a silly sort of girl," although "there is a very young appeal about her, and her great beauty disturbs and interests most people for a time" (19). Natty and Frances, both described as "queer," have a strong rapport (15, 17). A young man, Alec, "*tall and gay and conventional. Very well dressed. Nothing more*" (emphasis in original, 22), keeps asking Frances to marry him, but she is not interested. Gwen is engaged to John, a stooping bookseller who wears "dark flannels" (29), but she has had a fling with Alec. Gwen discovers she is pregnant and decides to marry Alec, telling him that the child is his; Alec declares that he is not the father, advises Gwen to have an abortion, and offers money. Gwen replies: "Money's no good to me. I can't have a baby unless I'm married. How can I? Alec, how can I?", and again replies to his protestations: "I must be married — I must. I must! I'm a respectable girl, I tell you!" (55). At the closing of the play, Frances persuades John to marry Gwen and give the child a father. Meanwhile, after a night of illicit passion, Natty kills himself. The play's characterization and plot resonates with other works by O'Brien, including *Mary Lavelle*.

The date of birth of Peter O'Mara is unknown, yet the consensus seems to be that the child was born some time after Kate O'Brien's marriage took place on May 17, 1923, with the implied suggestion that if there had been a child, and if Peter was that child, her husband, Gustav Renier, may have been the father. Eibhear Walshe has stated that, when Nance O'Mara adopted Peter "in the spring of 1927," he "was believed to be around eighteen months old. This means that he was born sometime in late 1924 or early 1925, in the year after the break up of Kate and Gustaaf's marriage" (*Kate* 36). There appears to be no birth certificate in existence, as Walshe points out, and the suggested dates must be taken with extreme caution. In fact, the original rumor, persistent at least up to 1978, when recorded by Elisabeth M. Hayes (see 6), was not that Kate O'Brien had a child in 1924–1925, but that she got pregnant in 1922–1923 and was pregnant when she left the Basque Country to return to London. O'Brien's sudden departure from the Areilza household was explained by herself in the 1964 *Self Portrait* as being due to "personal events" and by Walshe as being motivated by her giving in to pressure from Renier to get married (*Kate* 31). In my view, the most plausible explanation is that O'Brien left the Basque Country because she became/suspected-she-was pregnant, possibly with the intention of providing legitimacy for her child by marrying Renier. If we take *Mary Lavelle* to be a self-portrait, the persistent promise of Mary not to bother her Basque lover again, *no matter what may happen*, suggests the possibility of pregnancy. The repeated assurances are unnecessary within the time frame of the novel (Mary is, after all, gone from Juanito's life in the last chapter), and the emphasis is absolutely disproportionate to the situation: "I give you my word of honour I'll never trouble you again. I promise you that and I'll keep my promise.... I swear it won't be hell for you. I'll see to that" (*Mary* 306; compare to *Cloak* 419). If this is a reflection of a real incident with serious consequences, retold 15 years later, the (kept) promise of Mary/Kate acquires a different weight. However, if we see the "Denis and Christina" plot in *Without My Cloak* as autobiographical, it would suggest that O'Brien left the Basque Country and was then traced and followed by her former lover (perhaps to London), before they finally ended the relationship. Between 1924 and 1927, Kate O'Brien worked as a publications officer for the Sunlight League (see Walshe, *Kate* 37, 42), an organization set up to promote the health benefits of sunlight, which, as we know, is one of the areas in which Dr. Areilza was internationally known; it seems likely to me that either O'Brien secured the job *through* Enrique Areilza or she took it *because* she wanted to reestablish communication with him.

If we transpose onto Kate O'Brien's biography some of the information from *Mary Lavelle*, supplemented by what appears to be the treatment of a similar event in *The Anteroom*, *Without My Cloak*, and *Distinguished Villa*, we can perhaps glean that she may have arrived in the Basque Country in June or August 1922, may have started an affair with Enrique Areilza, and may have left him and the Basque Country in haste, perhaps in March 1923. O'Brien's marriage records in the University of Limerick archive give May 17, 1923, so if she had a child before then, the dates are tight. If an affair with Areilza began in November (four months after her arrival "in August"), the dates simply do not fit. John Jordan's claim that she lived in Bilbo for ten months gives us August 1922 to May 1923, which is by and large the most plausible timetable. It seems transparent to me, however, that there is an entirely unnecessary obfuscation of the dates of Kate O'Brien's stay in Bilbo and her marriage, as given by her, and as given/reproduced by other people. The confusion on the dates seems deliberate and may be consistent with a desire to produce an "alibi," if there was an event, such as childbirth, that needed to be kept secret. The perennial difficulties in accessing material related to Kate O'Brien may also be related to this. Throughout the years, several people (I am one) have made attempts to access certain personal information and archival material, in Ireland or the Basque Country, without success.

It is in Kate O'Brien's work, rather than in the available documentary evidence or in any public statements, that we can perhaps glean an approximation to the truth. According to Lorna Reynolds, Kate O'Brien "always spoke of marriage as an undertaking of desperate gravity" (*Kate* 36). There is no direct suggestion in *Mary Lavelle* that Mary/Kate was pregnant at the time of leaving Bilbo, although this should not be surprising in an autobiographical light. However, there are suggestive turns of phrase in the novel — "Yes, she was going away more laden than she had come," for example, or Mary's reflections on "fosterage" as she looks at Juanito saying goodbye to his wife and child, and in the travelogue — with O'Brien's odd emphasis on an El Greco *Annunciation* she saw in Bilbo (*Mary* 290, 172; see *Spain* 207). There may also be other references scattered throughout her books, in addition to the central plot of *Distinguished Villa*. In *Pray for the Wanderer*, for example, Tom Mahoney, who seems a double of the autobiographical Matt Costello, has an illegitimate child (80–1; see 84). Tina O'Toole has explored the fact that "surrogacy is a central concern to many of O'Brien's novels," focusing on *The Flower of May* ("Autonomy"). We find motherless children in a number of other works, from *A Broken Song* to *As Music and Splendour*. *A Broken Song* is a never-produced, undated screenplay about a young Irish tenor, Peter Cassidy, who has been told that his mother, Mary O'Shea, died in New York before he was three years of age. This could be a sequel to the "Christina and Denis in New York" subplot in *Without My Cloak* (with Cassidy as an illegitimate Considine), or indeed it could even be the "purged" section from the original draft, transformed into another text (Walshe catalogues *A Broken Song* as a "film scenario for *That Lady*, Northwestern collection" [*Kate* 62], but this is incorrect, certainly of the copy of the text in UL). I would tentatively date the script 1934; O'Brien did send it to her New York agent while she was living in 37 Gordon square, London — between 1930 and 1934. Throughout the story, Peter has repeated dreamlike visions of what appears to be his mother's face, singing to him Samuel Lover's "Fairy Boy," written between 1840 and 1849, on a background of a hawthorn tree in flower. Perhaps this was an early attempt at sketching some sort of testimonial narrative for a child O'Brien did not raise as her own. In the script, Peter's mother is called Mary and his father John, and another main character, an American music impresario, is called Emil Varonsk. The registered name of the child adopted by Kate's sister was Peter Johnson, perhaps an underlining of the connection to Gustav *Johannes Petrus* Renier. It seems impossible to me to ignore these connections. And yet, the presence of "orphaned" characters is perhaps less relevant to our discussion (given that O'Brien lost her own mother at an early age) than the fact that youths inheriting a double nationality are often key characters in her work — up to her last novel, *Constancy*, which was to be concerned with a Spanish-Irish couple divided in the aftermath of the Spanish Civil War, and with the progeny of that union. Peter Cassidy's status as a "fairy child" may also be relevant in this context. It is not without significance that, in Euskera, *hawthorn* is *arantza* (also the generic for *thorn*) and *hawthorn bush* is *arantzadi*, with the root *aran* meaning "currant," as we have discussed. If there was such a man as Juanito in Kate O'Brien's life, and if the man was Enrique Areilza, this would certainly explain a relatively puzzling feature in her recollections and lectures, and that is her insistent praise of José María Areilza. A special bond with this man and his family may explain O'Brien's attitude towards Dr. Areilza's son, who was, by all accounts, someone extremely unlikely to warrant her public eulogizing in ordinary circumstances. This bond may also illuminate other features of her work, big and small; I am reminded of a contrived and biblical-sounding aside in *Farewell Spain*: "Enrique who took up with Mary, as she in extreme folly with him" (ostensibly referring to Mary O'Neill and a Galizian boy — 86). As we have seen, in *Pray for the Wanderer* we are told that "romantic love is not an invention so much as a discovery, like America or radium" (O'Brien 188); it is also, however, subject to historical change, and the genuine love described in *Mary Lavelle* cannot last, because there is a different idiom of feeling in a "Victorian" man and in a "modern" woman, no matter how idiosyncratic and full of good intentions they both may be (see *Anteroom* 57). It is worth considering also Henry Archer (and the echo of Enrique Areilza's name is by now deafening), and his relationship with his daughter Helen, as another version of the relationship between Pablo/Juan and Mary Lavelle (who is referred to several times as "Ronsard's Helen") — with a young woman's traumatic introduction to sexuality, her enduring respect for her intellectual mentor, and the double temporality of lived/remembered experiences ... as "variations on a sin." In *Mary Lavelle*, then, Kate O'Brien may have managed to make a record of a crucial incident in her past, an affair with a married man based on mutual love, through the story of Mary and Juanito, while honoring her current life as a lesbian, through the subplot of Agatha's love for Mary, through the subtextual lesbian bildungsroman of Nieves/Mary/Agatha, and through the intertextual lesbian affair between Mary and Luisa. This alone makes *Mary Lavelle* an extraordinary piece of life-writing and a feat of fiction-writing.

The hypothesis that I would like to advance is that O'Brien wrote *Mary Lavelle* partly as a legacy for a child she gave birth to and had to give up for adoption in 1923. In the book, she gave a positive account of the child's father, the Basque surgeon and intellectual Enrique Areilza, and offered a relatively idealized summary of his family history (which was absolutely irrelevant to the main narrative). Also in the book, she showed that the romance had been genuine, that the partners had loved each other, however briefly, and that there had been no coercion — in fact, Kate/Mary had played an active part in the beginning of the affair. This information, presented in fictionalized form, was intended as a long letter of explanation to her child, in a way that was both discreet and accessible, and in a way that guaranteed that Kate O'Brien had the final say in relating the events which lead to the birth of the child (obviously, for the information to be accessible to this hypothetical child, the existence of some form of contact between O'Brien and the child would have been paramount). If this hypothesis is correct, O'Brien used *Mary Lavelle* as a store of memory that could be shared with her child. Uneasily interacting truths were presented simultaneously in *Mary Lavelle*. Only O'Brien herself, or someone who knew her life well, could access those truths in full. Yet at least, at last, she "said her say" (see *Teresa* 10). Kate O'Brien had every right to rewrite her life and, as *Mary Lavelle* proves, she had the ability to do it in a manner that was extraordinarily imaginative, courageous, and compelling.

Conclusion: Identity

Introduction

Identity is one of the main concerns in *Mary Lavelle*, a novel that reflects on how the self is formed, maintained, and presented to the world, and on how it needs to be confronted, abandoned, and remade. Kate O'Brien was very interested on the question of identity formation and development, including the describable qualities and process of a thinking self. In *Farewell Spain*, after a lengthy digression on Walter Pater's aesthetics, she refers to the "'multiplied consciousness' which is the daily bread of the artist" (*Spain* 12–13). Artists may be cursed or blessed with "multiplied consciousness," but how do ordinary people experience subjectivity? *Mary Lavelle* is the story of a few months in the life of an ordinary woman, a record of how external events affect her inner life. Ostensibly, the novel is concerned with the internal *development* in the protagonist. Mary claims to have been "changed" by her witnessing a bullfight for the first time (*Mary* 128). Also, in Madrid after she visits the Prado museum, Milagros suggests that Spain is "changing [Mary] in some absolutely visible way" (229). Mary seems to have very limited agency. For example, she claims to have made an "*accidental* escape from the accepted pattern of life as she knew it" (emphasis added, 128; see 140). Yet she had proven herself capable of independent thinking on at least two occasions: surprising everyone by taking a job as a governess and, if we get back further in her biography, defying her father's and her government's authority by helping the Irish Republican Army. When the narrative opens, we are told that Mary was "unpractised in writing or thinking about herself," and in fact "[s]he had been brought up in unself-conscious habits and therefore was not so much regretful as relieved that the mirrors' positions [in her bedroom in the Basque Country] made it impossible that she should see herself when arranged for sleep" (*Mary* 11, 12). But her Basque adventure will force her to face the mirrors and assess who she is. "From the cradle she had always been, without having to think of it, somewhat a person in her own obscure world. An eldest daughter, eldest sister; considered pretty, considered intelligent," Mary reckons; she had been "successful at school and some-what envied by schoolfellows for her natural graces; one of a family long respected in her native place; tentatively courted by more than one presentable young man, and loved by John MacCurtain" (72). She seems at this point a sum of "facts," a collection of other people's opinions. Her job as a governess is "[self-] obliterat-ing," and she gets the irony of that predicament for someone without a strong sense of self, in her first job in her first trip abroad, trembling on the brink of self-reliance (see 72). Six weeks ago, she thinks, "freedom from relationship to this one and that, freedom from being exactly what she circumstantially was and was glad to be, [was] the most ridiculous and unnecessary of conceptions" (73). "Ridiculous and unnecessary" are mental handcuffs, now that she has gained the freedom to *be* Mary Lavelle, whatever that may mean. I want to take a look at how Kate O'Brien deals with identity, which I will assume to mean *one's aware-ness of being a distinct being*. It is possible to refer to that awareness as "con-sciousness" or "subjectivity," and to that distinctiveness as "identity" or "self"; all these terms certainly have different meanings in different contexts, but for the sake of simplification in this section, the words will be often used inter-changeably. In *Mary Lavelle*, it is possible to discern three different approaches to identity: (a) the self as evolving entity (assuming change to be an in-built characteristic of consciousness, whether during the course of a single day or a lifetime); (b) the self as malleable material (being shaped by culture and the individual); and (c) the self as multiple (a mixture of chance, fate, and agency or, to put it another way, of essentialism and constructionism).

A changing self is crucial to Hegelian phenomenology, and it is also an assumption shared by both the modernist movement and the bildungsroman genre. *Mary Lavelle* is a bildungsroman, that is, it tracks the progression of a single subjectivity as it *evolves*. In addition, this modernist text uses stream of consciousness, a technique concerned with how subjectivity "moves," how it metamorphoses. This is different from the notion of a "synthetic" self (Sartre 58), the second approach to identity in *Mary Lavelle*, and a central idea in exis-tentialist philosophy, a school that claims that a complete, clean break is possible and necessary, that identity can and should be remade from scratch by the indi-vidual, and that this freedom to "choose/make" ourselves is what makes us human. Mary's decision to attend a bullfight is sudden and unaccountable; it is an existentialist decision, as is her initiation *of* a sexual encounter with Juanito, two of the moments that mark the novel as an existentialist work. The third approach to the self evident in *Mary Lavelle* is the notion of simultaneity of identities/realities of equal value, reflecting the new understanding of subjectivity suggested by quantum physics. Kate O'Brien is writing in 1935 of her *self of 1922*, and she deals with this double consciousness by duplicating her protagonist on the main text (Mary/Agatha) and by offering a negative photographic image of the protagonist in the subtext (heterosexual–Mary/lesbian–Mary); that is, the novel simultaneously presents incompatible "versions" of the same self. Finally, rather surprisingly, in the novel we also have yet another approach to subjectivity, as individual, static core; Mary begins by seeing her governessing job as a "shelter" and "veil" (72–3), but she will soon come to realize that it is the role of Mrs. MacCurtain which will obscure her self forever. In these ways, *Mary Lavelle* offers a variety of approaches to the nature of subjectivity, and it is important to consider them in turn, in order to elucidate a crucial part of the conceptual and philosophical scaffolding of the novel. In a sense, O'Brien's book is not *about* Mary Lavelle — it is an inquiry into who Mary Lavelle is, was, could have been, and may yet be.

The Self in Motion (Hegel, Modernism)

By 1935, at the time of writing *Mary Lavelle*, Kate O'Brien had a rich and long tradition of debate on the nature of identity to draw from. This was often framed within an investigation on the role of subjectivity in our experience of external reality. The Irish philosopher George Berkeley, for example, writing in 1710, declared that the outside world had no substance, that it was just ideas generated by our mind. David Hume, writing in 1739 and 1740, believed the opposite, that the self was an illusion, given that it cannot be empirically observed/analyzed, something which would also apply to other "concepts," such as God, the soul, or absolute moral values. Immanuel Kant attempted to bridge the gap between the two positions in 1881 by claiming that objectivity and subjectivity were in symbiosis. In his poetry, drama, and occult writings W.B. Yeats assumed an interrelationship between objective and subjective modes of being, but he saw them as taking turns rather than cooperating, and treated them as ordering principles rather than properties of all thought, all reality. G.W.F. Hegel and Friedrich Nietzsche had already suggested that we must overcome objectivity in order to be free — an idea that also applies to the external, "objective" reality of other individuals.

To Hegel, thought is the underlying basic substance making all reality, material and spiritual. It is the "first principle," a common building block, a philosophical term most often applied to pre–Socratic inquiries on the physical nature of the world — in *Without My Cloak*, as we have seen, Denis described money as the "first principle and holy grail" of American society (O'Brien 386). Within our discussion we are only concerned with the implications of Hegel's "thinking substance" for individual subjectivity. In Hegelian dialectic a thesis is opposed by an antithesis, after which a synthesis is arrived at, which will become the basis of a new thesis, which will then be challenged in turn. This progression was adapted by Karl Marx for his interpretation of the revolutionary process, referred to by Juanito in *Mary Lavelle*. In his *Phenomenology of Spirit*, of 1807, Hegel attempts to describe consciousness (spirit/mind/reality/the essence of the world), which he says is always "in motion." As Hegel explains, within each individual there are always two types of subjectivity at play: a "pure" one and another one that slowly grows attached to it, as a "slave," and eventually overcomes "its master" ("lord" and "bondsman" in some translations). This seems to be echoed when Lavelle wins the argument about leaving Ireland for a year, and John refers to their "slave-master" dynamic (O'Brien *Mary* 36). Hegel describes the process as a "duplicating of self-consciousness in its oneness" (115). Hegel is often charged with obscurity, and his central metaphor for subjectivity (for reality) is sometimes given as a prime example of his difficult style; yet it seems evident to me that, as Richard Wilhelm has suggested (73), Hegel based his theory on the remarkably easy to grasp ancient Chinese yin yang theory, which has had an immense influence on Western thinking despite regularly going unacknowledged. Considering this perpetual movement in psychological terms, we may say that each new confrontation with the world "dethrones" an assumption, which is then revised and "dethroned" in turn; that each certainty, each resemblance of stability, is a lord overcome by his bondsman. This may be encapsulated in the idea that "all thinking is learning," as O'Brien put it in a talk on education she gave in 1962 (5).

Mary's constant reviewing of her prejudices fits in with this model: the dominant view of Spain and the Iberian peninsula as "castanets and flowers in the hair" gives in to a new understanding of the realities of a Basque city, while the dominant understanding of life as a "quiet street" in rural Mellick gives way to an awareness of the chaos and violence of industrial capitalism. As importantly for Mary, the dominant view of love as simple and eternal gives way to an awareness of the suffering and uncertainty that come with being physical and emotional beings—that is, vulnerable beings. However, Hegel's description of consciousness, like the yin yang system, is based on *interlocked opposition*. Mary-Agatha, Juanito-Pablo (and, at another level, Spain and the Basque Country), may be doubles, but it is not so clear if they are opposites in any way, let alone symbiotic. For example, O'Brien's novel seems to be suggesting a progression, from the passionate, gregarious, communist Juan, towards the disillusioned, solitary, anarchist Pablo. Is this an example of yang turning yin? Of "lord" overcome by "bondsman"? If there is one example reminiscent of this model in the novel, it is the symbolic use of the bullfight — the lethal dance of beastly and sophisticated, instinct and deliberation, male and female circling the bullring, is not unlike the famous circular yin yang symbol which explained a whole philosophy before the invention of written language. Lavelle sums up the bullfight in Hegelian/yin-yang terms: "Movement, and its refusal, made absolutely beautiful by a formula of fantastic peril" (116). As we have discussed, at one level it is in fact the subordinate and harmless Mary who "kills" Juan/Pablo (see *Mary* 229), and it is in this surprising turn that the rotating wheel of personal history makes Mary (and O'Brien) master of her self.

According to Judith Butler, in the Hegelian model, "[t]o be a self is ... to be at a distance from who one is, not to enjoy the prerogative of self-identity ... but to be cast, always, outside one self, Other to oneself" ("Recognition" 148). This uncertainty, this difficulty in pinning down the fluttering moth of who one is at a given moment, was a prime concern of modernist writers. In *My Ireland*, Kate O'Brien referred to the self as being in motion: "The smug pleasure we may enjoy in this inescapable privacy [of our life's journey] is, however, soberly offset by our knowledge that we ourselves, the travellers, are never from day to day the same person that we think we know so well" (16). T.S. Eliot may have been thinking of Hegel when he developed his "theory of impersonality" in 1951, claiming that: "What happens [in artistic creation] is a continual surrender of [the artist] as he is at the moment to something which is more valuable. The progress of the artist is a continual self-sacrifice" (17). To Eliot, the good poet is just "a medium" (18), while a bad poet tends to be "personal" (21), a line of thinking that has shielded the academic bias against popular literature and film to this day, affecting the critical reception of, among others, Kate O'Brien. Poetry, Eliot continued, "is not the expression of personality, but an escape from personality" (ibid.). Notwithstanding that autobiographical interpretations of Eliot's own work can and have been made (see for example the 1994 film *Tom and Viv*), his approach is relevant to our discussion in another way. Eliot did not claim there was no stable self — and neither did other modernists. In fact, his theory assumes that individual artists have a self so distinct and weighty that it *can be put away* in a drawer, and it further assumes that a writer *can capture* someone else's self in writing. Arguably, the self was the moving target of the brand new stylistic artillery of modernism. Determined to realistically depict subjectivity, which realist writers had not succeeded in doing, the next generation had to adapt their tools to the task. That is, modernists were a furthering of the realist project, perhaps even its culmination.

But Eliot did not endorse an unchanging self — he referred to the artist "as he is at the moment" of creation (17), as he is at a given moment. The philosopher Henri Bergson's notion of internal, psychological, or "pure" time, as opposed to external, objective, or "scientific" time, developed in books published in 1889 and 1922, has been linked to modernist writing, as has the related notion of a "private" versus a "public" self. Michael Whitworth, for example, has discussed theories of consciousness derived from Bergsonian ideas in the context of Virginia Woolf's fiction (see 120–129). We know that Enrique Areilza, a contemporary of Bergson, had a number of books by him, probably in the original French, in his library. There is no evidence that O'Brien had read Bergson, but given her interest in philosophy, it is most likely that she was acquainted with his work; they had something in common — like Kate O'Brien and her beloved George Santayana, Bergson was also a non–Catholic who often endorsed and promoted values ascribed to the Catholic religion. The Bergsonian notion of the "élan vital," or "life energy," may not be unlike Hegel's conception of "geist" ("spirit" or "mind"). Bergson's proposal that consciousness is a flow of perpetually changing thoughts, obviously tuned to modernist writing, can be seen to follow on from Hegel's "subjectivity in motion." Bergson claims that "real" time (what he calls "durée," or "duration") is internal time — a shifting string of unordered thoughts and feelings that cannot be segmented or compartmentalized, because the nature of reality is shifting constantly, as are our thoughts with our experience of it. It is no wonder that Bergson has been linked to modernist art, given that he saw the exercise of freedom as a creative endeavor, claiming, in 1889: "We are free when our acts emanate from the whole of our personality, when they express it and when they have this kind of indefinable resemblance to it that we see sometimes between a work and the artist" (129 — quoted in Collinson 31). It may be an interesting exercise to think of Mary Lavelle's "experiments in freedom" as an aesthetic project, whereby Mary reshapes her sense of morality to express her changing experience of the world; a work in progress, with prejudices being chipped away as she faces yet another challenge: the café Alemán, love, the bullfight, the Prado, sex, grief, parting. Mary's engagement with these is perhaps also a creative process, "more real and exacting" than anything she had done before (*Mary* 116).

One of the notable features of modernist fiction is its narrative investment in the epiphany. O'Brien demystified the notion of a revelatory moment in a paper she gave in 1963, claiming that epiphanies are a continuing experience and an intrinsic part of the creative process (7). Arguably, a moment of revelation, a deepening of understanding, does not change who one is; it changes how a subject perceives an object; it "corrects" one's beliefs or "redirects" one's emotions, without turning one into a different person. Mary Lavelle has an epiphany at the bullfight. "[T]he most disconcerting experience of her life" (*Mary* 129) is an aesthetic experience, described in similar terms to Anna Murphy's epiphany in *The Land of Spices*, which is itself modeled on that of Stephen Dedalus in *Portrait of the Artist as a Young Man*. Through the bullfight, Mary has learned that "emotion at its most crude can by relation to a little art enchant, overwhelm, and seem eternal" (*Mary* 129). Also, in The Prado Museum, "'But these are so big!' she had answered herself in panic" before Rubens's *Three Graces*, painted around 1636–1638, wondering — the small irony is O'Brien's, not Lavelle's — how to read the language of these rotund figures and possibly also wondering how to interpret a narrative that suggests a lesbian scenario. As we have seen, the descriptions of art (and sex) in the novel are framed within the notion of the Burkean sublime, but it is likely that in drafting Mary's epiphanies O'Brien also had in mind Santayana's reflections on ethics and aesthetics in his book of 1896 *The Sense of Beauty*, where he claims that aesthetic experience is capable of bringing about a positive catharsis even if the experience was in itself sublime or "evil" and even if it was triggered by an "ugly" artistic object/event — defining ugliness as absence of pleasure. According to Santayana: "Truth is thus the excuse which ugliness has for being" (142). Mary's main realization is that life can be a dance of suffering, something suggested by the "crude" ceremony of the bullfight (*Mary* 140) and corroborated by her experience of sex in a similarly crude archetypal heterosexual initiation. In the context of subjectivity in motion, epiphanies are stagecoach inns arrived at in each individual's journey (I am paraphrasing Nicole Dowley, in correspondence August 2007). The modernist subject is never on her way to Damascus—momentary flashes, energizing jolts, disappointing blows abound, but they are followed by inner *adjustments*, not revolutions.

The Present Self (Existentialism)

As we have seen, the case can be made for *Mary Lavelle* to be considered an existentialist novel, with the themes of freedom from morality, anguish caused by infinite possibility, or the power of choice, being central to the story. Kate O'Brien is on record, in a lecture of 1966, hailing Jean Paul Sartre, the name most readily associated with existentialism, as a crucial thinker in the twentieth century and the supreme example of an avant-gardist. Sartre's most important work, *Being and Nothingness*, was first published in 1943, but we must keep in mind that the identification of an existentialist school of thought was retrospectively applied to philosophers from the nineteenth century, while thinkers as diverse as Heraclitus, Augustine, and Pascal are often named as forerunners. Also, existentialism is by no means circumscribed to philosophical treatises, and it seems clear to me that an existentialist strand of thought has survived in popular culture to the present day, in examples from popular literature such as "angst fanfic." The figure of the existentialist dilettante after the Second World War, partial to all things French, in black turtle-neck and Basque beret (borrowed from Basque peasant clothing), totally self-absorbed, detachedly musing on the meaninglessness of existence, was to become a caricature of a genuinely radical approach to life. Existentialist philosophy represented a new form of thinking, of being, and of thinking about being—the existentialist self was expected to change at will, an individual's personality or self-presentation could not be "cultivated," because of the unpredictability inherent to life that humans ought to embrace. Mary is, in this context, an existentialist heroine.

Death is the ultimate question; one can only assess one's life when it is about to end or, as Søren Kierkegaard put it, "life must be lived forward, but understood backwards" (quoted in Collinson 109). The idea is simple enough—one may say that it is impossible to appreciate *Mary Lavelle* as a work of art until one has reached the last page (which in this particular case may mean the last page of *As Music and Splendour*). At a microlevel, one may say that a paragraph or a sentence will not *be* unless it ends. With this novel, O'Brien is retrospectively coming to terms with the young woman she once was, making sense of her past from a vantage point. Most importantly, in existentialist terms, Mary becomes human for the first time when taking the "leap" of initiating a sexual encounter with Juanito, by risking her reputation, her livelihood, her bodily integrity, her ethical foundations—that is, by facing what is in effect a social, physical, and psychological death, after which a "new" Mary will emerge. There is an inherent risk in all choice, because of the uncertainty; by contrast, one's negation of one's freedom is a kind of prolonged death, yet the overwhelming majority of people opt for safety, for playing a single role within a tight script over and over and over again.

The tension between individuality and societal constraints is a common preoccupation of existentialists. Sartre memorably gave the examples of people who "act like a waiter" and "act like a heterosexual," and in *Mary Lavelle* we see how Mary abandons the pretence of acting "as a governess," "as a lady," "as an engaged woman." Kierkegaard famously declared in 1846 that "[a] crowd is untruth" (110)—explaining that "the truth consists precisely of that conception of life which is expressed by the individual" (117). Similarly, Friedrich Nietzsche referred to the majority of the population as "the herd," discussing the development of a Judeo-Christian herd mentality in his *Genealogy of Morals*, of 1878. *Mary Lavelle* explicitly states, as we have seen, the influence of Nietzsche on the generation of 98, and by implication his influence on Don Pablo. All the main characters in the novel depart from conventional morality at some point. One of Nietzsche's best known proposals is his hailing of an ideal "suprahuman" creature beyond moral constraints, in his book of 1885 *Beyond Good and Evil* (see O'Brien *Spain* 5). But O'Brien's characters are not amoral—quite the opposite; all the heroes in *Mary Lavelle* are committed to living by certain values, and even though those values may be individually set, all the main characters in the novel are ultimately consistent in the supreme respect they grant to each other's freedom. We are all free to make choices, in fact we are "condemned" to freedom, which is an inherent human characteristic. Sartre anticipated the objections, explaining in his *Being and Nothingness* that "'to be free' does not mean 'to obtain what one has wished' but rather 'by oneself to determine oneself to wish,'" and so, "we shall not say that a prisoner is always free to go out of prison, which would be absurd, nor that he is always free to long for release, which would be an irrelevant truism, but that he is always free to try to escape" (483–4).

According to Martin Heidegger, because of our mortality we are entities with a temporal dimension; in fact temporality and being are the same thing, as he explained in 1927 in *Being and Time*. Throughout *Mary Lavelle*, there is a constant movement back and forth, with the protagonists regularly revisiting their more or less distant past, and with the narrative itself constantly folding events. For example—and there are examples on practically every page of the novel—Mary retells the bullfight to John in a letter, in a way that anticipates her sexual encounter with Juanito, mocks her future confession to her fiancé, and throws a new light on her own final assessment of the sexual initiation: "It is terrible and inexcusable but it can be very beautiful too and one man did the most unforgettable things.... [O]nce it started I quite forgot to be sick. But I was awfully tired afterwards—" (*Mary* 129). In existentialism, the present is all there is, and we should concentrate all our energies on this moment, when everything begins. It is a powerful and dangerous idea. Existentialists revere new experiences and give themselves to them, or indeed, seek them out. In *Memoirs of a Dutiful Daughter*, of 1958, Simone de Beauvoir recalled how, as a young woman, she had stepped into a stranger's car merely because his invitation to do so offered the possibility of an unforeseen experience, which was of intrinsic value by virtue of being new. Existentialism was primarily about how to conduct your existence rather than about theoretical speculation. What role did ethics play in the behavior of existentialists is certainly open to question (see Louis Menand's article of 2005 on Sartre and de Beauvoir). Yet the incident retold by de Beauvoir shows how a respectable middle class young woman may intellectually and physically embrace risk. The same reckless attitude can be discerned in Mary Lavelle's striking claim about the bullfight (and implicitly, about the sexual encounter): "she had undergone it, which is all that matters about any experience" (*Mary* 129). This interest on fleeting, amoral novelties, was happening in the context of a speeding up of modernity and industrial capitalism; Heidegger's 1955 "Memorial Address" shows the connection particularly clearly. The new shapes of the material world and the new relationships it generated had an effect on subjectivity — the mechanization and alienation associated with industrial society needed a corrective return to an inquiry into the meaning of human existence. But the new breed of thinkers and artists had already been "contaminated," with an emphasis on the individual, the new, and the now.

The Multiple Self (Quantum)

Anne Banfield has highlighted how, in the early twentieth century, "the growth and dissemination of theory of knowledge required a wider intellectual setting [than logic and mathematics], a meeting-ground of philosophy not only with science, but, surprisingly, with a burgeoning artistic activity" (*Table* 5). In 1922, the year of Mary Lavelle, the philosopher Henri Bergson discussed the implications of Albert Einstein's relativity theory in his book *Duration and Simultaneity*. In 1936, the year of *Mary Lavelle*, the physicist Max Planck published *The Philosophy of Physics*, where he claimed that science moved "towards an aim which the poetic intuition may apprehend, but which the intellect can never fully grasp" (83 — quoted in Zukav 331). Studying the radiation of energy from heated objects, Planck discovered in 1900 that energy is emitted and absorbed in discrete units or packets, which he named "quanta."

This contradicted conventional views of the nature of radiation and energy, which was thought to behave like continuous waves rather than discrete units of energy. This meant that the accepted views set down by Newtonian physics were inadequate to explain the world at the sub-atomic level beyond human perception. It was the beginning of a thorough challenge to orthodox assumptions not just on matter and energy, but also on the nature of the human interaction with the world, on the possibility of knowledge, on agency, and on the making of consciousness. Arguably, the force of quantum physics rests in its metaphysical implications, which challenge, among other things, accepted logic. One of the key notions in quantum mechanics, for example, is the fact that matter can behave either as particles or as waves according to the observer's priorities. Put another way, it is possible to know exactly either the position or the momentum of a particle, but not both (Werner Heissenberg's "Uncertainty Principle"); as soon as one is measured, the other becomes impossible, so to decide on the objective of the experiment is to determine the actualization of the behavior to be observed — a self-fulfilling prophecy. This particle-wave duality is a characteristic of anything implicated in energy — in other words, a characteristic of everything in existence. In the quantum paradox, two contradictory behaviors are both possible until such a time when probabilities collapse into a resolution; further, two interlocked yet mutually exclusive modes of being are *both* necessary to make up the material world (yin yang theory again). As Niels Bohr suggested in his "Theory of Complementarity," this is not a property of matter but of human perception. That is, our experience of the world is not so much conditioned by matter behaving according to certain rules, but by the interaction between humans and matter, to the extent that there is no such thing as an accessible external world independent from us. So, reality is a set of relationships, and we *make* reality.

One of the approaches to consciousness discernible in *Mary Lavelle* is the notion of simultaneity. Kate O'Brien referred to the idea of multiple selves on a number of occasions; for example, when she claimed that Teresa of Avila had "lived several lives, and lived each one intensely and to its fullest exaction; she passed from plane to plane of human experience, always alert, always with all her mighty wits about her" (14). There may be an echo here of the quantum theories that were beginning to become popularized at this time, but her comment is a metaphor. However, simultaneous multiple subjectivities would be an intrinsic part of *Mary Lavelle* as writing experience and as reading text. A doubling is already implicit in any autobiographical account, since "[s]elf-consciousness implies the existence of two selves, one of them the object of the other's awareness" (Mermin 33). Writing in 1935, Kate O'Brien's raw material was her perception of herself in 1922. As a scientist (not just an artist) may have done, O'Brien set up a controlled environment in which to monitor the interplay of a number of events, thoughts, and emotions.

We have seen how, when Mary explains that Jorge has seen her double in San Martín, Rose replies, "Your double would take a bit of finding," and Agatha concludes, "And that's a fact" (200–1). When Mary first becomes interested in Juanito (little John), she asks herself: "Anyhow what do I know of him? Is he one-half so good a man as John?" (210). We have already discussed the "covert bildungsroman" of Nieves/Mary/Agatha. If at one level Mary *may* turn into Agatha and Juan *may* turn into Pablo, at another level it would be true to say that both Mary-Agatha and Juan-Pablo are double subjectivities existing *simultaneously*, the factual and the potential side by side on the same page. In the light of the autobiographical content, by the time we hold the novel in our hands, Agatha has stopped being the "potential" subjectivity to become the "factual" one: Kate O'Brien, the writer of the book. We find a further and even more extreme example of simultaneity in the remarkable authorial decision of redrafting characters from *Mary Lavelle* into the 1958 *As Music and Splendour* with a change of setting, time, and circumstance, including sexual orientation. The duplication of Mary Lavelle into Clare Halvey, and of Luisa Areavaga into Luisa Carriaga, is not an exercise in capturing the "essence" of an individual. Rather, it is the revision of a finished story, a move made with the ease of a hand substituting a figure on a chessboard — and with the same devastating effect. Mary and Luisa fall in love in the later novel, and it is impossible to return to their relationship in *Mary Lavelle* without feeling that the book has split into two irreconcilable stories, two contradictory versions of the same lives.

In terms of quantum theory, this is unremarkable. Contradictory events or behaviors are a key to the process by which individuals interact with the world. In the "Copenhagen interpretation" of quantum, an endlessly proliferating number of possibilities (always in mutually exclusive pairs) is generated by each bifurcation or choice. If two possibilities are of equal value and have an equal potential, is the discarded possibility of no further consequence to individual experience? According to the Everett-Wheeler-Graham theory (also known as the "Many Worlds Interpretation of Quantum Mechanics"), there is no such thing as a "lost possibility": Every single one of the possibilities at a given time/event actually occurs, and reality is perpetually split in parallel strands of experience inaccessible to one another. What we may feel to be our individual life — a set of experiences, thoughts, or emotions following one another — is in fact the only strand we are aware of — one of an ever-increasing number of existing lives. It may seem absurd in the face of experience that one, as an individual, could have had a radically different life. There cannot be the same likelihood that one may become a bitter lesbian emigrant trapped in a dreadful job in the Basque Country (Agatha) or that one may become a heterosexual woman wandering the cities of Europe and pursuing new experiences (one of the possible futures for Mary in *Mary Lavelle*). There cannot be the same likelihood that Mary has been introduced to love and sex through her liaison with Juanito (*Mary Lavelle*) or with his wife Luisa (*As Music and Splendour*). There cannot be the same likelihood that Mary walks away from her lover (Juanito) or that her lover (Luisa Carriaga) walks away from Mary. In autobiographical terms, there can't be the same likelihood that a young Kate O'Brien falls in love and has an affair with a Basque man or she doesn't, she has an illegitimate child or she hasn't, she is lesbian or she isn't, and she becomes a novelist or she doesn't. Even in the "multiple worlds" interpretation of quantum physics, where these things may happen at the same time, they cannot happen in the same plane of reality.

Throughout her life, Kate O'Brien cultivated a persona with the press, another with her friends, another with her relatives, and yet another with her partners, as Eibhear Walshe has documented in his biography. A number of "common sense contradictions" do not stand up to scrutiny. For example, "heterosexual" and "lesbian" are only mutually exclusive terms within a specific system of thought which assumes stable and fixed sexual identities. For example, "nationalist" and "internationalist" are only mutually exclusive within a specific definitional template that sees politics as based on border-management. The same applies to notions such as virginity, motherhood, literature, activism: One may have one form of emotional or sexual initiation with one person and a completely different initiation with another; one may be a mother and not behave or be perceived as such within a specific historical and cultural context; one may be a scribbler of autobiographical romantic novelettes and a major canonical writer; one may be a middle class bore and a revolutionary. We are all portmanteaus. I am myself Basque Irish, queer lesbian, and an anarchist who occasionally votes, and the present study reflects an interest in identity as grid rather than tag, as endeavor rather than given. According to quantum physics, the mere presence of a measuring device (an observer, whether human or not) in a laboratory experiment will cause the actualization of a single possibility among potential events. By contrast, *Mary Lavelle* is an "experiment in subjectivity" that expands reality rather than narrowing it down, a laboratory test designed to multiply the possibilities of what is and present all those possibilities side by side, actualized. Put another way, the "observer" (O'Brien), subjects memory, imagination, and present experience of a self (her own), to certain conditions, in order to produce a kaleidoscopic snapshot of quantum subjectivities.

"Who is Mary Lavelle?" is an existential and modernist concern. "There are multiple Marys" is one of the answers offered by the book. As we learned from modernism, the present moment constantly ceases to be; as we learned from existentialism, the present moment constantly comes into being — and a new set of possibilities emerges, to be ignored or wrestled with. What is distinctive about quantum theory is the agency (compulsive, unlike in existentialism), as well as the equal value, in ethical *and* utilitarian terms, given to opposing events and behaviors. We have a quantum model of consciousness seeking to explain brain function (see Stuart Hameroff's quantum "stream of consciousness" in "Funda-mentality," and the work of/with Roger Penrose). A quantum model of subjectivity could also be derived from the distinctive qualities of quantum reality. For example, one's awareness of possible interpretations of events and possible courses of action may be muted or forceful, constant or varying. Another difference with existentialism and modernism is the emphasis on interconnectedness in quantum theory. This peculiarity has been used among other things to suggest a new structural model for the European Union (see Danah Zohar's "quantum federalism," 285, 287). It also invites a new understanding of aesthetic practice. As David Finkelstein put it, "[o]ne of the features of quantum mechanics that leads to ... controversy is its concern with the nonexistent, the potential. There is some of this in all language, or words could only be used once..." (21). Kate O'Brien's last, unfinished novel is an apotheosis of quantum identities, with the author presenting herself in a number of very different characters existing simultaneously. Jean's explanation to the co-protagonist Catherine reads like the assessment of a lifetime of fiction:

> When you are my great age ... you will see a whole series of persons of your name ranging out behind you. You will know all the facts about these persons, and you will accept responsibility for them. But if my experience is any guide — you wont like anyone of them especially — and, what is really amusing — you wont feel much about them. Yes, they have all been you, at one time or another. It's disconcerting — but it keeps one quiet [18].

Conclusion

Kate O'Brien's *Mary Lavelle* can accommodate a number of theories of subjectivity, which itself indicates that the text prioritizes multivalence. How much power does the reader have to determine the meanings of this novel? Roland Barthes once suggested that a text was like a music score and a reader like a creative musician, so that any given text "solicits from the reader a practical collaboration" ("Work" 63). As Stanley Fish put it, "readers don't 'construe' texts, they construct them" (327), yet we may also agree with Hazel Rochman that "[r]eading makes immigrants of us all." In O'Brien's introduction to *Presentation Parlour*, of 1963, she explained:

> I had five aunts. So had my brothers and sisters, the same five in name and place. But my five aunts are not theirs any more than theirs are mine. All nine of us had each his own five aunts, in as much or as little as we possessed, observed or remembered them. Were there then forty-five aunts? Maybe. But they lived, conventionally and unassumingly, behind five names and five faces [7].

Not only is our reading unique to our abilities and temperament, each text we encounter — each new book, person, landscape, or experience — also interacts with us, "reading" us, transforming us. This is a dialogue, not a debate (quantic versus Newtonian, according to Zohar 292). Emmanuel Levinas, adapting Hegel to build an ethics of difference in his book of 1974 *Otherwise than Being*, proposed that any and every encounter undoes our identity, because one instantly assumes the new position and the vulnerability introduced by the other person. According to Levinas, the mental/emotional substitution of the "I" for "the other" is inevitable, in a sort of compulsive empathy (see Levinas 13). The reader of *Mary Lavelle* may choose one of multiple contradictory narratives, all equal in value until she picks up the book and brings her own experience and self-awareness into the reading. Conversely, *Mary Lavelle* will read the reader in a certain way, an active reading that will result in a new, unique text/person. I know I have become a more demanding reader, hoping for other books that will describe with the same sophistication and vividness the "wild adventure" of sitting alone on a bench in the leafy square of a Basque town, in perfect freedom to do anything, to be anyone (see O'Brien *Mary* 72, *Spain* 215).

There is a common thread running through the understanding of subjectivity in Hegelian phenomenology, modernist aesthetics, existentialist philosophy, and quantum theory: an emphasis on change. None of these approaches conceive of a static universe or a static subjectivity. *Mary Lavelle* may be a book that seeks to register — and encourage — transformation, but it is also an attempt to sculpt a mass of memory into a shape that will stand, indifferent to sun and rain, in a public space. Discussions on identity, in the last few years, have been framed near exclusively in terms of essentialism versus constructionism. After Agatha declares her love in the novel, Mary, observing the human traffic at San Geronimo/San Vicente and reflecting on self-repression (including the repression of her own feelings for Juanito), is shocked by a realization of the multitudes of people seeking to forgo "the essence of their own [lives]" (286). In poststructuralist contexts, essentialism is invariably seen as normative, yet Kate O'Brien here presents it as radically disruptive. In addition to the idea of a changing subjectivity, in *Mary Lavelle* we *also* find the notion of an essential, unchanging self. To understand how, it is necessary to abandon some of the critical parameters we are familiar with and their attached value judgments, including the assumption that essentialism and constructivism are incompatible. Essentialism is, in my view, a constant preoccupation in governess novels. The figure of "the governess" implies movement, a shift from one context to another, whereas her host home is the symbol of stasis. This is made evident in Iris Murdoch's 1973 *The Unicorn*, a sort of fictional essay on the governess genre. *The Unicorn* presents the dried-out ideological and philosophical bones that support the domestic epic of a governess's travails, by centering on the conflict between change and stasis— with the protagonists playing out an existentialist drama of subjectivity (including a textbook "death as revelation" scene). Mary Lavelle's trip to Bilbo to become a governess is presented in the novel as the external change that triggers the emergence of an unexpected self; yet her new attitude to life partly comes with a new *self-awareness*. That is, her identity is partly nonessential, partly nonconstructed. Similarly, the novel clearly states that Don Pablo and Agatha change after the "event" of meeting Mary, but there is a parallel suggestion that the blast had in fact unearthed a subterranean ore. After attending the bullfight, Mary becomes aware of "another, newer self " inside her (116). If the novel makes much of the transformative power of the bullfight ceremony, it also includes numerous, less spectacular (but not less lethal), stabs at the notion of a changing self. For example, when Mary ponders her new position as governess, "this curiously obliterating occupation" (72):

> She smiled now, thinking that after all one cannot be obliterated, but only hidden, disguised, and that it was pleasantly surprising to be Mary Lavelle, all clues and certainties thereto sealed within, and to sit unknown, unneeded, in the leafy square of a Spanish town. She anticipated no wild adventure; she wanted none. This was, to her simplicity, wild adventure. Six weeks ago, she had hardly been aware of the town of Altorno; six weeks ago Spain was as far as the mountains of the moon, and freedom from relationship to this one and that, freedom from being exactly what she circumstantially was and was glad to be, the most ridiculous and unnecessary of conceptions [72–3].

Perhaps the next pages don't mark an inner transformation, then, but an "awakening" (see Rosowski). In the opening pages of the novel, Mary describes her Basque adventure, in eager anticipation, as an "adventure in invisibility" (72). Like the "Giges ring" in Plato's parable of 360 BCE, governessing makes Mary invisible, it gives her a magic power to *be who she really is.*

Why does one become a governess? As we have seen, the protagonist of *Agnes Grey*, the 1847 novel by Anne Brontë, lists the reasons: "To go out into the world; to enter upon a new life; to act for myself; to exercise my unused faculties; to try my unknown powers; to earn my own maintenance" (12 — see Snowe's variation of this in *Villette* 57). "To go out into the world," implies there is a subjectivity in place, whereas "to try my unknown powers" clearly assumes already existing resources. Governess abroad novels are invariably classified as bildungsromans. Whether we understand the bildungsroman as linear progression (Dilthey [see Abel et al.]), as counter-narrative undoing (Fraiman), as socialization (Buckley), as philosophical quest to identify human attributes (Beddow), or as formation of a coherent self (Moretti), the fact of the matter is that the genre requires "bildung," development. After considering a number of governess abroad narratives, it seems impossible to find evidence of development in their protagonists. Agnes, Jane, Lucy, Jo, Rosina, Delia, Mary ... they *do not change*—they remain as stubborn or sensitive or outspoken or curious or secretive as they always were. The events they live through allow their personalities, their identities, to come to the fore more or less prominently, rather than causing them to evolve into new persons. These narratives of the self suggest that one may change direction, not vehicle; "[c]haracter is fate," we are told in *Pray for the Wanderer* (O'Brien 101). However, the governess gains agency from the moment she steps into her profession. She can now begin to "govern" herself, or at least she can motion herself towards self-government. *Mary Lavelle* is an "autoportrait" (like Tamara de Lempicka's 1925 painting of that title), mapping the route Kate O'Brien took in 1922 starting in the Basque Country, a route that brought her to 1936 and her commitment to the political future of Spain, to a certain outlook on life, to a certain sexuality, to a certain aesthetic practice. In modernist fashion, *Mary Lavelle* is also a sketch of "the" self, an attempt to describe subjectivity in action, as it moves. To an observer, the self is not apparent, only its manifestations are (as with subatomic particles) — but fiction can in fact show either or both. O'Brien's modernist take on the bildungsroman presents an individual protagonist who simultaneously changes and does not change. This is a Russian doll model, whereby a series of "truer" selves emerge in succession, having always been there, under an endlessly replicated painted surface (see Mary Morrissy's novel *The Pretender*). It is an essence model, whereby Mary Lavelle was always a "freelance" at heart, and the Basque experience has merely allowed her to give expression to her true, stable, unchanging self.

In light of this, we may have to conclude that despite its rhetoric of change and transformation, *Mary Lavelle* rests on an essentialist view of the self. Unless, that is, we understand development as outer, not inner development. Unless we understand development as a change in circumstances, in the adornments of the self. Unless we see development as change in financial situation, in status, in surroundings, in all the things that "surround" the self, be they a country, a job, a partner. Perhaps these outer changes allow us to become everything we already are. For how can we really know who and what we are, unless the circumstances change? And how can we stop knowing, learning, who we are, if the circumstances keep changing? If this is true, then, there is no end to this pouring out of the self, a pouring "out into the world" — out, into the *changing* world.

Works Cited

Abel, Elisabeth, Marianne Hirsh, and Elisabeth Langland. Introduction. *The Voyage In: Fictions of Female Development.* Elisabeth Abel, Marianne Hirsh, and Elisabeth Langland, eds. Hanover, NH: University Press of New England, 1983. 3–21.

Aberasturi, Luis J. [interviews Casilda Méndez Hernáez]. "Casilda, Miliciana. Historia de un Sentimiento." [Casilda, Militia Woman. History of a deeply felt conviction] (1985). *Los Anarquistas y la Guerra en Euskadi.* Luis Jiménez de Aberasturi ed. Andoain: Txertoa, 2009. 453–518.

Ackelsberg, Martha A. *Free Women of Spain: Anarchism and the Struggle for the Emancipation of Women* (1991). Oakland and Edinburgh: AK Press, 2005.

Ackland, Valentine. *For Sylvia: An Honest Account* [w. 1949]. London: Random House, 1989.

Adams, Michael. *Censorship: The Irish Experience.* Tuscaloosa: University of Alabama Press, 1968.

Alcott, Louisa May. *Good Wives.* Harmondsworth: Penguin, 1995.

_____. *Little Women* (1868). Harmondsworth: Penguin, 1989.

Allott, Miriam, ed. *Jane Eyre and Villette: A Casebook.* London: Macmillan, 1973.

Anasagasti, Iñaki. "José María de Areilza, o la variante ovóide de la occupación del espacio" [José María of Areilza, or the oval variant of filling up space]. Iñaki Anasagasti y Josu Erkoreka. *Dos Familias Vascas: Areilza/Aznar.* Madrid: Foca, 2003. 14–331.

The Anteroom. Television drama. Adaptation of Kate O'Brien's *The Anteroom,* by Tony Hickey. UTV, 1981.

Arana Goiri, Sabin. Carta a Engracio Aranzadi (sobre "El Discurso de Larrazabal," 3 Junion 1893) [Letter to Engracio Aranzadi (on the "Larrazabal Address," 3 June 1893)]. 20 December 1897. *Historia del Nacionalismo Vasco y sus Documentos* [History of Basque Nationalism and Its Documents]. Javier Corcuera and Yolanda Oribe, eds. Bilbao: Eguzki, 1991. 162–3.

Arantzadi y Etxeberria, Engracio de. *Ereintza: siembra de nacionalismo vasco 1894–1912* [Journal: seed of Basque nationalism 1894–1912] (1935). Donostia: Auñamendi, 1980.

Areilza, Enrique. *Epistolario.* Bilbao: El Cofre del Bilbaíno, 1999. 7–11.

_____. Prólogo [Prologue]. Vicente Blasco Ibáñez. *El Intruso.* Bilbao: El Tilo, 1999. 7–12.

Areilza, José María. "Cuatro libros de Bilbao" [Four books of Bilbo] (1984). *Tres batallas por Bilbao y otras páginas.* [Three battles for Bilbo and other pages]. Bilbao: El Tilo, 1997. 119–136.

_____. "El Doctor Areilza" [Doctor Areilza]. *Tres batallas por Bilbao y otras páginas.* Bilbao: El Tilo, 1997. 293–302.

_____. *Epistolario* [Selected correspondence] (1964). José María Areilza, ed. Bilbao: El Cofre del Bilbaíno, 1999.

_____. Introducción y Notas [Introduction and Notes] (1964). Enrique Areilza. *Epistolario.* Bilbao: El Cofre del Bilbaíno, 1999.

_____. "José Antonio Aguirre." *Tres batallas por Bilbao y otras páginas.* Bilbao: El Tilo, 1997. 335–344.

_____. "José María Areilza, alcalde de Bilbao, 'discurso pronunciado en el Coliseo Albia — 8 de Julio de 1937'" [José María Areilza, lord mayor of Bilbo, "address delivered in Coliseo Albia — 8 July 1937"]. Iñaki Egaña. *1936 — Guerra Civil en Euskal Herria; Volumen VI — La Ofensiva de Mola: Defensa y Caida de Bizkaia.* Andoain: Aralar Liburuak, 1999. 218–219.

_____. [José María Areilza to Kate O'Brien]. Letter. May 26, 1952. Kate O'Brien Papers, University of Limerick. Doc. 8 (1–3).

_____. [José María Areilza to Kate O'Brien]. Letter. May 13, 1960. Kate O'Brien Papers, University of Limerick. Doc. 9.

_____. "Kate O'Brien: A Personal and Literary Portrait" (1989). *With Warmest Love: Lectures for Kate O'Brien 1984–93.* John Logan, ed. Limerick: Mellick Press, 1994. 33–41.

_____. "Mary Lavelle" (n.d.a.). *Tres batallas por Bilbao y otras páginas.* Bilbao: El Tilo, 1997. 226–229.

_____. "Recuerdos del 'Lion D'Or'" [Memories of the "Lion D'Or"]. *Tres batallas por Bilbao y otras páginas.* Bilbao: El Tilo, 1997. 106–118.

_____. "El siglo y medio de la Sociedad Bilbaina" [The century and a half of the Bilbaina Association] (1989). *Tres batallas por Bilbao y otras páginas.* Bilbao: El Tilo, 1997. 137–146.

Arnold, Bruce. *Mainie Jellett and the Modern Movement in Ireland.* New Haven: Yale University Press, 1991.

Arriola, Nora. "Un hombre llamado Pedro Olea" [A man named Pedro Olea]. *Bilbao* 211 (January 2007): 41.

Art That Shook the World: Virginia Woolf's Orlando. Documentary film. Written by Jeannette Winterson. BBC, 2002.

Auden, W.H. "Spain" (1937). *Selected Poems.* London: Vintage, 1999.

Augustine, Saint Bishop of Hippo. *The Confessions of St. Augustine* [w. 397–8] (1907). Trans. E.B. Pusey. London: Everyman, 1966.

Austen, Jane. *Mansfield Park* (1814). Harmondsworth: Penguin, 1996.

Azorín. "Una doctrina feminista" [A feminist doctrine]. *Obras selectas.* Madrid: Austral, 1998. 604–8.

_____. "Feminismo" [Feminism]. *Obras selectas.* Madrid: Austral, 1998. 596–99.

_____. "El hombre y la mujer" [Man and woman]. *Obras selectas.* Madrid: Austral, 1998. 600–3.

Bacigalupe, Carlos. "'El Intruso,' la novela Bilbaina de Blasco Ibáñez, fue tambien pieza teatral" ["The Intruder," Blasco Ibáñez's Bilbaian novel, was also a play]. *Bilbao* 151 (May 2001): 38.

_____. "Triunfal visita del transformista Leopoldo Frégoli" [Triumphal visit by the gender-bender Leopoldo Frégoli (to Bilbao)]. *Bilbao* 210 (December 2006): 34.

_____. "Último adiós al Café Boulevard" [Last goodbye to the Café Boulevard]. *Bilbao* 208 (October 2006): 6.

Balzac, Honoré de. *The Girl with the Golden Eyes* (1835). New York: DeLuxe, 1931.

Balzano, Wanda. "The Question of the Foreigner—*Mary Lavelle.*" Unpublished paper, University College Dublin, 5 December 2002.

Banfield, Ann. *The Phantom Table: Woolf, Fry, Russell, and the Epistemology of Modernism.* Cambridge: Cambridge University Press, 2000.

Barandiaran, Alberto. *Gaizkileen faktoria—Ernest Hemingway euskaldunen artean* [Criminal factory—Ernest Hemingway among Basque people]. Bilbo: Euskandunon Egunkaria, 2000.

Barker, Michael. *Our Three Selves: A Life of Radclyffe Hall.* London: Hamish Hamilton, 1985.

Baroja, Pío. *Youth and Egolatry* (1917). Charleston, SC: Bibliobazaar, 2007.

Barthes, Roland. "The Death of the Author" (1968). *The Rustle of Language.* Oxford: Basil Blackwell, 1986. 49–55.

_____. "From Work to Text" (1971). *The Rustle of Language.* Oxford: Basil Blackwell, 1986. 56–64.

Battersby, Christine. *Gender and Genius: Towards a Feminist Aesthetics.* London: Women's Press, 1989.

Baza, Naiara. "Santutxu más cerca" [Santutxu closer]. *Bilbao* 208 (October 2006): 5.

_____. "Tradición y vanguardia" [Tradition and Avant Garde (in the Plaza Nueva)]. *Bilbao* 231 (November 2008): 4–5.

Beauvoir, Simone de. *Memoirs of a Dutiful Daughter* (1958). London: Penguin, 2006.

_____. *The Second Sex* (1949). London: Picador, 1988.

Beddow, Michael. *The Fiction of Humanity—Studies in the Bildungsroman from Wieland to Thomas Mann.* London: Cambridge University Press, 1982.

Bell, Clive. *Art* (1914). London: BiblioBazaar, 2007.

Bentham, Jeremy. "Offences Against One's Self" [w. 1785] (1931). *Journal of Homosexuality* 3.4 (1978): 389–405.

_____. *The Principles of Morals and Legisla-*

tion (1789). Oxford: Oxford University Press, 1996.

Bergson, Henri. *Duration and Simultaneity* (1922)—*Bergson and the Einsteinian Universe*. Manchester: Clinamen, 1999.

_____. *Time and Free Will: An Essay on the Immediate Data of Consciousness* (1889). London: Allen and Unwin, 1971.

Berkeley, George. *A Treatise Concerning the Principles of Human Knowledge* (1710). Oxford: Oxford University Press, 1998.

Berkman, Alexander. *ABC of Anarchism* (1929). London: Freedom Press, 2000.

Bersani, Leo. "Is the Rectum a Grave?" *October* 43 (Winter 1987): 197–222.

Beyond Rangoon. Feature film. Dir. John Boorman. 1995.

Bible [*see New Jerusalem Bible*]

Bilbao, Amaia. *Los Irlandeses de Bizkaia: "Los Chiguiris," siglo XVIII* [The Irish in Biscay: "The Chiguiris" (in the) eighteenth century]. Bilbao: BBK, 2004.

Binchy, Maeve. *Echoes* (1985). London: Arrow, 1994.

Blockade. Feature film. Dir. William Dieterle. 1938.

Blood and Sand. Feature Film. Dir. Fred Niblo, 1922.

Boland, Eavan. Introduction. Kate O'Brien. *The Last of Summer*. London: Virago, 1989.

_____. "Kate O'Brien." *Stony Thursday Book* 7. John Jordan, ed. Limerick: Limerick Arts Council, 1981. 46–53.

_____. "The Legacy of Kate O'Brien" (1985). *With Warmest Love: Lectures for Kate O'Brien 1984–93*. John Logan, ed. Limerick: Mellick Press, 1994. 1–14.

Boff, Leonardo. *Jesus Christ Liberator: A Critical Christology for Our Times* (1972). New York: Orbis Books, 1978.

Bookchin, Murray. *To Remember Spain: The Anarchist and Syndicalist Revolution of 1936*. Edinburgh and San Francisco: AK Press, 1994.

Bowen, Elisabeth. *The Hotel* (1927). New York: Cape, 1950.

_____. *The Last September* (1929). London: Virago, 1998.

_____. *The Mulberry Tree: Writings of Elisabeth Bowen*. Hermione Lee, ed. London: Virago, 1986.

Boylan, Clare. Introduction. Kate O'Brien. *The Land of Spices*. London: Virago, 2000. 7–12.

Bradley, Marion Zimmer. *The Mists of Avalon*. New York: Ballantine Books, 1982.

Brief Encounter. Feature film. Dir. David Lean. 1945.

Brontë, Anne. *Agnes Grey* (1847). Oxford: Clarendon, 1988.

Brontë, Charlotte. *Jane Eyre* (1847). Oxford: Oxford University Press, 2000.

_____. *Villette* (1853). Oxford: Oxford University Press, 2008.

Broughton, Trev, and Ruth Symes, eds. *The Governess: An Anthology*. Stroud: Sutton, 1997.

Buckley, Jerome Hamilton. *Season of Youth — The Bildungsroman from Dickens to Golding*. Cambridge, MA: Harvard University Press, 1974.

Burke, Edmund. *A Philosophical Enquiry into the Rising of our Ideas of the Sublime and Beautiful* (1757). Oxford: Oxford University Press, 1990.

Burney, Frances. *Evelina* (1778). [Originally published as *Evelina, or, the History of a Young Lady's Entrance into the World*]. Boston and New York: Bedford Books, 1997.

Burton, Richard. "The Sotadic Zone" (1886). *Sexology Uncensored: The Documents of Sexual Science*. Lucy Bland and Laura Doan, eds. Bodmin: Polity Press, 1998. 203–204.

Butler, Alison. *Women's Cinema: The Contested Screen*. London and New York: Wallflower, 2005.

Butler, Judith. "Critically Queer." *Bodies That Matter — On the Discursive Limits of "Sex."* New York and London: Routledge, 1993.

_____. "Longing for Recognition" (2000). *Undoing Gender*. New York and London: Routledge, 2004. 131–151.

Butler de Foley, Maria Isabel. "Each Other's Country: Some Twentieth Century Irish and Spanish Writers" (1989). *With Warmest Love: Lectures for Kate O'Brien 1984–93*. John Logan, ed. 15–31.

Butterfly. Feature film. Dir. Yan Yan Mak. 2004.

Byrne, Shannon. "Conflict in Consensus: Irish Suffragists and Nationalists, 1908–1910." Unpublished MA thesis, University College Dublin, 2006.

Byron, Catherine. "'This drawing-room: My prison.'" Unpublished paper delivered at "An Evening with Kate O'Brien," University College Dublin, 25 January 2006.

_____. "Towards my own 'Book of Changes': The Cap of Invisibility." Unpublished essay. [Sent to the author 6 February 2003.]

Cahalan, James M. *The Irish Novel*. Boston: Twayne, 1988.

El Calentito. Feature film. Dir. Chuz Gutiérrez. 2005.

Callaghan, Louise C. *Find the Lady*. Unproduced play. 2003.

_____. "Kate O'Brien." Unpublished paper delivered at "An Evening with Kate O'Brien," University College Dublin, 16 January 2003.

Calleja, Fernando. Fernando Calleja to Kate O'Brien. Letter, July 7, 1943. Kate O'Brien Papers, University of Limerick, document P12/209(1).

Camille. Feature film. Dir. Ray C. Smallwood, 1921.

Camille. Feature film. Dir. George Cukor, 1936.

Camus, Albert. *The Plague* (1948). New York: Vintage, 1991.

Cardwell, Richard A. "Modernismo frente a noventayocho: relectura de una historia literaria" [Modernism versus ninety-eight: rereading a literary history]. *Cuadernos interdisciplinarios de Estudios Literarios* 6.1 (1995): 11–24.

Carefree. Feature film. Dir. Mark Sandrich. 1938.

Carmen. Feature film. Dir. Cecil B. DeMille, 1915.

Castle, Terry. *The Apparitional Lesbian: Female Homosexuality and Modern Culture*. New York: Columbia University Press, 1993.

_____. "Sylvia Townsend Warner and the Counterplot of Lesbian Fiction." *Textual Practice* 4.2 (1990): 213–235.

Cawley, Patricia A. "Weapons of Independence: A Study of Kate O'Brien's Irish Heroines." Unpublished MA thesis, University College Dublin, 1981.

Charvet, John. *Feminism*. London: Dent, 1982.

Chiapuso, Manuel. El Gobierno Vasco y los Anarquistas. Bilbao en Guerra [The Basque government and the anarchists. Bilbo at War] (1978). *Los Anarquistas y la guerra en Euskadi*. Luis Jiménez de Aberasturi, ed. Andoain: Txertoa, 2009. 259–451.

Coleridge, Samuel Taylor. "Christabel" [w. 1787] (1800). *The Complete Poems*. London: Penguin Classics, 1997. 190–199.

Colette. *The Claudine Novels* (1900, 1901, 1902, 1903). Harmondsworth: Penguin, 1987.

Coll, Mary. Introduction. *Faithful Companions: Collected Essays Celebrating the 25th Anniversary of The Kate O'Brien Weekend*. Mary Coll, ed. Limerick: Mellick Press, 2009. xi–xiii.

Collins, Wilkie. *The Woman in White* (1859–1860). Harvey Peter Sucksmith, ed. New York: Oxford University Press, 1980.

Collinson, Diané. *Fifty Major Philosophers: A Reference Guide* (1987). London and New York: Routledge, 1997.

Conrad, Joseph. *The Secret Agent: A Simple Tale* (1907). London: Random House, 2004.

Corcuera Atienza, Javier. *Orígenes, ideología y organización del nacionalismo Vasco (1876–1904)*. [Origins, ideology and organization of Basque nationalism (1976–1904)]. Madrid: Siglo XXI, 1979.

Cortázar, Fernando García de. "En el centenario de José María Areilza" [In the centenary of José María Areilza]. *El Correo Español–El Pueblo Vasco*, 2 August 2009, 40–1.

Cossío, José María de. *Los toros: tratado téctino e histórico* [The bullfight: technical and historical treatise]. 12 vols. Madrid: Espasa Calpe, 1985–88.

Coughlan, Patricia. "Kate O'Brien: Feminine Beauty, Feminist Writing and Sexual Role." *Ordinary People Dancing: Essays on Kate O'Brien*. Eibhear Walshe, ed. Cork: Cork University Press, 1993. 59–85.

Cronin, Michael. "Moving Pictures: Kate O'Brien's Travel Writing." *Ordinary People Dancing: Essays on Kate O'Brien*. Eibhear Walshe, ed. Cork: Cork University Press, 1993. 137–150.

Cronin, Michael G. "Kate O'Brien's Women and the Exclusionary Limits of Liberal Critique." Unpublished paper delivered at the "Women in Irish Culture and History" Conference, University College Dublin, 21 October 2006.

Crosland, Margaret, ed. *The Marquis de Sade Reader*. London: Peter Owen, 2001.

Cuddihy, Geraldine Joan. "Towards an Archi-texture of the Body." Unpublished MA thesis, University College Dublin, August 2004.

Cullingford, Elisabeth Butler. "'Our nuns are not a nation': Politicizing the Convent in Irish Literature and Film." *Irish Post-*

modernisms and Popular Culture. Wanda Balzano, et al., eds. London: Palgrave, 2007. 55–73.

Dalsimer, Adele. *Kate O'Brien: A Critical Study.* Dublin: Gill and Macmillan, 1990.

Days of an Older Colour [Dias de Viejo Color]. Feature film. Pedro Olea. 1967.

Dickinson, Emily. Poem 505 [I would not paint — a picture — ...] [w. 1862]. *The Complete Poems.* Thomas H. Johnson, ed. London: Faber and Faber, 1975. 245–6.

_____. Poem 1129 [Tell all the truth but tell it slant] [w. 1868]. *The Complete Poems.* Thomas H. Johnson, ed. London: Faber and Faber, 1975. 506–7.

Díez, Isabel. "Dulce tentación" [Sweet temptation (in the pâtisseries of Bilbo)]. *Bilbo* 236 (April 2009): 28.

Donoghue, Emma. "Crossing Boundaries." [Review of Maureen Duffy's *Illuminations* and Jeanette Winterson's *Written on the Body.*] *Women: A Cultural Review* 5.1 (Spring 1994): 93–96.

_____. "Embraces of Love." *Faithful Companions: Collected Essays Celebrating the 25th Anniversary of The Kate O'Brien Weekend.* Mary Coll, ed. Limerick: Mellick Press, 2009. 16–31.

_____. "Noises From Woodsheds: The Muffled Voices of Irish Lesbian Fiction." *Volcanoes and Pearl Divers: Essays in Lesbian Feminist Studies.* Suzanne Raitt, ed. London: Onlywomen Press, 1995. 169–201.

_____. "'Out of Order': Kate O'Brien's Lesbian Fictions." *Ordinary People Dancing: Essays on Kate O'Brien.* Eibhear Walshe, ed. Cork: Cork University Press, 1993. 36–59.

Donovan, Katie. *Irish Women Writers — Marginalised by Whom?* Dublin: Raven Arts Press — Letter From the New Island Series, 1988.

Doyle, Bob. *Memorias de un rebelde sin pausa* [Memoirs of a continuing revolutionary]. Madrid: Asociación de Amigos de las Brigadas Internacionales, 2002.

Dracula's Daughter. Feature film. Dir. Lambert Hillyer. 1936.

Edelman, Lee. *No Future: Queer Theory and the Death Drive.* Durham: Duke University Press, 2004.

Edgeworth, Maria. *Castle Rackrent* (1800). Harmondsworth: Penguin, 1992.

Eisenstein, Sergei. "Through Theatre to Cinema." *Film Form: Essays in Film Theory.* New York: Harcourt Brace, 1977. 3–17.

Eliade, Mircea. *The Myth of the Eternal Return; or, Cosmos and History* (1949). New York: Princeton University Press, 1971.

Eliot, T.S. "Tradition and the Individual Talent." *Selected Essays.* London: Faber, 1951. 13–22.

Elliot, Katherine. *Rethinking the Novel/Film Debate.* New York: Cambridge University Press, 2009.

Emak Bakia. Short film. Dir. Man Ray. France: 1926.

The English Patient. Feature film. Dir. Anthony Minghella. 1996.

Enright, Anne. Introduction. Kate O'Brien. *As Music and Splendour* (1958). Dublin: Penguin Ireland, 2005. v–ix.

Enríquez, José Manuel. "La Falsa Contradicción del Homosexual Católico" [The False Contradiction of the Catholic Homosexual]. *El Homosexual Ante la Sociedad Enferma.* José Manuel Enríquez, ed. Barcelona: Tusquets, 1978. 101–122.

ER. Television series. Constant productions/Amblin Entertainment (1994–2009). "Rescue Me" (written by Neal Baer). Season 7, episode 7.

_____. "Sailing Away" (written by Jack Orman and Meredith Stiehm). Season 7, episode 19.

_____. "The Visit" (written by John Wells). Season 7, episode 6.

Erauso, Catalina de. *Historia de la Monja Alférez, Catalina de Erauso, Escrita por Ella Misma.* Madrid: Cátedra, 2002.

Espinosa, José María Lorenzo. *Gudari, una pasión útil. Eli Gallastegi (1892–1974)* [Gudari, a useful passion. Eli Gallastegi (1892–1974)]. Tafalla: Txalaparta, 1992.

Esteban, Ángel. Introducción [Introduction]. Catalina de Erauso. *Historia de la Monja Alférez, Catalina de Erauso, Escrita por Ella Misma.* Madrid: Cátedra, 2002. 11–90.

Etxebarria, Lucía. "Viajeras de sí a sí mismas — O del paso del viaje interior al exterior en la tradición literaria occidental" [Female travelers from self to self within — Or on the passage from internal to external voyage in the Western literary tradition]. *La Letra Futura — El Dedo en la Llaga: Cuestiones sobre Arte, Literatura, Creación, y Crítica.* Barcelona: Destino, 2000. 123–132.

Euskadiren Estatutu Politiko Berria: Nuevo Estatuto Politico de Euskadi [New national agreement for The Basque Country]. Vitoria-Gazteiz: Eusko Jaula-nitza: Gobierno Vasco, 2003.

Faderman, Lillian. *Chloe Plus Olivia: An Anthology of Lesbian Literature from the Seventeenth Century to the Present* (1994). Harmondsworth: Penguin, 1995.

_____. *Surpassing the Love of Men — Romantic Friendship and Love between Women from the Renaissance to the Present* (1981). London: Women's Press, 1985.

Farwell, Marilyn R. *Heterosexual Plots and Lesbian Narratives*. New York: New York University Press, 1996.

Feehan, Fanny. "Kate O'Brien and the Splendour of Music" (1979). *Ordinary People Dancing: Essays on Kate O'Brien*. Eibhear Walshe, ed. Cork: Cork University Press, 1993. 120–7.

Ferguson, Margaret, et al., eds. *The Norton Anthology of Poetry*. New York: Norton, 1996.

Fernández de la Sota, José. *Bilbao: literatura y literatos* [Bilbo: literature and literatti]. Bilbao: Laga, 2000.

_____. "A Través de Areilza (con Bilbao al fondo)" [Through Areilza (with Bilbo in the background)]. José María Areilza. *Tres batallas por Bilbao y otras páginas*. Bilbo: El Tilo, 1997. 9–33.

Finkelstein, David. Foreword (1978). Gary Zukav. *The Dancing Wu Li Masters — An Overview of the New Physics*. London: Rider, 1979. 19–21.

Fischerova, Jana. "The Writer and the Censor: Czechoslovakia and Ireland: The Case of Kate O'Brien and Frank O'Connor." Unpublished paper, CAIS conference, Maynooth, 24 June 2005.

Fish, Stanley Eugene. *Is There a Text in This Class? The Authority of Interpretive Communities*. Cambridge, MA: Harvard University Press, 1980.

Flaubert, Gustav. *Madame Bovary* (1857). Harmondsworth: Penguin, 1995.

Fogarty, Anne. "The Anteroom." Unpublished paper delivered at "An Evening with Kate O'Brien," University College Dublin, 16 January 2003.

_____. "Desire in the Novels of Kate O'Brien." *Ordinary People Dancing: Essays on Kate O'Brien*. Eibhear Walshe, ed. Cork: Cork University Press, 1993. 101–120.

_____. "Irish Novels into Spanish." *New Hibernian Review — A Quarterly Record of Irish Studies* 3 (Summer 1999): 142–146.

_____. "Translation and Notes." Kate O'Brien's *Mary Lavelle —: Rotas*. Barcelona: Edhasa, 1998.

For One Sweet Grape. Feature film. Dir. Terence Young. 1955.

Foster, Jeannette H. *Sex Variant Women in Literature* (1956). Tallahassee: Naiad, 1985.

Foucault, Michel. *The History of Sexuality: Volume One — The Will to Knowledge* (1976).

Fraiman, Susan. *Unbecoming Women: British Women Writers and the Novel of Development*. New York: Columbia University Press, 1993.

Freud, Sigmund. "Lucy R" (1901). *Three Case Histories*. New York: Touchstone, 1993.

_____. "Psychoanalytic Notes Upon an Autobiographical Account of a Case of Paranoia ('Dementia Paranoides')" (1911). *Three Case Histories*. New York: Touchstone, 1993. 83–160.

Gaines, Jane M. "Of Cabbages and Authors." *A Feminist Reader in Early Cinema*. Jennifer M. Bean and Diane Negra, eds. Durham and London: Duke University Press, 2002. 88–118.

Gallop, Rodney. *A Book of the Basques* (1930). Reno: University of Nevada Press, 1970.

Galvin, Miriam. "Masculinities and the Paedophile: Discursive Strategies in Irish Newspapers." PhD thesis, Department of Social Sciences and Humanities, University of Bradford, 2007.

García Lorca, Federico. "Poema doble del Lago Eden" [Double poem on Eden Lake]. *Poeta en Nueva York* [Poet in New York] (1929–30). Madrid: Cátedra, 2005. 165–167.

Giffney, Noreen. "Queer Theory: Key Concepts." Unpublished manuscript.

Gille, Vincent. "Love of Books, Love Books." *Surrealism: Desire Unbound*. Jennifer Mundy, ed. London: Tate, 2001. 125–135.

Gilman, Charlotte Perkins. *Herland* (1915). London: Women's Press, 2001.

God's Country and the Woman. Feature film. Dir. William Brant. 1936.

Godwin, William. *An Enquiry Concerning*

Political Justice and Its Influence on Modern Morals and Happiness (1793). Harmondsworth: Penguin, 1976.

_____. *Things as They Are, or The Adventures of Caleb Williams* (1794). New York: Oxford University Press, 1998.

Goldman, Alan H. "Plain Sex" (1977). *Applying Ethics.* Jeffrey Olen and Vincent Barry, eds. London: Wordsworth, 1996. 88–99.

Goldman, Emma. "Preface" (1917). *Anarchism and Other Essays.* London and Toronto: Dover, 1969.

González Abrisketa, Olatz. *Pelota vasca: Un ritual, una estética* [Basque handball: A ritual, an aesthetics]. Bilbao: Muelle de Uribitarte, 2005.

González de Durana, Javier. "Adolfo Guiard o la Flor del Suburbio." *Bilbao* 237 (May 2009): 12.

Gordon, Mary. "Chase of the Wild Goose" (1936). Reprinted as *The Llangollen Ladies— The Story of Lady Eleanor Butler and Miss Sarah Ponsonby, known as the Ladies of Llangollen.* Manchester: John Jones, 1999.

Gorky, Maxim. "Soviet Literature" (1934). *Soviet Writers' Congress 1934— The Debate on Socialist Realism and Modernism in the Soviet Union.* H.G. Scott, ed. London: Lawrence and Wishart, 1977. 27–72.

The Governess. Feature film. Dir. Sandra Goldbacher. 1997.

Grant, Linda. "Conflict of Interest." *Vogue* (March 2004): 171.

El Greco [Domenikos Theotocopulos]. *El Entierro del Conde Orgaz* [The burial of Count Orgaz]. Oil on canvas, 1586–88.

_____. *San Sebastian* [Cathedral Sacristy, Palencia]. Oil on canvas. 1555–78.

_____. *San Sebastian* [El Prado Museum]. Oil on canvas, 1600–14.

Guedes, Ann, and Eduardo Guedes. *Talk of Angels* [screenplay] (n.d.a.). Frank McGuinness Papers, Special Collections Library, University College Dublin. Folder 22.

Guezala, Luis de, ed. *El pensamiento de Sabino de Arana y Goiria* [sic] *a traves de sus escritos. Antología de textos 1893–1903.* [The thought of Sabino de Arana y Goiria (sic) through his writings. Anthology of texts 1893–1903]. Bilbo: Eusko Alderdi Jeltzalea/Partido Nacionalista Vasco, 1995.

Halberstam, Judith. *Female Masculinity.* Durham: Duke University Press, 1998.

Hale, C. Jacob. "Leatherdyke Boys and Their Daddies: How to Have sex Without Women or Men." *Queer Studies: An Interdisciplinary Reader.* Robert J. Coroler and Stephen Valocchi, eds. Bodmin, Cornwall: Blackwell, 2003. 61–70.

Hall, Radclyffe. *The Well of Loneliness.* London: Virago, 1982.

Hamel, Elisabeth, and Theo Vennemann. La Lengua Originaria de los Europeos Prehistóricos: [The original language of prehistoric Europeans]. *Investigación y ciencia.* (January 2007): 62–7. Reproduced in *La senda Aborigen.* Guillermo Piquero, ed. Bilbo: Linkiniano Elkartea, 2005. 175–180.

Hameroff, Stuart. "'Funda-mentality': Is the Conscious Mind Subtly Linked to a Basic Level of the Universe?" *Trends in Cognitive Science* 2 (1998): 119–127.

_____, and Roger Penrose. "Conscious Events as Orchestrated Space-Time Selections." *Journal of Consciousness Studies* 2.1 (1996): 36–52.

Hangstrum, Jean H. *The Sister Arts: The Tradition of Literary Pictorialism and English Poetry from Dryden to Gray.* Chicago: University of Chicago Press, 1958.

Hansen, Miriam Bratu. "The Mass Production of the Senses: Classical Cinema as Vernacular Modernism." *Modernism/Modernity* 6.2 (1999): 59–77.

Haranburu Altuna, Luis. *Historia de la alimentación y la cocina en el País Vasco* [History of food and cuisine in the Basque Country]. Alegia (Gipuzkoa): Hiria, 2000.

Haraway, Donna. "A Manifesto for Cyborgs: Science, Technology, and Socialist Feminism in the 1980s" (1985). *Feminism/Postmodernism.* Linda Nicholson, ed. New York and London: Routledge, 1990.

Harmon, Maurice, ed. *The Irish Writer and the City.* Gerrards Cross, Buckinghamshire: Colin Smythe, 1984.

Hartigan, Anne Le Marquand. "Kate O'Brien." Unpublished paper delivered at "An Evening with Kate O'Brien," University College Dublin, 15 January 2004.

Haverty, Anne. "Limerick's Liberated Lady." *The Irish Times,* Saturday, April 15, 2006, 12.

Hayes, Elisabeth M. "Kate O'Brien: An Approach." Unpublished MA thesis, University College Dublin, 1978.

Hegel, G.W.F. *Phenomenology of Spirit* (1807). Oxford: Clarendon, 1977.

Heidegger, Martin. *Being and Time* (1927). Oxford: Blackwell, 1962.

_____. "Memorial Address" (1955). *Discourse on Thinking*. New York: Harper Torchbooks, 1990. 43–57.

Hemingway, Ernest. *Death in the Afternoon* (1932). New York: Scribner's, 1960.

_____. *The Sun Also Rises* [or *Fiesta*] (1926). London: Arrow Books, 1994.

Hemmings, Clare. *Bisexual Spaces: A Geography of Sexuality and Gender*. London: Routledge, 2002.

Hennegan, Alison. Introduction. Radclyffe Hall. *The Well of Loneliness*. London: Virago, 1982. vii–xvii.

Hillen, Seán. "The Great Pyramids of Carlingford Lough, IRELANTIS." Photo-collage, 1994.

Hite, Shere. *The Hite Report on Female Sexuality* (1976). New York: Seven Stories Press, 2004.

Hogan, Desmond. Introduction. Kate O'Brien. *That Lady*. London: Virago, 1985.

_____. Introduction. Kate O'Brien. *Without My Cloak*. London: Virago, 1986.

Howe, Irving. *Politics and the Novel* (1957). New York: Fawcet Premier, 1967.

Hume, David. *A Treatise of Human Nature* (1739, 1740). Oxford: Oxford University Press, 1978.

Hurston, Zora Neale. *Their Eyes Were Watching God* (1937). London: Virago, 2005.

Huyssen, Andreas. "Mass Culture as Woman — Modernism's Other." *Studies in Entertainment: Critical Approaches to Mass Culture*. Tania Modleski, ed. Bloomington and Indianapolis: Indiana University Press, 1986.

Ibáñez, Vicente Blasco. *El Intruso* [The Intruder] (1904). Barakaldo: Ediciones de Librería San Antonio, 1999.

In Search of the Pope's Children. Documentary film. Written by David McWilliams. RTE, 13 November 2006.

Inckle, Kay. "Tragic Heroines, Stinking Lilies, and Fallen Women: Love and Desire in Kate O'Brien's *As Music and Splendour*." *Irish Feminist Review* 2: 56–73.

Irigaray, Luce. *An Ethics of Sexual Difference* (1984). Ithaca: Cornell University Press, 1993.

James, Henry. "The Princess Casamassima" (1886). *Novels 1886–189*. Daniel Mark Fogel, ed. New York: Library of America, 1989. 1–554.

_____. *The Turn of the Screw* (1898). London and New York: Norton, 1999.

Jamison, Anne. "An Exploration 'of memory, of imagination and of fact': Kate O'Brien's Archival Notes." Unpublished paper delivered at *Kate O'Brien Seminar*, Mary Immaculate College, Limerick, 23 February 2007.

Jemein y Lanbarri, Ceferino. *Historia ráfica del Nacionalismo*. [A Graphic History of (Basque) Nationalism"]. Bilbao: Editorial Vasca, 1935.

[Jimenez, Edorta]. *Hemingway y Urdaibai* [Hemingway and Urdaibai]. Basauri: Urdaibai Txatxi, 2001.

Jiménez de Aberasturi, Luis M. *Casilda Miliciana: historia de un sentimiento* [Militia woman: History of a deeply felt conviction] (1985). Interview with Casilda Méndez Hernaez. Andoain: Txertoa, 2009. 453–518.

Jordan, John. "Kate O'Brien" (1976). *Crystal Clear: The Selected Prose of John Jordan*. Hugh McFadden, ed. Dublin: Lilliput Press, 2006. 233–235.

_____. "Kate O'Brien" (1987). *Crystal Clear: The Selected Prose of John Jordan*. Hugh McFadden, ed. Dublin: Lilliput Press, 2006. 236–239.

_____. "Kate O'Brien: First Lady of Irish Letters" (1973). *Crystal Clear: The Selected Prose of John Jordan*. Hugh McFadden, ed. Dublin: Lilliput Press, 2006. 227–230.

_____. "A Passionate Talent" (*Hibernia*, 30 August 1974). *Crystal Clear: The Selected Prose of John Jordan*. Hugh McFadeen, ed. Dublin: Lilliput Press, 2006. 231–232.

_____, ed. *Stony Thursday Book* 7. Limerick: Limerick Arts Council, 1981.

Joyce, James. *A Portrait of the Artist as a Young Man* (1914–5). Ware: Wordsworth, 1992.

_____. *Ulysses* (1922). Harmondsworth: Penguin, 2000.

Kaijima, Akiko. "Female Characterization and the Theme of Love in Kate O'Brien's Novels." Unpublished MA Thesis, University College Dublin, 1979.

Kant, Immanuel. *Critique of Pure Reason* (1781). London: Macmillan, 1933.

Katz, Jonathan Ned. *The Invention of Heterosexuality*. New York: Dutton, 1995.

Keane, Molly. *Devoted Ladies* (1934). London: Virago, 2006.

_____. *Good Behaviour.* London: Andre Deutsch, 1981.

Kennedy, A.L. *On Bullfighting.* London: Random House, 1999.

Kennedy, S.B. *Irish Art and Modernism 1880–1950.* Belfast: Queen's University of Belfast, 1991.

Kent, Brad. "An Argument Manqué: Kate O'Brien's *Pray for the Wanderer.*" *Irish Studies Review.* 18.3 (2010): 285–298.

Kiberd, Declan. *Irish Classics.* London: Granta Books, 2000.

Kierkegaard, Søren. "Concerning the dedication to 'The individual'" [on the first page of *Edifying Discourses in Various Spirits*] (1846). *The Point of View for My Work as an Author.* New York: Harper, 1962. 109–119.

_____. *Concluding Unscientific Postscript to the* Philosophical Fragment (1846). Princeton, NJ: Princeton University Press, 1941.

The King and I. Feature film. Dir. Walter Lang. 1956.

Kinsey, Alfred, et al. *Sexual Behaviour in the Human Female.* Philadelphia: Saunders, 1953.

Koedt, Anne. "Lesbianism and Feminism." *Radical Feminism.* Anne Koedt, Ellen Levine, and Anita Rapone, eds. New York: Quadrangle, 1973.

Kornegger, Peggy. *Anarchism: The Feminist Connection* [pamphlet] (1976). London: "In the Spirit of Emma," 2003.

Kupfer, Joseph H. *Experience as Art — Aesthetics in Everyday Life.* New York: State University of New York Press, 1983.

Kurlansky, Mark. *The Basque History of the World.* (1999). London: Vintage, 2000.

Langland, Elisabeth. "Female Stories of Experience: Alcott's *Little Women* in light of *Work.*" *The Voyage In: Fictions of Female Development.* Elisabeth Abel, Marianne Hirsch, and Elisabeth Langland, eds. Hanover and London: University Press of New England, 1983. 112–130.

Lao Zi [Lao Tzu]. *Tao Te Ching.* D.C. Lau, trans. Harmondsworth: Penguin Classics, 2001.

Larronde, Jean-Claude. *El nacionalismo vasco: su origen y su ideología en la obra de Sabino Arana-Goiri.* [Basque nationalism: its origin and ideology in the work of Sabino Arana-Goiri]. San Sebastian: Txertoa, 1977.

Laverty, Maura. *No More than Human* (1944). London: Virago, 1986.

Lawrence, D.H. *Lady Chatterley's Lover* (1928). Harmondsworth: Penguin, 1990.

_____. *The Plumed Serpent: Quetzalcoatl* (1926). Cambridge: Cambridge University Press, 1982.

_____. *Women in Love* (1921). Harmondsworth: Penguin, 1996.

Lawrence, Margaret. *We Write as Women* (1936). London: Michael Joseph, 1937. [Originally published as *The School of Femininity: A Book For and About Women as they are Interpretated* (sic) *Through Feminine Writers of Yesterday and Today*].

Lee, Hermione. *Elizabeth Bowen* (1981). London: Vintage, 1999.

_____. *Virginia Woolf* (1996). London: Vintage, 1997.

Le Fanu, Joseph Sheridan. "Carmilla" (1872). *In a Glass Darkly.* Oxford: Oxford University Press, 1999. 243–319.

_____. *Uncle Silas: A Tale of Bertram-Haugh* (1864). Harmondsworth: Penguin, 2000.

Legasse, Mark, Jakue Paskual, Jimy Olaizola, and Marta Karlos. *Anark-Herria* [Basque Anarkountry]. Donostia: Txertoa, 1986.

Le Guin, Ursula K. *The Dispossessed* (1974). London: Millennium, 1999.

Lempicka, Tamara de. *Autoportrait (Tamara in the Green Bugatti).* Oil on wood. 1925.

Leonardo da Vinci. *Virgin of the Rocks.* Oil on panel. c. 1508.

Letts, Winnifred M. *Knockmarron — Sketches.* London: Murray, 1933.

Levinas, Emmanuel. *Otherwise Than Being — or Beyond Essence* (1974). London: Martunus Nijhoff, 1981.

Lewis, Mathew Gregory. *The Monk* (1796). Oxford: Oxford University Press, 1998.

Lynam, Shevawn. *The Spirit and the Clay.* Boston: Little, Brown, 1954.

Litvak, Lily. "La Buena Nueva. Cultura y Prensa Anarquista (1880–1913)." *Revista de Occidente* 305 (October 2006): 5–18.

Logan, John, ed. *With Warmest Love: Lectures for Kate O'Brien 1984–93.* Limerick: Mellick Press, 1994.

Lombroso, Cesare. *Criminal Man* (1876). Durham: Duke University Press, 2006.

Lorenzoni, Giulia. "Powerful Visions: New Geometries of Family in Kate O'Brien's Fiction." Unpublished paper for "The Kate O'Brien Weekend," Limerick, 1 March 2003.

MacManus, Seumas. *The Story of the Irish Race* (1921). Old Greenwich, CT: Devin-Adar, 1991.

Madariaga, Salvador de. *Spain*. London: Ernest Benn, 1930.

Magnus, Laurie. *A History of European Literature*. London: Ivor Nicholson and Watson, 1934.

Major Barbara. Feature film. Dir. Gabriel Pascal. 1936.

Malinovski, B. *The Sexual Lives of Savages*. London: Routledge and Kegan Paul, 1932.

Malory, Thomas. *Le Morte Darthur: The Winchester Manuscript* [w. 1465]. New York: Oxford University Press, 1998.

Mansfield, Katherine. "The Little Governess." *The Stories of Katherine Mansfield*. Antony Alpers, ed. Auckland: Oxford University Press, 1984.

Maraña, Félix. "Ernestina de Champourcin, misterio, memoria, poesía." *Pérgola*, Bilbao 1999, xiii

Marler, Regina. *Bloomsbury Pie* (1997). London: Virago, 1998.

Marshall, Peter. *Demanding the Impossible: A History of Anarchism* (1992) [revised edition]. St. Ives: Fontana Press, 1993.

Martí, José. "Amor de ciudad grande" [Big city love] (1882). *Ismaelillo/Versos Libres/ Versos Sencillos*. Madrid: Cátedra, 2001. 125–128.

McCourt, Frank. *Angela's Ashes: A Memoir* (1996). London: Flamingo, 1999.

McFadden, Hugh, ed. Introduction and Notes. *Crystal Clear: The Selected Prose of John Jordan*. Dublin: The Lilliput Press, 2006.

McGuinness, Frank. *Talk of Angels* [screenplay] (n.d.a.). Frank McGuinness Papers, Special Collections Library, University College Dublin. Folder 22.

McNeill, John. *The Church and the Homosexual*. Kansas City: Sheed Andrews and McMeel, 1976.

Mead, Margaret. *Coming of Age in Samoa: A Study of Adolescence and Sex in Primitive Societies* (1928). Harmondsworth: Penguin, 1977.

_____. *Growing up in New Guinea: A Study of Adolescence and Sex in Primitive Societies* (1930). Harmondsworth: Penguin, 1965.

_____. *Male and Female* (1950). Harmondsworth: Penguin, 1970.

_____. *Sex and Temperament in Three Primitive Societies*. London: William Morrow, 1935.

Meaney, Gerardine. "Regendering Modernism: The Woman Artist in Irish Women's Fiction." *Women: A Cultural Review* 15.1 (2004): 67–82.

_____. "Territory and Transgression — History, Nationality and Sexuality in Kate O'Brien's Fiction." *Irish Journal of Feminist Studies* 2.2 (December 1997): 77–92.

Menand, Louis. "'Stand by Your Man'— The Strange Liaison of Sartre and Beauvoir." *The New Yorker*, 26 September 2005. <http://www.newyorker.com/archive/ 2005/09/26/050926crbo_books>

Mentxaka, Aintzane L. " A Catholic Agnostic — Kate O'Brien." *Breaking the Mould: Literary Representation of Irish Catholicism*. Eamon Maher and Eugene O'Brien, eds. Oxford: Peter Lang, 2011. 87–104.

_____. "Kate O'Brien." *Berria*, 25 September 2009, 5.

_____. "Politics and Feminism: The Basque Contexts of Kate O'Brien's *Mary Lavelle*." *Irish University Review* 39.1 (Spring/Summer 2009): 65–75.

_____. "The Witch, the Nun, and the Goddess— Some Basque Lesbians of History and Myth." Mary McAuliffe and Sonja Tiernan, eds. *Historicising the Lesbian — Volume I*. Cambridge: Cambridge Scholars Press, 2007.

Mercier, Vivian. "Kate O'Brien." *Irish Writing* 1(1946): 86–100.

Meredith, Isabel [Helen and Olivia Rossetti]. *A Girl Among the Anarchists* (1903). Lincoln and London: University of Nebraska Press, 1992.

Mermin, Dorothy. *Godiva's Ride: Women of Letters in England, 1830–1880*. Bloomington: Indiana University Press, 1993.

Merriman, Brian. *Cúit an Mheán Oíche* ["The Midnight Court"] (w. c. 1790). There are two translations: (1) Trans. and Introduction by Frank O'Connor. Dublin: O'Brien Press, 1989. (2) Trans. by Cosslett O'Cuinn. Dublin and Cork: Mercier Press, 1982.

Mesa, María Jesús Cava. "Mujeres en la sombra" [Women in the Shadows (in turn-of-the-century Bilbao)]. *Bilbao* 231 (November 2008): 16–7.

_____. "Usos y arquetipos en la historia de Bilbao" [Customs and archetypes in the history of Bilbao]. *Bilbao* 163 (August 2002): 52–3.

Metropolis. Feature film. Dir. Fritz Lang. 1926/2010.

Mill, John Stuart. *The Subjection of Women* (1869). Indianapolis: Hackett, 1988.

_____. "Utilitarianism" (1861). Indianapolis: Hackett, 2001.

Miller, Henry. *Black Spring* (1936). New York: Grove, 1991.

Mills, Jackie. "*The Land of Spices* onto Film." Unpublished paper delivered at "An Evening with Kate O'Brien," University College Dublin, 16 January 2003.

Milton, John. *Paradise Lost: Books I & II*. J. Sargeaunt, ed. London and New York: Edward Arnold, 1900.

Mir, Gregori. Introducción. *La Literatura del Desastre*. Miquel S. Oliver. Barcelona: Ediciones Península, 1974. 7–57.

Mr. Deeds Goes to Town. Feature film. Dir. Frank Capra. 1936.

Mittermaier, Ute. "Images of Spain in Irish Literature, 1922–1975." Unpublished Doctoral thesis, Trinity College Dublin, 2009.

Modern Times. Feature film. Dir. Charles Chaplin. 1936.

Moglen, Helene. *Charlotte Brontë: The Self-Conceived* (1976). *Villette — Contemporary Critical Essays*. Pauline Nestor, ed. London: Macmillan, 1992. 16–31.

Montalbán, Josu. *El Doctor Areilza: Médico de los Mineros*. Bilbao: Muelle de Uribitarte, 2008.

_____. "Kate O'Brien: Mucho más que una institutriz" [Kate O'Brien: much more than a governess] *Pérgola*, suplemento cultural del periódico *Bilbao*, 247 (April 2010): 10.

Montefiore, Janet. "Listening to Minna: Realism, Feminism, and the Politics of Reading." *Volcanoes and Pearl Divers: Essays in Lesbian Feminist Studies*. Suzanne Raitt, ed. London: Onlywomen Press, 1995. 123–46.

Montero, Manuel. *La California del hierro: las minas y la modernización económica y social de Vizcaya* (1994) [The California of iron: mines and the economic and social modernization of Biscay]. Bilbao: Beta III Milenio, 2005.

_____. *Mineros, banqueros y navieros* [Miners, bankers, and ship-owners] (1990). Bilbao: Beta III Milenio, 2005.

_____. Prólogo [Prologue]. Vicente Blasco Ibáñez. *El Intruso*. Bilbao: Ediciones Librería, San Antonio, 1999. 9–33.

Moore, George. *A Drama in Muslin* (1886). Dublin: Appletree Press, 1992.

Moore, Thomas. *Utopia* (1516). Harmondsworth: Penguin, 1965.

Morales Ladrón, Marisol. "Banned in Spain? Truths, Lies and Censorship in Kate O'Brien's Novels." *ATLANTIS, Journal of the Spanish Association of Anglo-American Studies* 32.1 (June 2010): 51–72.

Moretti, Franco. *The Way of the World — The Bildungsroman in European Culture*. London: Verso, 2000.

Morrissy, Mary. *The Pretender* (2000). London: Vintage, 2001.

Mulford, Wendy. Introduction (1989). Silvia Townsend Warner. *After the Death of Don Juan*. London: Virago, 1989. v–xvii.

Murdoch, Iris. *The Red and the Green* (1965). London: Vintage, 2002.

_____. *Three Arrows*. London: Chatto and Windus, 1973.

_____. *The Unicorn* (1963). London: Virago, 2000.

Nashe, Thomas. "The Unfortunate Traveller" (1594). *The Unfortunate Traveller and Other Works*. Harmondsworth: Penguin, 1985.

Navarre, Marguerite de. *The Heptameron* (1559). Harmondsworth: Penguin, 1984.

The New Jerusalem Bible — Study Edition. Henry Wansbrough, ed. London: Darton, Longman, and Todd, 1994.

Newell, Peter E. "Alexander Berkman: An Introduction" (1970). Alexander Berkman. *ABC of Anarchism*. London: Freedom Press, 2000.

Nicholson, Nigel. *Portrait of a Marriage*. London: Weidenfeld and Nicholson, 1973.

Nietzsche, Friedrich. *Beyond Good and Evil* (1886). New York: Vintage, 1967.

_____. *The Gay Science* (1882). New York: Random House, 1974.

_____. *Towards a Genealogy of Morals* (1878). New York: Vintage, 1967.

O'Brien, Donough, ed. *For a Special Occasion in the University of Limerick: Some Writings by Kate O'Brien, Lorna Reynolds, Michael O'Toole*. Limerick, May 2005.

O'Brien, Kate. *The Anteroom* (1934). London: Virago, 2006.

_____. "The Art of Writing." *University Review* 3.4 (1963): 6–14.

_____. *As Music and Splendour* (1958). Dublin: Penguin, 2005.

_____. "As to University Life." *University Review* 1.6 (Autumn 1955): 3–11.

_____. "Aunt Mary in the Parlour" [Lecture to Spanish Society, UCD]. *University Review* 3.2 (1963): 7.

_____. *A Broken Song*. Undated film Script. Kate O'Brien Papers, University of Limerick. Doc. 185.

_____. "Constancy." Novel draft. Kate O'Brien Papers, University of Limerick. Doc. 165. [Partly printed as "Constancy" in *Winter's Tales from Ireland*, Kevin Casey, ed. (Dublin: Gill and Macmillan, 1972)].

_____. *Distinguished Villa: A Play in Three Acts*. London: Ernest Benn, 1926.

_____. *English Diaries and Journals*. London: William Collins, 1947.

_____. *Farewell Spain* (1937). London: Virago, 1985.

_____. *The Flower of May*. London: Heinemann, 1953.

_____. "George Eliot: A Moralizing Fabulist." *Transactions of the Royal Society of Literature*. G. Rostrevor Hamilton, ed. London: Oxford University Press, 1955.

_____. *Gloria Gish*. Undated unpublished typescript. National Library of Ireland.

_____. "Ireland and *Avant-Gardisme*." Unpublished lecture delivered as part of a series of lectures [unidentified] to honor Douglas Hyde. Unidentified location. Undated; date in "Kate O'Brien Papers' University of Limerick catalogue: May 1966. Doc. 157.

_____. "Irish Writers and Europe." *Hibernia*, March 1965. Reprinted in *Stony Thursday Book* 7. Limerick: Limerick Arts Council, 1981. 36–7.

_____. *Kate O'Brien: Self-Portrait*. [Documentary]. RTE. Broadcast, 28 March 1962.

_____. "Kate O'Brien's Journalisms. Selected Gleanings." *Stony Thursday Book* 7. Limerick: Limerick Arts Council, 1981. 33–5.

_____. *The Land of Spices* (1941). London: Virago, 2000.

_____. *The Last of Summer* (1943). London: Virago, 1989.

_____. [Leningrad Address: The Writer Must Be Left Alone]. Untitled and unpublished address delivered to an [unidentified] international conference of writers, Leningrad, August 1963. Kate O'Brien Papers, University of Limerick. Doc. 153.

_____. "Long Distance." *Irish Times* [see "Kate O'Brien's Journalisms"].

_____. "Manna" (1962). Unpublished short story. Kate O'Brien Papers, University of Limerick. Doc. 145.

_____. *Mary Lavelle* (1936). London: Virago, 2000.

_____. *Mary Magdalen*. Undated filmscript. National Library of Ireland. Doc. 19,703.

_____. *My Ireland*. London: B.T. Batsford, 1962.

_____. *Pray for the Wanderer*. London: Heinemann, 1938.

_____. *Presentation Parlour* (1963). London: House of Stratus, 2001.

_____. "La prosa imaginativa o fictional en Irlanda a partir de 1800." Lecture. December 1971, University of Valladolid. Kate O'Brien Papers, University of Limerick. Doc. 165. [Published in English as "Imaginative Prose of the Irish." *Myth and Reality in Irish Literature*. J. Ronsley, ed. Waterloo: Wilfrid Laurier University Press, 1977].

_____. "Singapore Has Fallen." *The Spectator*, 27 February 1942, Doc. 141.

_____. ["Spain"]. Untitled and unpublished lecture delivered to the Association of Professional and Businesswomen, Canterbury, 10 March 1972. Kate O'Brien Papers, University of Limerick. Doc. 166.

_____. *Teresa of Avila* (1951). Cork and Dublin: Mercier Press, 1993.

_____. *That Lady* (1946). London: Virago, 1985.

_____. ["That's William Yeats!"]. Undated, unpublished autobiographical sketch. "Kate O'Brien Papers," University of Limerick. Doc. 151.

_____. "UCD as I Forget It." *University Review* 3. 2 (1962): 6–11.

_____. "Why the Rage for French Films?" *The Star*, 1 February 1938, n.p. Kate O'Brien Papers, University of Limerick. Doc. 134, 12.

_____. *Without My Cloak* (1931). London: Virago, 1986.

Oliver, Miquel dels Sants. "El Culto a la Tristeza" (1907). *La Literatura del Desastre*. Barcelona: Ediciones Península, 1974. 61–9.

_____. "La Literatura del Desastre" (1907). *La Literatura del Desastre*. Barcelona: Ediciones Península, 1974. 69–122.

Olney, James. "Autobiography and the Cultural Moment: A Thematic, Historical, and Bibliographical Introduction." *Autobiography: Essays Theoretical and Critical*.

James Olney, ed. Princeton, NJ: Princeton University Press, 1980. 3–27.

_____. *Metaphors of Self: The Meaning of Autobiography.* Princeton, NJ: Princeton University Press, 1972.

O'Neill, Mary. Introduction. Kate O'Brien. *Farewell Spain.* London: Virago, 1985. ix–xxi.

Oppenheim, Lois. *The Painted Word — Samuel Beckett's Dialogue with Art.* Ann Arbor: University of Michigan Press, 2000.

Oppenheim, Meret. *Object* (Le Déjeuner en Fourrure) [Object (Fur Breakfast)]. Sculpture/Object. Fur-covered cup, saucer, and spoon. 1936.

O'Riordan, Michael. *Connolly Column: The Story of the Irishmen Who Fought for the Spanish Republic 1936–1939* (1979). Torfaen: Warren and Pell, 2005.

Ortiz Alfau, Angel. "Palabras para esta edición" ['Words for This Edition'] (1997). Enrique Allott, Miriam, ed. *Jane Eyre and Villette: A Casebook.* London: Macmillan, 1973.

Orwell, George. *Animal Farm* (1945). Harmondsworth: Penguin, 1996.

_____. *Homage to Catalonia* (1938). Harmondsworth: Penguin, 1989.

_____. *The Road to Wigan Pier* (1937). Harmondsworth: Penguin, 1989.

O'Toole, Michael. "The Art of Writing — Kate O'Brien's Journalism." *Ordinary People Dancing: Essays on Kate O'Brien.* Eibhear Walshe, ed. Cork: Cork University Press, 1993. 128–136.

_____. Foreword. Kate O'Brien. *Presentation Parlour.* London: House of Stratus, 2001. 1–6.

_____. "Peasants to Princes." *Management — Journal of the IMI.* December 1995. [Reproduced in *For a Special Occasion in the University of Limerick: Some Writings by Kate O'Brien, Lorna Reynolds, Michael O'Toole.* Donough O'Brien, ed. Limerick, May 2005].

O'Toole, Tina. "Kate O'Brien." Unpublished paper, delivered at "An Evening with Kate O'Brien," University College Dublin, 15 January 2004.

_____. "Sexual and Political Autonomy in Kate O'Brien's Fiction." Unpublished paper, delivered at the "Kate O'Brien Seminar," Mary Immaculate College, Limerick, 23 February 2007.

Our Relations. Feature film. Dr. Harry Lachman, 1936.

Panofski, Erwin. *Early Netherlandish Painting: Its Origins and Character.* Cambridge, MA: Cambridge University Press, 1966.

La Pelota Vasca: la Piel Contra la Piedra/ Euskal Pilota: Harria Larruaren Kontra [Basque ball: Skin Against Stone]. Documentary film. Dir. Julio Medem. 2003.

Penrose, Roger. *The Emperor's New Mind: Concerning Computers, Minds, and the Laws of Physics.* Oxford: Oxford University Press, 1989.

_____. *Shadows of the Mind: A Search for the Mixing Science of Consciousness.* Oxford: Oxford University Press, 1994.

Peterson, M. Jeanne. "The Victorian Governess: Status Incongruence in Family and Society." *Suffer and Be Still: Women in the Victorian Age.* Martha Vicinus, ed. London: Methuen, 1980. 3–20.

Pí y Margall, Francisco. *Unitarismo y federalismo* [Unitarianism and federalism] (1890). Madrid: Emiliano Escolar, 1981.

Picasso, Pablo R. *Guernica.* Oil on panel. 1937.

Pine, R. "Where Is This Place? Kate O'Brien, Autism and Modern Literature." *With Warmest Love: Lectures for Kate O'Brien 1984–93.* John Logan, ed. Limerick: Mellick Press, 1994. 77–98.

Planck, Max. *The Philosophy of Physics.* New York: Norton, 1936.

Plato. *The Republic* [w. 360 BCE]. Harmondsworth: Penguin, 2003.

_____. *The Symposium* [w. 360 BCE]. Harmondsworth: Penguin, 2003.

Pramaggiore, Maria. "Epistemologies of the Fence." *RePresenting Bisexualities: Subjects and Cultures of Fluid Desire.* Maria Pramaggiore and D. E. Hall, eds. New York: New York University Press, 1996.

Preston, Paul. "A Life Adrift: Indalecio Prieto." *¡Comrades! — Portraits from the Spanish Civil War.* London: Fontana, 1999. 235–275.

_____. "Pasionaria of Steel: Dolores Ibárruri." *¡Comrades! — Portraits from the Spanish Civil War.* London: Fontana, 1999. 277–318.

Proust, Marcel. *Sodome et Gomorrhe* (1921–22). London: Penguin, 2003.

Quilligan, Maureen. *The Language of Alle-*

gory: Defining the Genre. Ithaca: Cornell University Press, 1979.

Rabinowitz, Nancy Sorkin. "'Faithful Narrator' or 'Partial Eulogist': First-Person Narration in Brontë's *Villette*" (1985). *Villette — Contemporary Critical Essays.* Pauline Nestor, ed. London: Macmillan, 1992. 68–82.

Radek, Karl. "Contemporary World Literature and the Tasks of Proletarian Art" and "Speech in Answer to the Discussion" (1934). *Soviet Writers' Congress 1934 — The Debate on Socialist Realism and Modernism in the Soviet Union.* H.G. Scott, ed. London: Lawrence and Wishart, 1977. 73–184.

Ramblado, Cinta. "Farewell Spain: Running Away from Fascism." Unpublished paper delivered at the "Kate O'Brien Seminar," Mary Immaculate College, Limerick, 23 February 2007.

_____. ["Kate O'Brien and Spain"]. Unpublished paper delivered at "An Evening with Kate O'Brien," University College Dublin, 20 January 2005.

Rambuss, Richard. "Pleasure and Devotion: The Body of Jesus and Seventeenth-Century Religious Lyric." *Queering the Renaissance.* Jonathan Goldberd, ed. Durham: Duke University Press, 1994. 253–279.

Rank, Otto. *The Double — A Psychoanalytical Study* (1914). London: Maresfield Library, 1989.

Rath, R. John. "The *Carbonari*: Their Origins, Initiation Rites, and Aims." *The American Historical Review* 69. 2 (January 1964): 353–370.

Reynolds, Lorna. "The Image of Spain in the Novels of Kate O'Brien." *Literary Interrelations — Ireland, England and the World. 3 National Images and Stereotypes.* Wolfgang Zach and Heinz Kosok, eds. Tübingen: GNV [Gunter Narr Verlag], 1987. 181–188.

_____. "Irish Women in Legend, Literature and Life." *Woman in Irish Legend, Life and Literature.* S.F. Gallagher, ed. London: Colin Smythe, 1983. 11–25

_____. *Kate O'Brien — A Literary Portrait.* Gerrards Cross, Buckinghamshire: Colin Smythe, 1987.

_____. "Kate O'Brien: Artist and Feminist" (1990). *With Warmest Love: Lectures for Kate O'Brien 1984–93.* John Logan, ed. Limerick: Mellick Press, 1994. 51–62.

_____. "Kate O'Brien and Her 'Dear Native Place.'" *Ireland of the Welcomes*, September–October 1990, 33–35.

Rhys, Jean. *Voyage in the Dark* (1934). Harmondsworth: Penguin, 1969.

Rich, Adrienne. "Compulsory Heterosexuality and Lesbian Existence" (1980). *Adrienne Rich's Poetry and Prose.* Barbara Charlesworth Gelpi and Alobert Gelpi, eds. New York and London: Norton, 1993. 203–24.

Richardson, Dorothy. *Pilgrimage 1* (1915–19). London: Virago, 1979.

Rigby, Mair. "'A Strange Perversity': Bringing Out Desire Between Women in *Frankenstein.*" Unpublished paper delivered at "The(e)ories: Advanced Seminars for Queer Research 2003," University College Dublin, 25 March 2003.

Rivera, Diego de. *Man at the Crossroads.* Painted mural. 1934.

Riviere, Joan. "Womanliness as Masquerade" (1929). *Formations of Fantasy.* Victor Burgin, et al., eds. London: Routledge, 1989. 35–44.

Roberts, Michèle. Introduction. Kate O'Brien. *Mary Lavelle.* London: Virago, 2000. ix–xiv.

Roche, Anthony. "The Anteroom as Drama." *Ordinary People Dancing: Essays on Kate O'Brien.* Eibhear Walshe, ed. Cork: Cork University Press, 1993. 85–101.

Rochman, Hazel. "Against Borders." *Horn Book Magazine*, March/April 1995. <http://www.hbook.com/exhibit/article_rochman.html>.

Rodríguez, Txani. "'La mujer Bilbaina tiene la elegancia interior de quien sabe lo que quiere'" [The Bilbaian woman has the inner elegance of one who knows what they want]. *Bilbao* 241 (September 2009): 24.

Romano, Juanjo. "Adiós a 'La Palanca'" ["Goodbye to 'La Palanca'" (the old red light district)]. *Bilbao* 215 (May 2007): 28.

Rosemont, Penelope. *Surrealist Women: An International Anthology.* Austin: University of Texas Press, 1998.

Rosowski, Susan J. "The Novel of Awakening." *The Voyage In: Fictions of Female Development.* Elisabeth Abel, Marianne Hirsh, and Elisabeth Langland, eds. Hanover, NH: University Press of New England, 1983. 49–68.

Rossetti, Christina Georgina. "In an Artist's

Studio" (1896). *The Norton Anthology of Poetry.* Margaret Ferguson, et al., eds. New York: Norton, 1996.

Rubin, Gayle. "Thinking Sex: Notes for a Radical Theory on the Politics of Sexuality" (1984). *The Lesbian and Gay Studies Reader.* Henry Abelove, et al., eds. London and New York: Routledge, 1993. 3–44.

_____. "The Traffic in Women: Notes Toward a Political Economy of Sex." *Toward an Anthropology of Women.* Rayna Reiter, ed. New York: Monthly Review Press, 1975. 157–210.

Ruppert, Peter. "Technology and the Construction of Gender in Fritz Lang's *Metropolis.*" *Genders* [online journal] 32, 2000. www.genders.org/g32/g32_ruppert.html.

Ryan, Joan. "Class and Creed in Kate O'Brien." *The Irish Writer and the City.* Maurice Harmon, ed. Gerrards Cross, Buckinhamshire: Colin Smythe, 1984. 125–135.

Sachs, Maurice. *Witches' Sabbath* (1953, 1960). London: Cape, 1965.

Sackville-West, Vita. *The Eagle and the Dove: A Study in Contrasts: St. Teresa of Avila, St. Thérese of Lisieux.* New York: Doubleday, 1944.

_____. *Saint Joan of Arc* (1936). London: Michael Joseph, 1948.

Sade, Donatien Alphonse-François, Marquis de. *The Marquis de Sade Reader* (1991). Margaret Crosland, ed. London: Peter Owen, 2001.

Salkeld, Blanaid. "As for Me." *Experiment in Error.* Ashford, Kent: Hand and Flower Press, 1955. 29.

Saña, Heleno. "Filosofía del anarquismo Español" [Philosophy of Spanish anarchism]. *Revista de Occidente* 305 (October 2006): 35–55.

Santayana, George. *The Sense of Beauty; Being the Outline of Aesthetic Theory* (1896). New York: Dover, 1955.

Sartre, Jean-Paul. *Being and Nothingness— An Essay on Phenomenological Ontology* (1943). London: Methuen, 1957.

_____. *The Nausea* (1938). London: Penguin, 2000.

Scott, H.G., ed. *Soviet Writers' Congress 1934— The Debate on Socialist Realism and Modernism in the Soviet Union* (1935) [originally published in English as "Problems of Soviet Literature"]. London: Lawrence and Wishart, 1977.

The Seashell and the Clergyman. Feature film. Dir. Germaine Dulac, France, 1926.

Sedgwick, Eve Kosofsky. *Between Men: English Literature and Male Homosocial Desire* (1985). New York: Columbia University Press, 1992.

_____. *The Coherence of Gothic Conventions.* New York: Arno, 1980.

_____. *Epistemology of the Closet.* Berkeley and Los Angeles: University of California Press, 1990.

_____. "Queer and Now." *Tendencies.* Durham: Duke University Press, 1993. 1–20.

Segal, Lynne. "Rethinking Heterosexuality: Women with Men." *Straight Sex: The Politics of Pleasure.* London: Virago, 1994. 213–66.

Serna, Emiliano. *Un anarquista de aalón* [An armchair anarchist]. Bilbao: Beitia, 2005.

Sévigné. Feature Film. Dir. Marta Balletbò-Coll. 2004.

Shaddock, Jennifer. Introduction. Isabel Meredith. *A Girl Among the Anarchists.* Lincoln: University of Nebraska Press, 1992.

Shakespeare, William. "Sonnet 34" (1609). *Shakespeare's Sonnets.* Katherine Duncan-Jones, ed. London: Arden, 2005. 178–9.

Sheridan, Richard. *La Duenna* (1775). Oxford: Oxford University Press, 1998. 87–146.

Shostakovich, Dmitri. *Lady Macbeth of the Mtsensk District.* Opera. 1934.

Shostakovich Against Stalin: The War Symphonies. Documentary film. Dir. Larry Weinstein Rombhus/ZDF Film, 1997.

Smith, Bernard. *Modernism's History— A Study in Twentieth-century Art and Ideas.* Sydney: University of New South Wales Press, 1998.

Sommerville, Edith, and Martin Ross. *Through Connemara in a Governess Cart.* (1892). London: Virago, 1990.

Soueif, Ahdaf. *The Map of Love* (1999). London: Bloomsbury, 2000.

The Sound of Music. Feature film. Dir. Robert Wise. 1965.

Stein, Gertrude. *The Autobiography of Alice B. Toklas* (1933). London: Vintage, 1990.

Stetsky, A.I. "Under the Flag of the Soviets, Under the Flag of Socialism" (1934). *Soviet Writers' Congress 1934— The Debate on Socialist Realism and Modernism in the Soviet Union.* H.G. Scott, ed. London: Lawrence and Wishart, 1977. 261–274.

Stowe, Harriet Beecher. *Uncle Tom's Cabin* (1851–2). New York: Kessinger, 2000.

Sucksmith, Harvey. Introduction and Notes. Wilkie Collins. *The Woman in White*. New York: Oxford University Press, 1980.

Sunrise — A Song for Two Humans. Feature film. Dir. F.W. Murnau. 1927.

Swinburne, A.C. *Lesbia Brandon* [w. 1864–7]. London: Falcon, 1952.

Swing Time. Feature film. Dir. George Stevens. 1936.

Sylvia Scarlett. Feature film. Dir. George Cukor. 1936.

Táin bó cuailnge [The cattle raid]. Mary Anne Hutton, trans. Dublin: Talbot Press, 1907.

Táin bó cuailnge [The Cattle Raid]. Thomas Kinsella, trans. Dublin: Dolmen Press, 1969.

Talk of Angels. Feature film [adaptation of *Mary Lavelle*]. Dir. Nick Hamm. 1998.

That Lady. Feature film. Dir. Terence Young. 1955.

Things to Come. Feature film. Dir. William Cameron Menzies. 1936.

Thomas, Calvin. "Straight with a Twist: Queer Theory and the Subject of Heterosexuality." *Straight with a Twist: Queer Theory and the Subject of Heterosexuality*. Calvin Thomas, ed. Urbana: University of Illinois Press, 2000. 11–44.

Three Colours: Blue. Feature film. Dir. Krzysztof Kieślowski. 1993.

Thunder in the Sun. Feature film. Dir. Russell Rouse. 1959.

Tiernan, Sonja. "The Journal *Urania*: An Alternative Archive of Radical Gender Masquerade." *Essays in Irish Literary Criticism: Themes of Gender, Sexuality, and Corporeality*. Deirdre Quinn and Sharon Tighe-Mooney, eds. Lewiston, NY: Edwin Mellen, 2008. 55–70.

Tighe-Mooney, Sharon. "Sexuality and Religion in Kate O'Brien's Novels." *Essays in Irish Literary Criticism: Themes of Gender, Sexuality, and Corporeality*. Deirdre Quinn and Sharon Tighe-Mooney, eds. Lewiston, NY: Edwin Mellen, 2008. 125–140.

"To Spain." Episode from the documentary series *Time in Their Hands*. RTE. February 2007.

Tobar-Arbulu, Joseba Felix. "Kate O'Brien Euskal Herrian" [Kate O'Brien in the Basque country]. *Gara*, 13 August 2009, 11.

_____. "Kate O'Brien Euskal Herrian" [sic] [Kate O'Brien in the Basque Country]. *Karmel*. No. 267. Uztaila-Iraila 2009. <http://bibliotecadigitalportugaluja.com/pdf/articulos/Memorias/Kate%20OBrien%20Euskal%20Herrian.pdf>

_____. "Kate O'Brien Euskal Herrian" [Kate O'Brien in the Basque Country]. *Karmel*. No. 267 Zenb. (2009–3 Uztaila-Iraila): 45–53.

Tóibín, Colm. "Introduction." *The Penguin Book of Irish Fiction*. Colm Tóibín, ed. Harmondsworth: Penguin, 1999. ix–xxxiv.

Tolkien, J.R.R. *The Lord of the Rings* (1937, 1954–5). New York: Houghton Mifflin, 1999.

Tolstoy, Leo. "The Kingdom of God Is Within You" (1894). *Tolstoy's Writings on Civil Disobedience and Non-Violence*. London: Peter Owen, 1968.

_____. "A Reply to Criticisms" (1897). *Tolstoy's Writings on Civil Disobedience and Non-Violence*. London: Peter Owen, 1968. 173–179.

_____. *Resurrection* (1899). London: Oxford University Press, 1966.

Tom and Viv. Feature film. Dir. Brian Gillbert. 1994.

Tomalin, Clare. *The Life and Death of Mary Wollstonecraft*. Harmondsworth: Penguin, 1977.

Tomás Benítez, Mariano. *Las claves de la tauromaquia* [The keys to the art of bullfighting]. Villares de la Reina (Salamanca): Caja Duero, 2005.

Trumbo, Dalton. *Johnny Got His Gun* (1939). London: Doubleday, 1984.

Truong, Monique. *The Book of Salt* (2003). London: Vintage, 2004.

Turgenev, Ivan. *A Sportsman's Sketches* (1852). New York: Kessinger, 2004.

Turner, Paul. Introduction. Thomas More. *Utopia*. Harmondsworth: Penguin, 1965. 7–23.

Turpin, John. "Visual Marianism and National Identity in Ireland: 1920–1960." *Art, Nation, and Gender: Ethnic Landscapes, Myths, and Mother-figures*. Tricia Cusack and Síghle Bhreathnack-Lynch, eds. Burlington, VT: Ashgate, 2003. 67–78.

Twice Two. Short film. Dir. James Parrot. 1933.

Ugalde, Martin de. *Síntesis de la historia del País Vasco* [Brief history of the Basque

Country] (1974). Zarauz: Ediciones Vascas, 1977.

Unamuno, Miguel de. *Del sentimiento trágico de la vida* [On tragic sentiment in life]. Buenos Aires: Alianza, 1986.

_____. "Poema" [Poem] (1907). *Antología poética* [Selected poetry]. Barcelona: Austral, 2003.

_____. *Paz en la guerra* [Peace in war] (1897). Madrid: Cátedra, 1999.

Uriarte, Iñaki. "Patrimonio, memoria e identidad en la Ría." *Bilbao* 198 (November 2005): 36.

Urriz, Begoña Rodríguez. "Novecentismo Bilbaino" [Bilbaian "Novecentismo" (and *Hermes*)]. *Bilbao* 236 (April 2009): 15.

_____. "San Vicente." *Bilbao* 222 (January 2008): 7.

Valdelande, Victor Manteca. "Afición taurina en la semana grande de Bilbao" [Bullfighting interest at the "big festival week" of Bilbo]. *Bilbao* (August 2002): 27.

Vampyr — Der Traum des Allan Grey. Feature film. Dir. Carl Theodor Dreyer. Germany, 1932.

Vanita, Ruth. *Sappho and the Virgin Mary: Same-Sex Love and the English Literary Imagination.* New York: Columbia University Press, 1996.

Vega, Suzanne. "On Masculinity." *Squire.* October 1991.

Velasco, Sherry. *The Lieutenant Nun: Transgenderism, Lesbian Desire, and Catalina de Erauso.* Austin: University of Texas Press, 2000.

Vicinus, Martha, ed. *Suffer and Be Still: Women in the Victorian Age.* London: Methuen, 1980.

Vitoria Ortiz, Manuel. *Vida y obra del Doctor Areilza* [Life and work of Doctor Areilza]. Bilbao: La Gran Enciclopedia Vasca, 1975.

Walshe, Eibhear. "Biographical Note." *Ordinary People Dancing: Essays on Kate O'Brien.* Eibhear Walshe, ed. Cork: Cork University Press, 1993. 11–4.

_____. "Invisible Irelands: Kate O'Brien's Lesbian and Gay Social Formations in London and Ireland in the Twentieth Century." *SQS* 1 (2006): 39–48.

_____. *Kate O'Brien: A Writing Life.* Dublin: Irish Academic Press, 2006.

_____. "Lock Up Your Daughters: From Ante-Room to Interior Castle." *Ordinary People Dancing: Essays on Kate O'Brien.* Eibhear Walshe, ed. Cork: Cork University Press, 1993. 150–166.

_____. "'Us writing chaps': Kate O'Brien and Irish Gay Men's Writing." Unpublished paper Delivered at the "Lesbian Lives Conference XI: The Lesbian Postmodern," University College Dublin. 14 February 2004.

Ward, Colin. *Anarchism — A Very Short Introduction.* New York: Oxford University Press, 2004.

Warner, Michael. "New English Sodom" (1992). *Queering the Renaissance.* Jonathan Goldberg, ed. Durham and London: Duke University Press, 1994. 330–357.

_____. *The Trouble with Normal: Sex, Politics, and the Ethics of Queer Life.* New York: Free Press, 1999.

Warner, Sylvia Townsend. *After the Death of Don Juan* (1938). London: Virago, 1989.

_____. *Summer Will Show* (1936). London: Virago, 1994.

Weekes, Ann Owens. *Irish Women Writers — An Uncharted Tradition.* Lexington: University Press of Kentucky, 1990.

Whitworth, Michael. *Authors in Context: Virginia Woolf.* New York: Oxford University Press, 2005.

Wilde, Oscar. "The Critic as Artist" (1890). *Complete Works of Oscar Wilde.* London: Collins, 2001. 1009–1059.

_____. "De Profundis" [w. 1897]. *De Profundis, The Ballad of Reading Gaol, and Other Writings.* Ware: Wordsworth, 2002.

_____. "Salome" (1893). *The Complete Works of Oscar Wilde.* London: Collins, 2001. 552–575.

_____. "The Soul of Man Under Socialism" (1890). *Complete Works of Oscar Wilde.* London: Collins, 2001. 1079–1104.

_____. "Vera, or The Nihilists" (1880). *Complete Works of Oscar Wilde.* London: Collins, 2001. 647–688.

Wilhelm, Richard. "Commentary: The Teaching of Lao Zi" (1925). Lao Tzu, *Tao Te Ching.* Harmondsworth: Penguin Arkana, 1989. 65–114.

Wiseman, Jay. *SM 101: A Realistic Introduction* (1992). San Francisco: Greenery Press, 1996.

Wittig, Monique. *The Guerrilleres* (1969). London: Picador, 1971.

_____. "The Straight Mind" (1980). *The Straight Mind and Other Essays.* New York and London: Harvester Wheatsheaf, 1992. 21–32.

Wollstonecraft, Mary. *Mary, A Fiction* (1788). Oxford: Oxford University Press, 1977.

Woodcock, George. *Anarchism* (1962). Harmondsworth: Penguin, 1970.

Woodworth, Paddy. *The Basque Country: A Cultural History*. Oxford: Signal, 2007.

Woolf, Leonard. *Downhill All the Way: An Autobiography of the Years 1919–1939* (1967). Slough: Readers Union and the Hogarth Press, 1968.

Woolf, Virginia. "Mr. Bennett and Mrs. Brown." *The Nation and Athenaeum* 34 (December 1923): 342–3.

_____. *Mrs Dalloway* (1925). Harmondsworth: Penguin, 1992.

_____. "A Room of One's Own" (1929). *A Room of One's Own/Three Guineas*. Harmondsworth: Penguin, 2000.

_____. "Three Guineas" (1938). *A Room of One's Own/Three Guineas*. Harmondsworth: Penguin, 2000.

_____. *To the Lighthouse* (1927). Harmondsworth: Penguin, 2000.

_____. *The Waves* (1931). London: Vintage, 2004.

_____. *The Years* (1937). Oxford: Oxford University Press, 1992.

Wordsworth, William. "The Oak of Guernica" (1908). *The Poems: Volume One [1770–1850]*. John O. Harden, ed. New Haven: Yale University Press, 1981. 838–9.

Wright, William. *The Brontës in Ireland: Or, Facts Stranger Than Fiction* (1893). Brooklyn, NY: Haskell House, 1971.

Yeats, William Butler. *The Collected Plays*. London: Macmillan, 1952.

_____. "The Second Coming" (1920). *The Poems*. London: Everyman, 2001. 235.

_____. "A Vision" (1925). *A Critical Edition of Yeats's* A Vision *(1925)*. Mills Herper and Walter Kelly Hood, eds. London: Macmillan, 1978.

_____. *A Vision*. London: Macmillan, 1962.

Young Indiana Jones Chronicles. Television series. Amblin Entertainment (1992–3). "Ireland, April 1916" (written by Jonathan Hales, Dirs. Gilles Mackinnoy and Carl Schultz). Season 2, episode 1, 1993.

_____. "London May 1916." Story by George Lucas, written by Rosemary Anne Sisson, Dirs. Carl Schultz and Ellery Ryan. Season 2, episode 2, 1993.

Zettl, Karin Eva. "'In Search of a Personal Position': Women's Quest for Individuality in Kate O'Brien's Novels *The Anteroom* (1934), *Mary Lavelle* (1936), and *That Lady* (1946)." Unpublished MA Thesis, University College Dublin, 1993.

Zhdanov, A. "Soviet Literature — The Richest in Ideas, the Most Advanced Literature" (1934). *Soviet Writers' Congress 1934 — The Debate on Socialist Realism and Modernism in the Soviet Union*. H. G. Scott, ed. London: Lawrence and Wishart, 1977. 15–26.

Zohar, Danah. "A Quantum Vision for European Cultural Integration." Danah Zohar and Ian Marshall. *The Quantum Society — Mind, Physics and a New Social Vision*; London: Flamingo, 1994. 282–294.

Zola, Emile. *Nana* (1880). New York: Random House, 1990.

Zukav, Gary. *The Dancing Wu Li Masters: An Overview of the New Physics*. London: Rider, 1979.

Zulaika, Joseba. *Basque Violence: Metaphor and Sacrament*. Reno: University of Nevada Press, 1988.

Index

Woolf, Virginia 15, 16, 21, 41, 70, 71, 101, 103, 104, 105–7, 108, 110–1, 124, 184, 204, 239; and anarchism 16; donates *Three Guineas* manuscript to Basque refugees 51; influence on/affinity with Kate O'Brien 15, 16, 71, 104, 105–6, 110–11; middle class "daughters of educated men" 5, 29, 52
Wordsworth, Dorothy 73
Wordsworth, William 142, 161–2; "The Oak of Guernica" 142
Wright, William 32

Yeats, William Butler 42, 54, 103, 219, 237
Yin Yang theory 224, 238, 244

Young, Terence *see* *That Lady* (1955)
Young Indiana Jones Chronicles 67

Zettl, Karin Eva 27, 82–3, 141
Zhdanov, A. 40
Zimmer Bradley, Marion 20
Zohar, Danh 247–8
Zola, Emile 84, 92
Zukav, Gary 243
Zulaika, Joseba 95, 144
Zuloaga, Ignacio 175, 195